The World the Sixties Made

Politics and Culture in Recent America

In the series

CRITICAL PERSPECTIVES ON THE PAST

edited by Susan Porter Benson, Stephen Brier, and Roy Rosenzweig

The World the Sixties Made

Politics and Culture in Recent America

Edited by
VAN GOSSE
AND RICHARD MOSER

TEMPLE UNIVERSITY PRESS
Philadelphia

Temple University Press, Philadelphia 19122
Copyright © 2003 by Temple University
All rights reserved
Published 2003
Printed in the United States of America

⊗ The paper used in this publication meets the requirements of the
American National Standard for Information Sciences—Permanence
of Paper for Printed Library Materials, ANSI Z39.48-1984

Library of Congress Cataloging-in-Publication Data

The world the sixties made : politics and culture in recent America /
    edited by Van Gosse and Richard Moser.
        p.   cm. — (Critical perspectives on the past)
    Includes bibliographical references.
    ISBN 1-59213-200-6 (cloth : alk. paper) — ISBN 1-59213-201-4 (pbk. : alk. paper)
      1. United States—Politics and government—1989– . 2. United States—Social
conditions—1980– . 3. Popular culture—United States—History—20th century.
4. Political culture—United States—History—20th century. 5. United States—
History—1961–1969. 6. Nineteen sixties. 7. New Left—United States—History.
8. Social movements—United States—History—20th century. 9. Social change—
United States—History—20th century. I. Gosse, Van. II. Moser, Richard R., 1952– .
III. Series.

    E839.5.W67 2003
    973.92—dc21

                                                                        2003044048

2 4 6 8 9 7 5 3 1

Contents

Acknowledgments

This book began as a panel at the 1997 annual meeting of the American Historical Association. We wish to thank the other panelists, Anne Enke and Komozi Woodard (whose fine book on black power, *A Nation Within a Nation,* has since been published), as well as our commentator Ellen Schrecker. Since then it has gone through several incarnations and names, but we have stuck with our intent to re-think the history of the recent past and challenge stereotypes about the death or collapse of the social movements that made up the New Left and the "long Sixties" posited here.

We express our gratitude to Janet Francendese of Temple University Press for her support of this project, and also to series editors Roy Rosenzweig, Steve Breyer, and Susan Porter Benson. The criticisms of the anonymous reviewers for the press helped improve many of the essays, not least our own, for which we thank them. On a personal note, Van Gosse sends his love and gratitude to fellow historian Eliza Jane Reilly, an unflagging backer of this project, who contributed, among other things, its final title. Richard Moser acknowledges the passing of his old friend and colleague Ronn Eugene McGee, and thanks Galina Lewis for her patient instruction in the ways of compassion, quiet fortitude, and love.

Finally, we dedicate this book to the History Department of Rutgers University, where we were both trained to question conventions. Long may it reign.

The World the Sixties Made

Politics and Culture in Recent America

Van Gosse

Introduction I

Postmodern America

A New Democratic Order in the Second Gilded Age

ANYONE WHO teaches the history of the United States in the last quarter of the twentieth century knows the available historiography is thin indeed. These decades have seen constant change and contestation in all areas of historical inquiry, covering the gamut of diplomatic, political, social, cultural, business, women's, labor, and intellectual history. During the 1990s it became common to speak of dizzying technological and cultural revolutions that had occurred since one was a child. Yet the teacher of the nearly three decades since the falls of Richard Nixon in August 1974 and Saigon nine months later—as close to a historical break as one can find—must rely upon books by journalists, political scientists, and sociologists. When it comes to historical scholarship, there are few studies that treat the 1970s or 1980s, let alone the Clinton era.

Why is there little serious history yet written about a generation of vast demographic, economic, and cultural shifts, including the greatest surge in immigration in a century, the transition to a postindustrial economy, and the eclipse of the normative patriarchal family? One explanation can be found in Richard Moser's introduction to this book, which examines the apocalyptic tendency written into U.S. culture; he and I characterize this type of history as *declensionist,* following Perry Miller's analysis of how the Puritans mythologized their own trajectory. In this scenario, the Sixties failed in their millenarian purpose and now Americans have stepped outside their own history, lost their groove, and forgotten what Todd Gitlin called their "common dreams."[1] Thus there is no real need for ongoing historical exploration, for the case studies, revisions, new syntheses, and rediscovery of old arguments leading to a dense, overdetermined series of explanations—a historiography.

1

Another reason for the dearth of history writing is the absence of any accepted periodization. Historians have not yet agreed that the decades since the Nixon presidency constitute a historical period equivalent to the post-1945 "long boom" that mutated into the high Sixties of 1966–74, or the Depression and World War II era framed by the crash in October 1929 and Hiroshima in August 1945. This is underlined by the problem of naming: If the period is a coherent whole, what should we call it, what are its defining features, and when does it end? Some of us get by with makeshift phrases like "post-Sixties," "late" or "post–Cold War" America, but they lack explanatory weight and carry no evident associations, unlike "the Progressive Era," "Depression," "the New Deal" or "Cold War America." Given this historiographical limbo, recent decades become just "the present," and there are few things more likely to warn historians off than the possibility of being proved wrong by "current events." Certainly, the events of September 11, 2001, are likely to make historians very wary. Was this the close of one period and the beginning of another, or just one terrible moment in a long post–Cold War era of U.S. hegemony stretching far into the future?

Above all, there is the professional inclination of historians to let the dust settle. One suspects the same complaint was made in 1965, when scholars were just beginning to examine the vast changes since D-Day. Even now, many U.S. historians do not teach past 1968 or 1976, and the final chapters of U.S. history textbooks rely on summaries derived from the essays and polemical accounts of journalists like Haynes Johnson, Kevin Phillips, Thomas Byrne Edsall, and Sidney Blumenthal.[2]

This book's purpose is to initiate scholarly debate and begin filling in the blanks for the end of the American Century. Our hope is that combining case studies of particular places with synthetic arguments about longer-term political shifts will stimulate further research and productive arguments. This introductory essay's goal is to propose a periodization of, and a name for, the historical time since the Sixties "ended," looking closely at what constitutes current historiography. A central focus will be to challenge the assertion of a "Reagan" or "conservative" revolution, since the claim of a decisive shift to the right is a constant in both textbook and journalistic accounts of what I call "Postmodern America." It starts with questions, rather than premises. First, from 1980 on, have the politics, society, and culture of the United States been realigned in a conservative direction, and if so, what are the results?

Second, what was the New Right, stripped of its pretensions? Third, what happened to the New Left, the pluralist "movement of movements" that some claim "died" circa 1970, but whose legacies and effects surround us.?[3]

LOCATING POSTMODERN AMERICA

Why use the ubiquitous, much-abused term "postmodern?" In this case, both its negative and positive connotations are appropriate. Whereas the modern age assumed a driving imperative of industrial development and progress, "postmodernism" has come to signal drift, fragmentation, and the sense that no center can hold. In that sense, the United States after Vietnam is the epitome of a postmodern capitalist-democratic state, where an extreme liberalism regarding personal liberty coexists with a rigorous corporate-driven regime of consumption. The visceral impulse of such a society is to plunder its own past for styles and cultural artifacts that can be marketed to precisely defined niches of the public. This is the face that America presents to the world—the truncated kind of freedom promised by "have it your way."

There is an undeniable reality to this image of a strip-mall America that is homogenized, alienated, and selling itself off to the highest bidder. Much that was authentic or at least "local" has faded fast in the past generation under the onslaught of Wal-Mart and other chains. Nor is this sense of commodified uniformity and vulgarity restricted to what we see, hear, wear, buy, and eat. The ambience of dislocation reaches into the core of our politics and is barely touched by the post-9/11 crisis and official calls for a renewed spirit of national sacrifice. What passes for public life at the millenial moment has a cartoonish cast, a cheapness symbolized by the descent in scale and gravity from one impeachment to another. However frightening and sordid, Watergate was about genuine abuses of power that amounted to a slow-motion coup, as government police agencies were corrupted to neutralize the political opposition at the president's direct order.[4] Contrast that with the attempted removal of another president for lying about his sexual dalliance with an intern, which threatened no one. Of course, the Monica Lewinsky affair raised the question of post-Sixties sexual libertinism and the supposed corruption of our culture, but it did so in prurient, pornographic terms dictated by Kenneth Starr and the ham-handed Republican inquisitors, which explains why large majorities rallied to the Clintons' side—few Americans of any background welcome someone poking into their sex lives.

But defining late-twentieth-century America as "postmodern" has other resonances that are more positive. To start with, the "diversity" and fracturing of experience that a postmodern, fiercely pluralist United States fosters in schools, churches, workplaces, and even the armed forces is more than a slogan. It is a reasonable representation of one of history's most ethnically complex societies, now changing before our eyes as urban (and some rural) areas teem with new Americans from Asia and Latin America. The politics of "diversity" and "multiculturalism" may be amorphous and hypocritical, submerging differences and inequalities into a mass of deferential mutuality—lists of religious and ethnic holidays, each with its own food. But hypocrisy is, after all, the tribute that vice pays to virtue. The recognition of diversity and the constant evocation of multiculturalism are the public faces of our highly unequal society's accommodation with a kind of "social" democracy, one too hard-won to be sneered at.

Second, it is true that postmodern pluralism defines Americans as consumers first and citizens second. Many citizens have simply opted out of "politics," with only a minority bothering to vote in presidential elections, and old-style radical "mass movements" like those of the Sixties seem unimaginable now. Yet the dense, fluid networks of age, taste, and polycultural identity possible under postmodern conditions provide constant opportunities for political organizing.[5] These nooks and crannies may be less familiar than those of the recent past, but they are fully equal to the ethnic lodges, saloons, union halls, and parish churches of the old industrial America, circa 1877–1948. The long-building upsurge against corporate neoliberalism that broke into the open at the November 1999 World Trade Organization meeting in Seattle, and earlier global solidarity movements for southern African and Central American liberation during the 1970s and 1980s, have all relied on new technologies and multiplying avenues for communication across borders and hemispheres that sharply distinguish the post-Sixties era. Certainly the New Right has never accepted that "postmodern" meant "postpolitics," which is why it has generated a series of genuine mass movements via these technologies.

Thus we arrive at this book's central argument: *a primary reason for the fragmentation and alienation of Postmodern America is that we are more dem-*

ocratic than any America that came before. Since the 1960s, conservatives have dismissed the civil rights movement, feminism, and even, on occasion, gay rights as the latest stage in a "natural" progress toward toleration, while appealing via coded language ("law and order" and, later, "family values") to resentment of these movements. But manipulation by the Right, resentment among sections of the public (especially white men), and weariness on the Left cannot obscure the fact that we live in a world the Sixties made. We are still fighting over that legacy in ways that matter deeply, no matter how mindlessly partisan and trivialized those struggles sometimes appear. It behooves us, therefore, to examine those huge changes.

Given this country's origin in slavery and the extermination of native peoples, any discussion of democracy and its limits should begin with race. On this front the second half of the twentieth century marks a political and cultural revolution both unfinished and undefeated.[6] Within the memory of the majority of Americans, any person of color faced open, rampant discrimination in schools, housing, employment, and all aspects of the public sphere, de facto or de jure, and the threat of violence by agents of the state or other groups acting with impunity. No one could claim this castelike burden has disappeared, and in some respects the complex of racial oppression has intensified in perverse, insidious ways. So what has changed? First, since the 1970s (for the first time since Reconstruction) this society has proclaimed an enforceable equality before the law, while acknowledging that that equality does not yet exist. Pronouncements by themselves mean little, however. Far more important is that legislatures, judiciaries, police forces, and the administrative apparatus of local, state, and federal governments are now filled by people whose assumed origins once guaranteed their exclusion. The rise of a "prison industrial complex" focused on incarcerating black men, the constant threat of "profiling" that leads to police brutality, and persisting discrimination in education, housing, and the workplace cannot obscure the fact that white supremacy must hide its face, and the assertion that this is a "white man's country" can no longer be made in mainstream venues. "More democratic than any America that came before" may be setting the bar very low, but it also recognizes how far we must advance to overcome a legacy written into our national identity as a settler and slaveholding republic.

The same argument for a sweeping democratic transformation can be made, from a different angle, for the newest recognized "minority," gay and lesbian Americans, who have moved from the lowest possible status as a despised medical and criminal category to a contested but potent level of recognition.[7] By their insistence not on assimilation but on the right to be, and be visible, across all the usual boundaries of race, ethnicity, and class, homosexuals have confronted our assumptions about how to categorize people. Lacking any radical past, any nineteenth-century symbols equivalent to Frederick Douglass, Seneca Falls, or the Knights of Labor, the "out" presence of gay women and men may be the sharpest indicator of how radically this country has changed.

Last and most obvious is the profound democratization of relations between the sexes, brought about by one of the longest-lived movements in U.S. history, the second-wave feminism that germinated from the 1940s on, burst forth between 1968 and 1972, and continues into the new century.[8] Nothing remains more fought over, as conservative politicians bob and weave around the distinctions between equality and difference, celebrating women's slow ascent to political leadership and workplace parity while invoking the tattered shreds of "separate spheres" ideology. No one can claim that the female majority has gained its fair share of power, and basic feminist tenets remain more prescriptions than accurate descriptions of how family and sexual lives are led. Yet the tide has turned—like Humpty Dumpty, it is exceedingly difficult to see how patriarchy could be restored, short of a counterrevolutionary scenario like that in Margaret Atwood's *Handmaid's Tale*.[9]

If there has been a revolution that changed the lives of the majority— women, gays, lesbians, African Americans, Latinos, Native Americans, Asians Americans—why is it still constantly asserted that "the Sixties" failed and we live in a conservative era? Here's why: The hope of generations of radicals, socialists, and progressives was that a new democratic, revolutionary order would strike at the basis of state and private power in the capitalist system. Self-evidently, nothing like that has transpired. Defying predictions, "late" capitalism proved capable of accommodating, absorbing, and even welcoming revolutions in racial, sexual, and gender relations. Indeed, the essence of Clintonism and the boom times of the 1990s was to represent that enthusiastic accommodation. Disturbed by this surprising resilience, some pundits on the Left assert that the still-roiling democratic upsurge of our era is nothing more than "identity politics," affecting various subsets of the population but not, presumably, the real America, which is white, heterosexual, and politically moderate. Some even argue that post-Sixties struggles over race, gender, and sexuality—the "cultural war" named by Pat Buchanan in his infamous speech to the 1992 Republican Convention—are neither progressive nor democratic, instead only dividing the majority of the country so it can better be conquered.[10]

The term "identity politics" stood for a transitional moment, but, like "politically correct," it has turned into a meaningless pejorative. We suggest that "democratic politics" is more useful, and that the coming forward of new political communities claiming their own social, cultural, and political identities constitutes the birth of *a new democratic order,* which in the early twenty-first century is reaching maturity after a generation defending the fragile egalitarianism catalyzed by the New Left of 1955–75.[11]

Of course, we are aware of the dangers of a neo-Whig history that asserts the best of all possible worlds is just around the corner. Rather than vindicating the Sixties, we seek a judicious balance. Our responsibility in this volume is to avoid the twin pitfalls of an unwarranted progressivism, seeing only sunny vistas and final victories, and that romantic declensionism which does not bother to investigate the reality of politics since 1975 (or even 1968). There have been powerful reactionary currents since the Sixties, impressively assembled under the big tent of Reagan Republicanism. But it is profoundly wrong to suggest the New Left led to a resurgence of racism, greater sexism, more oppression of homosexual people, or increased imperialism. All of these dynamics were there all along, part of the warp and woof of Americanism, and the success of "the Sixties" was to make visible and vocal what was largely unseen or ignored. Such visibility produces discomfort, and not only among self-defined conservatives.

We are also conscious of the risk in characterizing this transitional period as similar to the first Gilded Age in terms of the fallout from a bitter revolutionary war combined with sweeping political-economic shifts at all levels of society.[12] But the more one extends the analogy of "a second Gilded Age" into the practicalities of partisan politics, the more apt it seems. The late-twentieth-century Democratic Party strongly resembles the old post-abolition, post-Reconstruction, nominally antiracist and thoroughly probusiness Republicans after 1877, while the GOP has taken up the mantle of the solid (white) South. Like the late nineteenth century, this is a period of partisan stalemate, with control of Congress shifting back and forth as presidents eke out pluralities while trying to squelch third-party schisms within and around their own parties. One notes also the avoidance of debate over the political economy in favor of unchallenged nostrums (Herbert Spencer then, Francis Fukuyama now). Finally, there is the power of certain totems, whether "free silver" as a common man's panacea then, or "free choice" as a leitmotif for the most recent wave of women's sexual liberation. It remains to be seen whether this second Gilded Age will continue or will fall prey like the first to a depression and another great wave of reform. Or did it end with the crash of the Twin Towers? Only time will tell.

THE END OF THE SIXTIES:
LIBERALISM BREAKS RIGHT AND LEFT

Historians may be wary of periodizing the years since 1968, but most accept the argument that in 1980, with Ronald Reagan's election, the United States took a major shift rightwards for the first time since the 1920s. This is the premise of the most influential work of historiography on twentieth-century America published in the past twenty years, *The Rise and Fall of the New Deal Order, 1930–1980*.[13] But the endpoint of that book's title suggests the problem with this argument. Just as one cannot end an assessment of the New Deal with the realigning election of 1936 and the epochal reforms of 1935–37 (social security, the Wagner Act and so on), one should not make claims about the New Right's rise without extending the narrative forward into the 1980s and 1990s. To accomplish this requires clarity about what came before, and the radical shifts *to the left* in U.S. politics and culture in the long decade from 1964 to 1976, in many cases institutionalized even further during Jimmy Carter's presidency, 1977–1980. A brief reprise is in order.[14]

From the mid-1960s through Nixon's presidency, liberal government steadily expanded its scope and reach, because of continuous pressure from grassroots social movements and the unleashed inclinations of a governing class raised on the premises of the New Deal. Old hopes of the Thirties, Forties, and Fifties became realities in the early 1970s, including a massive influx of black voters' upending of the South's white power structure, and the new environmentalist movement challenging big business's prerogatives in the name of the whole citizenry.

But liberal government faced sharp challenges on its ideological flanks. Best known is the repudiation of "corporate liberalism" by the movements grouped under the New Left's banner. Even as the Nixon administration introduced affirmative action, the Democratic Party was democratized, opening doors to blacks and women, and environmental, gay, and antiwar activists. Outside of Congress and partisan politics, numerous social movements pushed beyond liberal premises and began to talk openly about issues that New Deal left liberals had never considered: the division of labor in the family, whether black people constituted a "nation within a nation" and should separate themselves, the right of homosexuals to live as couples with the same legal protections as heterosexuals.

The catalyst to this cascading radicalism moving the political center leftward from 1964 to 1976 was the Vietnam War, the "liberals' war," as it was dubbed. For a significant minority, there could be no common cause with leaders who countenanced the year-in, year-out bombing of a peasant country half a world away to maintain geopolitical credibility. This insurgency turned the Democratic Party into an ideological free-for-all. By 1972, two remarkably opposing figures competed as its leading presidential candidates—Alabama governor George Wallace, avatar of white pseudopopulism, and South Dakota senator George McGovern, leader of antiwar forces in Congress, with former vice president Hubert Humphrey (once the shining star of Cold War liberalism) caught in the middle as a late-blooming afterthought. Analogous to such a split would be the Republican Party in 2004 choosing between a feminist and a conservative evangelical Christian.

In short, the static version of liberalism that held sway from 1948 to 1968 was overturned, and the guardians of Cold War liberalism became a disgruntled center-right rump in a party splitting at the seams. The submerged "progressive" liberalism that had been a major bipartisan current in the century's first half, with its crusading style and preference for single-issue "causes," resurfaced via Eugene McCarthy's candidacy in 1968, McGovern's in 1972, and the profusion of liberal champions whom the centrist Jimmy Carter edged out for the 1976 Democratic nomination (including Morris Udall, Fred Harris, Birch Bayh, Frank Church, and Jerry Brown). Carter's presidency awaits proper historical consideration and was too contradictory and amateurish to summarize here. But the efforts to incorporate activists connected to social movements into high-level administration posts (Andrew Young, Pat Derian, Virginia Apuzzo, and Sam Brown are among the best known), the im-

mediate amnesty for draft resisters, and the global "human rights policy" all suggested a recognition that "the Sixties" must be accepted, and
the past expiated.

At the same time, a deep-rooted conservative movement based in
opposition to the waves of reform from the Progressive Era on also gar-
nered new adherents and political power. In the later 1970s and 1980s,
this movement took over parts of the Republican Party, elected as president the charismatic orator Ronald Reagan, and passed legislation reversing much of the New Deal and the Great Society. Ever since then,
scholars and commentators have dissected the "New Right," the "Religious Right," the "Neoconservative Right," and so on, trying to untan-
gle the origins of the Reagan Revolution.

THE INTENTIONS AND ACCOMPLISHMENTS
OF THE REAGAN REVOLUTION

That U.S. politics underwent a watershed in the 1980s is not in question.
The premises of liberal "big government" fell into disrepute, and a
right-wing administration and party dominated governance for the
first time since the 1920s. But what the Reagan Revolution actually accomplished and the extent of its revolution, and how it took power in
the first place, are still in dispute. The safest assertion is that Reaganism
responded to a genuine mobilization and represented a significant social
base—the primacy of one group over another (southern white evangel-
icals versus northern white "ethnics"; "paleoconservatives" of the Old
Right versus cosmopolitan, often Jewish neoconservatives) remains
murky, as political disputes muddy the water. What makes the Reagan
Revolution most difficult to interpret is that it is hardly over. The 1994
Republican sweep of Congress and a majority of statehouses represented a more complete "realignment" of electoral power than Reagan
ever achieved. Then Clinton handily turned back the Republican drive
on the White House in 1996, and cut deeply into their congressional
majorities, sparking a counter-attack on his physical person led by Kenneth Starr, which in turn mobilized core Democratic constituencies
(African Americans and pro-choice women) to flock to the polls. The
bizarre 2000 election only confirmed the partisan stalemate and the un-
relenting conservative push for power by any means necessary, but in
2001 this sparked a one-man insurgency within the Senate itself, as Vermont Senator James Jeffords, "the last of the Mohicans" of New England

liberal Republicanism, left his party and returned the majority to the Democrats, only to see control shift back after November 2002.

As the new century unfolds, political gridlock persists. No new progressive model of governance has emerged to challenge the promise of Reaganism—to "get government off the backs of the American people"—but the Republicans appear unable to assemble a durable electoral majority.

To understand what conservative organizers, Republican Party leaders, and Ronald Reagan himself hoped to accomplish, we need to step back to the post-World War II era, when New Deal policies and Franklin Delano Roosevelt's posthumous presence dominated American political life. Ironically, this liberal golden age became a touchstone for the New Right of the 1970s and 1980s.[15] America was at the peak of its global economic, military and political power, and domestically conservative cultural values seemed triumphant. In 1945, the U.S. had more than half of the world's industrial capacity, and over the next twenty years the average American family doubled its real income because of that economic supremacy. Until the late 1950s the U.S. faced no serious competition in the nuclear arms race, and the CIA routinely fixed elections and overthrew governments outside the Soviet orbit. Rather than competitors, the Western Europeans and Japanese were suppliants, desperate for Marshall Plan aid to rebuild their countries. The idea of peasant guerrillas stalemating the U.S. Army would have seemed absurd: the U.S. waged effective "counter-insurgency" in the Philippines, as did our British allies in Kenya, Malaysia and elsewhere. Few could imagine the rise of Ho Chi Minh, Fidel Castro, and the "Third World."

At home, the social order seemed unassailable, as none of the New Left's insurgencies were yet visible. Though segregation was clearly a problem that was tearing at the Democratic Party as early as 1948, hardly anyone in white America imagined that within a few years hundreds of thousands would march, tens of thousands would be arrested, and Dr. Martin Luther King, Jr., would become the greatest American leader of his time. To most whites, black Americans were invisible, a troubling side issue at best. Even harder to imagine was a feminist renascence, as vast new suburbs and a flight from Depression and wartime insecurity re-established the patriarchal nuclear family, where husbands went to work and women raised children and kept house. The clearest marker of the Fifties, however, was the position of homosexual men and women. Black people and women could evoke earlier struggles and partial victories. Gays and lesbians had no such history and barely existed as a recognized social group until after World War II, when their presence in urban areas was seized upon as evidence of decadence and cultural degradation. No one in America, and few gays, could imagine that they would emerge as a recognized community within a few decades.

The intentions of Reaganism can be summed up as restoring this vanished world of the Fifties. Its political genius lay in evoking both the imagined past *and* its chaotic coming apart, not just an argument about what should be, but a vision of what had been, tying its destruction to Democratic liberals' capitulation to radicalism. Over and over, Reagan and his followers hammered away, finding specific policies and people to blame. Indeed, this appeal to resentment first surfaced at the 1960s' climax, in the 1968 presidential campaign when Richard Nixon and George Wallace between them took 57 percent of the vote, with Nixon offering a kindler, gentler version of Wallace's racialized call for "law and order."

Reaganism offered three solutions to the uncertainties and change faced by Americans in the 1970s and 1980s. First, it promised to restore America as a dominant world power, no longer accepting military parity with the Soviet Union, defeat at the hands of revolutionary guerrillas, or disrespect from NATO allies and the Japanese. Second, it promoted the idea of an older moral order, based explicitly in the heterosexual, patriarchal family and (slightly less openly) in the cultural authority of white Americans. Finally, it promised to sharply limit the federal government's role as a re-distributor of wealth and regulator of business—functions crucial to the legitimacy of the New Deal Order consolidated by Franklin Roosevelt and extended by Lyndon Johnson. The scope of these claims exceeded those of any of Reagan's predecessors. Neither FDR nor LBJ, nor Theodore Roosevelt or Woodrow Wilson earlier, asked for a sweeping mandate to remake the nation. Unlike Reagan, all of these presidents styled themselves progressives, and the conservative has a great advantage in offering the familiar past rather than an uncertain future.

To what extent did the Reagan Revolution meet its aims? Conservatives still argue over that question, masking their disputes in veneration of Reagan the man. That the Reagan Administration and a bipartisan majority in Congress diminished government's role as an agent of social equality by shifting the focus of federal spending cannot be doubted. Between 1980 and 1988, spending on all domestic social programs dropped by more than a third, while military spending skyrocketed, to nearly half-a-trillion dollars per year (in 1999 dollars). The tax cuts of 1981 and subsequent economic policies constituted a massive deregulation in favor of business, which encouraged a shift in income to the wealthy without precedent in American history. In that sense, the Reagan Revolution was successful: it got government "off the backs of" American capitalism, while maintaining the panoply of corporate welfare via the military-industrial complex. The rich and to a lesser extent the 20 percent of the population that Kevin Phillips designated "Upper America" got a lot richer, the working classes and poor got a lot poorer, and the middle classes barely hung on. By one basic measurement, the New Deal was reversed, as the shares of national income held by the top and bottom 20 percent of the population returned to the levels of inequality of the 1920s.[16]

It is inaccurate to claim, however, that Reaganism abolished the welfare state, as "movement conservatives" had hoped. However straitened, the host of liberal programs mainly lived on, either because of wide middle-class popularity (Social Security, Medicare, the Clean Water Act, Pell Grant college scholarships) or through stubborn resistance by activists and their congressional allies (Legal Services, Head Start, Food Stamps). In that sense, rather than a "revolution," Reaganism was one more wave of reform, in this case backwards instead of forwards. The depths of disillusionment can be seen in Newt Gingrich's bitter gibe in the late 1980s that Senate Majority Leader and Republican stalwart Robert Dole was merely the "tax collector for the welfare state."

If Reaganism enjoyed success at home, by reversing a half-century of federal policy aimed at regulating capitalism, it also claimed victory internationally. Invoking a passionate anti-Communism stretching back to the 1917 Russian Revolution, it celebrated the Soviet Union's collapse in 1989–1991. The president and his supporters claimed all the credit, and without doubt the arms race of the 1980s intensified the economic strains destabilizing the Soviets, though their system had been declining for decades, and a Democrat might just as easily have presided over the "victory." Yet the ambitious foreign policy of the Reagan years, intended to "roll back" Communist revolution around the globe, produced numerous calamities, which threatened Reagan's presidency and consolidated significant domestic opposition.

For reasons ranging from geopolitical credibility to wounded imperial pride, the Reaganites wanted to re-fight the Vietnam War in this hemisphere, making a test case of Central America. When Reagan took office in January 1981, leftist guerrillas had taken power in Nicaragua and threatened the military dictatorships in Guatemala and El Salvador. Throughout the 1980s, the Reagan and Bush Administrations invested enormous political capital in winning these proxy wars and proving they could defeat Marxist revolutions. Ultimately, Reagan overplayed his hand, illegally circumventing Congress and the Constitution by funding "Contras" trying to overthrow the Sandinista government in Nicaragua. The resulting Irangate scandal of 1986–87 tarnished Reagan's authority, and high Administration officials faced trial and conviction. Aid to the anti-Sandinista opposition produced a pro-U.S. government in Nicaragua's 1990 elections, but the Bush Administration was shaken by a 1989 rebel offensive in El Salvador, and deferred to a United Nations-brokered peace settlement that ended death-squad rule and brought the guerrillas into the political system. After a decade of war, hundreds of thousands of civilians killed by U.S.-supported militaries, and widespread protest and solidarity movements, few could say that the Vietnam Syndrome had bit the dust.[17]

Nor was the Central American debacle the only major defeat in foreign policy. Despite their success in expanding the military-industrial complex through expensive new weapons systems, the New Right was hamstrung in its ability to exert force and rearrange the geopolitical order. In the early 1980s, a trans-Atlantic movement for a "nuclear freeze" made arms-control a political imperative, and it is an irony of the Cold War that Ronald Reagan and then George Bush pushed through major treaties with the Soviets reducing weapons of mass destruction. Despite the desire of the U.S. Right for a "constructive engagement" with South Africa's anti-communist *apartheid* regime, the liberation struggle there crested in the late 1980s, in large part because millions of Americans believed they were carrying forward the civil rights movement by insisting on economic sanctions that forced the Africaners to give up power. The Reaganites did trumpet a clear win in CIA funding and direction of the bloody Afghani war of resistance against Soviet occupation, but it was an odd kind of victory, consolidating an international network of well-trained Islamic militants that came back to haunt the United States in the late 1990s (and perhaps for the foreseeable future).

The greatest failure of Reaganism came at home, however, not in the electoral or legislative arenas, but in the ordinary give-and-take, the "personal politics," of daily life and mass culture. Despite the cant of traditional morality and "family values," American culture became more tolerant of difference of all kinds, more genuinely polycultural, and more liberated (or just libertine) in its sexual mores. Even if all one did was watch television or movies, it would be impossible to call this a conservative era. Some scholars and conservatives have concluded therefore that the Reagan Revolution was a sham, and that religious and "social" conservatives were simply manipulated. The truth seems more complex. In practical terms, the votes were simply not there for overturning the 1973 *Roe v. Wade* decision legalizing abortion, or weakening Title VII of the Civil Rights Act of 1964. However haltingly, people of color, women, and gay people continued to advance as distinct political constituencies, and the most canny conservatives recognized this political reality. Whenever they needed reminding, the voters provided incentives, as in the sweeping repudiation of the Republican Party by Latinos following California Governor Pete Wilson's leadership in passing a ballot initiative that sharply restricted immigrants' rights to public services. In terms of policy-making, the New Right could claim success for its fiscal, regulatory and economic policies, while suffering significant defeats in its efforts to reverse the liberalism of American culture and the official egalitarianism written into American society in the Sixties.

The best indicator of this failure is the focus of George W. Bush's campaign, from 1998 through the post-Labor Day 2000 endgame (when it eroded Al Gore's solid majority through relentless blandness), on banishing the image of the Republican Party as a collection of ideological zealots. Bush's strategists emulated Bill Clinton's opportunistic manipulation of multiculturalism, though relying more on gestures and tableaux than the apparatus of patronage that kept the Democratic Party running in the 1990s. Thus radical intellectuals were blind to the central role of Colin Powell's speech to the July 2000 Republican Convention, and the insistence on giving the podium to the one openly gay Republican congressperson, Jim Kolbe of Arizona, while Pat Robertson, Pat Buchanan, James Dobson, Bob Barr, Newt Gingrich and other heroes of the hard Right were put out of sight. It may be a bitter pill to call "compassionate conservatism" a tribute to the Left, but that is the practical reality of U.S. politics.

INTERPRETING THE NEW RIGHT

The best-known account of Reaganism focuses not on where it came from, but what it did: Kevin Phillips' *The Politics of Rich and Poor: Wealth and the American Electorate in the Reagan Aftermath.* The former Republican strategist charts the extent to which Reaganism succeeded in eliminating taxes and regulations upon the very wealthiest in American society, and the extent to which the top ten percent of Americans profited during the 1980s because of the speculative fever instigated by right-wing resurgence. Phillips's arguments became foundational for everything written about the rise of the Right, since he demonstrated irrefutably the probusiness perspective that drives conservativism. But Phillips had little to say about the movements that placed Reagan in power, or the complex ideologies regarding race, gender, culture, sexual morality, and the world that drove those movements. His is a balance-sheet, bottom-line traditional kind of muckraking about results rather than causes.

Godfrey Hodgson's *The World Turned Right Side Up: A History of the Conservative Ascendancy in America* offers the "movement" perspective of the New Right's rise.[18] Hodgson focuses on how disparate streams of conservative thought, from antistatist libertarianism to Burkean social conservatism, fused in the 1950s and 1960s into a simple, effective electoral message. His willingness to take conservatives seriously as rational political actors rather than provincial reactionaries makes the book very useful. But he ignores the rawer, antidemocratic aspects of the U.S. Right—its deep roots in northern (especially Midwestern) nativism and antisemitism and the southern commitment to white supremacy. Leaving the hard Right out of the story of conservatism is equivalent to leaving Communists and other leftists out of the New Deal, or confining the story of the black freedom struggle to Dr. King while pretending Malcolm X and Stokely Carmichael did not exist. It misses the importance of uncompromising militancy in redefining the terms of debate.

Thomas Byrne Edsall's account in *Chain Reaction: The Impact of Race, Rights, and Taxes on American Politics* is similar to Hodgson's in positing that the Right rose to power through a process of accretion, layering constituencies into a working electoral majority.[19] But Edsall puts Democratic Party radical liberalism at the center. In his view, the Democrats' errors are the cause of conservative resurgence because, since the 1960s, Democrats have stepped away from an inclusive politics based on class interests and taken the side of various minorities, particularly black people, against the interests of working-class white Americans. Identifying themselves with racial minorities, feminists, gays, and antiwar activists, says Edsall, the Democrats destroyed the New Deal's electoral majority and handed power to a "top-down coalition" of conservatives.

There is an overriding problem with Hodgson and Edsall, located in their evasion of the centrality of race to U.S. politics. Hodgson does not see how racialized fears inform nearly all organizing on the Right, perhaps because since the 1970s these fears are conveyed in a "code" (crime, drugs, immorality, shiftlessness, and so on versus traditional or "American" values). Edsall's version is superior to Hodgson's because race dominates his narrative, as the wedge breaking up the New Deal coalition in which whites and blacks had submerged their differences. But Edsall matches Hodgson in his inability to acknowledge the depth of racism among white people, including the working-class "Reagan Democrats" whom he considers the lost protagonists of U.S. politics. This myopia is clearly delineated in each author's assertion that northern whites supported equality for blacks until the supposed excesses of black militants frightened them away. The unavoidable conclusion is that, however laudable morally, the Democratic Party's association with the civil rights movement was a political disaster—*and should have been avoided.*

Recent studies provide useful foils to the conventional narratives just described, showing that the roots of the Right's resurgence go back much further, to the early Cold War years—long before the emergence of civil rights, black power, Vietnam, women's liberation, gay rights, and other radical causes commonly cited as provoking a conservative reaction. Each of these books also shares a common taproot in the recognition that whiteness itself (as fear, as pride, as a cross-ethnic "Americanism") was a basic organizing principle for right-wing politics.

The starting place for conservative politics as a postwar social movement is the career of George Corley Wallace, the charismatic southern Democrat who was governor of Alabama and a four-time presidential candidate (running in the Democratic primaries in 1964, 1972, and 1976, and as an Independent in the general election in 1968). Dan Carter's recent biography examines his enormous influence on both Democrats and Republicans.[20] By demonstrating the nationwide appeal of a message that combines anti-elite and racist sentiments, Wallace inserted a new dynamic. He broke the mold, and in his wake followed Richard Nixon, Ronald Reagan, Newt Gingrich, and a host of others repeating the same message in quieter tones.

Carter's insistence on the centrality of unreconstructed white supremacism among white Southerners and others is complemented by Sara Diamond's *Roads to Dominion: Right-Wing Movements and Political Power in the United States,* which makes a striking contrast to Hodgson's book covering the same period.[21] Though he gingerly covered the John Birch Society, Hodgson ignored the web of profascist and extremist groups that dated from World War II and persisted into the postwar era, forming the infrastructure of Wallace's campaigns. The anti-Semite Willis Carto's Liberty Lobby, the constellation of Ku Klux Klan groups, and the proliferating "Christian Identity" networks, with their violent offshoots like the Aryan Nation and the so-called "militias," are all carefully examined by Diamond.

Two major studies of the Barry Goldwater phenomenon show how the New Right incubated outside the traditional Deep South, in the "old America" of the Midwest and the nouveau southwestern terrain later dubbed the Sunbelt. Rick Perlstein's definitive biography of the Arizona senator places his movement's extraordinary takeover of the Republican Party between 1959 and 1964 into a larger cultural context that stretches back to the New Deal, while Lisa McGirr's study of Orange County, California's "suburban warriors" is the first in-depth study of "movement conservatives" in their natural social location, the postwar suburbs.[22]

A notable revision of conservatism's rise is Thomas Sugrue's *The Origins of the Urban Crisis*.[23] Until Sugrue, scholars of the northern, white working and lower-middle classes assumed that racial anger expressed electorally was a distinctive feature of the late 1960s on, a response to the civil rights movement. Sugrue turns this hypothesis on its head. In Detroit, the heartland of blue-collar politics in the 1930s and 1940s via the United Auto Workers, white aggression against black assertions of equality surfaced violently during World War II and increased steadily throughout the postwar era. Focused on the issue of "open housing," it spawned a massive movement, recruiting thousands of whites into homeowners' associations and electing a mayor committed to protecting white privilege. Year after year, organized mobs protected racial turf by driving out new black residents with little police intervention.

If white working-class communities shared and acted on a fear and hatred of blacks *before* the civil rights movement, then the New Deal was founded not on common interests but on black submission and was inherently fragile. The sad story of Detroit also explains what white politicians and journalists have long proclaimed irrational: the insurrections that shook northern African American "ghettoes" just as the civil rights movement reached its peak of influence between 1964 and 1968. Just when blacks had the greatest sympathy from white America, goes the story, they threw it all away by burning and looting and following "extremists" like the Black Panther Party. Sugrue shows how decades of "white flight," continued residential segregation, acute housing shortages for African Americans, and deindustrialization—removing the unionized factory jobs that provided black men a route to security—made cities like Detroit into tinderboxes of mutual resentment. Certainly, the Great Society and practical assertions of black power mattered, especially the breakthroughs in black electoral representation, but these were not catalysts of legitimate white resentment against a loss of status (as Edsall, Jonathan Rieder, and others argue) but rather the latest stages in an explicitly racial war for urban control in which whites were the aggressors.

THE WHITE PARTY

Taken together, this historiography suggests that the conservative triumphs after 1980 are the product of a long germination, rather than a response to immediate conditions. Looking back over modern America since the Civil War, it is clear that the preservation of white privilege is a defining resentment knitting together disparate classes, ethnicities, and regions. This requires overturning the shibboleth that the "liberal" New Deal smashed traditional conservatism, and only periodic appeals to crude anticommunism combined with the liberal Republicanism championed by figures like Thomas Dewey, Dwight Eisenhower, and Nelson Rockefeller allowed the Republicans to maintain electoral power after World War II. *The New Deal itself, as a Democratic Party–led coalition, contained within it the core ultraconservative constituency of twentieth-century U.S. politics—the white supremacist voters and political apparatus of the South.* They briefly went along with the activist national state and radical reforms of the 1930s because of dire economic necessity, as long as their regional power was unchallenged. Once postwar prosperity took hold, the Democrats were forced to confront their contradictions because of pressure from the emerging bloc of northern black voters. From 1948 to 1964, in fits and starts and motivated by a potentially crippling black swing to the Republicans, the Democrats gave up their historic identity as a "white man's party." In response, the solid South began a long migration that over time birthed a new conservative coalition, built from a southern base and using "southern" methods of cross-class racial mobilization. In 1948, Mississippi governor Fielding Wright led his state's delegation out of the Democratic National Convention when a pro–civil rights plank was adopted. The Mississippians organized their own convention, never acknowledging they had bolted the party, and ran South Carolina governor Strom Thurmond as a "states rights Democrat" (or "Dixiecrat"). He carried the four states where he was listed as the official Democratic candidate, a premonition of the New Right to come decades later, as the South moved into the Republican column.

By itself, however, the possible defection of southern Democrats did not guarantee a new conservative alignment. Northern Republicans had a deep antipathy to associating with the Confederacy's heirs (and vice versa). The historic identification as the "party of Lincoln" still meant something, not primarily as a commitment to black equality—though until 1965, northern Republicans joined Democrats in bipartisan support for civil rights bills, and the twentieth century's first African American senator was Massachusetts Republican Edward Brooke, elected in 1966—but because of inherited sectional hostility. The white South stood for backwardness, corruption, ignorance, and lawlessness. Therefore a central concern of New Right operatives, the little-known professionals who infiltrated the Republican Party in the 1960s, was reconciling the historic division between conservative constituencies.[24] In the postwar era, there were two regionally defined right-wing voting blocs: segregationists defending their white supremacist fortress, and traditional Midwesterners who anchored the Republican Party but did not control it, losing out every four years in the presidential selection process to the "eastern establishment" identified with Wall Street and elitist liberalism, personified in the 1960s by New York governor Nelson Rockefeller. Assembling a new majority required moving all of these natural allies into a single ideological home, breaking down the traditional overlap of liberals and conservatives spread across both parties.

The Goldwater presidential campaign of 1959–64 was a failed attempt at this new conservative coalition. Goldwater as a "man of the West" could transcend old regional and partisan divisions, it was hoped. He repudiated the New Deal but in language that suggested a newfangled individualism, not just old-fashioned fiscal probity. The core of Goldwater's message was not racial but political: anticommunism married to antistatism as a holy cause. During the Fifties, this was the creed that drew together the scattered fragments of intellectual conservatism, especially the cadre of polemicists, fundraisers, and organizers around William F. Buckley's skillfully edited *National Review*. For a moment, it seemed the ghosts of Herbert Hoover and the Great Depression were finally banished.

But the Goldwaterites' commitment to stopping the Soviet threat obscures the base of this "new" conservative movement. In 1964, when Lyndon Johnson monopolized the political center and claimed the allegiance of the liberal Left, the only states where Goldwater won a majority (other than Arizona) were in the deepest South, Democratic since the 1870s. Commentators claimed this proved Goldwater's irrelevance, but it portended a fundamental shift in voter alignments: Every Democratic president and congressional majority for a hundred years relied on the "solid" white South. If the GOP could take Dixie, all standard electoral calculations were off. Republican losses in 1964 could be made up, as the party rebounded spectacularly in 1966, but the Democrats, now defined as the party of racial liberalism, had lost their historic base. From 1964 through the present, conservatism's rise has been a three-pronged offensive anchored by the politics and ethos of southern whiteness. First, whole sections of the old Democratic Party machines that controlled the South turned Republican. Second, among the Republicans, a bureaucratic contest festered to move the party to the Right and southward, depriving the northeastern moderates of power. Finally, a series of single-issue movements have been recruited into the Republican Party, mainly via a politicized evangelical Protestantism spreading nationwide from southern bases.

This summary raises an obvious point: The conservative ascendance is really the story of the Republicans more than a narrative of social movements. Why? From the beginning, conservative activists have focused on winning elections and controlling government machinery, not as a means to an end, but as *the* end. The labor movement of the 1930s wanted to change conditions on the factory floor and even democratize capitalism itself, seeing government as a vehicle. The civil rights movement of the 1960s wanted black people to live with dignity and the basic rights of U.S. citizens and needed federal power to make it happen. The New Right was different and more revolutionary—from the first it wanted to control government so as to determine the course of U.S. society.

The internal Republican battle is the least visible aspect of this story. The party has existed since 1854. A conscious attempt to take it over, using ex-Democrats, caused much bitterness. The conservatives had their own resentments, stemming from the repeated denial of the presidential nomination from 1940 to 1952 to their standard bearer, Ohio senator Robert Taft ("Mr. Conservative"), in favor of Wendell Wilkie, Thomas Dewey, and Dwight Eisenhower. The public refusal of many northeastern GOP leaders to support Goldwater after he won the nomination in 1964 set off a blood feud. By the late 1990s, liberal Republicans in Congress could be counted on the fingers of one hand: Representatives Connie Morella of Maryland and Jim Leach of Iowa, perhaps a few others. Vermont senator James Jeffords's defection in 2001 to "independent" status signaled the probable extinction of this wing of the Grand Old Party.

The intraparty war for survival was complicated by Richard Nixon's presidency. Nixon's willingness to implement liberal social policies while using Vice President Spiro Agnew as a mouthpiece for right-wing sentiments confused conservatives and slowed their coalescence, and of course the Watergate affair hurt the Republicans badly. But Nixon advanced the Right's long-term interests by narrowly winning in 1968 and sweeping to reelection in 1972 through a "southern strategy," using calculated appeals to white southerners to leave their Democratic home. This plan included two failed attempts to put segregationists on the Supreme Court (he knew they would lose but relished the symbolic political gain), a go-slow policy on school desegregation, and demonstrative opposition to busing, the main racial issue of the 1970s. Nixon paved the way for the ascendance of conservative Republicans in that pivotal decade, as Ronald Reagan moved from the Sunbelt fringe to become the central party leader, and abortion became a key political litmus test. A host of movements surged to block the Equal Rights Amendment, defeat local ordinances banning discrimination against gays, and advance aid to anticommunists abroad. The evangelical renaissance among white Protestants gathered force; hundreds of new religious television and radio stations went on the air. Building on all of these elements, a self-conscious "New Right" announced itself. As Goldwater veterans, they nursed skills and grudges and pioneered the techniques of mass mobilization and direct-mail fund-raising that put the liberal mainstream on the defensive. Between 1978 and 1980, New Rightists defeated a host of senior liberal Democrats in Congress through gut-level political attacks, sending shock waves through the bipartisan establishment. In 1980, they helped elect a president. Ever since, they have operated as a permanent insurgency, never achieving total control of the GOP but forcing it sharply to the right. Only the threat of repudiation by centrist voters—as in President Bush's stunning 1992 loss—kept the Republicans from complete co-optation by "movement conservatives."

A party-centered narrative of right-wing politics misses major developments. The "pro-life" movement, for instance, is certainly more than a tool of Republican politicians. Based in Catholic and fundamentalist Protestant infrastructures, it is an unlikely alliance between historical adversaries committed to maintaining the patriarchal family based on women's chastity and service. Few scholars have yet investigated this powerful movement's relationship to partisan politics, so we are left with the evidence of its effects. As recently as the late 1970s, major Republicans endorsed "family planning" and supported Planned Parenthood. By the 1990s, no Republican aspiring to national office would publicly identify with a pro-abortion organization, outside of scattered urban areas. The shift in a once pluralist party can be extended to other areas. Northeastern Republican senators like New York's Jacob Javits and Maryland's Charles Matthias were leaders in passing legislation to end discrimination and protect black voters. Even Midwestern conservative Robert Dole helped extend the Voting Rights Act during the Reagan years in alliance with liberal bogeyman Ted Kennedy. Nowadays, it hard to imagine a senior Republican corralling votes to extend basic constitutional protections to people of color when a pro-Confederate rightist with a record of opposing desegregation, Missouri's John Ashcroft, was approved as attorney general in January 2001 by a solid bloc of Republican votes.

That the past three decades have seen the rise of a technologically advanced, diversified right-wing political coalition is not in doubt. The source of its dynamism, however, is much less understood. Hard as it is for both liberals and leftists to believe, the Right sees itself as permanently beleaguered. Though often manipulated for purposes of fundraising and mobilizing, conservatives share a worldview of moral, familial, and national (or imperial) collapse abetted by an organized Left. From their perspective, this view of the United States *after* Vietnam, *after Roe v. Wade, after* black power and gay liberation, makes total sense. Therefore, to understand the Right requires understanding the equally entrenched brand of progressive politics within the structure of parties and interests. Acknowledging this balance of power means letting go of the Left's myths of heroic marginalization but brings us closer to an accurate picture of U.S. politics and society since the 1960s.

RADICAL LIBERALISM AND THE BALANCE OF POWER

With this tracing of the outlines of the New Right, one fact must be underlined. What has unified conservative forces, from 1972 to 2002, is the conviction that they face a formidable enemy—a tide that threatens the home, the school, the workplace, the church, and even the armed forces. They give various names to this ideological and social force, from "radical liberalism" in the 1970s (the most accurate description) to "San Francisco Democrats" in the 1980s (in Jeanne Kirkpatrick's formulation at the 1984 Republican Convention), to "McGovernism" in the 1990s, as when Newt Gingrich labeled the Clintons "McGoverniks." Most often, conservative activists have painted with the broadest brush, using the terms "liberals" and "the Left" interchangeably, to sow confusion.

Many self-described radicals ignore the Right's tendency to conflate different stances, as if Bill Clinton and Jesse Jackson (or Al Gore and Ralph Nader) were on the same team. But this deliberate mystification, whatever its intended purposes, points to a truth hidden in plain sight. *Conservatives have never believed that the New Left died, or that their own ascendance was predetermined. To them, the social movements of the Sixties, from black power to women's and gay liberation to the antiwar coalition, survived and prospered in the 1980s and 1990s, with disastrous results. In this conviction, they are closer to grasping the main currents of U.S. politics than are most on the Left.*

To understand why the New Right often is the greatest booster of "the Left," we must turn to outlining radicalism's contours since the 1960s. We begin by looking at the two definitions of the Left in U.S. politics over the past generation. When conservatives use the term, they mean, first, the solidly social-democratic voters of black America, who often function as a party within the Democratic Party. Second, they mean the militant sectors of the labor movement: those unions that represent public employees and service workers, and what remains of the old industrial union powerhouses like the United Auto Workers. That the AFL-CIO and the National Education Association deploy the country's most effective voter-mobilization operations guarantees that conservatives have something to fear on Election Day. Finally, the Right uses "the Left" most broadly to describe the host of well-funded organizations that deal with reproductive and civil rights, environmental and consumer protection, and social justice, plus their congressional allies in the Democrats' "progressive" wing.

Conversely, when most scholars (and leftists) talk about "the Left" in recent America, they decry its decline from the halcyon past of Debsian socialism in the 1910s, the Communist-led Popular Front in the 1930s, or the New Left's "beloved community" in the 1960s. It is an article of faith among radicals that they are a tiny minority ignored by the vast majority. To keep asserting this, they have to minimize the weight of the actually existing Left of blacks, labor, feminists, gays, and environmentalists. The earlier schema is dismissed as mere "liberalism" yoked to the Democratic Party, without ideological coherence. There is a clear contradiction between these two views, and the Right's version is considerably more accurate. The least-told story of U.S. history in the late twentieth century is how the social movements of the Sixties institutionalized themselves, as documented by the essays in this book: a pattern of irreversible democratization of political and personal life over three decades—the "new democratic order" of this essay's title.

Am I suggesting that the NAACP, the National Organization for Women, Planned Parenthood, the AFL-CIO, the National Abortion and Reproductive Rights Action League, the League of Conservation Voters, the Sierra Club, the Human Rights Campaign Fund, the National Council of La Raza, the National Gay and Lesbian Task Force, the American Civil Liberties Union, People for the American Way, Handgun Control, Greenpeace, the American Friends Service Committee, the Public Interest Research Groups (PIRGs), Amnesty International, the Association of Community Organizations for Reform Now (ACORN), and the Children's Defense Fund (to list only some of the best-known organizations denoted as "liberal," "leftwing," or "progressive") constitute the Left in U.S. politics? Yes and no. Certainly, these are the institutions defending the gains staked out by the New Left between 1964 and 1976 and expanded since then. Among them, they have millions of supporters, many of whom not only support a "single issue" but also share a larger commitment to civil and human rights for all people, women's rights to control their own bodies, the preservation of the natural world from corporate despoliation, social justice for working people and the poor, and opposition to militarism. However hedged with qualifications, these overlapping constituencies constitute the Left in U.S. politics, the "radical liberalism" that so enrages the Right.

What conservatives miss, though, is that the combination of professionalized national advocacy groups with urban black, feminist, gay, and labor voters is only one expression of progressive politics in Postmodern America. Space precludes a thorough analysis of the patchwork of the residual past and emerging future that constitutes the current Left. The crucial distinction is between "national" and "local," since many of the national advocacy groups have a limited relationship to grassroots activism. Anyone familiar with progressive organizing knows there exists more openly radical layers of activism at the city and county level, focused on issues like police brutality, immigrant rights, environmental racism, the death penalty, sweatshops, corporate globalization, and abortion clinic defense. Many activists commute between the "national" and the "local," as the grassroots is where organizers usually begin before moving on to national offices. Often, the two spheres remain separate, because of the name recognition and clout among press, policy makers, and the public reserved for the long-established national organizations. During the November 1999 protests against the World Trade Organization in Seattle, one could see the explosive consequences when radicals, from nuns to students, converged with the institutional Left, represented by John Sweeney of the AFL-CIO and Carl Pope of the Sierra Club.

Of course, this brief narrative leaves out much, like the dozens of Jobs with Justice coalitions and "living wage" campaigns, and attempts to build viable electoral formations outside of the Democrats like the New, Labor, and Green Parties. And over the past generation the Left has had a third leg: its influence in sectors of higher education, where many social science and humanities disciplines are led by scholars who identify publicly with the Left. The goal of demonizing the academic Left, with its access to institutional resources and the minds of millions of young Americans, underlay the 1990s campaign against "political correctness." But the general population at least knows about the existence of the academic Left, if only through the age-old stereotype of "bearded professors" and indictments of "tenured radicals" by neoconservative academicians like Roger Kimball. Less visible but ultimately more consequential are the thousands of progressive churches and other places of worship, including the "mainline" Protestant denominations (Methodist, United Church of Christ, Lutheran, Presbyterian, Episcopal, and others), a significant number of Catholic parishes, many synagogues, and, of course, the "peace churches" (Friends, Church of the Brethren, and Mennonites). In large parts of rural and suburban America, they are the Left, the voices for tolerance, social justice, and opposition to war.

Despite claims of conservative dominance, solid support for core progressive issues should not require demonstrating. As one example, to counteract the voter mobilization by groups like the Christian Coalition, a systematic effort began in 1994 to combine statewide "voter files" of progressives, merging into one database the memberships of related organizations for lobbying and get-out-the-vote drives. This project was initiated by the League of Conservation Voters in the environmental community and largely funded by Ted Turner. It moved to the national level during 1999 and 2000, after successful coalitions were built in almost thirty states, generating a voter file with more than three million names. Before the 2000 election, Turner funded a similar effort by feminist organizations that rapidly assembled more than two million pro-choice women voters.

The larger question is the extent to which single-issue commitments overlap: Are "pro-environment" voters generally "pro-choice"? Are the latter supporters of gay and lesbian rights? Do commitments to civil liberties extend to support for trade unions or global human rights? Certainly, most progressive organizations see themselves as mining the same seam, bartering membership lists for fund-raising appeals, drawing on the same celebrity endorsements, and supporting the same candidates for office. Locally, there is considerable overlap and mutual aid. Whether their constituencies identify as a larger "progressive" sector of society is less clear. This possibility has never been adequately tested and may never be, given the frozen quality of the current standoff, reminiscent of the Gilded Age when Democrats and Republicans sparred ritually over the bloody shirts of partisan interest.

Radicalism's post-Sixties segmentation should not be seen, however, as the conscious preference of the current and former activists, self-identified "liberals," and less ideological single-issue supporters that back the major progressive groups. That would constitute blaming the victim—the error of those writers who attack the supposed divisiveness of "identity politics." Rather, the dispersed, pluralist Left is the result of how U.S. politics function after the decline of the political parties and voting since 1945. To effect legislation, garner any notice from a cynical press, and build anything lasting, the Left must operate by the rules of interest-group politics. Since the 1960s, that engagement with the terms of power has moved radical causes far away from left-wing modes of operation and traditions of confrontation.[25]

A chief reason it is hard to recognize the progressive "communities" as an extension of the New Left is their reliance on carefully focused discourses ("choice" rather than "liberation"), with funding from wealthy individuals via private foundations, and a larger mass of middle-class professional/technical workers giving small donations. The core national organizations (and hundreds of others lesser known but similar) are almost all centralized entities run by a full-time professional staff. They rarely relate to explicitly radical groups. Only a few of the oldest, like the NAACP and the Sierra Club, maintain traditional volunteer-based local structures at city, congressional district, and state levels. Many operate solely as "national" organizations—sophisticated fundraising machines that undergird communications and legislative "shops" inside the Beltway, and electoral arms devoted to "issue advocacy" aimed at forcing candidates to bend to their wills.[26] Most are tied to the Democratic Party and give short shrift to overturning the closed two-party system through a "multi-issue" challenge to structures of privilege. One need only cite the anger expressed by the leaders of most progressive groups regarding Ralph Nader's candidacy in 2000, and their attempts to suppress that effort.

This is not an indictment. The single-issue progressive phalanx is not corrupt, accommodationist, or insufficiently radical. When fewer and fewer people will devote time as volunteers to building organizations from the bottom up, there are few recourses for activists who seek to advance a particular cause. To defend the hard-won legal and social gains of the 1960s and 1970s—and "defense" is the main mode of activism— the only option is to professionalize via highly rationalized fundraising apparatuses that will produce money sufficient to support a competent lobbying, communications, and field staff. In terms of the oppositional militancy associated with the Left, it is hard to see this trend as part of the radical tradition—but it is. Can one imagine a NARAL (National Abortion and Reproductive Rights Action League) or Sierra Club field organizer dragged off a soapbox and threatened with lynching, or board members in these organizations hiding an escaped slave, or PIRG canvassers confronting U.S. Steel or Ford goons outside a plant gate? Perhaps not, but they must confront the challenges that exist now, rather than the enemies of the past. The state violence, paramilitary gangs, legal injunctions, and blacklisting once routinely endured by radical agitators are no longer legally acceptable, and that marks a sea change in U.S. history. As a recent development, we should celebrate that legalization and "pacification" of political struggle, rather than bemoan it in favor of the repression and resistance of the past.

The array of progressive issue constituencies and organizations are necessary but not sufficient to defining the Left in Postmodern America, but it is with these organizations and constituencies that we must start. Otherwise, we are reduced to artificial distinctions between radical goals, like full equality for gay men and women, including the civil protections of marriage, versus militant means, such as disrupting a service at a church espousing homophobic policies. Propelled by grassroots organizers with high expectations, the progressive establishment continues to pursue radical goals: Anyone who thinks that civil rights for homosexuals, a woman's right to control her own body, or public control over the natural environment are "mainstreamed" liberal issues is not paying attention or inhabits one of the bicoastal enclaves like Boston, New York, the Bay Area, Los Angeles, or Seattle, where much of radicalism is now conventional wisdom.

One more analogy sums up the role of progressives today: Since the 1960s the Left has gradually reclaimed the role it played in earlier periods, specifically the Popular Front of the 1930s and 1940s, when an array of well-established institutions, from the Congress of Industrial Organizations to the National Negro Congress to myriad peace, youth, women's and ethnic groups were vital to the ascendance of the New Deal coalition. Then, as now, no one could claim that the Left runs the Democratic Party. Progressives and radicals remain both indispensable and subordinate within a larger center-left political bloc, a difficult position to maintain and one that is constantly renegotiated, especially since "New Democrats" associated with the Democratic Leadership Council, like Bill Clinton and Al Gore, began working in the later 1980s to limit the power of progressives within the party. But the ascendance of Clintonism also included the cold-eyed recognition that Democratic electoral victories required the all-out mobilization of constituencies (African Americans, feminists, gays and lesbians, committed labor voters, environmentalists) who remain firmly on the Left. Early in the twenty-first century, the paradox only intensifies. The Democrats have programmatically lost their bearings, scared of the Republicans and holding desperately to a mythical "vital center." They rely on the Left but run away from it. How long this alliance of convenience can persist is an open question.

How do the essays in this collection contribute to our understanding of the complex "war of position" characterizing U.S. politics and culture since the 1970s? They illuminate a vast field of change by what I denote, with deliberate ambiguity, as either a post–New Left or a radicalized liberalism.

First, there is the field of memory and representation, where conservatives are sharply aware of their inability to reestablish the moral order. Several essays bring into relief the impact of Sixties movements upon the most visible aspects of public culture. The contrast between mass-market movies and federally funded history exhibits underlines the ubiquity of cultural shifts. In quite different essays, our contributors demonstrate that addressing U.S. history on other than triumphalistic terms has radical implications. First, in "The Movement Inside: BBS Films and the Cultural Left in the New Hollywood," Andrew Schroeder explores how the independent filmmaker Bert Schneider and his cohorts built upon their 1969 hit *Easy Rider* to change the Hollywood studio system and inaugurate a vastly expanded space for socially critical films seeking a mass market. In their joint essay "Holding the Rock: The 'Indianization' of Alcatraz Island, 1969–1999," Tina Loo and Carolyn Strange explore the history of the ex-prison museum-island of Alcatraz, popular because of its movie-made associations, where Park Service personnel have worked to incorporate the 1969 Native American occupation, one of the New Left's signature confrontations, into a genuinely multicultural narrative. Future studies will undoubtedly expand this investigation of democratized cultural production to other areas of public life and entertainment—television, radio, parades, ceremonial gatherings, conventions and funerals, monuments, religious institutions, eating and drinking, neighborhoods and streets and parks, and, most obviously, popular music and the rise of the web.

Turning to how the Sixties inflect recent politics, it is difficult to assert which wing of the New Left had the greatest impact, since so much changed so fast. Yet it seems indisputable that, just as gender cuts across the most intimate tissues of society, so the effects of second-wave feminism are the most pervasive, regardless of class, racial, or ethnic position. As Sara Evans demonstrates in "Beyond Declension: Feminist Radicalism in the 1970s and 1980s," the women's movement not only became a permanent presence, but also maintained its radical edge. Evans's argument is complemented by two other essays. In "Taking Over Domestic Space: The Battered Women's Movement and Public Protest," Anna Enke shows how one of the first women's shelters, founded in Minneapolis during the 1970s, managed class and cultural antagonisms among women and the resistance of municipal authorities to provoke basic changes in public policy that curtailed the male prerogative of physical abuse. Looking at this same transitional moment, Natasha Zaretsky argues in "In the Name of Austerity: Middle-Class Consumption and the OPEC Oil Embargo of 1973–1974," that the new gendering of politics had sweeping effects during the energy crisis, which seemed to augur permanent declines in both the nation's political economy and the myth of family harmony. Zaretsky probes how gender concerns intruded into conventional politics, surfacing in coded references to women's liberation as the cause of disorder.

Another take on how post-Sixties social movements changed the body politic can be found in a third set of essays, also concerned with gender and sexuality. In "Fabulous Politics: Gay, Lesbian and Queer Movements, 1969–1999," Jeffrey Escoffier analyzes "the identitarian moment" in gay and lesbian life and politics. He argues that once gay liberation with its utopian universalism declined, a more particularistic, ethnic-group politics was the practical option, but one containing inherent limitations. Christopher Capozzola's "A Very American Epidemic: Memory Politics and Identity Politics in the AIDS Memorial Quilt, 1985–1993" looks at one of the most successful campaigns for gay dignity, the quilt project that spread nationwide during the 1980s, incorporating large parts of Middle America otherwise hostile to gay people. Finally, Kitty Krupat's semi-autobiographical essay, "Out of Labor's Dark Age: Sexual Politics Comes to the Workplace," looks at being "out" on the job, and the resulting requirement for traditional union structures to defend gays against discrimination. She shows how committed trade unionists in a progressive New York union stretched over time to understand this new discourse, while gay activists became an explicit interest group within labor, leading to a formal commitment to gay rights by the new AFL-CIO leadership in the 1990s.

Krupat's essay points to one of the least understood shifts of recent decades—the rise of a new social unionism opposed to the hierarchical, Cold War–oriented conservatives who ran U.S. labor in the post-1945 era. Her analysis of the accrual of reform forces shows that the 1995 election of John Sweeney as AFL-CIO president was no sudden coup but the culmination of a long effort. In this context, co-editor Richard Moser's study, "Autoworkers at Lordstown: Workplace Democracy and American Citizenship," demonstrates the potency of working-class solidarity at a time of supposed class collaboration and gives the lie to those who have written off the labor movement.

The remaining essays each illustrate a major development of the postmodern, post-Vietnam era. In "Unpacking the Vietnam Syndrome: The Coup in Chile and the Rise of Popular Anti-Interventionism," I look at the mid-1970s transition from Vietnam-era protest to the more enduring brand of resistance that made life difficult for Washington policy makers during subsequent decades, especially when they attempted to reimpose an imperial order in Latin America. Andrew Feffer's essay, "The Land Belongs to the People: Reframing Urban Protest in Post-Sixties Philadelphia," explores a central shift in electoral dynamics: a new urban majority politics based on an energized black electorate. Focusing on Philadelphia in the late 1970s, Feffer examines political conflict over housing and municipal space in which the militants, putatively outside the system, included the man who would be elected mayor two decades later, John Street. His essay constitutes an ethnography of black power in action, the sort of local study that is sorely needed. James Livingston's "Cartoon Politics: The Case of the Purloined Parents" forces us to take seriously the complicated narrative substructure of some of the biggest movie hits in recent years, the new-style Disney movies *The Little Mermaid* and *Toy Story*. Livingston demonstrates the sophistication and political depth of these films, which go well beyond cartoon stereotypes of "feminism." Eliot Katz concludes our volume with "At the End of the Century." Balancing the elegiac with the prophetic, his poem surveys the century's tragedies but finds in jazz music and social movements metaphors for hope that "sometime . . . our sketches will come to life."

An astute reader will quickly grasp all the possible topics this collection does not address. A few bear particular watching. First, respectful attention should be paid to the phenomena grouped under the heading New Age, including organic food production and consumption, alternative medicine, and the search for spirituality. Second, the "social movement" character of right-wing insurgency needs attention, as groups from Operation Rescue to the Christian Coalition mimic the rights-centered discourse (and sometimes the protest tactics) associated with the Left. Third, while I have just sketched the structural character-istics of progressive, left, and liberal organizing since the Sixties, such as the reliance on fund-raising rather than old-style membership building, we need historians prepared to grapple with this history. Journalists and therefore the "political public" know the New Right expanded its power outside of traditional Republican politics via innovative direct-mail operations led by Richard Viguerie and others in the 1970s, build-ing new donor bases in the millions (for Jesse Helms's Congressional Club originally, and then for many other organizations). But many en-gaged liberal and radical intellectuals are ignorant of the parallel tech-nological breakthrough that built the post–New Left political machines like Greenpeace, Citizen Action, and the PIRGs: door-to-door canvasses that recruited millions of small donors, at the same time training hun-dreds of new organizers every year (how to compress a salient political argument into a simple short message; how to ask for money without fumbling).

Finally, even in terms of this collection's specific focus—politics and culture since the Sixties that fall outside the shibboleths about "the rise of the Right"—we have not addressed continuing activism among Puerto Ricans, Chicanos, and other Latinos/Latinas in the United States; the politics of the Asian American community; the roiling "sex wars" that have swept through and polarized the feminist and gay move-ments (to invoke the title of Lisa Duggan's and Nan Hunter's excellent book); the Rainbow Coalition as the great failed hope of independent left electoralism (both Manning Marable and Adolph Reed Jr. have written extensively on this and related subjects); and more. Much re-mains to be done, if we are to recover this quarter century of low-level ferment and high-level skullduggery, "old" middle-class and new Yup-pie complacency, and constant brushfire confrontation. We hope our readers will see this volume as the beginning of a long conversation and respond themselves with new interpretations and further investi-gation.

NOTES

1. Todd Gitlin, *The Twilight of Common Dreams: Why America Is Wracked by Culture Wars* (New York: Metropolitan Books, 1995).
2. Examples of these authors' recent work include Haynes Johnson, *Sleep-walking through History: America in the Reagan Years* (New York: Anchor Books, 1992) and *Divided We Fall: Gambling with History in the 1990s* (New York: Norton, 1994); Sidney Blumenthal, *Our Long National Daydream: A Political Pageant of the*

Reagan Era (New York: Harper & Row, 1988) and *Pledging Allegiance: The Last Campaign of the Cold War* (New York: HarperCollins, 1990); Kevin Phillips, *The Emerging Republican Majority* (Garden City, N.Y.: Anchor Books, 1970), *The Politics of Rich and Poor: Wealth and the American Electorate in the Reagan Aftermath* (New York: Random House, 1990); Thomas Byrne Edsall, *The New Politics of Inequality* (New York: Norton, 1984) and (with Mary Edsall), *Chain Reaction: The Impact of Race, Rights, and Taxes on American Politics* (New York: Norton, 1991). Before Reagan left office, Blumenthal and Edsall had edited a still-useful collection of essays, *The Reagan Legacy* (New York: Pantheon Books, 1988). Phillips and Edsall are the preeminent journalistic interpreters of politics in this era. For representative textbook treatments, see John Mack Faragher et al., *Out of Many: A History of the American People* (Englewood Cliffs, N.J.: Prentice Hall, 1994); Gary Nash et al., *The American People: Creating a Nation and a Society*, vol. 2, *Since 1865*, 3d ed. (New York: HarperCollins, 1994); James A. Henretta et al., *America's History*, 2d ed. (New York: Worth, 1993). All three cite Johnson's *Sleepwalking through History* and Phillips's *The Politics of Rich and Poor*, and one cites the Blumenthal and Edsall volume.

3. For a critical assessment of the historiography of the New Left, see Van Gosse, "'A Movement of Movements': The Definition and Periodization of the New Left," in Jean-Christophe Agnew and Roy Rosenzweig, eds., *Blackwell Companion to Post-1945 America* (Malden, Mass.: Blackwell, 2002), 277–302; a compressed narrative can be found in Gosse, *The American New Left: A History* (New York: Bedford/St. Martin's, forthcoming).

4. See Stanley I. Kutler, *The Wars of Watergate: The Last Crisis of Richard Nixon* (New York: Norton, 1992).

5. For a specification of "polycultural" identity more useful than the bagginess of multiculturalism, see Robin D. G. Kelley, "People in Me," *Color Lines*, winter 1999, 5–7.

6. A starting point for understanding the roots of racialized political and cultural identity in the United States is Edmund Morgan's magisterial *American Slavery, American Freedom* (New York: Norton, 1975). See also Alexander Saxton, *The Rise and Fall of the White Republic: Class Politics and Mass Culture in 19th Century America* (New York: Verso, 1990); Theodore W. Allen, *The Invention of the White Race*, vol. 2, *The Origin of Racial Oppression in Anglo-America* (New York: Verso, 1997); David R. Roediger, *The Wages of Whiteness: Race and the Making of the American Working Class* (New York: Verso, 1991); and Michael Goldfield, *The Color of Politics: Race and the Mainsprings of American Politics* (New York: New Press, 1997).

7. See John D'Emilio, *Sexual Politics, Sexual Communities: The Making of a Homosexual Minority in the United States, 1940–1970* (Chicago: University of Chicago, 1983); Jeffrey Escoffier, *American Homo: Community and Perversity* (Berkeley: University of California Press, 1998); Barry D. Adam, *The Rise of the Gay and Lesbian Movement* (Boston: Twayne, 1987); Martin Duberman, *Stonewall* (New York: Dutton, 1993); Dudley Clendinen and Adam Nagourney, *Out for Good: The Struggle to Build a Gay Rights Movement in America* (New York: Simon and Schuster, 1999).

8. See Sara Evans, *Personal Politics: The Origins of Women's Liberation in the Civil Rights Movement and the New Left* (New York: Knopf, 1979) and *Born for Liberty: A History of Women in America* (New York: Free Press, 1989); Ruth Rosen, *The World Split Open: How the Modern Women's Movement Changed America* (New York: Viking, 2000); Susan M. Hartmann, *The Other Feminists: Activists in the Liberal Establishment* (New Haven, Conn.: Yale University Press, 1998); Leila J. Rupp and Verta Taylor, *Survival in the Doldrums: The American Women's Rights Movement, 1945 to the 1960s* (Columbus: Ohio State University Press, 1990); Flora Davis, *Moving the Mountain: The Women's Movement in America since 1960* (Urbana: University of Illinois Press, 1999).

9. Margaret Atwood, *The Handmaid's Tale* (Boston: Houghton Mifflin, 1986).

10. Gitlin's *Twilight of Our Common Dreams* is the best known of these polemics. See also Jim Sleeper, *The Closest of Strangers: Liberalism and the Politics of Race in New York* (New York: Norton, 1990) and *Liberal Racism* (New York: Viking, 1997); Michael Tomasky, *Left for Dead: The Life, Death, and Possible Resurrection of Progressive Politics in America* (New York: Free Press, 1996); and, verging on absurdity, Ronald Radosh, *Divided They Fell: The Demise of the Democratic Party, 1964–1996* (New York: Free Press, 1996). Jonathan Rieder's *Canarsie: The Jews and Italians of Brooklyn against Liberalism* (Cambridge: Harvard University Press, 1985) is the foundational book for this argument.

11. Joel Rogers's article, "How Divided Progressives Might Unite" (*New Left Review*, March–April 1995, 3–32), is a balanced account of these defensive wars of position that have occupied the institutional apparatus born of the Sixties social movements, as well as a call to transcend particularism and go on the offensive.

12. Kevin Phillips was the first to label the late twentieth century another Gilded Age, in his still-powerful *The Politics of Rich and Poor*.

13. Steve Fraser and Gary Gerstle, eds., *The Rise and Fall of the New Deal Order, 1930–1980* (Princeton: Princeton University Press, 1989).

14. An exception to treating the 1970s as mere prelude to "conservative ascendance" is Peter Carroll, *It Seemed Like Nothing Happened: America in the 1970s* (New Brunswick, N.J.: Rutgers University Press, 1990), which stresses the continuities of social mobilization since the 1960s. Recently, Bruce J. Schulman has also advanced a provocative thesis about the 1970s' importance in *The 1970s: The Great Shift in American Culture, Society, and Politics* (New York: Free Press, 2001). Schulman's insistence that "the Sixties" ended with Richard Nixon's ascension to power in January 1969 diverges sharply from our understanding of the period. He claims much of the New Left and the Sixties for an elongated "1970s," to substantiate the "great shift" of his title, and then pushes what we would see as a very short "decade," 1975–1980, into Ronald Reagan's first term. Ultimately, this desire to establish an identity around a particular decade seems strained.

15. For an explicit assertion of this perspective, see the book by Republican congressman William Dannemeyer, *Shadow in the Land: Homosexuality in America* (San Francisco: Ignatius Press, 1989).

16. Phillips, *The Politics of Rich and Poor*, catalogues the upward redistribution of wealth under Reagan to great effect.

17. The literature on the United States and Central America in the 1980s is vast. Three sober treatments from scholars engaged on different sides of the domestic policy conflict are Cynthia Arnson, *Crossroads: Congress, the President and Central America, 1976–1993* (University Park: Pennsylvania State University Press, 1993); Robert Kagan, *A Twilight Struggle: American Power and Nicaragua, 1977–1990* (New York: Free Press, 1996); and William LeoGrande, *Our Own Backyard: The United States in Central America, 1977–1992* (Chapel Hill: University of North Carolina Press, 1998).

18. Godfrey Hodgson, *The World Turned Right Side Up: A History of the Conservative Ascendancy in America* (Boston: Houghton Mifflin, 1996).

19. Thomas Byrne Edsall with Mary B. Edsall, *Chain Reaction: The Impact of Race, Rights and Taxes on American Politics* (New York: Norton, 1991).

20. Dan T. Carter, *The Politics of Rage: George Wallace, the Origins of the New Conservatism, and the Transformation of American Politics*, 2d ed. (Baton Rouge: Louisiana State University Press, 2000). See also Dan T. Carter, *From George Wallace to Newt Gingrich: Race in the Conservative Counterrevolution, 1963–1994* (Baton Rouge: Louisiana State University Press, 1996).

21. Sara Diamond, *Roads to Dominion: Right-Wing Movements and Political Power in the United States* (New York: Guilford, 1995). Also Sara Diamond, *Not By Politics Alone: The Enduring Influence of the Christian Right* (New York: Guilford, 1998) and *Spiritual Warfare: The Politics of the Christian Right* (Boston: South End, 1989).

22. Rick Perlstein, *Before the Storm: Barry Goldwater and the Unmaking of the American Consensus* (New York: Hill and Wang, 2001); Lisa McGirr, *Suburban Warriors: The Origins of the New American Right* (Princeton: Princeton University Press, 2001).

23. Thomas J. Sugrue, *The Origins of the Urban Crisis: Race and Inequality in Postwar Detroit* (Princeton: Princeton University Press, 1996).

24. Mary C. Brennan, *Turning Right in the Sixties: The Conservative Capture of the GOP* (Chapel Hill: University of North Carolina Press, 1995).

25. For the crumbling of traditional party structures, see Walter Dean Burnham, *The Current Crisis in American Politics* (New York: Oxford University Press, 1982).

26. There are many variations: Greenpeace eschews lobbying in favor of superbly publicized "direct actions," while others only lobby. The PIRGs rely on door-to-door canvassing, while others are direct-mail specialists, and some avoid the labor-intensive acquisition of members and rely on foundation grants and "major donors." Depending on their tax status, self-image, funding sources, and willingness to maintain multiple legal entities, organizations do or do not lobby or engage electorally. The AFL-CIO and individual unions are a special case, because of their size and clout and because local unions still have an immediate economic functionality.

RICHARD MOSER

Introduction II

Was It the End or Just a Beginning?

American Storytelling and the
History of the Sixties

DID THE Sixties die a quick and quiet death? Can the final de-cades of the American Century be accurately labeled a "conservative era," as so many left and liberal academics and analysts insist? The most widely influential treatments of the 1960s see a wave of popular protest that crested in 1968, followed by the rapid decline of social movements and a national trend toward conservatism, co-optation, backlash, and quiescence.[1] We intend to challenge this interpretation by investigating significant elements of continuity between the social movements and cultural trends of the 1960s and later political and cul-tural developments. Rather than endorsing the idea that the period be-tween 1970 and the end of the century was a time of decline and cyni-cism (or of the ascendance of a triumphal conservatism), this volume examines the many ways that Americans continued to advance impor-tant aspects of the Sixties' unfinished agenda.

Certainly, the movements of that thirty-year period often seemed on the defensive. The battles, for instance, against aid to the Nicaraguan Contras and Robert Bork's nomination for the Supreme Court lacked the iconoclastic drama of the free-speech movement or Mississippi Free-dom Summer. But from the 1980s to the new century, Mississippi Free-dom Summer inspired new seasons of activism in Redwood Summer, Union Summer, and Democracy Summer. The peace movement that greeted the first Gulf War did not became an engine of social change like its predecessor, yet it was an effective, broad-based, and spirited re-sponse that successfully asserted very real constraints on U.S. policy.

It is valuable, indeed refreshing, to consider the trench-warfare of the 1970s, 1980s, and 1990s from the perspective of the Right. However much conservatives possessed an insurgent élan, they recognized that the constituencies of the post-1960s social movements held the cultural high ground. It was this painful recognition that energized the New Right and their desire for the restoration of what they imagined to be a superior traditional world. In this sense, then, we are more in agreement with those New Right conservatives who waged prolonged war against what they called "the Left" than with historians who write of the Sixties' death.

During the 1990s, the renaissance of the labor movement and the wave of demonstrations that started with Seattle 1999 convinced many that a resurgent movement for change was afoot. These new democratic movements continue and are impossible to explain without reference to the various political currents and alternative cultures that blossomed during the Sixties.

The essays in this volume demonstrate that social changes unleashed during the Sixties continued to shape American life until the end of the century. The attacks on New York and Washington, the subsequent war on terrorism and the wars in Afghanistan and Iraq are world-historic events but their meanings and consequences are far from clear. If these political and armed conflicts proceed as U.S. leaders have projected, they could be analogous to the Cold War in duration and character and could become what John F. Kennedy once described as a "long, twilight struggle." The Cold War had multiple, ambiguous and unintended consequences ranging from anticommunist hysteria to the civil rights movement and gave rise to both the New Right and the New Left. Given the doctrine of preemptive war, the rise of a grassroots antiwar movement, and the conflicting understandings of freedom and empire such polarization implies, it may well be that social movements similar to those we describe in this volume will continue to be a major influence in the politics and culture of the United States.

To see the Sixties and the movements that followed as part of an American tradition we must broaden the scope of our analysis beyond recent events and place the late-twentieth-century United States within the grand narratives of its own history. Scholars such as Richard Slotkin and James Gilbert have already begun to create accounts that understand recent history as rooted in many of the values, ideals, and social trends that reach back to the nation's earliest times.[2] We may join that exploration by listening closely to old stories of new beginnings.

New Frontiers, Apocalypse Now, and the Mirage of Paradise

All interpretations of the 1960s borrow from our inherited ways of understanding new beginnings. The reigning historical accounts explain that time as a utopian moment in which America's rebellious sons and daughters strove for authenticity and sought to perfect the world with moral and political ideals that envisioned an almost apocalyptic change. In this view, Sixties activists were the descendants of radical pacifists, existentialists, radical intellectuals, millennialists, abolitionists, utopian communards, and finally the original protest reformers of the new frontier, the Puritans.[3] As with their forebears, the fantastic hopes of Sixties activists were dashed, followed by a lament of loss and decline. Scholars called this slipping away of the Puritan vision "declension," and we use the same concept to draw attention to the continuity between historical events and historians' interpretations of them.[4]

Declensionist readings of the Sixties unconsciously replicated a view of historical and social change that derived its logic, emotional power, and narrative form from the culture of the frontier and from the apocalyptic strain in American religious culture. While these interpretive metaphors do resonate deeply with certain aspects of the 1960s, an alternative, equally compelling interpretation of the period could look instead to the American Revolution, Civil War, and Reconstruction, and the prophetic tradition of Judaism and Christianity. Interpretations that appreciate the sensibility of American revolutions and believe that people shape their own destiny by using the past, not fleeing from it, allow for a more open-ended story that can encompass the social movements and cultural changes of the 1970s, 1980s, and 1990s. Such a history disallows claims of certain triumph or defeat and acknowledges contingency, possibility, and conflict.

Stories of decline recast essential elements of two enduring and intertwined narratives that have been used to explain endings and new beginnings since America itself began. Early European colonists looked at the new land and imagined it as a wild frontier where their apocalyptic hopes for a godly community could be fulfilled. The idea of the frontier and the apocalypse have shaped the national character and American storytelling traditions ever since. Most scholars discuss the frontier as the cradle of empire, a master narrative of domination and a source of violence in the United States. That is only half the story. The frontier also calls us to a great, if ultimately misguided, adventure. Its vast untouched spaces promise spiritual renewal, freedom, and material wealth.

In 1702, when Cotton Mather wrote the first history of this country, he pictured the Puritans "flying from the deprivations of Europe to the American Strand" and inaugurated a lasting view of history that understood renewal as the product of departure and flight.[5] Frederick Jackson Turner's famed "frontier thesis" first granted the frontier a premier role in scholarly explanations of U.S. history and culture. William Appleman Williams elaborated Turner's conception of the frontier as a "gate of escape from the bondage of the past" into a theory that explained how Europeans, then Americans, attempted to evade social and political problems or oppressive institutions by leaving them all behind and starting over fresh.[6] Richard Slotkin's mighty study of the frontier argued that the political ideas, military doctrines, and cultural genres that shaped America's response to the world all replicated a process of "separation, regression to a more . . . 'natural' state and regeneration through violence" that originated in the frontier experience.[7] All these interpretations agree that deeply imbedded in U.S. culture is the presumption that the first step on the path to change begins with escape, departure, and separation.

While the physical frontier is no longer a viable resort for most Americans, the logic of the frontier lives on most forcefully in the imperial spirit but also remains a powerful mode of comprehension and identity that shapes social and political activity across what are otherwise profound political divisions. Frontier mythology leads us to find our problems and their solutions along the outside edge of our country rather than within. Thus, NSC 68, written in 1950, defined Cold War policy by locating a global borderline between freedom and communism that required policing and containment. Internal dissenters could not be accepted as authentic and so were attacked as "un-American."[8] Following this logic, liberal leaders of the 1960s convinced themselves that the creation of a new anticommunist nation in distant Vietnam was crucial to U.S. domestic security and prosperity.

During these same years, youthful hippies felt such a profound revulsion for urban commercial life that many withdrew to rural communes. Other kinds of retreats—psychological, cultural, and pharmaceutical—were far more common. At the height of radical engagement, some of the most committed and active cultural and political radicals adopted the stance of outsider, and the pose of permanent withdrawal remains a marker of dissent.

Frontier thinking satisfies the desire for newness and experimentation, most starkly articulated in the impulse to tear it all down and start over again, but directs the movement for change away from reforming existing political, cultural, and social institutions. Living on the edge is a kind of psychic utopia that thrives on feelings of release and freedom from the constraints of society, but it also guarantees that all sorts of seemingly radical actions and criticisms play themselves out without creating fundamental political change.

The focus on escape may produce resistance but weakens the capacity of social movements to propose practical alternatives and positive programs. Radicals are often attracted to frontier metaphors because they offer the most culturally ready modes of rebellion, but they are distracted by them as well because the frontier focus on the margin and periphery misdirect efforts away from reforming the core political institutions and culture understandings that most forcefully shape U.S. policy and history. Using the rhetoric of the frontier, John F. Kennedy was able to wed the optimistic hope for change to conventional politics. His appeal for Americans to "bear any burden" and rise to the challenges of a "New Frontier" enlisted reforming energy unleashed by the civil rights movement in the service of anticommunism abroad and the status quo at home.[9]

When the metaphors of escape and renewal are applied to historical time rather than physical space, as they now most often are, the frontier spirit encourages us to think that we must shed our past on the way to the future. History or tradition becomes the "old country" to be recalled sentimentally, then forgotten and cast aside. Attempts to bring about change interpreted through the lens of frontier mythology appear to be outside the currents of history: new, unique, original, unprecedented, and unrepeatable. Stories told in this vein have a closed circular quality that strips the 1960s of their historical context and leaves them "hermetically sealed off from what came before . . . and what has come since."[10] Historical accounts that measure the 1960s solely by the standards of escape and total change cannot help but see decline.

Ultimately, the frontier is able to operate so successfully as a symbolic substitute for revolution because both are metaphors of freedom.[11] The frontier promises freedom *from* the world, while revolution promises freedom *to participate* in it. This tension between opposing understandings of freedom can be read across virtually all the movements of the midcentury.

The values of the frontier and their power to displace revolutionary thinking are fortified by America's apocalyptic leanings. For the Puritans, frontier thought was fused with the expectation that as God's chosen people they would either suffer God's wrath for their sins or be rewarded for their virtue with salvation and a good earthly life in a perfect "city on the hill." Puritanism proposed that history turned on a delicate balance between the miraculous acts of God and studied, sweaty human striving. Some Puritans tilted toward the apocalyptic and collapsed human efforts for moral perfection into an instant and dramatic conversion experience they believed gave them a new birth in God's grace. They considered salvation a predestined act of God that no one could alter or prepare for. This style of apocalyptic belief was an important strain within Puritan religious attitudes that contributed to the American Revolution and over time became secularized into a way of viewing the world.[12]

As popular culture, apocalyptic thought directs our understanding of history and expectation of the future toward a binary of utopia or dystopia. We vacillate between a new world order of moral certainty and security and one of anarchy and Armageddon. Both are unknown worlds that follow an endtime that destroys the existing order. Apocalyptic thinking anticipates a "radical discontinuity of history," with the future bursting in on, rather than arising out of, the past or present.[13] History loses its power to explain and is reduced to a record of human corruption or a romantic recollection of lost innocence. Apocalyptic logic insists on a clean break between past and future but ultimately produces social passivity, because its adherents have no way to imagine the connection between what was, what is now, and what ought to be.

"Yet," as Christopher Rowland observed about early Christians, "life on the brink of the millennium is psychologically and politically impossible to sustain."[14] When a new dawn fails to materialize, apocalyptic hopes tend to return to more conventional preexisting beliefs or to degenerate into despair and cynicism. The wars, moral outrages, and religious uncertainty of the twentieth century have colored the apocalyptic imagination with a decidedly dismal cast.[15]

The apocalyptic posture did indeed shape some aspects of the 1960s and has certainly influenced historical thinking about the decade.

Whether declensionist accounts despise the Sixties and the social movements or sympathetically bemoan the latter's presumed failure, these arguments belong to the same culture of apocalyptic desire that drove moralistic reformers, except that now their millennialist vision has soured into a sense of disaster, pessimism, or ironic detachment. As Perry Miller suggested about the Puritans, their very lament functioned as a cultural and psychic purge that "serves as a token payment upon the obligation" to their ideals and so "liberates the debtors" to return to the more immediate tasks of building empires and making money.[16] Some declensionist readings of the 1960s still cling to a vision of social change, but their deep sense of resignation implies that people can only wait for, not create, its coming.

The apocalyptic rupture from the past and the frontieresque departure toward new spaces and exotic cultures can actually predispose radicals to return to the fold and abandon their project. When political action is conceived of as striving for a world that has no practical connections to the past, or to what already exists, activism often comes to naught or devolves into adventure, repudiation, and piety. In the declensionist version of the Sixties, the past (or "the system," or "liberalism") is abandoned for a fresh start, rather than changed, and so remains intact to beckon as an attractive destination for disillusioned seekers. The radical frontiersman may head out boldly but, finding paradise a mirage, returns home to relive the past.[17]

Told in this light, the story of the 1960s came to its inevitable end as the covenant that bound the true radicals together was torn apart with their return to liberalism, conservatism, or the Marxism of the Old Left. What little remained after 1968, by this account, was the false radicalism of identity politics forever blinkered by its own narrow interests and vision. This version of the Sixties labors under a weighty sense of predestination as it moves inexorably toward declension.[18] There can be no denying its powerful resonance with significant groups of former activists. These narratives of total change and defeat do describe an important dimension of the 1960s but also leave much unsaid and unseen.

AMERICAN REVOLUTIONS, THE PROPHETIC VISION, AND THE TRANSFORMATION OF TRADITION

The existing stock of American stories contains vitally important, if less appreciated, accounts of historical change that shift our attention from endings and failure to new beginnings by articulating the links between continuity and discontinuity, between destruction and creation, between human agency and the possibility for a better world.

The Revolution and Civil War destroyed empire and slavery but also served as acts of creation that gave birth to democratic traditions. The history of revolution, reconstruction, and reform are enormously complex human events that contain a frontier and apocalyptic dimension—but, for the purposes of understanding the legacy of the 1960s, these founding movements are even more useful because they lend themselves to narrative forms that defy the logic of declension with counterthemes of transformation and reconstruction.

By using ideas of transformation and reconstruction, we can better envision the processes of historical change as the play between continuity and discontinuity or between tradition and innovation. Not some nagging residue that must be overcome, cultural and historical traditions instead represent the inevitable grounds on which social change occurs and the raw materials from which new consciousness is constructed. Revolutions succeed when new, more inclusive, and compelling versions of worn-out traditions take root by assuming the latent power and liberating vision of some frayed but classic ideal. A better telling of the 1960s will investigate the worklike processes of social movements that embrace histories and traditions and simultaneously change them through intellectual inquiry and citizen activism.[19]

In the years just before the American Revolution, New England's radical ministers touched the hearts and minds of their congregations by investing the new meanings of liberty, natural rights, and reason into the old form of the Puritan sermon known as the jeremiad.[20] Jefferson's rhetorical strategy in the Declaration of Independence succeeded so well because its affinity with the jeremiad's themes of crisis, corruption, anxiety, and salvation allowed criticism of the king and the call to independence to be communicated with familiar syntax and style. Jefferson and the other signatories vowed allegiance to the cause with a solemn pledge and exhorted their audience to action "with a firm reliance on the Protection of Divine Providence." In so doing, they relied on a mode of comprehension deeply embedded in the American mind to marshal a nation toward the attainment of a lofty yet earthly destiny.[21] Tom Paine's *Common Sense* similarly adopts the rhetorical forms of traditional American Protestantism, as did some writings of Benjamin Franklin, John Adams, and Samuel Adams.[22] In the crisis of the Revolution, political actors resorted to the jeremiad as the best available model of persuasive speech but invested it with new political energy.

In the mid-1770s, revolutionary leaders across the political spectrum sought to forge a new national identity by evoking the heroic past. They revised the original Puritans' "errand into the wilderness" and the Revolution into commensurate episodes of the historic struggle of freedom against tyranny. As Sacvan Bercovitch tells us: "The revolution was the movement linking the two quintessential moments in the story of America—twin legends of the country's founding fathers—The Great Migration and the War of Independence."[23] The sense of continuity with the past was so profound in the imaginations of revolutionary Americans that Franklin and Jefferson proposed that the seal of the new nation depict not simply the Puritans, but the Puritans' own imaginary forebears. An image of Moses leading his people to the Promised Land and inscribed with the legend "Rebellion to Tyrants Is Obedience to God" united biblical, colonial, and revolutionary content into a symbol of liberation.[24]

James Madison typified revolutionary transformation when he turned the classic arguments against large republics into the basis of a lasting modern republic and reconceived the English constitution of monarchical, aristocratic, and common representation into three branches of popular government.[25] Madison's intellectual achievement mirrored the mass transformation of a people who initially undertook armed conflict intent on reclaiming the narrow rights of freeborn Englishmen, but subsequently produced a new American identity based on the promise of universal principles.

Abraham Lincoln's "mystic chords of memory" enunciated revolutionary patriotism as the heroic measure of his generation of citizen-soldiers and claimed the American Revolution as his "ancient faith" and the only standard by which the reconstruction of the nation could be rightly judged.[26] For Frederick Douglass, slavery betrayed the ideals of the republic and only slavery's destruction could fulfill America's revolutionary vision. Douglass's critical embrace of American religious and political traditions formed the organizing principle of his widely read slave narrative and 1852 oration, "What to a Slave Is the Fourth of July?"[27]

These revolutions transformed and reconstructed the past, and we would do well to remember that some of the most influential figures of Sixties radicalism, from Robert F. Williams to Martin Luther King, from Ho Chi Minh to the Vietnam Veterans Against the War, repeatedly evoked this tradition of revolution in damning the contemporary U.S. government.[28]

Narrative strategies that make transformation and reconstruction their analytical metaphors will both reconfigure the historical lineage of the 1960s and resist notions of the decade's decline because they allow us to see that social movements do not destroy or repudiate the past but rather are bound to rewrite the past. At their best, the social movements of the 1960s salvaged the universal values that republicanism, liberalism, and socialism once championed. When continuity with classic political traditions is confirmed, the reflex for return to current and more decrepit versions of these traditions is diminished. If the social movements of the 1960s and after are understood as the best representations of U.S. political traditions, then connections to, and continuations of, the past are enhanced, and there is less risk of turning to some new form of conservatism or orthodoxy. Once we recognize that the historical antecedents of the 1960s are located deep within the contours of U.S. history, then its legacy in the 1970s, 1980s, and 1990s also becomes more visible.

Like the transformative approach derived from the Revolution, the Puritan legacy can also help us to place new beginnings in historical time characterized by both continuity and discontinuity. Interwoven with apocalyptic yearnings was a prophetic vision also deeply rooted in Judeo-Christian traditions and equally influential on secular conceptions of social change.[29] "Prophetic" here does not imply adherence to biblical predictions of Armageddon, or the ability to see the future. Rather prophecy shifts our attention from endtimes to beginnings and asserts the human ability to create a better future in this world. The prophetic view held that the good and godly life was attainable through human action and choice.

Some Puritans saw conversion as a gradual process that stressed human preparation for God's grace rather than relying on God's will alone.[30] Eighteenth- and nineteenth-century post-millennialists continued the prophetic tradition. They believed that Christ would return only after people made Christianity an earthly truth and lived a thousands years in peace.[31] From 1830 until the Civil War, widespread reform movements, from abolitionism to women's rights to temperance, expressed the belief that the world could be improved, perhaps even perfected, by taking action.

In modern secular terms, the prophetic consciousness of political actors becomes apparent when they articulate a path between what now exists and the world that ought to be and insist that this path can be constructed by human activity and choice. While the apocalyptic view waits for a swift end to the old world and an immediate start for the new, the prophetic engages history as a gradual, unfolding, and challenging struggle that is worth the effort because a new world is possible.[32] Within the prophetic vision, history is seen as transition.

Prophetic interpretations can minimize declensionist readings of the 1960s precisely because they do not require a total break with history for justice to be achieved. John Wiley Nelson suggests that inherent in the prophetic is the idea that "the new age continues and fulfills the possibilities of the old age, rather than inaugurating a totally different world."[33] Put another way by James Darsey, prophets are "simultaneously insider and outsider." "Prophetic discourse," he argues, "seeks to . . . re-create the audience in accordance with a strict set of ideals . . . assented to in principle but unrealized by the audience."[34] Prophet actors give voice to the discord between ideals and reality.

This perspective finds American ideals damaged but still viable despite their tainted origins in slavery and their marginalization under the current corporate and imperial order. Democracy, justice, and freedom are worthy ideals for political action precisely because they remain unfulfilled. Much of the 1960s and its legacy can be interpreted through the prophetic lens as a movement that pursued a future whereby the values of the Declaration of Independence and the Bill of Rights might be finally realized. Certainly the civil rights movement borrowed heavily from the prophetic traditions of black Christianity in articulating a revolutionary vision rooted in the American idiom.

The transformative, reconstructive, and prophetic modes of understanding social change also differ from the frontier and apocalyptic perspectives in allowing us to embrace open-ended contingency and complexity rather than stark opposites and sealed fates. Like the America Revolution and Civil War, the promise of the 1960s was both won and lost. Ironically, it was the very anxiety of the uncertain historical transition of the late twentieth century that produced the desire to impose conclusive outcomes on the decade's legacy. Apocalyptic, frontier, and declension metaphors appeal most powerfully when old standards and expectations no longer apply, but new ones are still uncertain or unformed.[35] In this sense, the declensionist accounts of the 1960s are a response to both the failure of utopian hopes and the real if ambiguous outcomes of popular activism. The current stalemate has lingered on, but activists endure despite the absence of total victory because they read history as a record of successes as well as setbacks. Instead of decline, the abundance and variety of social movements in the last three decades should yield an abundance of interpretations. Of course, even using the transformative and prophetic modes of analysis, historians will have to investigate for movements below the radar screen of mainstream media.

The essays in this volume join a number of existing works that see 1968 as a kind of beginning rather than a kind of ending. Works that move in this direction are *Reclaiming Democracy* by Meta Mendel-Reyes, and Sara Evans's classic *Personal Politics. Citizen Action and the New American Populism* by Harry C. Boyte, Heather Booth, and Steve Max chronicles the activism of the 1980s and also sees modern citizenship as the "re-emergence" of America's "most ancient" democratic vision. Ronald Fraser's *1968: A Student Generation in Revolt* is of particular interest because it deals with a history most conducive to declensionist thinking. In the U.S. edition of *1968*, by Ron Grele and Bret Eynon, the concern for social transformation wins out and as a result the narrative resists closure. The authors of *1968* present an "unfinished history" and so invite us to consider how its next chapters may be written. *The World the Sixties Made* contributes to this unfinished history of cultural change and political action.

The essays herein demonstrate that the movements of the 1960s created a durable, if variegated, alternative American public. Existing notions of citizenship were cast into doubt but not thoroughly dissolved, and people initiated the process of reconstructing the practice of citizen activism. This new public made possible the wars of position evident in the cultural and political history of the subsequent decades. In this view, then, the 1960s and 1970s appear as a halfway revolution that produced conflict and meaningful debate for the rest of the century. By recasting the dissent of the last half of the twentieth century as an effort to reconstruct citizenship, we may both rewrite the historiographic interpretations of recent social movements and better contribute to the ongoing renovation of the grand narratives of U.S. history.

NOTES

1. The works that most powerfully represent this view are: James Miller, *Democracy Is in the Streets: From Port Huron to the Siege of Chicago* (New York: Simon & Schuster, 1987); Todd Gitlin, *The Sixties: Years of Hope, Days of Rage* (New York: Bantam Books, 1987); Tom Hayden, *Reunion: A Memoir* (New York: Random House, 1988); Maurice Isserman, *If I Had a Hammer: The Death of the Old Left and the Birth of the New Left* (Urbana: University of Illinois Press, 1993); Kirkpatrick Sale, *SDS* (New York: Random House, 1973). One of the first works of this type was by ex-SDS leader Greg Calvert, tellingly titled *A Disrupted History: The New Left and the New Capitalism* (New York: Random House, 1971). For works that investigate the continuity between the Sixties and later decades, see Jack Whalen and Richard Flacks, *Beyond the Barricades: The Sixties Generation Grows Up* (Philadelphia: Temple University Press, 1989); Lauren Kessler, *After All These Years: Sixties Ideals in a Different World* (New York: Thunder's Mouth Press, 1990); and Bret Eynon "Look Who's Talking: Oral Memoirs and the History of the 1960s," *Oral History Review*, 19 (spring 1991): 99–107. For a thorough historiography see Van Gosse, "A Movement of Movements: The Definition and Periodization of the New Left," in Roy Rosenzweig and Jean-Christophe Agnew, eds., *A Companion to Post-1945 America* (London: Blackwell, 2002).

2. Richard Slotkin, *Gunfighter Nation: The Myth of the Frontier in Twentieth-Century America* (New York: HarperPerennial, 1992). James Gilbert, "New Left: Old America," in Sohnya Sayres, Anders Stephanson, Stanley Aronowitz, and Fredric Jameson, eds., *The 60s Without Apology* (Minneapolis: University of Minnesota Press in cooperation with Social Text, 1984), 244–47.

3. Gilbert, "New Left: Old America," 244–47; Eynon, "Look Who's Talking," 101, 103; Rick Perlstein, "Who Owns the Sixties?" *Lingua Franca*, May–June 1996, 33.

4. The original declension theme was articulated by Perry Miller in *The New England Mind: The Seventeenth Century* (Cambridge: Harvard University Press, 1939), 396, 400, and in his second volume, *From Colony to Province* (Cambridge: Harvard University Press, 1953), 484–85; Philip Greven, *The Protestant Temperament: Patterns of Child-Rearing, Religious Experience, and the Self in Early America* (New York: Knopf, 1980), 5–6; Van Gosse, *Where the Boys Are: Cuba, Cold War America, and the Making of a New Left* (Verso: New York, 1993), 7–10. See also Perlstein, "Who Owns the Sixties?" and Winifred Breines, "Whose New Left?" *Journal of American History*, 75, 2 (September 1988): 528–29.

5. Cotton Mather, "Magnolia Christi Americana" in Kenneth B. Murdock, ed., with the assistance of Elizabeth W. Miller, *Magnolia Cristi Americana: Books I and II* (Cambridge: Belknap Press, 1977), 1.

6. William Appleman Williams, *The Contours of American History* (Chicago: Quadrangle Books, 1961), 257, 377–78, 472–73; James Livingston, *Pragmatism and the Political Economy of Cultural Revolution, 1850–1940* (Chapel Hill: University of North Carolina Press), 273–79.

7. Slotkin, *Gunfighter Nation*, 12.

8. National Security Council Document 68 was a top secret government report and one of the most influential policy statements of the Cold War.

9. Slotkin, *Gunfighter Nation*, 1–5.

10. Gosse, *Where the Boys Are*, 9–10. See also Bret Eynon, "Cast upon the Shore: Oral History and New Scholarship on the Movements of the 1960s," *Journal of American History*, 83, 2 (September 1996): 562.

11. Edmund Morgan made this point about the great migration of Puritans to America; cited in Sacvan Bercovitch, *The American Jeremiad* (Madison: University of Wisconsin Press, 1978), 24.

12. Greven, *Protestant Temperament*, 354–61; Frank Kermode, *The Sense of an Ending: Studies in the Theory of Fiction* (New York: Oxford University Press, 1966), 1–9 and chap. 4; Bercovitch, *The American Jeremiad*, 17–19; Paul Boyer, *When Time Shall Be No More* (Cambridge: Harvard University Press, 1992), preface, prologue, 122–23; Nathan O. Hatch, *The Sacred Cause of Liberty: Republican Thought and the Millennium in Revolutionary New England* (New Haven, Conn.: Yale University Press, 1977); Ruth H. Bloch, *Visionary Republic: Millennial Themes in American Thought, 1756–1800* (New York: Cambridge University Press, 1985).

13. Lois Parkinson Zamora, "The Myth of Apocalypse and the American Literary Imagination," in Zamora, ed., *The Apocalyptic Vision in America: Interdisciplinary Essays on Myth and Culture* (Bowling Green, Ohio: Popular Press, 1982), introduction, 98.

14. Christopher Rowland, "'Upon Whom the Ends of the Ages Have Come': Apocalypse and the Interpretation of the New Testament," in Malcolm Bull, ed., *Apocalypse Theory and the Ends of the World* (Cambridge, Mass.: Blackwell, 1995), 55.

15. Krishan Kumar, "Apocalypse, Millennium, and Utopia Today," in Bull, *Apocalypse Theory*, 202–6.

16. Perry Miller, "Errand into the Wilderness," in *Errand into the Wilderness* (Cambridge: Harvard University Press, Belknap Press, 1956), 8–9. See also Kenneth Burke, *Attitudes toward History* (Los Altos, Calif.: Hermes, 1939), 44.

17. Martin Sklar, *The United States as a Developing Country: Studies in U.S. History in the Progressive Era and the 1920s* (New York: Cambridge University Press, 1992), 176–96, 207–8; J.G.A. Pocock, *The Machiavellian Moment: Florentine Political Thought and the Atlantic Republican Tradition* (Princeton: Princeton University Press, 1975), 550.

18. Maurice Isserman, "The Not-So-Dark and Bloody Ground," *American Historical Review* 94, 4 (October 1989): 994–97, 1008.

19. Sklar, *United States*, 196.

20. Hatch, *Sacred Cause of Liberty*, 69–71; Bercovitch, *American Jeremiad*, chaps. 3, 4.

21. Bloch, *Visionary Republic*, 93.

22. Bercovitch, *American Jeremiad*, 118–25; Hatch, *Sacred Cause of Liberty*, 91–95.

23. Bercovitch, *American Jeremiad*, 132; Hatch, *Sacred Cause of Liberty*, 76–81.

24. Richard Moser, *The New Winter Soldiers: GI and Veteran Dissent during the Vietnam Era* (New Brunswick, N.J.: Rutgers University Press, 1996), 165; Bercovitch, *American Jeremiad*, 124.

25. Alexander Hamilton, James Madison, and John Jay, *The Federalist Papers* (New York: Mentor Books, 1999), 10 and 51; Gordon Wood, *Creation of the American Republic, 1776–1787* (Chapel Hill: University of North Carolina Press, 1969), 61–63, 608–14; Greven, *Protestant Temperament*, 354–61.

26. Livingston, *Pragmatism*, 287–89.

27. Linda Jimison, *The Frederick Douglass Fourth of July Oration at Rochester, New York, July 5, 1852* (Indianapolis, Ind.: Lifestar Enterprises, 1994).

28. Moser, *New Winter Soldiers*.

29. James Francis Darsey, *The Prophetic Tradition and Radical Rhetoric in America* (New York: New York University Press, 1997); Bercovitch, *American Jeremiad*, 94–103.

30. Norman Pettit, *The Heart Prepared: Grace and Conversion in Puritan Spiritual Life* (New Haven, Conn.: Yale University Press, 1966), cited in Greven, *Protestant Temperament*, 8–9.

31. Boyer, *When Time Shall Be No More*, 67–68.

32. Debra Bergoffen, "The Apocalyptic Meaning of History," in Zamora, ed., *Apocalyptic Vision in America*, 26.

33. John Wiley Nelson, "The Apocalyptic Vision in American Popular Culture," in Zamora, ed., *Apocalyptic Vision in America*, 166.

34. Darsey, *Prophetic Tradition and Radical Rhetoric*, 202.

35. Charles Lippy, "Waiting for the End: The Social Context of American Apocalyptic Religion," in Zamora, ed., *Apocalyptic Vision in America*, 38.

SARA M. EVANS

1   Beyond Declension

*Feminist Radicalism in the
1970s and 1980s*

THE EVOLUTION of the feminist movement in the 1970s and
1980s challenges most of the dichotomies that have framed discussions
of the legacy of activism in the 1960s. Despite the declension implied by
stories of the "rise and fall" of feminist radicalism in the 1970s, it is no
simple matter to plot on a liberal/left continuum the range of radical/
socialist/lesbian/cultural/reform/Marxist and postmodern feminisms.
As measured by public demonstrations, feminism peaked in the mid-
1970s, but the seeds it scattered continued to sprout. This evolution was
not a simple matter of decline. Step away from stereotypes and you will
find that many leading "liberal" feminists, defined by their focus on
working through traditional political, legislative, and judicial institutions, have intellectual and activist roots in the left. Some of the most
militant feminist leaders (people the popular culture perceives as "radicals") are steeped in liberal tradition, while leftists have frequently
withdrawn from public activity into the professional comforts of academia. It was radicals who led the turn to an entrepreneurial, countercultural feminism and fostered a plethora of women's businesses while
others, having built alternative institutions to provide social services,
survived the Eighties by accepting state funding, with its accompanying
restrictions, and shifting away from volunteerism toward professionalism. As a result, despite regular pronouncements of its "death," feminism has not only weathered the right-wing backlash during the past fifteen to twenty years but also continued to grow.

A YEAR of cataclysm for so many, 1968 was the year that wom-
en's liberation burst into public consciousness with a demonstration at
the Miss America Pageant in Atlantic City. A small group managed to
get inside the auditorium and unfurl a huge "Women's Liberation"

banner from the balcony, while their cohorts outside crowned a live sheep, auctioned off an effigy of Miss America ("the 1968 model: she walks, she talks, AND she does housework"), and tossed objects of female torture (bras, girdles, curlers, and issues of the *Ladies Home Journal*) into a "freedom trashcan." August 1968 was the same month as the Democratic Convention debacle in Chicago, where police assaulted protesters. The women in Atlantic City were feisty but not violent. They had fun with their anger because it was infused with a utopian hope. The truth of their critique, they believed, was unassailable. With their assertion that "the personal is political," they exposed the power dynamics of the most private relationships and forced onto the political agenda issues rooted in personal life, such as reproductive freedom, domestic violence, child care, and the cultural definitions of "male" and "female" imbedded in law and tradition. For almost a decade their movement seemed invincible.

At the end of the Sixties, feminism was just getting started as a mass movement. It reached its heyday in the middle 1970s and continued as a powerful force in U.S. society to the end of the century and beyond. Indeed, the label for the proliferation of groups, organizations, and ideas that constituted the renewed struggle for women's rights—"the second wave"—offers a useful image with which to challenge declension narratives. Historians and activists alike have quibbled over the accuracy of this designation, but most would accept its metaphoric power. Waves are surface evidence of powerful forces that cannot always be seen or understood—underwater earthquakes, changing climate, storms, or just prevailing winds. They can be gentle swells that wear away rocks molecule by molecule, or they can be tidal waves that rearrange the landscape overnight. The sea, whose surge a wave is, remains always, and another crest will inevitably develop as it reacts to change. The "first wave" of feminism, the struggle for woman suffrage, waxed and waned through almost a century. It would be a mistake to think that the latest resurgence would fade away even more quickly. At the same time, it is important to recognize how dramatically the second wave has already reshaped U.S. society. To understand its power, it is essential to recognize that as a social movement, it defies most of the dichotomies that social movement historians and activists alike have tried to impose.

Because the second wave was a movement with two distinct branches in the beginning, one liberal and one radical, its history has tended to be told in a dichotomous way. Certainly in the early years, radicals were greatly concerned to maintain their distinctive perspective, to avoid co-optation. Similarly, liberals feared that the radicals would alienate women with their anger and issues like abortion and lesbianism. By the middle to late seventies there were some radicals who believed that their movement had been hijacked by liberals and by cultural feminists.[1] They failed to understand the transforming power of feminist radicalism, however, and the interactive way in which these branches shaped and reshaped each other. It is, in part, the broad political spectrum of the second wave that clarifies its power to reshape U.S. social, political, and cultural landscapes and its continuing influence at the turn of the century. This was a movement that drew on the deepest wells of U.S. liberalism (individualism, egalitarianism, democracy) while simultaneously challenging them all the way to their patriarchal foundations.

FOUNDATIONS IN THE 1960s

The founding stories of both initial branches have deep roots in the 1960s. They have been told many times, so I will offer brief summaries here.

Liberal Feminism

The National Organization for Women (NOW) was founded in 1966 out of networks built in the President's Commission on the Status of Women and the subsequent state commissions on the status of women. Initially, they sought to build an effective lobbying network. The civil rights movement had demonstrated that effective lobbying required grassroots pressure and activism. As a result, early actions included picketing campaigns against segregated want ads, and soon local chapters began to initiate direct-action campaigns against all manner of public symbols of discrimination. Around NOW grew a plethora of more specialized policy organizations: the Women's Equity Action League (WEAL), highly focused on using the courts to challenge economic discrimination and to insist on enforcement of Title VII; policy think tanks like the Center for Women Policy Research in Washington, D.C. (founded in 1972); the National Women's Political Caucus (founded in 1971), centered on building women's power in electoral politics.[2]

Women's Liberation

The Women's Liberation Movement (so named in early 1968 when Jo Freeman began to edit the first newsletter, "Voice of Women's Liberation") erupted spontaneously among New Left activists in several cities in the fall of 1967.[3] Modeled in some ways on the black power movement, it engaged in serious internal debates from the outset about the degree of separation from the Left, but most of its activists shared an intense disdain for the liberal feminists. Rather than collaborate with "the system" in any way, they set out to understand the root causes of women's oppression by pooling their personal experiences in "consciousness-raising" sessions. Using the methods of consciousness raising, the fluid forms of the small group, and the preexisting networks of antiwar/student/civil rights activism, women's liberation spread like wildfire across the nation. Consciousness-raising groups were seedbeds for what grew into diverse movements around issues that ranged from women's health, childcare, violence, and pornography to spirituality and music.

Even in the early years, it was often the case that liberals and radicals joined forces for major demonstrations and events. Whoever called a demonstration, the full spectrum of feminist activists was likely to show up. NOW veteran Jacqui Ceballos, for example, can be seen in news clips of the Miss America demonstration in Atlantic City organized by New York Radical Women. Two years later, Ceballos was the key organizer for the NOW-inspired National Women's Strike on August 26, 1970.

The leadership in each branch was anxious to maintain a distinctive public image untarnished by "radicals" (on the one hand) or "bourgeois liberals" (on the other). Yet by 1970 the boundaries between liberal and radical feminism were seriously blurred. The fact was that the thousands of women who were drawn to the movement frequently did not know or care which direction they went. In cities where NOW was the only feminist organization, it became a center for radical activism. Where women's liberation groups predominated, they frequently drew in women who were militant but not self-consciously leftist.

THE RADICALISM OF THE LIBERALS

The radicalism of early liberal feminists can be illustrated in multiple ways. Many liberals, like Congresswoman Bella Abzug and Betty Friedan, had strong activist roots in left/labor movements from the 1940s. It is only the erasure of the McCarthy era that has obscured this connection.[4] Furthermore, liberal groups were often more hospitable spaces for interracial organizing than were radical groups. Their somewhat greater clarity about structure, and their focus on specific policy issues, made it easier to work with people who were not "the same" but who wanted to be at the table and to have their say. Early NOW activists, for example, included EEOC member Aileen Hernandez and civil rights lawyer Pauli Murray.[5] Gloria Steinem, through the 1970s, insisted always on sharing speaking platforms with black women.[6] The crossover between liberal organizations (both feminist and mainstream) and government agencies also facilitated the career paths of a multicultural feminist leadership that functioned, frequently, behind the scenes.

Liberals also included a substantial cohort of labor union organizers and activists. United Auto Workers staff Olga Madar, Dorothy Haener, and Milly Jeffrey and Addie Wyatt of the Meatcutters were involved in NOW from the beginning and ultimately became the initiators of the Coalition of Labor Union Women (CLUW). These were activists closely allied to the civil rights movement and the farmworkers' grape boycott who also had strong connections to the President's Commission and numerous state commissions on the status of women.

Militancy characterized liberals as much as it did radicals. From the outset, NOW disrupted legislative hearings and sat in at all-male clubs. While they focused on specific policy changes (as opposed to "revolution"), such as equal pay, the ERA, enforcement of Title VII, passage of Title IX, the Women's Educational Equity Act, and the Equal Credit Opportunity Act, they did not shrink from using demonstrations, pickets, guerrilla theater, and other tools from the tactical toolbox of the radicals.

Finally, liberal groups were effectively radicalized by the dynamism of the radical movement. NOW chapters, YWCAs, even local churches began offering "consciousness-raising" groups. Self-consciously feminist organizations focused increasingly on "process" and a view of feminism as inherently anti-hierarchical. An example of this confluence was the National Women's Political Caucus (NWPC) founded in 1971 by many of the same women who founded NOW. On the one hand, NWPC was clearly the creature of liberal political activists. Its purpose was to influence the political parties both nationally and at the grass roots. Radicals, deeply disillusioned with electoral politics in the wake of the civil rights movement and Vietnam, felt that this was gross co-optation and maintained their distance. And yet, the women's liberation movement had already set a new tone, one that placed a powerful emphasis on flattening hierarchies and on inclusive representation. The NWPC founding convention was far more inclusive both racially and economically than most feminist gatherings up to that point. That gathering included novelist Toni Morrison, civil rights leader Fannie Lou Hamer, leaders from the National Welfare Rights Organization, and strong caucuses of Chicanas, Native American women, and Puerto Rican women. In its caucus structure, in its emphasis on local autonomy, in its concern about hierarchy and "stars," it incorporated central concerns and practices of the radical movement.

Within NOW there was always a fierce contest for leadership that was frequently framed in "radical v. liberal" terms. Early battles over the ERA and abortion led those who considered such issues "too radical" to create WEAL. Subsequent struggles over lesbianism and organizational style deeply radicalized the organization. By the mid-1970s a battle over leadership at the national convention revolved around the slogan, "Out of the mainstream and into the revolution." While many radicals still saw NOW as mainstream, NOW activists cast themselves as revolutionaries.

THE LIBERALISM OF THE RADICALS

Just as liberals used militant and radical methods, radicals found themselves employing the tools of liberalism as they grappled with the problem of creating genuine and lasting change on specific issues. Springing from and embattled with the Left, feminist radicals challenged not only liberalism but also the gender hierarchies imbedded in both theory and practice on the Left. They challenged the idea that some structural inequalities (e.g., class) were more fundamental than others (e.g., sex) and demanded a movement that lived up to its vision in every respect. They also sought practical, active ways to address women's oppression and to mobilize for change. In doing so, they employed liberal or radical tactics for ideological reasons and out of pure serendipity in equal measure. For example, numerous women's liberation groups engaged in underground abortion counseling and referral in the years before *Roe v. Wade*. One in Chicago, "Jane," went so far as to begin providing illegal abortions itself. Another in Austin, Texas, started Sarah Weddington on the journey that would lead her to help initiate the case of *Roe v. Wade*. At the age of twenty-five, Weddington stood before the Supreme Court to argue that a woman's decision to have an abortion in the early months of pregnancy was constitutionally protected as a private decision between the woman and her doctor. The resulting decision in 1973 legalized abortion overnight.[7]

Throughout the 1970s, socialist-feminist groups (often called Women's Liberation Unions) flourished across the country. Formed by feminist radicals, who criticized the efforts of some radical feminists to define sex as the primary source of all oppression and men as "the enemy," they were nonetheless strong advocates of an autonomous movement of women. Socialist feminists were among the most critical of "bourgeois feminists," who, in their view, sought equal access for women to systems that remained inherently unequal (e.g., the corporate ladder). Yet their dedication to moving beyond ideological dispute toward practical organizations capable of winning real victories led them to actions which, in many ways, paralleled those of NOW chapters.

For example, members of the Chicago Women's Liberation Union who founded Women Employed in Chicago soon discovered that some of their strongest allies for organizing clerical workers were in Chicago NOW. Their sister organization in Boston, Nine to Five, ultimately joined forces with a national labor union, the Service Employees International Union (SEIU). Numerous radical groups set out to create alternative institutions such as day care centers or shelters for battered women under the institutional wings of a local YWCA or church. At the same time, a growing number of activists with radical roots found themselves drawn to the possibilities of work within the government in the Carter administration. Leslie Wolf, on the staff of the Civil Rights Commission, always thought of herself as someone with radical roots and a radical agenda, but her place of operation was a federal agency. From there she could work on building a multiracial feminism long before that had become the mantra of feminist organizations.[8]

One of the great contributions of the women's liberation movement was the creation of an enormous range of counterinstitutions in response to social problems discovered through the consciousness-raising process. Hundreds of journals, newsletters, publishing houses, shelters for battered women, rape crisis hot lines, health clinics, coffeehouses, and multipurpose women's centers appeared across the country. Their very success created crises of institutionalization by the late 1970s. Volunteers "burned out," weary of eighteen-hour days and voluntary poverty. Founders and newcomers clashed over philosophy, divisions of labor, and professionalization. Rent and taxes had to be paid and forms filed to receive nonprofit status. Government funding and grants from liberal foundations frequently filled the gaps, but each required a series of compromises and loss of "purity." Nonprofits, for example, had to prove that they were not engaged in political activity in order to receive the exemption from taxes that also made them eligible for most foundation grants. The institutions that survived did so by incorporating efficient business practices, engaging in effective fundraising, and looking more and more like their nonprofit (or even profit-making) liberal counterparts. One of the most radical separatist groups—the Furies Collective in Washington, D.C. (1971–72)—had multiple offshoots in the realm of new feminist institutions, ranging from Olivia Records to Diana Press to *Quest: A Feminist Quarterly.*

Many radicals turned toward the policy arena in search of changes that could affect large numbers of women. One of the most important Marxist feminist theorists, economist Heidi Hartman, headed a National Academy of Sciences study on the issue of comparable worth. She and her colleagues demonstrated with scientific precision that female-dominated jobs receive lower pay than comparable male-dominated jobs. Her work laid the theoretical ground for a series of pathbreaking policy initiatives in states throughout the country in the early 1980s. There is no doubt that comparable worth, or pay equity, could be framed as a radical, structural reform that promised to increase the economic independence of women in the very lowest-paid jobs. It could also be framed as simple fairness, and its use of managerial technologies to measure "worth" meant that it challenged pay systems that discriminated on the basis of gender or race but it did not in any way challenge the idea of hierarchies of pay based on some measure of a job's "worth." Thus, in the 1980s, the issue of comparable worth made allies of feminist radicals and feminist liberals who had been doing grassroots work on state commissions on the status of women, in labor unions, through the NWPC or the League of Women Voters. Indeed, in many instances it would be difficult to say precisely who was who.[9]

By the late 1970s, radicals had also joined the battle for the Equal Rights Amendment, something for which they had little use a decade before. The symbolic issues that framed the debate (unisex bathrooms, alimony, women in the military, abortion) reflected cultural anxieties about the possible erasure of traditional sex roles. As the ERA became a focal point for the newly aroused right-wing backlash, by the end of the decade many radicals had come to see the symbolism of the ERA as important to them too.

While many radicals over the course of the seventies turned to reform and a reengagement with public policy and the state, a substantial number also moved into academia. Women's caucuses formed in most disciplines in the early 1970s, and women's studies programs came into being by the hundreds. By the 1980s feminist scholarship was flowering in virtually every discipline of the humanities and social sciences. Armed with new knowledge, feminist scholars inaugurated a massive effort to transform the entire curriculum in the humanities and social sciences. Women's studies programs and centers for research on women (many initially funded by the Ford Foundation) became institutionalized at most universities, complete with journals, majors, minors, and tenure-track faculty. The National Women's Studies Association made a serious effort to replicate the anti-hierarchical, inclusive ethos of women's liberation. Like other national organizations that did the same, it foundered on deep internal splits and multiple agendas. At the same time, the sheer intellectual power of the feminist critique and the outpouring of new research sparked a series of intellectual revolutions. Among the most powerful analyses from the late 1970s through the 1980s came from scholars who had been activists in women's liberation and socialist-feminist groups, and in particular in a series of Marxist-feminist study groups in the late 1970s and early 1980s.[10]

THE PERSISTENCE OF FEMINIST RADICALISM

Contrary to stories of decline, feminism retained its radical edge through the conservative backlash of the Eighties. One reason is that second-wave feminism challenged a fundamental underlying structure of U.S. culture. While liberal feminism sought, at the outset, to confine women's claims to the terrain of equal rights, the radical challenge to the definitions and language of gender and the gendered division of labor, permeated virtually all feminist issues. The result, however, was a kind of diffusion of radicalism. It is important, therefore, to track its various paths and to recognize that conflicts within feminism cannot be understood in a dichotomous way.

In the late 1970s and early 1980s a series of debates emerged that illustrate the diffusion of radicalism into positions that sit most uncom-
fortably on a Left/Right continuum. Indeed, both sides frequently had
liberal and radical versions. One such argument had to do with
whether women and men were fundamentally the same or essentially
different. Another focused on sexuality and pornography. A third prob-
lematized the category "woman" in light of the massive differences
among women in terms of race, class, religion, nationality, sexuality,
and so forth.

The "sameness/difference" debate took many forms and can be
found in almost every feminist venue by the late 1970s. Initially, both
radicals and liberals perceived that arguments based on women's difference (presuming some essential female nature) were at the root of
most discriminatory practices, and that first-wave activists who embraced such arguments had in fact traded short-term rhetorical gains for
long-term loss. Protective laws, for example, that limited women's
working hours and imposed weight-lifting restrictions had allowed
employers to discriminate and exclude women from higher-paying
jobs. Liberals insisted that women and men be treated the same under
the law. Radicals went even further to claim that most research on "sex
differences" was so infused with bias that the outcomes were virtually
predetermined.[11] Radical feminists' insistence on the eradication of sex
roles on the one hand, and on the designation of men as "the enemy" on
the other, set up a contradictory polarity, however. The former claimed
sameness as its critical ground. The latter asserted a fundamental difference as the basis for political solidarity.[12]

By the mid-1970s, however, the power of women's communities,
the growth of feminist artistic expression in music, poetry, painting,
sculpture, and other visual and performing arts, and the articulation of
lesbian feminism meant a widespread exploration and celebration of
womanhood. Cultural feminism was related to the emergence of identity-based cultural politics among numerous marginalized groups, especially racial minorities. And in every case, the celebration of unique
cultural attributes flowed easily into assertions of essential difference.

While other radicals—most notably socialist-feminists—continually
challenged the essentialist premises of cultural feminism, liberals frequently embraced them, flocking to retreats and workshops by charismatic psychologists like Anne Wilson Schaef and arguing in settings

from corporations to classrooms that there is a "women's way" of doing things.[13]

Similarly, the issue of pornography provoked an intense, acrimonious debate in which both sides had liberal and radical versions. Radical feminists like Robin Morgan, Andrea Dworkin, and legal theorist Catherine MacKinnon built an anti-pornography movement on the analyses of sexual violence that had emerged from the women's liberation movement. In consciousness-raising groups and in a wide variety of publications women named the violence against them as fundamental to their oppression. Exposure to the routine use of violence and degradation in pornography, in fact, became an important tool in the process of consciousness raising. Yet there were other radicals for whom sexual expressiveness and challenges to cultural boundaries on female desire were central elements of their concept of feminism. In their view, suppression of one form of sexual fantasy (pornography) could only lead to suppression of other forms. These two views clashed most overtly at a conference at Barnard College in 1982, where anti-pornography activists accused "pro-sex" feminists of betraying the movement, and subsequently in connection with a series of legal initiatives intended to grant women individual rights to sue pornographers. Interestingly, the anti-pornography activists often found themselves allied with right-wing conservatives. The "pro-sex" radicals, on the other hand, found their strongest allies among civil libertarians and the ACLU.

Like the "sex wars," debates about race, class, and gender also took place most fiercely within universities, where they assumed a strongly theoretical cast. Certainly the migration of feminist radicals into universities made for an audience well prepared to take seriously the challenges issued by women of color in the late seventies. It was minority women—e.g., bell hooks, Bonnie Thornton Dill, Darlene Clark Hine, Gloria Anzaldua—who posed the problem most starkly, accusing feminist theorists of generalizing to all women from the experiences of white, Western, middle-class females.[14] While the debates were sometimes acrimonious, for the most part they were serious and tough, and the result very quickly was that concerns about race and class moved to the center of feminist theory and of a growing proportion of feminist scholarship.

It is important to note that this massive growth in sheer scholarship and institutionalization took place in the hostile atmosphere of the Eighties. It was the radicalism of liberal feminism—as Zillah Eisenstein has argued—that provoked such a sharp right-wing backlash.[15] Indeed, the second wave reshaped the political landscape not only by introducing new issues under the rubric of "the personal is political" but also by serving as the foil and the chief antagonist of the New Right, which made cultural issues—family, abortion, gay rights, and opposition to affirmative action and welfare—its central concern. Once elected, Ronald Reagan sought to systematically eliminate the large number of feminists who were working within government agencies and to starve the programs focused on education, childcare, the poor, and race or gender equity in any form.

Conclusion

Late-twentieth-century feminism had (at least) two wellsprings, one liberal and the other New Left. Its liberalism, however, was never invested in Cold War anticommunism (as, for example, the labor movement was), and its roots in the Left were tempered—or perhaps more accurately, driven—from the outset by critique. At the level of theory, feminist theory exposes deep flaws in both liberal and radical traditions. These were, not unexpectedly, similar flaws, by the way, as both traditions sprang from an enlightenment view rooted in gendered notions of public and private. When liberals advocated "civic equality" and leftists called for "liberation," each assumed that politics had to do with public life and that the public was primarily a male domain. Thus, by pronouncing that "the personal is political," feminists demanded a redefinition of "the political" across the board. Marxism and classical liberalism alike employed concepts of "the worker" and "the citizen" that were inherently male. They presumed that politics and public life were male domains. When liberals and radicals included the personal within their definitions of the political, they reconfigured U.S. politics across the political spectrum. Feminism released a passion for change among U.S. women, who came to the movement without ideological preconditions and predilections but with a deeply personal sense of anger and hope. The result was a remarkably fluid relationship between "Left" and "liberal" in the 1970s, and indeed ever since.

Thus the second wave, in all its variety, offered a radical (in the sense of going to the root) challenge regardless of the arenas in which actions occurred. Furthermore, many of the changes that "radicals" articulated have been incorporated into U.S. culture. Language has shifted to become more inclusive. The designator "Ms." avoids labeling women by their marital status. Occupations are no longer linguistically coded male and female (e.g., "firefighter" replaces "fireman"). The double standard for sexual behavior no longer has the power to destroy women's lives— a power that had endured for millennia. Lesbians and gay men now constitute a publicly visible (though far from universally accepted) political force. The definition of "family" has been challenged profoundly by single parents, by gay and lesbian couples, and by reproductive technologies that separate biological from social parenthood, sex from conception, and conception from gestation. Laws now provide defenses against not only employment discrimination but also marital rape and sexual harassment.

Feminism persisted because of its breadth. Rooted in the liberal values of equality, democracy, and individual rights, feminists also challenged the patriarchal bias of that tradition that has distorted those very values throughout U.S. history. Under attack, feminists have succumbed from time to time to the splintering effects of identity politics and to the illusory power of moral self-righteousness rooted in claims of victimhood. The resulting damage and fragmentation are real, but that anything survived is also remarkable. The fact is that feminist radicalism has continued to produce nodes of experimentation and activism that proceed inside and outside of mainstream institutions. Not so out of fashion as it was in the mid-Eighties, the feminist infrastructure of research and policy institutes, academic programs, and national organizations coexists with an ever-shifting layer of associational life and a younger generation that is extremely impatient with older divisions.

This new generation has begun to claim the mantle of leadership and the right to (re)define feminism. Designating themselves a "third wave," some of them are young women of color who use the term to designate their challenge to white feminists. Others—frequently daughters of feminists—critique the "second wave" as rule-bound, rigid, and uptight. For example, some argue that wearing makeup is not necessarily a form of collaboration with cultural prescriptions to be pleasing to men; rather it can be a method of trying on and playing with identities or simply fun. Similarly they reject rigidly identity-based definitions of lesbianism and heterosexuality, embracing a more fluid spectrum. In general young women accept the postmodern theoretical challenge to positivist epistemology and the assumption that fixed categories ("women," "reality") can be defined, grasped, and made the basis of action.[16] And yet even they yearn to employ the "we" of feminism, despite their acute awareness of its difficulty.

NOTES

1. See Redstockings, eds., *Feminist Revolution* (New Paltz, N.Y.: Redstockings, 1975), and Alice Echols, *Daring to Be Bad* (Minneapolis: University of Minnesota Press, 1989).

2. See Ruth Rosen, *The World Split Open: How the Modern Women's Movement Changed America* (New York: Viking, 2000), and Flora Davis, *Moving the Mountain: The Women's Movement in America since 1960* (New York: Simon & Schuster, 1991).

3. See my extended analysis of these origins in *Personal Politics: The Roots of Women's Liberation in the Civil Rights Movement and the New Left* (New York: Vintage, 1980).

4. See Daniel Horowitz, *Betty Friedan and the Making of the Feminine Mystique: The American Left, the Cold War, and Modern Feminism* (Amherst: University of Massachusetts Press, 1998).

5. Susan Hartmann (*The Other Feminists: Activists in the Liberal Establishment* [New Haven, Conn.: Yale University Press, 1998]) found substantial leadership among African American feminists within liberal organizations such as the ACLU, labor unions, and the National Council of Churches.

6. Historian Susan Hartmann has documented numerous additional examples of women working within mainstream liberal organizations in ways that furthered goals of gender and racial equality. Places like the ACLU, the National Council of Churches, the Ford Foundation, and progressive labor unions, in fact, provided the most expansive opportunities for African American women to assert leadership on feminist issues.

7. See Laura Kaplan, *The Story of Jane: The Legendary Underground Feminist Abortion Service* (New York: Pantheon, 1995), and Sarah Weddington, *A Question of Choice* (New York: Putnam, 1992).

8. *Civil Rights Digest*, 6, 3 (spring 1974).

9. See Sara Evans and Barbara Nelson, *Wage Justice: Comparable Worth and the Paradox of Technocratic Reform* (Chicago: University of Chicago Press, 1989).

10. Members of these groups included numerous well-known feminist academics such as Heidi Hartmann, Alice Kessler-Harris, Linda Gordon, and Rosalind Petchesky. One should also note that *Feminist Studies,* one of the two leading journals in the field of women's studies, was self-consciously socialist-feminist in orientation.

11. See Naomi Weisstein's classic article, "'Kinder, Kuche, Kirche' as Scientific Law: Psychology Constructs the Female," in Robin Morgan, ed., *Sisterhood Is Powerful* (New York: Random House, 1970).

12. I must distinguish here between "radical feminists" and "feminist radicals." There were many varieties of feminist radicals, one group of whom called themselves "radical feminists." They are most associated with ideological posi-

tions on the eradication of sex roles, men as "the enemy," and the "pro-woman line." See Anne Koedt, Ellen Levine, and Anita Rapone, eds., *Radical Feminism* (New York: Quadrangle Books, 1973).

13. See Anne Wilson Schaef, *Women's Reality: An Emerging Female System in the White Male Society* (Minneapolis: Winston Press, 1981).

14. See Gloria Hull, Patricia Bell Scott, and Barbara Smith, eds., *All the Women Are White, All the Blacks Are Men, But Some of Us Are Brave* (New York: Feminist Press, 1982); Gretchen M. Bataille, Kathleen Mullen Sands, and Gloria Anzaldua, eds., *Making Face, Making Soul: Creative and Critical Perspectives by Feminists of Color* (San Francisco: Aunt Lute Books, 1990); Gloria Anzaldua and Cherrie Moraga, eds., *This Bridge Called My Back: Writings by Radical Women of Color* (Watertown, Mass.: Persephone Press, 1981); bell hooks, *Ain't I A Woman: Black Women and Feminism* (Boston: South End Press, 1981) and *Feminist Theory: From Margin to Center* (Boston: South End Press, 1984).

15. Zillah R. Eisenstein, *The Radical Future of Liberal Feminism* (New York: Longman, 1981).

16. See, for example, Barbara Findlen, ed., *Listen Up: Voices from the Next Feminist Generation* (Seattle: Seal, 1995); Rebecca Walker, ed., *To Be Real: Telling the Truth and Changing the Face of Feminism* (New York: Doubleday, 1995); Leslie Heywood and Jennifer Drake, eds., *Third Wave Agenda: Being Feminist, Doing Feminism* (Minneapolis: University of Minnesota Press, 1997).

ANDREW FEFFER

2   The Land Belongs to the People
    Reframing Urban Protest in
    Post-Sixties Philadelphia

For the third Thursday in a row, hundreds of poor, mainly black Philadelphians filed into the weekly session of City Council, as police formed a cordon between the gallery and the main floor. The crowd, comprised largely of residents of Philadelphia's impoverished North Central ward, was assembling to contest the city's 1979 application for federal community development funds, which they maintained funneled federal resources into downtown redevelopment at the expense of neighborhood rehabilitation. The atmosphere was tense. The previous week nearly one thousand protesters had filled the fourth floor of City Hall while others were forcibly evicted from council chambers for disrupting earlier hearings. Council leaders had declared they would not tolerate further disruptions.

No sooner did President George X. Schwartz open the session, however, than a melee began. As blackjack-wielding police waded into onlookers, housing activist and state representative Milton Street dove over a brass railing onto the council floor, followed quickly by his brother and fellow activist John. Both were dragged from the room shouting. As police beat and arrested protesters in the gallery, a white council member attacked a black colleague, punching him in the face before others pulled them apart. The civility of council was shattered, and its ability to govern the city ended, not to be restored for several weeks.[1]

From the Bicentennial until the first year of the Reagan administration, dramatic scenes of social protest like the one just described regularly disrupted the conduct of Philadelphia's municipal government. Such events were unmistakable signs of deep social rupture over urban policy, growing impoverishment, and political disfranchisement. Yet when framed by conventional narratives, which describe America settling into complacency and ideological drift after the turbulence of the

67

1960s, the scenes that unfolded in Philadelphia's City Council chambers in February 1979 appear incongruous and out of place. Were these protests the residue of "Sixties activism"? Were they an aberration in the complacent Seventies, a last gasp of protest before the Reagan Revolution?[2] The origin of these confrontations and the vehemence with which they were engaged suggest a negative answer to both questions, and a different picture of left politics after 1968 than implied by the narrow frame of standard historical accounts.

Indeed, it is only when one extends the narrative frame of recent Philadelphia history back well before the 1960s that events like the City Council fracas of 1979 become comprehensible. Rather than simply prolonging the movements of the previous decade or anticipating the travails of the next one, the protests that wracked Philadelphia in the late 1970s were part of a story of deindustrialization, suburban migration, and the transformation of the social and racial geography of the city.[3] The near riots in City Council chambers marked the climax of a citywide housing movement that brought redevelopment programs under closer public scrutiny and mounted dramatic squatting campaigns that involved hundreds of poor Philadelphians. Attacking the "pro-growth" policies of professional city planners, downtown businesspeople, and liberal politicians, who hoped to make local residential and commercial real estate attractive to investors, housing activists called for equalizing power in the economy and the use of public resources for redistribution rather than growth. Similar popular responses to related structural dislocations emerged in cities as disparate as New York, Boston, San Francisco, Cleveland, and Chicago. The primary resources at stake were shelter and land. They belonged, housing activists declared, "to the people."[4]

Expanding the historical frame in this manner restores the relationship between the recent past and long-term structural trends that occupied the background of Vietnam-era political life. It would be a mistake, however, to view Philadelphia's housing movement primarily as a futile popular reaction against relentless post-Fordist forces of global economic change. Many Philadelphians experienced urban restructuring as part of the enduring legacy of racial discrimination and institutionalized racial inequalities, recognizing them as matters of personal and political responsibility for which alternatives were possible. Philadelphia's housing movement, comprised primarily of African Americans and Latinos, disrupted city government in large part because city

officials over the previous two decades conceived and implemented redevelopment strategies that were racially discriminatory in effect and
intent. Not only did liberal policy perpetuate the spatial segregation of
the postwar city; but also it was enacted on a terrain of constant racial
polarization, in which the geographic and occupational mobility of
black Philadelphians was regularly blocked by the use of force and in-
timidation.[5]

That racism and restructuring went hand in hand suggests a break
with yet another conventional narrative, that of a civil rights protest cycle in which the respectable demands for political equality and desegregation in the 1950s and 1960s were exceeded by black nationalism,
rising expectations of public entitlements, and a "rights revolution" in
the 1970s (all setting the stage for a white backlash in the 1980s). Racial
politics in Philadelphia was considerably more complex than such conventional wisdom would have it, involving a concerted public response
to liberal urban policy that evolved over the decades from the struggle
for civil rights to the assertion of political self-determination. By the
1970s, caught between planners on the one hand and the aggressive defense of racial boundaries on the other, activists addressed long-standing, acutely intolerable, and remediable injustices in the economic and
racial geography of the city. And they demanded far more than rights
and entitlements.[6]

REDEVELOPMENT, 1952–1976

The City of Philadelphia's redevelopment program took shape in the
period immediately after World War II. A liberal "pro-growth coalition,"
the Greater Philadelphia Movement (GPM), led by Democrats Richard-
son Dilworth and Joseph Clark, mobilized reform-minded business
leaders to support a successful bid to take control of city government in
1951, revise the city charter to minimize ward-based political patronage
and graft, and prepare a plan for the rebuilding of the city's downtown.[7]
But the reform years under the Clark (1952–56) and Dilworth (1956–62)
administrations, while they brought temporary order and honesty to
city government, could not stem the outflow of jobs and population.
Long a center for the production of nondurable consumer goods, Philadelphia suffered more than many other northeastern cities as textile, garment, and similar manufacturing moved to the suburbs, to the South,
and overseas. Between 1958 and 1986 Philadelphia, a city of roughly two

million in 1950, lost 200,000 manufacturing jobs.[8] By 1960, the city was already showing a clear population loss, and with it a loss in the residential as well as the commercial tax base. By the 1980s, Philadelphia (smaller by nearly half a million residents) could be declared a "post-industrial" city, more concentrated in lower-paying service and retail occupations than in manufacturing, situated in a "diversified, multi-centered metropolitan region," no longer part of a "core-dominated industrial metropolis."[9]

Meanwhile, the composition of the city's population followed the pattern of other northern industrial cities, with people of color, primarily African Americans, replacing whites, until by 1960 one in every four Philadelphians was black. As Kenneth Kusmer points out, the influx of African Americans "coincided with the reshaping of the metropolis," including the suburbanization of industry and business, and the large-scale, federally subsidized displacement of white urban populations to the suburbs.[10] Philadelphia's net population loss was almost entirely white, comprised of families that followed employment and residential development beyond the city limits.[11] While white out-migration was limited only by the availability of economic resources, for blacks it was a different matter. Numerous studies by the Philadelphia Commission on Human Relations (PCHR), established in 1953, and the nonprofit Philadelphia Housing Association (PHA) found suburban housing closed to blacks (and other racial and ethnocultural minorities) by severe and persistent racial discrimination.[12] The changing metropolitan political economy combined industrial relocation, highway development, and housing subsidies with a pervasive culture of racism to concentrate people of color within the boundaries of the city.[13]

Few if any planners were overtly racist, instead couching their concerns in terms of the perceived socioeconomic liabilities of the black population. As one Planning Commission study put it, "[D]ifferences between the white and nonwhite races in social characteristics make it important to distinguish the two in connection with any planning that bears upon economic and social problems."[14] Nevertheless, redevelopment projects hatched during the Clark and Dilworth administrations aimed to change the composition of the city's resident population. On the surface only the socioeconomic consequences of economic restructuring seemed to motivate and guide redevelopment strategies, such as the 1960 Comprehensive Plan, initiated shortly after Clark entered the mayor's office in 1952. The basic framework for redevelopment through the next quarter century, the plan combined federally subsidized urban renewal projects in the central business district (CBD) and sixteen neighborhoods targeted for middle- and lower-income housing development.[15]

The breadth of this approach earned the Philadelphia planning officials, led by liberals such as Edmund Bacon and William Rafsky, a reputation among reformers for unusually careful and creative attention to neighborhoods and shelter. Liberal activists associated with the GPM through the Philadelphia Housing Association had high expectations of the city's ability to balance downtown revitalization with housing, through the private market supplemented by public projects.[16] However, in practice, city government found that its resources were most effectively spent on rebuilding the CBD. And to the extent that there was a successful "housing program," it also emerged downtown, in historic districts such as Society Hill, adjacent to Independence Mall, renovated with substantial public investment to serve the tax-paying upper middle class that reformers hoped to keep in the city.[17]

Redevelopment projects like Society Hill symbolized for many Philadelphians the misapplication of public funds for private gain. Orchestrated by the Old Philadelphia Redevelopment Corporation, a public-private partnership set up by the GPM and controlled by downtown corporations and real-estate interests, Society Hill's financial underpinnings included nearly $40 million in federal funds directly subsidizing private developers by absorbing the cost of demolition and site improvement. As local housing reformer Cushing Dolbeare recognized in 1961: "Because most current redevelopment proposals are based on the premise that the city must recapture the upper income group, we are in reality subsidizing this group."[18] Conversely, a substantial cost of the Society Hill project was born by existing residents of the district, more than six thousand of whom were forced out by demolition of cheap rental property and the inflation of housing costs. That many of them were black suggested to some critics that the interest of the city officials in economic revitalization was in what housing activists called the "whitening" of downtown.[19]

HOUSING CONDITIONS IN NEIGHBORHOODS

Meanwhile, housing conditions deteriorated in other parts of the city, including areas on the periphery of the CBD slated for redevelopment.

African Americans bore the brunt of the deterioration. A housing survey of selected districts conducted for the city in the late 1940s found blacks living in housing with four times the number of deficiencies of those occupied by whites.[20] The Philadelphia Housing Association similarly found that by 1950 roughly 35 percent of the black population lived in dilapidated housing or housing that lacked a private bath. Only 8 percent of whites lived under similar conditions.[21] This disproportion in substandard housing for blacks could not be explained solely by the operation of filtering mechanisms in the housing market, which reserved older, more deteriorated real estate for more recent (and usually poorer) arrivals to the city (as blacks were in the 1940s). As the PHA and the city's Human Relations Commission demonstrated, discrimination, which one human relations researcher declared "a daily, commonplace practice in Philadelphia," determined the distribution of housing in the private market, closing access for blacks to better real estate. Between 1940 and 1950, 140,000 housing units were built in the Philadelphia area, but only 1,044 were available to African Americans, and only 466 of those were in the suburbs. As in other northern cities, black and Latino Philadelphians searched fruitlessly for home financing. Mortgages were available to them neither for suburban housing nor for the purchase or renovation of inner-city real estate.[22]

Liberal planners decried housing discrimination. Indeed, to the extent that discrimination blocked the movement of African Americans to the suburbs, housing desegregation was in the interest of those who wanted to "revitalize" the city. Suburbanization allowed many whites to withdraw resources from the city, leaving its residents and businesses to cover the residual costs of deindustrialization.[23] But fair-housing advocates fought an uphill battle. Deindustrialization and neighborhood deterioration brought with them an increase in racial polarization and conflict that broke out in race-related violence on a number of occasions. Residents often used violence to police the boundaries between so-called transitional and white neighborhoods in northeast and southwest Philadelphia and the surrounding suburban communities, severely limiting the ability of blacks to follow the migration of earlier inner-city ethnic groups.[24]

Federal policy, discrimination, and racial violence thus combined to keep African Americans from the better-paying jobs, superior schools, and newer housing of the suburbs and the outer neighborhoods of the city, confining them to those that were decrepit, more rapidly deteriorating, and, as officials and activists agreed, more expensive to live in.[25] A chronic absence of cheap rental units in black neighborhoods was exacerbated by the massive abandonment of housing that began in the 1960s and accelerated through the 1970s. By 1972, the city estimated that around 35,000 units or more than 5 percent of the housing stock had been abandoned. According to one calculation, during the 1970s the city contained a constant 22,000 abandoned structures, with 10,000 residential buildings being demolished each year. Roughly 10 percent of housing units disappeared by the end of the 1980s, despite the building of middle-class housing in gentrifying neighborhoods. While abandonment occurred throughout the city, it was most severe in areas such as North Philadelphia that had been settled by blacks within the previous two decades.[26] These abandonment and demolition statistics indicate that good housing was not filtering down to lower-income renters and buyers, as predicted by conventional theories. Vacancy rates in districts with substandard and crowded housing (such as North Philadelphia) remained high, as often did the rents. The effect of this shortage in cheap dwellings was that Philadelphia's urban poor were spending far more of their income on shelter than was recommended by the federal government, and many of them were on long waiting lists to enter the dwindling supply of public housing.[27] Redevelopment projects, ostensibly meant to revitalize neighborhood housing, neither stemmed the rate of abandonment nor aided resident black communities. Despite the official commitment to providing shelter, redevelopment increasingly resorted to slum clearance, removing abandoned and blighted structures rather than rehabilitating or building new housing, of serious consequence for African Americans, who constituted a disproportionate number of the residents in redevelopment zones.[28]

NEIGHBORHOOD RESPONSES TO URBAN RESTRUCTURING

As it grew plain in the late 1960s that abandonment and redevelopment were palpably degrading the quality of life of inner-city neighborhoods, mobilization over housing issues began to pick up momentum. According to Thad Mathis, a longtime activist in the African American community, a turning point in housing conflicts came with the 1967 rent strike against the Jefferson Manor apartment building in North Philadelphia, an early and prominent effort at collective bargaining in local landlord-tenant relations.[29] The collective-bargaining strategy became the centerpiece of the North West Tenants Organization (NWTO), founded that same year as a nonprofit representative of tenant interests and a "federation of tenant unions" in the Germantown section of the city. NWTO launched its first collective bargaining effort at the Green Street apartment complex in Germantown in the fall of 1971. By February 1972 the organization had forced a settlement with the landlord that addressed the primary concerns of building maintenance and the arbitration of landlord-tenant disputes.[30]

According to North West Tenants organizer Rudy Tolbert, the centralized and accessible Green Street complex was "an organizer's dream. " The group's success in the rest of North Philadelphia, however, was limited. The large number of relatively small and widely dispersed rental properties made trade-union-style organizing among Philadelphia tenants difficult.[31] By the early 1970s, as the housing crisis intensified, activists became increasingly aware of the need for a citywide housing movement that would address the structural transformation of the market and mobilize poor Philadelphians for better municipal regulation of housing.

Such a citywide movement did not successfully coalesce until North West Tenants activists established the Tenant Action Group (TAG) in 1974, founded explicitly to engage in political advocacy and militant grassroots organizing.[32] Run by a board comprising housing activists, tenants, and neighborhood representatives, TAG knitted together tenant grievances, as well as concerns about housing and redevelopment policy, from African American, white, and Latino communities across the city. Meanwhile, other organizations formed to address the inequities of redevelopment and its damaging effects on poor neighborhoods. The Philadelphia Housing Association, long associated with the liberal Greater Philadelphia Movement, drifted leftward as the city's progrowth coalition fell apart under the political pressures of the late 1960s. In 1968, PHA combined with the Fair Housing Committee of the Delaware Valley to form the Housing Association of the Delaware Valley (HADV), which soon embarked on a more activist course that included opposition to the war in Vietnam. In 1971 the board appointed Shirley Dennis, a former real-estate agent and NAACP activist, as executive director. Bringing neighborhood representatives into the decision-making process, Dennis quickly aligned the organization with TAG and other more militant groups, though it largely remained dedicated to its original service and fact-finding mission. By 1974 a coalition of more conventional and less militant neighborhood organizations had emerged as well under the leadership of a Catholic priest, Father Joseph Kakalec. With the venerable HADV, Kakalec's Philadelphia Council of Neighborhood Organizations (PCNO) lent a politically respectable and melioristic voice to the ensuing struggle over redevelopment.[33]

In 1974 TAG entered a rent-control bill into City Council, its first effort to force greater regulation of the housing market. Four years later, after much wrangling, rent control died, but TAG's mobilization directed public attention to the city's housing crisis and to the need for legislation to address the restructuring of the urban economy. TAG was more successful in forcing the passage of a Tenant Bill of Rights, an ensemble of municipal laws that by 1978 included a model lease and a statute forbidding housing discrimination against single parents.[34] Unlike the HADV and PCNO, TAG explicitly dedicated itself to mobilizing "direct action" throughout the city to force legislation protecting the rights and interests of the poor. Unafraid of militant displays of discontent and "rule-violating" behavior, often in City Council chambers and the offices of city government, TAG called on housing activists to "escalate their activities beyond polite petitioning." "If the lives of the poor are to be transformed," declared Tolbert, then "forces superior to those which resist change must be mobilized to counteract them." Conflict and confrontation were necessary. In many respects, TAG simply reasserted the public right to control municipal resources and to hold elected officials accountable. Yet, while the organization primarily confined itself to such collective-consumption organizing, it nonetheless addressed housing as a political issue and understood the housing crisis as a systemic problem, defined in some part by the conflict of irreconcilable class interests and by racial inequality and discrimination.[35]

As TAG, HADV, and PCNO built the organizational framework to respond to the deepening housing crisis, several factors added momentum to citywide organizing. First, as did other U.S. industrial cities during this period, Philadelphia suffered a fiscal crisis that intensified with the economic downturn after 1973. While the city was never put into virtual receivership as New York was, Philadelphia's budget woes mounted nonetheless. In 1972 the combined deficit of the municipal government and the school district topped $90 million. The Federal Reserve Bank of Philadelphia projected a fivefold increase in three years.[36] Creative accounting and deferred debt service kept the city afloat; however, constant downward pressure on spending, as well as the constant need to raise revenues and stabilize and rebuild the tax base, became ever-present limiting conditions for city planning.

Second, the credibility of the city's planning community, especially with people of color and the poor, began to dissolve. It is not clear exactly when this happened. The tenuous synthesis of redevelopment and housing upon which liberal planners had built an international reputation did not long survive the final demise of the GPM's pro-growth regime. Yet even as late as 1975, city planners and redevelopment officials enjoyed a residue of public trust left over from the days of the Clark-Dilworth reform coalition. That trust began to crumble when evidence emerged in the mid-1970s that the administration of former police commissioner Frank Rizzo, elected in 1971, consciously engaged in a policy of "recycling" poor and largely black neighborhoods for business and middle-class residential use. While elements of such a recycling strategy were implicit in downtown redevelopment from the start (and even in the optimistic projections of progressive city planners), city officials began publicly to endorse the withdrawal of city services in poor districts to encourage abandonment and depreciation of property, and to foster the displacement of poor populations that discouraged real-estate investment. The suspicions of housing activists were confirmed in early 1973 when the chair of the city planning commission, Bernard Meltzer, bluntly declared that the city should recycle "nonviable" neighborhoods, withdrawing services and demolishing abandoned properties (regardless of their potential for rehabilitation).[37]

Meltzer's statement entered "recycling" into the city's political lexicon, yet city officials still insisted that it did not reflect official policy. In early 1975, the Rizzo administration became even less guarded about its intentions and revived Meltzer's earlier proposal, assigning $10 million in federal community development money for razing up to four thousand houses a year and landscaping and fencing off vacant lots, as part of a highly publicized program to remove "urban blight" in preparation for the following year's Bicentennial celebration. Housing and redevelopment officials estimated that twenty thousand dwellings could be removed over the course of five years.[38] Even worse, the press quoted city officials predicting the "eventual loss of North Central Philadelphia," where the city's black population was concentrated. Declaring in response that the city "never had a housing program," the normally circumspect director of HADV, Shirley Dennis, accused officials of consciously trying to push poor blacks out of districts that bordered on prime real estate and predicted a "dilution of black political strength."[39] Although Rizzo later cut the demolition program back by half in response to the public outcry, neighborhood activists continued to suspect that under Rizzo the city had abandoned earlier commitments to sheltering the poor in favor of recycling poor neighborhoods.

To some extent, housing policy in the city was being determined at the federal level, a third factor in the unfolding confrontation over urban space. The imbroglio about recycling began at public hearings about the city's Year I application for funding under the new federal Community Development Block Grant (CDBG) program, instituted under the Housing and Community Development Act of 1974. Part of the Nixon administration strategy to shift responsibility for human services and resources to the local level, CDBG replaced the grants-in-aid system of the Johnson administration with largely undifferentiated blocks of funding that would be administered by municipal agencies. So, even if it essentially marked the death of Johnson's Model Cities program, CDBG gave much greater latitude to municipalities in determining the application of federal funds, with relatively few guidelines and restrictions. City governments therefore tended to support it.[40]

Perhaps more importantly, the Nixon administration together with the federal courts drastically limited the availability of public housing. Nixon's 1973 moratorium on rental and purchase subsidies directly affected poor Philadelphians, many of whom could find shelter only in the projects or through government assistance. The housing authority served as a landlord to fully 3 percent of the city's population, most of whom were black. While public housing cost the city virtually nothing (it was built and maintained with federal funds and rent), the racial composition of the projects made it a delicate political issue. According to historian John Bauman, Philadelphia's public housing, innovative as it was in pursuing scattered-site and used-house programs, nevertheless followed a familiar path of least resistance determined by suburban zoning, neighborhood racism, and political pressure. During the 1950s and 1960s, planners, some of them reluctantly, increasingly concentrated housing projects in black neighborhoods, areas with the least desirable real estate and limited political power, and often moved blacks there from redeveloped neighborhoods close to downtown.[41] When in 1972 HUD, under court order, tightened site selection criteria for public housing, requiring its location in "nonimpacted" (i.e., white and middle-class) areas, circumstances were set for a virtual blockage of large-scale public housing construction in the city.[42]

While the courts and HUD merely set conditions for public-housing construction, Rizzo used those conditions as a pretext for stalling it altogether by allowing neighborhoods the right of refusal on the location of projects. Not surprisingly white districts took Rizzo up on his offer, and together they drew a racial boundary on the dispersal of public housing around a long-delayed project in the south Philadelphia neighborhood of Whitman. First approved in 1956, construction of Whitman Park Homes began with housing demolition, displacing low-income residents, 46 percent of whom were black. This action effectively removed black residents from the blocks south of Snyder Avenue, one of the area's informal racial boundaries. White residents thereafter obstructed the efforts of planners to finish the project. As in other parts of the city, in Whitman the combination of restrictive site selection and racism contributed to the overall shortage of low-income housing, whether public or private. Though only a small number of units were at stake, for years the city's failure to complete Whitman Park symbolized to Philadelphia blacks official complicity with communal racism to defend racial boundaries and restrict the geographical and occupational mobility of people of color. The Rizzo administration's intentions were unmistakable when, in 1977, the mayor (on behalf of local residents and using racially inflammatory language) illegally used an injunction to stop the project's construction.[43] Meanwhile, Rizzo's housing authority neglected maintenance on existing high-rise projects, making many units almost uninhabitable, spurring tenants (mainly black) to organize tenant councils and engage in rent strikes, the most visible of which occurred at the Schuylkill Falls project in northwest Philadelphia in early 1976.[44]

The ascent of the Rizzo regime in 1971 also heightened a long-brewing sense of urgency about institutionalized racism and racial violence, a fourth impetus to the emerging housing movement. Installed as police commissioner by Mayor James Tate (1964–72) as a concession to conservative voters in blue-collar ethnic wards, Rizzo won the 1971 election on the thinly veiled racism of a "law-and-order" campaign. His reputation for keeping the city relatively free of openly violent racial confrontation contributed to his electoral fortunes. So too did his notoriety for tough treatment of black nationalists and their sympathizers during the mid-1960s, with spectacular contempt for civil rights evidenced in the public strip searching of Black Panthers in a night-time raid on their headquarters in 1970. The fact that the federal Civil Rights Commission considered Commissioner Rizzo's approach to police-community relations incendiary did not stop voters in predominantly white south and northeast Philadelphia from voting for him in large numbers.[45]

Evidence indicates some escalation in police abuse after Rizzo's ascent to power in police headquarters and city hall. Reports of police brutality brought the intervention of the federal government as early as 1971, when the Civil Rights Commission held hearings on problems in the department. That study reported the routine beating and verbal abuse of suspects, the regular harassment of black citizens, and a protective code of silence that extended from the officers' ranks to the district attorney's office. The Civil Rights Commission also reported a dramatic increase in the shooting of black civilians by police officers in 1970 alone. By 1978, when the housing movement was at its height, incidents of police violence were reported in the press on a weekly basis, and demonstrations on the issue by civil rights activists took place with regularity at city hall. A *Philadelphia Inquirer* investigation in early 1975 revealed that the practices about which witnesses testified in 1971 had continued and worsened. One state official complained that "police in this town are out of control." In 1976, the Public Interest Law Center of Philadelphia (PILCOP) reported a threefold increase in police brutality complaints during just one year (1975) of the Rizzo regime. The following year PILCOP found a 38 percent increase.[46]

Meanwhile there was every indication that the spatial segregation that had defined urban life for African Americans in the North continued and even intensified, a fifth factor in the emergence of the city's housing movement. We now know, from Douglas Massey and Nancy Denton's exhaustive comparative study of census data, that racial discrimination unrelentingly locked African Americans into the inner city through the 1970s. As Massey and Denton point out, throughout the postwar period "there was widespread support among whites for racial discrimination in housing and for the systematic exclusion of blacks from white neighborhoods."[47] Philadelphia was no exception, as housing activists were aware at the time. Racial violence marked the periphery of many black neighborhoods, as well as the border between black Philadelphia and the white suburbs, especially along the boundary between northwest Philadelphia and Montgomery County, where occasional white-supremacist activities reminded blacks that geographical mobility brought unexpected costs.

COMMUNITY DEVELOPMENT, 1976–1980

These conditions set the stage for the dramatic confrontations of the late 1970s, focusing on applications for the city's annual federal Community Development Block Grants. In July 1976, the CDBG program was in its second year of funding and already beset by controversy. For more than a year, community activists had severely criticized Philadelphia's funding applications in public hearings and the press. That winter several prominent housing and neighborhood coalitions, including Tenant Action Group and the Housing Association of the Delaware Valley, formed the Ad Hoc Committee on Housing and Neighborhood Revitalization to challenge the city's CDBG applications and to consolidate citywide opposition to redevelopment.[48]

At the center of the Ad Hoc Committee stood Milton Street, a young, dynamic street vendor and state legislator, whose North Philadelphia Block Development Corporation soon would provide the core of activists for the city's squatting movement. With relatively little political experience, Street had entered the public arena in the fall of 1974 in a conflict with the city over the availability of sidewalk space for street merchants. Initially a dispute over the placement of Street's hotdog and pretzel stands at locations around the city, the controversy quickly developed into a struggle over who would be represented in the revitalized public life of the downtown. Street and other vendors laid claim to downtown sidewalks, while city officials tried to control the symbolic and commercial space of the streets through legislative and police authority, in part responding to pressure from conventional downtown businesspeople who liked neither the competition from vendors nor the visual aesthetic of a virtual bazaar stretched along the streets in front of their shops.

Street's theatrical manner of confrontation, which included well-orchestrated disruptions of City Council meetings, set the tone for the battles over housing and redevelopment that would follow, many of which he would lead. Upstaging the city fathers, Street displayed an uncanny sense for the appropriateness of dramatic and comic confrontation at a time when the city's primary concern was to restore prosperous civility and decorum to the downtown in preparation for the Bicentennial. By February 1975, Street and his fellow vendors were able to mobilize an effective interracial opposition to a proposed bill severely restricting vendors' licensing rights.[49] As the vending issue died down in the press, Street and many of his followers shifted their attention to the pressing need for services and housing in poor districts of Philadelphia, initiating campaigns demanding more frequent trash removal and the boarding up of houses in Street's north Philadelphia neighborhood. Soon Street turned his attention back to city hall, joining the ongoing campaign to force redistribution of the city's federal block grants to include more housing and services for the poor.[50]

Street, the Ad Hoc Committee, and other critics attacked the community development program for two general failings. First, the city was not meeting the requirements of the act for full community disclosure and participation, which mandated well-publicized open hearings on yearly applications and proposed budgets. Community organizations complained from the start that the city neither offered sufficient notice of public meetings, nor incorporated in CDBG applications citizen concerns expressed at those meetings and elsewhere. Such criticism got to the heart of the CDBG strategy, which as one housing activist pointed out, circumvented existing forms of neighborhood control, notably the Project Area Committees set up under urban renewal and maintained through the Model Cities program. "The real effect" of the Housing and Community Development Act of 1974, he argued, was "to take power over planning and development away from the people in the neighborhoods, and . . . centralize [it] in City Hall."[51] Such indifference to neighborhood concerns and public criticism created especially acute problems in the Philadelphia program, as the Rizzo administration became increasingly defensive and recalcitrant, favoring, according to some critics, the needs of conservative white neighborhoods that endorsed Rizzo's authoritarian and racially incendiary politics.

The community development program's second general failing, according to critics, was that the city was avoiding public scrutiny because only a small fraction of the federal money was going to the neighborhoods. That which did, as housing officials acknowledged, was not effectively applied to rehabilitation of low-income housing.[52] As HADV pointed out in testimony to City Council, the "so-called housing program set forth in [the Year II] application is not rightfully a housing program at all, but a program of housing demolition." Furthermore, that small portion of money applied to housing rehabilitation offered limited benefits to the poor, concentrating mainly on complete reconstruction of buildings that would enter the market at prices too high for low-income residents to afford.[53] However, as activists tirelessly pointed out, whatever money went into housing and neighborhood revitalization was a pittance compared to that which the city was using for administration, for police and fire services, and for downtown commercial development, including the building of a new shopping mall.[54] A proposed commuter tunnel underneath that mall, linking rail lines into a continuous service between suburbs and city, elicited the most concerted early opposition. Receiving a substantial portion of community development funding, the tunnel, a centerpiece of the planning commission's 1960 blueprint, would be of little benefit to inner-city neighborhoods. Opposition to the tunnel merged in the winter of 1977 with neighborhood protests over declining transit service, as well as with rank-and-file mobilization by left-wing militants in the transit workers union. That March more than four hundred people packed City Council for hearings on the tunnel project, which a local left-liberal think tank estimated would use up more than half of available funds for capital improvements in regional transportation.[55]

Meanwhile, activists maintained intense public and political pressure on HUD in the press and the courts to block the city's Year II and Year III applications (for fiscal years 1976 and 1977).[56] They claimed not only a failure to meet the mandate of the act to supply low- and middle-income housing, but also "a strong pattern of racial discrimination and destruction of minority neighborhoods."[57] By the spring of 1977, the pressure brought a warning from HUD, reinforced by a vote of no confidence from the regional planning commission and embarrassing revelations in local papers that the city's new housing director, John Gallery (a protégé of the Greater Philadelphia Movement's Edmund Bacon), favored withdrawing services and funds from "hardcore" areas of the city (most of them black), allowing them to "fall apart." In an April letter to the Rizzo administration, Robert Clement, HUD director for the Philadelphia area, threatened the rejection of Philadelphia's Year III application if more effective provision of low-income housing were not worked into the city's redevelopment plans.[58] To placate his increasingly vocal and effective critics, Gallery publicly offered a "special effort" to apply funds to the housing problem in north Philadelphia. Privately, the city's defense of its application revealed the fundamental disagreement of principle between officials and activists. Arguing that

Philadelphia's program technically fulfilled the requirements of the 1974 act, Gallery conceded that low-income housing was not a priority for his office. For him, community development primarily served urban revitalization; it was not an assistance program. The conflict that had emerged between housing activists and planners such as Gallery, then, was not just between neighborhood and downtown, but between competing views on policy goals and metropolitan models.[59]

HUD's responsiveness encouraged housing activists to step up their pressure for the following year's application, packing City Council and disrupting city government with increasing regularity. To some extent their expectations were raised by the entry of Jimmy Carter into the White House in 1977. Under Patricia Harris, Carter's HUD tightened guidelines for and oversight of the use of community development funds and sent a clear message to municipalities to raise local commitments to low- and moderate-income housing programs.[60] A suit challenging distribution of block grant funds, charges of police brutality, and stonewalling on public-housing construction combined with sit-ins at regional HUD offices and high-profile squatting in several Philadelphia neighborhoods to draw the attention of national political leaders, who brought pressure on HUD officials at the highest level to do something about the situation in Philadelphia.[61]

SQUATTING, 1977–1981

By 1977 housing advocates had spent six years wrangling with an intransigent city government. It was partly to underscore this indifference to the housing woes of poor Philadelphians and to force the hand of federal officials that first Street and then other housing activists began squatting.

In June 1977 Street announced that his North Philadelphia Block Development Corporation would begin to help local residents break into abandoned homes and demand squatters' rights. Actually, by that summer Street and his organization had been discretely placing people for more than a year in vacant houses around his north Philadelphia neighborhood. Choosing only those houses that obviously had been abandoned by their owners, Street avoided confrontation with the city over the disposition of the real estate, terming the new residents merely temporary tenants. They were there, he argued, to prevent vandalism and further deterioration of the housing stock.[62] By the summer of 1977,

however, Street had moved beyond neighborhood preservation, leading crowds of people to snip the padlocks off the front doors of federally owned buildings with a large pair of bolt cutters. Choosing homes
under FHA foreclosure and currently controlled by HUD, Street demanded the sale of vacant HUD homes to poor families through his
organization.[63] At first HUD agreed in principle to lease some of its
properties, declaring squatting an admirable "direct action" to deal
with a problem inherited from Republican predecessors. But HUD
failed to deliver on promises of reasonable rents for a sufficient number of habitable buildings. By September Street's organization claimed
to have settled 110 families, in defiance of HUD threats to evict.[64] As
HUD's tolerance of Street waned, the north Philadelphia activist esca-
lated the confrontation, leading a three-day sit-in at the Philadelphia
HUD offices, and harassing HUD secretary Patricia Harris in her Washington, D.C., headquarters. Meanwhile, Street moved on to buildings
owned privately and by the city, broadening the scope of the unfolding
conflict to include the Rizzo administration, from whom Street had no
reason to expect cooperation. HUD soon abandoned any efforts to re-
start negotiations with Street, beginning to evict squatters in late September.[65]

The squatting movement followed closely on the heels of federal
court decisions ordering the Rizzo administration to build the Whitman Park project, legitimating claims by Street and others that the city's
federally funded housing programs were racially motivated. Squatting
also appeared as moderate housing activists expressed frustration and
disgust with such showcase projects as Urban Homesteading, long pursued as a means of converting abandoned property into habitable shelter by housers such as Dennis.[66] It was not surprising then that when
Street began squatting, which in his penchant for comic appropriation
he called "walk-in homesteading," Dennis and other moderates supported the action fully, adding institutional respectability to his blatant
disregard for public authority and private property rights. So too did
City Councilmen Lucien Blackwell (of west Philadelphia) and Cecil
Moore (of north central), as well as Edmund Bacon, the former executive
director of the planning commission, whose association with the liberal
GPM put him at odds with Rizzo. And they would continue to do so as
squatting spread across the city. "We applaud Mr. Street's efforts to try
to provide housing for people who need it desperately," declared Den-

nis, "people who have been discarded by the city who uses their existence to gain greater federal funds, then uses those funds to try to eliminate them."[67]

Some housing experts criticized the north Philadelphia squatters for setting poor people up in houses that they had insufficient resources to rehabilitate and maintain (a problem that also plagued the urban-homesteading program). But Dennis recognized Street's squatting campaign for what it actually was: a dramatic effort to force the hand of city government and bring down public (and federal) opprobrium on local housing authorities for failing to address the housing crisis and abrogating their responsibility to the poor. The objective, she wrote, was "a turn-around by government at all levels. Housing must be provided and can be provided if only the commitment [from government] were there. But the commitment is not there so conflict and confrontation is where we are."[68] Always oriented toward center city, Street and his supporters were relentless in their harassment of municipal and federal agencies, regularly packing City Council chambers and disrupting its proceedings. On one occasion they set up a bureau in city hall to "process" squatting claims on HUD houses, mocking the pompous spectacle with which federal and municipal government doled out a tiny supply of rehabilitated properties.[69] Squatting demonstrated that neither the city nor HUD had any intention of addressing the need for affordable housing and forced HUD and the city to evict families en masse. One sweep came in the middle of a frigid December. As the list of abandoned properties lengthened, federal and local authorities found themselves in the position of removing one needy family from a house to (at best) replace it with another.[70]

In part because of high-profile publicity, the walk-in homesteading campaign expanded through the neighborhoods to include Latinos and whites as well as blacks, making it, as Street often argued, an act on behalf of the poor, for economic as well as racial justice. By 1979, multiethnic squatting campaigns from the Kensington section of the city joined forces with Street, as did poor black and Latino squatters across the Delaware River in Camden, New Jersey, two years later. As it spread across the metropolitan area, squatting combined the salvaging of shelter with the creation of public spectacle, stabilizing neighborhoods while pressuring local, state, and federal governments to grant more vacant properties to poor families and people of color. The numbers were substantial and impressive. While activist claims of having appropriated one thousand houses in Philadelphia may be exaggerated, Camden squatters can document the permanent walk-in homesteading of nearly two hundred in a city one-twentieth the size.[71] Yet, housing activists across the city had no illusions about stemming the tide of abandonment through squatting. Fifteen hundred homes saved from demolition and recycling did not supply the persistent need for affordable shelter, which HADV and others estimated required the rehabilitation of roughly six thousand properties a year, and thus a massive federal and local spending program.

Indeed it was evident from their range of targets that squatters' dramatic transgression of property rights addressed a larger set of issues than merely local building abandonment and housing shortages. Many of the same people involved in appropriating houses throughout Philadelphia took part simultaneously in the continuing spectacle of protest against downtown redevelopment and the political authoritarianism of the Rizzo administration. The goal for many housing activists was the mobilization of public sentiment against a political regime that had evident contempt for the poor and for racial minorities and was interested in displacing such undesired populations from a gentrified urban landscape. Thus, downtown projects such as the Gallery shopping mall, completed in 1977, represented all that was unsavory and unjust in the history of redevelopment and all that was dangerous in the Rizzo administration's championship of urban revitalization. Incorporated in the planning commission's original blueprint for the downtown redevelopment zone, the Gallery was heavily funded by public investment, including portions of several federal community development block grants. While it was legal for the city to invest CDBG money in commercial development, many Philadelphians, especially those from deteriorating neighborhoods, considered it an injustice to construct a downtown mall during a severe housing crisis and a moratorium on subsidized housing.

While its designers conceived of the Gallery as a commercial public square, they had no idea that it would become a political one as well. In the summer of 1978, on the first anniversary of its completion and as squatters continued to break into houses throughout the city, the new mall became a magnet for protest by the same coalition of neighborhood activists that comprised the Ad Hoc Committee, whose grievances had by that time expanded to include inadequate housing, the misappropriation of public resources, the Rizzo administration's corruption and racism, and Rizzo's attempt to change the city charter to allow himself an unlimited number of terms in office. In the midst of tumultuous political disturbances over housing and the charter change, the Rizzo administration added a final provocation: the unannounced storming and destruction in early August 1978 of the headquarters of MOVE, a radical environmentalist and predominantly black commune that had beleaguered a West Philadelphia neighborhood for the previous year. One police officer was killed in the fusillade of bullets let loose in the confrontation (the source of the bullet was never determined), and news cameras caught officers brutally beating a MOVE member taken into custody. Although few Philadelphians, white or black, had much sympathy for MOVE at the time—the MOVE members let garbage collect in their backyard and went about violently haranguing Philadelphians on obscure doctrinal matters—many were shocked by the brutality of the police action. The attack served as the final convincing evidence of the Rizzo administration's violent racism and corruption.[72]

In the weeks leading up to the MOVE incident, Philadelphians had futilely struggled to avert a tragedy. So it was partly in frustration and anger with Rizzo's authoritarianism that on the occasion of a massive protest at City Hall over the MOVE affair, Milton Street officially announced a boycott of the Gallery to commence the following week (August 25). The boycott targeted the proposed charter revision, added by City Council to the ballot in early September, and the absence of black businesses in the new mall.[73] It lasted through the next spring, with as many as one thousand picketers at a time paralyzing the mall's commercial activity. Legal action, upheld by the U.S. Supreme Court, ended the boycott and resulted in Street's prosecution by District Attorney (and future mayor) Ed Rendell on charges of criminal contempt.[74] The spectacle of social protest came to a head that February 1979 as Street and his allies stopped City Council proceedings for nearly two months in displays of extraordinary public contempt for the authority of city government, recounted on an almost daily basis in the press. Packing the weekly City Council meetings with as many as a thousand supporters at a time, Street's well-scripted antics had become a centerpiece of Philadelphia life and of the regular business of government, and TV viewers were tuning in nightly to make sure they didn't miss the latest episode.[75]

CONCLUSION

By the time of the City Council fracas, much already had changed in city politics that measured the success of a decade of popular protest. In May 1978, HUD released a report finding Philadelphia had widely discriminated against minorities and the poor in community development programs since 1975. The result of its first review of a city's civil rights compliance under the 1974 Housing and Community Development Act, HUD's revelations confirmed the accusations of Street, Dennis, and the Ad Hoc Committee. The following year HUD was forced to impound 90 percent of the city's nearly $70 million in community development funding until housing officials submitted a viable program for sheltering the poor by building and renovating subsidized housing.[76]

Meanwhile, voters blocked Rizzo's effort to extend his term. Rizzo's departure in 1980 deflated authoritarian backlash even as the nation experienced the ascendancy of Reaganism, which had been prefigured on a local level by political leaders such as Philadelphia's former police commissioner. Meanwhile, another vacuum in the upper reaches of political leadership appeared almost simultaneously. That chaotic February of 1979 witnessed the death of City Council member Cecil B. Moore, head of the militant branch of Philadelphia's fragmented NAACP and a major force in earlier struggles against racial discrimination. Moore's death opened a seat on City Council for Milton Street's brother John, who won election that fall. John Street would go on to lead an informal progressive caucus in council (four members of which entered office in 1980), eventually becoming council president and using that position to launch his successful candidacy for mayor twenty years later.[77]

John Street's rise to power in municipal government marked, with Rizzo's departure, the transition to a new black political leadership and a reconfiguration of progressive politics in the city. Street owed his ascendancy in part to the successes of his brother and the housing movement, whose assaults on the public square yielded a margin of greater space for the expression of dissent and the shaping of urban policy. The social protests of the late 1970s manifested a broad and intense opposition to established urban regimes, uniting diverse groups in a citywide movement that defied predictable alignments of power among urban constituencies. By the early 1980s that movement had essentially removed a racist mayor from office, helped change the political composition of city government, and, far from exhausting the "political energies" of the 1960s, laid a durable foundation in city institutions and in the city's left political culture on which opposition to Reaganism could be maintained into the early 1990s. With the 1983 election of Wilson Goode, the city's first black mayor and a longtime housing activist with ties to the GPM, some of the goals set in the housing protests of the previous decade were reached. Goode redistributed federal funding to previously neglected districts, shifted the focus of housing development from demolition to construction, and encouraged the growth of community development councils as neighborhood-based administrators of housing money.

Yet Philadelphia's political opening of the early 1980s reached definite structural and political limits characteristic of such urban movements, stopping short of institutionalizing community advocacy, substantial resource redistribution, or even reliable oversight of the planning and policing of urban space. Efforts by the Black Political Convention (BPC), a coalition of black nationalists, neighborhood populists, and Marxists, to mount a left challenge against Rizzo, as well as against remnants of the GPM machine (represented by the winning 1979 mayoral candidate, William Green), based on an alternative to pro-growth planning failed the same fall that John Street won office. Though the BPC-endorsed mayoral candidate, Lucien Blackwell, fared well in the election (garnering more than 15 percent of the vote), his defeat, together with the retiring of Rizzo as a common enemy uniting progressive activists, began a decline in grassroots mobilization against redevelopment and recycling.[78] By the time of Goode's election—an event that could not have happened without the political and social movements of the late 1970s—places for progressives opened at all levels of city government. As a result, much of the previous decade's progressive momentum disappeared into a newly formed centrist regime, which included descendents of the GPM (Goode and Rendell, who succeeded Goode in 1991), as well as younger and more militant activists such as John Street, TAG's Maisha Jackson, and the leader of Kensington squatting, Mike DeBerardinis (who would serve as Rendell's commissioner of recreation).

This power shift in city government was surprisingly durable and to some extent can be credited with laying the foundation for more enlightened urban management under the Goode, Rendell, and Street administrations. Yet, as progressive activists entered city government, the restructuring of urban space continued, as did pro-growth policy. Philadelphia still competed for corporate and real-estate investment, while steadily hemorrhaging population. An addition to the Gallery was completed in the mid-1980s, as was a huge convention center nearby (the funding of which was engineered by Goode). Huge new redevelopment projects transformed other parts of the downtown, which appeared to flourish even as north and west Philadelphia continued to decline. Thus, it was not surprising that opposition to the use of public money to revitalize the downtown continued, including additional waves of squatting in 1981 and 1982. Tragically, Goode achieved his greatest notoriety for the 1984 bombing of another MOVE house in another part of the city, resulting in the incineration of an entire block and widespread condemnation of Goode's own version of municipal authoritarianism.

Even such a mixed political legacy should not tempt us to resurrect conventional narratives in which a dissipating urban activism in the 1970s merely extended the protest cycle of the 1960s beyond its natural life span. As the reframing presented here suggests, Philadelphia housing activists addressed a transformation of the urban political economy that had been occurring for decades, in terms that recognized a broader and more enduring set of issues than those usually associated with the politics of 1968. Street, his followers, and their opponents experienced and enacted that social transformation in racial terms, along the boundaries of neighborhoods, in housing and community development agencies, along the thin blue line of police authority. Yet, in recognizing the instrumental role of redevelopment in shaping the racial and economic geography of the city, they drew together the struggle for black liberation and efforts to restore public control to the management of the city. Their concerns and aspirations far exceeded the demand for rights and entitlements, reaching for a more fundamental, democratic reorganization of city life.

NOTES

1. *Philadelphia Bulletin,* January 23, 1979, 16, and February 9, 1979, 1; Philadelphia *Tribune,* January 26, 1979, 1, February 2, 1979, 1, and February 9, 1979, 1.

2. Even those who celebrate the emergence in the 1970s of the "neighborhood revolution," "new social movements," and "antiregime" urban political coalitions have tended to situate them in the stream of history whose sources are the social and political disruptions of Vietnam and civil rights. On neighborhood movements see Robert Fisher, *Let the People Decide: Neighborhood Organizing in America* (Boston: Twayne, 1984), 125–26. Harry Boyte argued that during the

1970s an "identifiable social movement," a "renaissance in citizen activism was beginning to be visible at every hand" (Harry C. Boyte, *The Backyard Revolution: Understanding the New Citizen Movement* [Philadelphia: Temple University Press, 1980], xiv, 3, 33). For similar assessments from urbanologists see Manuel Castells, *The City and the Grassroots* (Berkeley: University of California Press, 1983), xv, and John H. Mollenkopf, *The Contested City* (Princeton: Princeton University Press, 1983), 257.

3. For the leading examples of this argument see Arnold Hirsch, *Making the Second Ghetto: Race and Housing in Chicago, 1940–1960* (Cambridge: Cambridge University Press, 1983); Thomas Sugrue, *The Origins of the Urban Crisis: Race and Inequality in Postwar Detroit* (Princeton: Princeton University Press, 1996); Kenneth Kusmer, "African Americans in the City since World War II: From the Industrial to the Post-Industrial Era," *Journal of Urban History,* 21, 4 (May 1995): 458–504.

4. On antiregime politics in other cities during the 1970s see Richard Edward DeLeon, *Left Coast City: Progressive Politics in San Francisco, 1975–1991* (Lawrence: University Press of Kansas, 1992); Todd Swanstrom, *The Crisis of Growth Politics: Cleveland, Kucinich, and the Challenge of Urban Populism* (Philadelphia: Temple University Press, 1985); Barbara Ferman, *Challenging the Growth Machine: Neighborhood Politics in Chicago and Pittsburgh* (Lawrence: University Press of Kansas, 1996); Larry Bennett, *Neighborhood Politics: Chicago and Sheffield* (New York: Garland, 1997). For a summary see Pierre Clavell and Nancy Klienewski, "Space for Progressive Local Policy: Examples from the United States and the United Kingdom," in John Logan and Todd Swanstrom, eds., *Beyond the City Limits: Urban Policy and Economic Restructuring in Comparative Perspective* (Philadelphia: Temple University Press, 1990), 199–234.

5. On the post-Fordist city see David Harvey, *The Condition of Post-Modernity: An Enquiry into the Origins of Cultural Change* (Oxford: Basil Blackwell, 1989), chap. 4; Margit Mayer, "Politics in the Post-Fordist City," *Socialist Review,* 21, 1(January–March 1991): 119. For a useful critique of such analyses, see Edmond Preteceille, "Political Paradoxes of Urban Restructuring: Globalization of the Economy and Localization of Politics," in Logan and Swanstrom, *Beyond the City Limits,* 27–59.

6. On the rights revolution and rising demand for entitlements, see Thomas Byrne Edsall and Mary D. Edsall, *Chain Reaction: The Impact of Race, Rights, and Taxes on American Politics* (New York: Norton, 1991), chap. 1. For the evolution of black nationalism from struggle with pro-growth liberals in the civil rights movement, see Mathew Countryman, "Civil Rights and Black Power in Philadelphia, 1940–1971" (Ph.D. diss., Duke University, 1998).

7. Todd Swanstrom defines a "liberal" pro-growth coalition as one in which government plays an active role in planning, development, and the management of social costs (such as displacement). Conservative pro-growth strategies rely primarily on market mechanisms. Both try to reconstruct urban economies to attract investment, maintain growth, and protect real-estate values (*Crisis of Growth Politics,* 4). See also John Bauman, *Public Housing, Race, and Renewal: Urban Planning in Philadelphia, 1920–1974* (Philadelphia: Temple University Press,

1987), 97–98, 102–3; Carolyn Teich Adams, David Bartlet, David Elesh, Ira Gold-stein, Nancy Kleniweski, and William Yancey, *Philadelphia: Neighborhoods, Division, and Conflict in a Postindustrial City* (Philadelphia: Temple University Press, 1991), 113.

    8. Adams et al., *Philadelphia*, 31, 39; William J. Stull and Janice Fanning Madden, *Post-Industrial Philadelphia: Structural Changes in the Metropolitan Economy* (Philadelphia: University of Pennsylvania Press, 1990), 27.

    9. Joseph S. Clark Jr. and Dennis J. Clark, "Rally and Relapse: 1946–1968," in Russell F. Weigley, ed., *Philadelphia: A 300-Year History* (New York: Norton, 1982), 668; William J. Stull and Janice Fanning Madden, *Work, Wages, and Poverty: Income Distribution in Post-Industrial Philadelphia* (Philadelphia: University of Pennsylvania Press, 1991), 128–29; Stull and Madden, *Post-Industrial Philadelphia*, 11, 21. On the characteristics of a postindustrial city see John Hull Mollenkopf and Manuel Castells, *The Dual City: Restructuring New York* (New York: Russell Sage Foundation, 1991), 6–10.

    10. Adams et al., *Philadelphia*, 103; Kusmer, "African Americans in the City," 461; Simon Kuznets, *The Population of Philadelphia and Environs* (Philadelphia: City Planning Commission, 1946), 24.

    11. The percentage of blacks outside the city proper remained constant at 6.5 percent through 1960, and to the extent it grew at all, it was in the satellite cities of Camden, New Jersey, and Chester, Pennsylvania. Martha Lavell, *Philadelphia's Non-white Population, Report No. 1: Demographic Data* (Philadelphia: Commission on Human Relations, November 1961), 1, 3.

    12. See, for instance, Philadelphia Housing Association (PHA), *Philadelphia's Negro Population: Facts on Housing* (Philadelphia: Commission on Human Relations, October 1953), 36; also Dennis Clark, *Intergroup Problems in Housing: 1958–1960* (Philadelphia: Commission on Human Relations, August 1961).

    13. See Kusmer, "African Americans in the City," 461–62, 477, for an excellent multilayered analysis of these trends. For a similar analysis of Detroit, see Sugrue, *Origins of the Urban Crisis*, chap. 7.

    14. Kuznets, *Population of Philadelphia*, 23, 25.

    15. Philadelphia City Planning Commission (PCPC), *Center City, Philadelphia: Major Elements of the Physical Development Plan for Center City, 1960* (Philadelphia: PCPC, 1960), 1. See also Adams et al., *Philadelphia*, 103–4.

    16. Bauman, *Public Housing, Race, and Renewal*, 80, 98–99. Statements that balance housing with CBD revitalization can be found in David Wallace, "Beggars on Horseback," in Cushing Dolbeare, ed., *Ends and Means of Urban Renewal: Papers from the Philadelphia Housing Association's Fiftieth Anniversary Forum* (Philadelphia: Philadelphia Housing Association, 1961), 47–56. In the same volume, see also William L. C. Wheaton, "The Feasibility of Comprehensive Renewal," 59–75.

    17. As Carolyn Teich Adams and her associates write: "[R]edevelopment aimed to change the distribution of the population in the metropolitan area to correspond with the changing function of the city" and "to increase Philadelphia's white middle-class population and thereby lessen the proportion of the poor, unemployed, and minority groups living in the city" (Adams et al.,

Philadelphia, 104); see also PCPC, *Center City Housing Market Study: Conclusions: Policy Paper No. 5* (Philadelphia, June 1984), 4.

18. Bauman, *Public Housing, Race, and Renewal*, 181. Cushing N. Dolbeare, "Synthesis of Forum Discussions," in Dolbeare, *Ends and Means*, 97. On public subsidy of Society Hill see Neil Smith, *The New Urban Frontier: Gentrification and the Revanchist City* (London: Routledge, 1996), 54, 123, 126, 137.

19. The nonwhite population of center city declined from 23 percent in 1950 to 6 percent in 1980 (Lavell, *Philadelphia's Non-white Population*, 19); PCPC, *Population Characteristics: 1960 and 1970 Philadelphia Census Tracts* (Philadelphia: PCPC, 1972), 12–13; PCPC, *Population and Housing Characteristics: Technical Information Paper* (Philadelphia: PCPC, 1983), 10; Adams et al., *Philadelphia*, 118–19. Such figures were in the press in 1975. See "Blacks Being Pushed Out of Center City?" *Philadelphia Inquirer*, January 7, 1975.

20. PCPC, Redevelopment Authority, and PHA, *Housing Quality Survey* (Philadelphia, 1951), 31. A copy is in the Philadelphia City Archives, Redevelopment Authority Papers, RG 161.1, box 675.

21. PHA, *Philadelphia's Negro Population*, 7, 15–16.

22. Ibid., 38. In 1976 the Housing Association of the Delaware Valley (HADV) completed a study of redlining in four Philadelphia neighborhoods that effectively showed the continued withholding of private mortgage financing from blacks, regardless of their socioeconomic standing (*Infill*, 4, 1 [winter 1976]: 6–11). For comparison to Chicago, see Hirsch, *Making the Second Ghetto*, chap. 1.

23. Dolbeare, "Synthesis of Forum Discussions," 90; see also Walter F. Naedele, "Gallery Wants Suburbs to Assist Poor in City," *Philadelphia Bulletin*, July 19, 1977.

24. According to Bauman, "Philadelphia's numerous incidents of racial conflict warned blacks to beware of trespassing in white neighborhoods" (*Public Housing, Race, and Renewal*, 162); Commission on Human Relations, *Intergroup Problems*, 1, 5, 7, and *Some Factors Affecting Housing Desegregation* (Philadelphia, December 1962), 1, 5. On racial tension and deindustrialization in Philadelphia, see Adams et al., *Philadelphia*, 22, 24; Clark and Clark, "Rally and Relapse," 668–78; also Ira Goldstein and William Yancey, "Neighborhood Disputes and Intergroup Tension Events in Philadelphia: 1986–1988," in *The State of Intergroup Harmony in Philadelphia—1988* (Philadelphia: Commission on Human Relations, 1988), 56–58.

25. Swanstrom, *Crisis of Growth Politics*, 70. See also Kusmer, "African Americans in the City," 461–62, and Adams et al., *Philadelphia*, 55. PHA, *Philadelphia's Negro Population*, 7; Commission on Human Relations, *Intergroup Problems*, 3.

26. Adams et al., *Philadelphia*, 72; *Infill*, 1, 4 (winter/spring 1973): 6. HADV, *Housing Abandonment: The Future Forgotten* (Philadelphia: HADV, 1972), 2, 7, 13.

27. Press release, Tenant Action Group, March 10, 1975, box 15, TAG Papers, Urban Archives, Temple University, Philadelphia (hereafter, TAG Papers). Adams et al., *Philadelphia*, 72.

28. Planners were aware of this problem in 1953, when the Commission on Human Relations warned that blacks would be dislocated in large numbers by

slum clearance (PHA, *Philadelphia's Negro Population*, 12–13). The PHA found that "almost no" cheap private rental housing was available to displaced African Americans in the city, despite a relatively high vacancy rate (PHA, *Relocation in Philadelphia* [Philadelphia: PHA, November 1958], i, 22–23).

29. Interview by author with Thad Mathis, February 6, 1997 (in personal possession of the author). On the Jefferson Manor strike see "Tenants Agree to Rent Rise If Conditions Are Improved," *Philadelphia Bulletin*, April 12, 1967, and "20 Picket Jefferson Manor in Protest over Conditions," *Philadelphia Bulletin*, July 6, 1967.

30. *Infill*, 1, 4 (winter/spring 1973): 8–13.

31. Ibid., 13. Eva Gladstein to Joe Cirincione, May 22, 1974, and Gladstein and Brenda [Maisha] [Jefferson] Jackson to Dennis J. Gesker, March 9, 1977, box 15, TAG Papers.

32. On the effort to establish the City-wide Tenants Council, see "City-wide Tenants Council Proposal" (n.d., probably 1970), box 7, TAG Papers. As Eva Gladstein put it: "We have not been able to produce a situation in which the tenant's activities proceed from one level of struggle to another level of struggle" (Gladstein to Cirincione, May 22, 1974). See also TAG open letter to "Friends," June 4, 1974, box 15, TAG Papers.

33. Bauman, *Public Housing, Race, and Renewal*, 197–99. *Infill*, 1, 1 (spring 1972): 2–5. PCNO was initially founded as Council of City-Wide Organizations ("Program and Priority Development," November 12, 1974, box 5, Philadelphia Council of Neighborhood Organizations Papers, Urban Archives, Temple University, Philadelphia [hereafter, PCNO Papers]).

34. *Tenants' Advocate*, 3, 5 (September–October 1975): 8. Copies of *Tenants' Advocate* are dispersed throughout the TAG Papers and the PCNO Papers. On the history of TAG's municipal legislative campaign see "History of the Tenant Action Group's Efforts to Achieve Rent Control," October 1978, box 15, TAG Papers.

35. Gladstein to Cirincione, May 22, 1974. As with many housing organizations, among themselves the TAG steering committee and staff debated the proper balance of neighborhood-oriented service and issue-oriented activism (see Minutes of TAG Steering Committee, September 27, 1981, box 15, TAG Papers). On militancy see *Tenants' Advocate*, 3, 6 (November–December 1975): 7. Tolbert's remarks, delivered by him as the director of NWTO, were reported in *Tenant Advocate* as representing the views of TAG (*Tenants' Advocate*, 5, 3 [May–June 1976]: 2). On class rhetoric see for instance TAG, press release of December 4, 1974, box 4, TAG Papers; "TAG Rips Switch of Schwartz in Rent Control Bill Hearing," *Philadelphia Tribune*, February 15, 1975, and "TAG Claims Council Trying to Stoewall," May 10, 1975; Brenda Jefferson (Maisha Jackson), letter to editor, *Philadelphia Daily News*, August 9, 1975. In many respects, TAG advocated, as did HADV and PCNO, populist development strategies similar to the advocacy planning Norman Krumholz briefly instituted in Cleveland during the Kucinich years (Swanstrom, *Crisis of Growth Politics*, 115). This use of the term "rule-violating" comes from Frances Fox Piven and Richard Cloward, "Normalizing Collective Protest," in Aldon D. Morris and Carol McClurg

Mueller, eds., *Frontiers in Social Movement Theory* (New Haven, Conn.: Yale University Press, 1992), 301–3.

36. Conrad Weiler, *Philadelphia: Neighborhood, Authority, and the Urban Crisis* (New York: Praeger, 1973), 56.

37. Meltzer's remarks were reported in an interview with the *Philadelphia Bulletin* in "Shall We Abandon 'Unlivable' Neighborhoods?" February 4, 1973. Laura Murray, "Landbanking Idea for Abandoned Property Is Hit," *Philadelphia Bulletin*, June 18, 1974.

38. "Rizzo Steps Up Program to Raze, Fix Empty Homes," *Philadelphia Inquirer*, January 26, 1975.

39. Shirley Dennis attributed the "whitening of center city" to the redlining practices of banks as well as to the policies of the city planning commission: It "wasn't a conspiracy in the classic sense, meaning that some people met in secret to map out their plans. . . . In fact, the banks, the universities and the urban renewal people were all quite open about it" ("Blacks Being Pushed Out of Center City?" *Philadelphia Inquirer*, January 7, 1975). "City Writes Off North Phila. as Incurable," *Philadelphia Inquirer*, February 16, 1975.

40. Dennis R. Judd and Todd Swanstrom, *City Politics: Private Power and Public Policy* (New York: Addison Wesley Longman, 1998), 271, 273, 283–84. For a local criticism of CDBG as undemocratic, see Conrad Weiler, "Testimony on the City of Philadelphia Application for Funding under the Housing and Community Development Act of 1974," November 18, 1974, box 5, PCNO Papers.

41. The Philadelphia Housing Authority abandoned initial efforts to locate integrated projects in white neighborhoods in 1957, after violent reactions to the presence of black families in local projects (Bauman, *Public Housing, Race, and Renewal*, 36, 39, 47, 169).

42. Weiler, *Philadelphia*, 117; Bauman, *Public Housing, Race, and Renewal*, 200.

43. The city's black press recognized the complexity of the Whitman Park issue, hailing the court of appeals decision against the city in the fall of 1977 as a victory not only for blacks but also for the poor in general. This was not mere political rhetoric, since the failure to complete projects in white neighborhoods prevented the city from building any concentrated public housing at all. Whitman, according to the *Tribune*, was a clearly visible message to Rizzo's "white friends" that "he's capable of keeping Blacks and poor whites out of their neighborhood" (*Philadelphia Tribune*, "Whitman Decision Is Major Victory for Minorities, Low-income People," September 3, 1977, 6); "Mayor, Press Blamed for Resistance to Whitman Park Project," *Philadelphia Tribune*, November 20, 1976, 18; *Infill*, 4, 3 (summer/fall 1976): 7, and 4, 4 (winter/spring 1977): 7–8.

44. According to TAG, Philadelphia Housing Authority data showed that only 2,823 new units added during the first years of the Rizzo administration. Only 837 of those were new construction and most were for senior citizens (*Tenants' Advocate*, 3, 6 (November–December 1975): 7). See also *Infill* 1, 1 (spring 1972): 7–8; *Tenants' Advocate*, 5, 1 (January–February 1976): 5.

45. Joseph R. Daughen and Peter Binzen, *The Cop Who Would Be King: Mayor Frank Rizzo* (Boston: Little, Brown, 1977), 149–50. Weiler, *Philadelphia*, 88–92.

46. *Report of Hearings before the Pennsylvania State Committee to the United States Commission on Civil Rights, Philadelphia, March 4, 5 and 23, 1971* (Washington, D.C.: U. S. Government Printing Office, 1972). The *Inquirer* series ran February 16–18, 1975. Public Interest Law Center of Philadelphia, "Second Annual Report on Police Abuse Complaints Received by the Police Project of the Public Interest Law Center of Philadelphia—for the Calendar Year 1976," in *Judiciary Committee Hearings of United States Senate, Ninety-Fifth Congress, Second Session* (Washington, D.C.: U. S. Government Printing Office, 1978), 471–82.

47. Indices of black-white segregation and black isolation remained high and roughly constant in Philadelphia through the 1970s (Douglas S. Massey and Nancy A. Denton, *American Apartheid: Segregation and the Making of the Underclass* [Cambridge: Harvard University Press, 1996], 44, 64).

48. The Ad Hoc Committee was founded in late 1976. Its members included TAG, HADV, PCNO, the Philadelphia Welfare Rights Organization (PWRO), representatives of public-housing tenants, and Milton Street's North Philadelphia Block Development Corporation (see "Charge City Planning to Develop North Phila. into Society Hill North," *Philadelphia Tribune*, January 15, 1977).

49. "Vendors Are Given Reprieve," *Philadelphia Bulletin*, February 5, 1975. "300 Jam Council Hearing," *Philadelphia Bulletin*, February 4, 1975.

50. Pete Dexter, "Street Launches Canned Protest," *Philadelphia Daily News*, September 10, 1976; John Dubois, "300 Volunteers Pledge to Spruce Up North Philadelphia," *Philadelphia Bulletin*, October 18, 1976; Joe Davidson, "City Slighting North Phila., Citizens Say," *Philadelphia Bulletin*, November 23, 1976.

51. Father Joseph Kakalec to Board of Directors, Delaware Valley Regional Planning Commission, January 29, 1976, Hearings Folder, box 3, PCNO Papers; CCWCO, "Citywide Hearings and the Community Development Year II Application: An Analysis," March 19, 1976, Acc. 425, box 10, Housing Association of the Delaware Valley Papers, Urban Archives, Temple University, Philadelphia (hereafter, HADV Papers); Weiler, "Testimony."

52. Walter F. Naedele, "Let Slums 'Fall Apart,' Aide Urged Rizzo," *Philadelphia Bulletin*, April 28, 1977.

53. Testimony of Rev. Robert T. Strommen before Philadelphia City Council, February 18, 1975; Shirley Dennis, "Report on the Housing Rehabilitation Programs of the Community Development Act of 1974," August 1974; Memo, Noreen Shanfelter to HADV staff, "Summary of the Neighborhoods Project Report on Community Development Funding," n.d. HADV and others favored inexpensive partial rehabilitation that allowed cheaper resale (see "Objections by the Ad Hoc Committee to Philadelphia Year IV Community Development Application" [n.d., probably 1978]). All sources listed in this note are in Acc. 425, box 10, HADV Papers.

54. David Runkel and Joe Davidson, "Only 11.4% of HUD Grants Went to City Housing," *Philadelphia Bulletin*, March 4, 1979. Allocation of funds was only part of the problem, as the Ad Hoc Committee pointed out. Much of the disproportion between housing and other community development programs resulted from the city's failure to spend housing funds fully (around 30 percent

was used in the first three years), while nearly exhausting budgets for neighborhood security and administration (see "Objections by the Ad Hoc Committee"). See also "The Housing Agenda for 1979" (n.d., but probably written by TAG staffers in late 1978), box 15, TAG Papers. Restrictions on CDBG use were lax from the start, allowing funds to be used in affluent districts and for policing (Swanstrom, *Crisis of Growth Politics,* 181; Judd and Swanstrom, *City Politics,* 286–87).

55. On tunnel opposition see "Residents Urged to Pressure City Council on Tunnel," *Philadelphia Tribune,* February 15, 1977. A Coalition for Better Transportation in the City began protesting the withdrawal of transit services from north Philadelphia in the fall of 1976, led by Henry DeBernardo, a housing activist and collaborator with Milton Street ("More SEPTA Protests Threatened," *Philadelphia Inquirer,* October 5, 1976, and "Transit Coalition Mounts Protest Drive Against SEPTA," *Philadelphia Tribune,* January 11, 1977). The tunnel was finished in 1984.

56. Joe Davidson, "Community Groups Want U.S. to Reject $61 Million for Philadelphia," *Philadelphia Bulletin,* February 4, 1976; "Suit Seeks to Bar City Getting $57M Grant," *Philadelphia Tribune,* March 1, 1977.

57. Milton Street to Robert Embry, Undersecretary of HUD, May 10, 1977, Acc. 425, box 10, HADV Papers. At issue was in part the designation of white areas in the city's river districts and neighboring the CBD as preferential recipients of rehabilitation funds (John Gillespie, "Blacks File Suit to Get Funds for North Phila.," *Philadelphia Bulletin,* February 26, 1977).

58. Naedele, "Let Slums 'Fall Apart'"; Walter F. Naedele, "U.S. Tells Phila. to Provide More Low-Income Housing," *Philadelphia Bulletin,* May 13, 1977.

59. Memorandum from John Gallery to "all community organizations," September 1, 1977; John Gallery to Robert J. Clement, April 20, 1997, both in Acc. 425, box 10, HADV Papers.

60. But Urban Development Action Grants, a Carter program to attract private investment for economic redevelopment, required minimal oversight, providing "an even more glaring example of writing conservative growth politics into the very structure of federal programs" (Swanstrom, *Crisis of Growth Politics,* 182, 235; Judd and Swanstrom, *City Politics,* 284–86). *Infill* 4, 3 (summer/fall 197[7]): 4–5 (the dateline on this issue was incorrectly printed; *Infill* volume numbers are not chronologically consistent). See also Mollenkopf, *The Contested City,* 279.

61. The suit was brought by the PWRO (Harmon Y. Gordon, "Welfare Group Sues Phila. to Force Housing for Poor," *Philadelphia Bulletin,* May 18, 1977). On higher-level pressure, see, for instance, a series of letters concerning Philadelphia Urban Development Action Grants: William Proxmire to Pat Harris, February 20, 1978; John Gallery to William Proxmire, March 6, 1978; Henry DeBernardo et al. to William Proxmire, March 13, 1978, all in Acc. 425, box 10, HADV Papers. The last letter was from members of the Ad Hoc Committee.

62. John DuBois, "300 Volunteers Pledge to Spruce Up North Phila.," *Philadelphia Bulletin,* October 18, 1976.

63. Walter F. Naedele, "Phila. Squatters Seize Empty U.S. Houses," *Philadelphia Bulletin,* June 5, 1977; Walter F. Naedele, "Squatters to Pay Rent in HUD Agreement," *Philadelphia Bulletin,* July 27, 1977.

64. Walter F. Naedele, "Housing Activist Ends U.S. Deal on Squatters," *Philadelphia Bulletin,* August 17, 1977; Kit Konolige, "There *Are* Houses on His Street," *Philadelphia Daily News,* September 9, 1977.

65. "Squatters Vow to Continue Program," *Philadelphia Bulletin,* August 2, 1977; "100 Picket HUD Over 4 Evictions," *Philadelphia Tribune,* November 12, 1977; "Homestead Mother of 7 Evicted from HUD House," *Philadelphia Tribune,* October 1, 1977.

66. The Urban Homesteading bill passed City Council July 19, 1973, and was administered by a board of Rizzo appointees selected from a council list, explaining in part the persistent corruption in the program (*Infill,* 2, 1 [fall 1973]: 9). In the summer of 1975 HADV published complaints by homesteaders of mistreatment and corruption ("Hear the Other Side of the Urban Homestead Story: A Presentation by Urban Homestead Families," July 12, 1975, Acc. 439, box 1, HADV Papers). In the first three years the Philadelphia homesteading program placed 335 families, with an average income of $13,000 (*Infill,* 5, 2 [summer/fall 1978]: 13).

67. *Infill,* 4, 4 (winter/spring 1977): 13. On Blackwell and Moore's support, see "2 Councilmen Voice Support for Walk-in Homesteaders," *Philadelphia Tribune,* October 4, 1977. On Bacon, see Walter F. Naedele, "Planner Supports Seizure of Abandoned Homes," *Philadelphia Bulletin,* June 7, 1977.

68. Shirley Dennis, "The Environment, Sufficient Energy, Decent Housing, Accessible Transportation: Making Black Families Comfortable," *Special Memorandum No. 75,* November 4, 1977, Acc. 439, box 1, HADV Papers.

69. "Squatters Invade Council Caucus," *Philadelphia Tribune,* September 27, 1977.

70. "Evicted Sqautters Have No Place to Call Home," *Philadelphia Tribune,* December 6, 1977.

71. HADV claimed that by late September 1977, two hundred families had squatted houses with Street (Infill 4, 4 [winter/spring 1977]: 13). Leaders of the Kensington and Camden movements noted that Latino residents brought experiences with squatting in their home countries and generally comprised the majority of permanent households. Kensington Joint Action Committee claims eight hundred successful takeovers. Neither KJAC nor the squatting projects run by Street kept complete records of squatting activities; however, one study by PCPC in West Kensington revealed a fairly high number (thirty-four) of squatted houses in early 1984 (PCPC, West Kensington Area Strategy, Report 86-2 [Philadelphia: PCPC, May 1984]). Activists associated with Concerned Citizens of North Camden, which kept good records, did most of that city's squatting. It should be noted that squatters in both Camden and Kensington, while addressing the political questions raised by Dennis, also intended from the start to occupy housing permanently (Michael DeBerardinis [KJAC] and Tom Knoche [CCNC], interviews by the author, July 29, 1997, Philadelphia, and October 15, 1996, Camden, N.J.; Knoche to author, August 13, 1999).

72. "MOVE Sympathizers March on City Hall," *Philadelphia Bulletin*, August, 17, 1978; A. W. Geiselman Jr. and David Runkel, "Protest Focuses on Ousting Rizzo," *Philadelphia Bulletin*, August 18, 1978.

73. Newspapers reported roughly 50 percent of the employees were African American (Bruce Boyle, "Black Employees Face 2 Kinds of Pressure," *Philadelphia Bulletin*, August 29, 1978).

74. "DA Planning to Cite Street for Contempt," *Philadelphia Bulletin*, March 29, 1979. Again in the comic tradition, Street theatrically attempted to serve his sentence in early 1980, appearing at the doors of Holmesburg prison, only to be thwarted by an indifferent and embarrassed criminal justice system, which dropped Street's ninety-day sentence (David Runkel, "Street Gets a No in Bid for Prison," *Philadelphia Bulletin*, January 3, 1980).

75. A similar breakdown occurred the following spring, again over CDBG appropriations (Stephen Franklin, "Council Becoming the Best Show in Town," *Philadelphia Bulletin*, April 13, 1980).

76. Kitty Caparella, "$63M Housing Fund to Receivership?" *Philadelphia Daily News*, April 3, 1978; Walter F. Naedele, "HUD Report Finds Housing-Funds Bias," *Philadelphia Bulletin*, May 4, 1978. Joe Davidson, "Phila. Bows to Pressure by U.S., Unveils Subsidized Housing Plan," *Philadelphia Bulletin*, October 6, 1979.

77. Cynthia Burton, "Street Bids Council a Fond Farewell," *Philadelphia Inquirer*, December 18, 1998.

78. Ronald Goldwyn, "Blackwell Is Drafted for Mayoralty Race," *Philadelphia Bulletin*, July 16, 1979. For a discussion of the structural limits of antiregime political movements, see DeLeon, *Left Coast City*, 5–11. A copy of the BPC's "Human Rights Agenda" is in the author's files.

3   Unpacking the Vietnam Syndrome
     The Coup in Chile and the Rise of
     Popular Anti-Interventionism

BESIDES SUFFERING military defeat by a "fourth-rate power," in Henry Kissinger's words, the long-term impact of the Vietnam War at home was that, from 1967 on, major institutions of civil society, including professional and academic associations and leading religious denominations, linked their antiwar demands to those of radicals. Suddenly, opposition to U.S. foreign policy became pervasive instead of marginal—a part of life in major urban centers. In this context, the ambitious and the brilliant were drawn in through the mixture of high purpose and opportunism that distinguishes crises like wars and revolutions. Bill Clinton's trajectory from helping organize the 1969 Moratorium to serving as Texas director of the 1972 McGovern campaign demonstrates the attraction of the antiwar side in a polarized United States, even for those seeking power within the mainstream. The failure of U.S. political-military strategy in Southeast Asia, and the ensuing systemic crisis, produced a free fall where the mainstream had no consensus, legitimating sharp public disagreements unknown since the debates over entry into World War II before Pearl Harbor.

Out of this ferment emerged a new political coalition opposed to the Cold War's basic premises: containment of revolutionary nationalism in the Third World; covert action as a principal policy instrument; support for reactionary (usually military) dictatorships as bulwarks against the "two, three, many Vietnams" across Africa, Asia, and Latin America prophesied by Ernesto Che Guevara. This coalition represented the successful fusion of the antiwar movement and the heterogeneous New Left with the post-1968 radicalization of Democratic Party liberalism.

The Vietnam War was the starting point, rather than the culmination, of effective anti-interventionist politics in the Cold War era, and the consolidation of a radical-liberal bloc against the Cold War consensus came at the war's end, after U.S. troops withdrew from Indochina in early 1973. Congressional and grassroots activism against U.S. backing of military dictatorships in places like Greece, Brazil, and Guatemala had grown from 1968 on, as demonstrated by a series of legislative hearings, the first restrictions on U.S. aid to governments that abused human rights, and the formation of small activist groups like the American Friends of Brazil and the American Friends of Guatemala. International outrage focused especially on Brazil in the early 1970s, with a Bertrand Russell Tribunal in Rome in July 1973. All of this was a prelude, however, to protest against the Nixon administration's role in the September 11, 1973, coup that toppled Chile's elected Marxist government, which kept growing in the months after the coup because of the brutality of the junta led by General Augusto Pinochet. Activism around Chile played a central role in cohering the new anti-interventionist coalition from 1974 to 1976. From then on, during the late 1970s and the 1980s, until the end of the Cold War between 1989 and 1991 and military triumph in the 1991 Gulf War, it placed real limits upon the "national security state" by redefining the relationship between the public, Congress, and the Executive. In sum, *this* was the Vietnam syndrome: not just an unarticulated public malaise and a gun-shy senior-officer corps, but the establishment of a well-grounded foreign policy opposition.

Historians have documented that the premises of Cold War diplomacy came under attack after 1965 because of a mushrooming antiwar movement with a Capitol Hill lobby led by liberal churches and traditional peace groups, and political scientists have noted the significance of the Chilean coup to the development of a new, post-Vietnam foreign policy ethic.[1] In 1981, Lars Schoultz examined how by 1977 "the combined interest groups concerned with the repression of human rights in Latin America had become one of the largest, most active, and most visible foreign policy lobbying forces in Washington" and that "Chile became the focus of the human rights movement in the United States."[2] Later, Paul Sigmund assessed the long-term effects of revelations about CIA activities, outlining how a series of sensational congressional hearings coinciding with the Watergate crisis ratcheted up pressure to assert congressional control over foreign policy. This process began in March 1973, before the coup, when Idaho senator Frank Church exposed the International Telephone and Telegraph (ITT) company's attempts to use the CIA to block the Socialist Salvador Allende's 1970 ascension to Chile's presidency. It extended through 1976, when Congress cut off all military and most economic aid to the Pinochet junta—at that time, an unprecedented step. In between came the 1975 hearings on intelligence activities by Senate and House committees (headed, respectively, by Church and Representative Otis Pike) that were the worst humiliation ever suffered by the Cold War elite, worse even than that spring's final collapse of "South" Vietnam. The Church and Pike Committee hearings ruined the careers of two directors of Central Intelligence and exposed decades of routine CIA political corruption, destabilization, and assassination in the Third World. As Sigmund reminds us, the lever that forced this grand show-trial was outrage over revelations of U.S. complicity in the destruction of Chilean democracy.

But there is an ellipsis, a gap, in these studies. Why? Why the Church Committee? Why the intense focus on state terror in Chile, when repression, torture, and murder had been the norm in Latin America since the U.S.-backed coup in Brazil in 1964? Certainly Chile's Socialist president Dr. Salvador Allende was a compelling figure, and his Popular Unity government's experiment in "socialism with freedom" by a coalition of Socialists, Communists, and radical Christians engaged global sympathy. But asserting major public and congressional outrage without explaining the sources of that protest begs the question of causality. Sigmund essentially ignores the anti-intervention mobilizations "in solidarity" with Chile.[3] Schoultz takes the organized opposition seriously but limits his investigation to Capitol Hill, alluding only briefly to diverse constituencies outside Washington that were the ground troops for human rights lobbyists like the Washington Office on Latin America and the Coalition for a New Foreign and Military Policy. His account of how "humanitarian values" intersected with "bureaucratic politics" points us in the right direction, however, by listing the factors that changed U.S. policy after 1973, a sequence from Vietnam through Watergate to "the 1973 coup in the nation that had been the pride of Latin American democracy."[4]

My goal in this essay is to reconsider the role of dissent so as to show how organized activism is sometimes central to the making of foreign policy. The congressional heroes of the "human rights years" in the mid-1970s, Senator Edward Kennedy and Representatives Donald Fraser, Michael Harrington, and Tom Harkin, and the groups that collaborated with them to write vital new legislation responded to specific constituencies, including three distinct sectors with their own institutional bases: first, intellectuals organized by their profession or discipline, including professors, doctors, and lawyers; second, the self-identified

Left (both New and Old); finally, the vast web of Christian denominations, with the United States Catholic Conference (USCC) as a leading voice.

The intelligentsia was quickest off the mark in responding to the coup. In the first months after September 11, 1973, professors and doctors played the leading role. Without a chorus of respectable but impassioned voices that labeled the new junta as beyond the pale, Chile might never have become a celebrated human rights cause. At first, even liberal opinion was hardly unanimous. In the coup's immediate aftermath, the *New York Times* gave repeated excuses for the junta, which had bombed and then militarily assaulted Chile's presidential palace, the Moneda. On September 12, 1973, the day after a democratically elected president had died gun in hand, it editorialized that "a heavy share [of blame] must be assigned to the unfortunate Dr. Allende" because "he persisted in pushing a program of pervasive socialism for which he had no popular mandate." On September 20, four days after publishing an Amnesty International report that thousands of leftists had been summarily shot, the *Times* asserted "it was inevitable that lurid rumors of mass executions would circulate" and "it was incorrect to refer to what had happened there as a fascist coup" because "there is no reason to doubt that the military leaders moved against Dr. Allende with great reluctance, and only because they genuinely feared a polarized Chile was headed for civil war."

In this context, the prompt reaction of academics and other professionals made a real difference. The first national protests against the coup were led by professors. On Sunday, September 23, the Chile Emergency Committee placed a full-page ad in the *New York Times* under the headline "Santiago: the Streets Are Red with Blood." Besides denouncing the "reign of terror" in Chile, it detailed the U.S. destabilization of Allende, with numerous quotations from ITT memos and *New York Times* and *Washington Post* articles. The bulk of the text was a list of nearly a thousand sponsors. Along with the usual suspects on the antiwar liberal-Left, from Congresswoman Bella Abzug to Susan Sontag, Daniel Ellsberg, Jules Feiffer, Tom Hayden, Joan Baez, Philip and Daniel Berrigan, Jane Fonda, Fannie Lou Hamer, Country Joe McDonald, Huey P. Newton, and Jann Wenner, this list was dominated by contingents of professors from campuses like Antioch, California State at Los Angeles, Catholic University, Columbia, George Washington, Hampshire, Harvard, MIT, New York University (NYU), Rutgers, Stanford, Berkeley,

Santa Cruz, the University of Maryland, the University of Massachusetts, American University, and various City University of New York colleges. Evidently the organizing took place school by school, which was clarified when two of those professors, Donald and Margaret Bray, announced in the *Nation* a "Week of Solidarity with the Popular Forces in Chile" for October 8 through 14, naming themselves as coordinators.[5]

On September 28, the *New York Times* also ran stories announcing that the six-thousand-member Authors League of America had sent cablegrams to the Chilean Writers Society deploring "the book burning and suppression of writers by the Chilean Government," and that the Committee for Latin American Studies at Harvard, joined by the president of MIT, Jerome Wiesner, and John P. Lewis, dean of the Woodrow Wilson School at Princeton, had appealed to the U.S. government to "exert the strongest pressure" on the junta "to stop its reign of terror." A few days later it was announced that the Latin American Studies Association (LASA, which turned sharply left in the early 1970s) and various universities such as NYU were joining with Amnesty International and the office of Senator Edward Kennedy to find academic positions for newly exiled Chilean scholars. Read together, the effect of this concerted institutional denunciation was to effectively stigmatize the Pinochet junta, a burden from which it never recovered.[6]

Of all these protests, what irritated the junta most was an ad campaign begun on January 27, 1974, by the Emergency Committee to Save Chilean Health Workers, which charged in yet another *New York Times* ad, over the names of several hundred doctors, that the junta had killed pro-Allende doctors and initiated a "policy that closed health centers, cut back milk and supplemental health programs, burned libraries, decimated the faculties of medical schools and schools of public health and placed them under military control." This committee grew from an established leftwing New York medical group, the Physicians Forum. In response, the Pinochet regime ran its own advertisement on February 24, 1974, "The Real Story of the Persecution of Doctors in Chile." Its fabrications were rebutted in another ad by the Emergency Committee on September 15, 1974, commemorating the coup's anniversary, which suggested that "it is as if American military and economic aid had been used to support the Nazis, fund the Gestapo, and maintain Auschwitz, Belsen and Dachau." A week earlier the news had broken of the CIA's committing $8 million to overturn Allende through what *New York*

Times columnist Tom Wicker called "gangster schemes of bribery, violence and even assassination," so this language did not seem especially inflammatory.

Intellectuals were not limited to these expressions of professional sympathy, or to the conventional forms of activism like the stream of articles on torture and repression in the *New York Review of Books* and *Harper's*. They also acted directly. The murders of Charles Horman and Frank Teruggi by the Chilean military in late September 1973, in the context of the arrests, beating, and expulsions of numerous U.S. citizens, were key events in catalyzing public outrage and congressional intervention. The primary goad in making the Horman and Teruggi cases a public scandal was a prominent Latin Americanist, Professor Richard R. Fagen of Stanford, vice president of LASA. He and three other LASA officers went to Washington, D.C., immediately following the coup, to pressure Assistant Secretary of State for Inter-American Affairs Jack Kubisch. Fagen then flew to Santiago, where he "uncovered a whole series of outrages." He led the effort to contact the victim's families (in Teruggi's case, the State Department had told them nothing) and to bring the case to the attention of U.S. reporters, who pursued it with a vengeance.[7] Fagen also wrote a nine-page letter to Senator Fulbright, chair of the Senate Foreign Relations Committee, spurring high-level congressional pressure on the State Department.

Fagen was the first of many North Americans to fly down to Chile, conducting personal diplomacy on behalf of established institutions openly at odds with U.S. policy. When the trials of former Socialist and Communist officials began in the spring of 1974, a Lawyers Committee on Chile was set up in New York, which delegated as "observers" at the trials Orville Schell, head of the Bar Association of the City of New York, and Paul O'Dwyer, former U.S. Senate candidate and head of the New York City Council.[8] It is not surprising that when the junta moved to improve its public relations through a contract with a subsidiary of the J. Walter Thompson ad agency, it stipulated that the major targets would be "government leaders, intellectuals and other decision-makers in the United States."[9]

While academics, doctors, and lawyers mobilized immediately around Chile, the uncredentialed Marxist Left moved more haltingly. In the weeks after the coup, there were dozens of protests, but they were relatively small in comparison to the scale of the antiwar movement of the early 1970s. The *Guardian* weekly, the newspaper of record for the

New Left, reported rallies in New York, San Francisco, Detroit, Chicago, Los Angeles, Washington, D.C., Pittsburgh, Ann Arbor, Philadelphia, Boston, St. Louis, Baltimore, Austin, Iowa City, Indianapolis, Denver, and Memphis between September 12 and 18, most involving a few hundred people. Several weeks later, thirty-five cities were claimed to be participating in the "Week of Solidarity with the Popular Forces of Chile," with an emphasis on teach-ins and memorial services, but no major national demonstrations were called.[10]

The divisions of the later Chile Solidarity Movement were apparent even at this stage, however. Since leftist infighting was a significant factor in the 1970s, it is worth briefly examining, as it undermined not only solidarity organizing for Chile, but also many other radical campaigns in those years. The same *Guardian* that reported "Thousands Protest Coup" also carried a long analysis by Steven Torgoff, "Revisionism and Counter-Revolution in Chile." At the very moment that hundreds of Chilean Communists were being hunted down and shot, Torgoff indicted the "revisionist" Chilean Communist Party for betraying the workers because of its "petty bourgeois" orientation. How does one explain this seeming betrayal (or blaming the victim) to a later generation?

The year 1973 was the climax of the "new communist" movement, an attempt to build a new Marxist-Leninist party out of the hard core of the New Left, and the *Guardian* was key to this doomed effort. The central principle uniting the thousands of youthful "new communist" party builders was attacking the Soviet Union and the "old Communists" who supported it around the world, including the Communist Party USA (CPUSA). The debilitating rivalry between "new communists," who were highly critical of Allende, and the more moderate CPUSA, which identified closely with the Popular Unity government, persisted throughout the consolidation of an organized Chile solidarity network in 1974 and 1975.[11]

Between 1974 and 1975, U.S. Communists established leadership over the heterogeneous local groups that sprang up after the coup, such as the Los Angeles Coalition for the Restoration of Democracy in Chile, the Michigan Committee for a Free Chile, the Colorado May Chile Be Free Committee, and the Chicago Citizen's Committee to Save Lives in Chile. Two national conferences were held, from which a National Coordinating Center in Solidarity with Chile was established under the leadership of an experienced CPUSA organizer, Susan Borenstein. Key to the party's ability to bring together this broad network was its status as the only U.S. organization with formal ties to Allende's coalition, via the Chilean Communists. As a consequence, when prominent exiles such as former government ministers and Allende's widow visited the United States, it was Communists who organized their tours and hosted them. Many of these local Communist activists were well established in the antiwar movement, in unions, and even in Democratic Party circles, where their CPUSA affiliations were not publicly admitted.

The New York–based National Chile Center, as it became known, effectively tied together many different strands of activism. It recruited Cynthia Buhl, a young human rights activist from Oregon who would become the principal Washington, D.C., lobbyist on Latin America in the 1980s, and its board of directors included Mary Ann Mahaffey, a Detroit City Council member, and a prominent historian of Latin America, John Coatsworth, who in the 1990s served as president of the American Historical Association. It organized speaking events by exiled Popular Unity leaders and 1977–78 concert tours by the famous "Nuevo Cancion" groups Quilapayun and Inti-Illimani that included celebrity appearances by Jon Voight; Leonard Bernstein; Jane Fonda; Peter, Paul and Mary; and Senators Edward Kennedy, James Abourezk, and George McGovern. A Chile Legislative Center was opened in Washington, staffed by the Reverend Charles Briody, and considerable emphasis was put on lobbying, with close but unpublicized relations maintained to Senator Kennedy's office—the command post for antijunta work on the Hill.

Throughout this period, however, there was a different strain of solidarity activism that rejected the pragmatic emphasis on human rights, the legislative focus, and the alliances with liberals championed by the National Chile Center. The national Chile Solidarity conferences always included a minority Anti-Imperialist Caucus led by supporters of Chile's clandestine Movement of the Revolutionary Left (MIR), which had refused to join Allende's coalition and criticized it as insufficiently revolutionary. In late 1975, the anti-imperialists split off to form an organization called Non-Intervention in Chile (NICH), committed to a more militant style of protest and to making the connections between U.S. corporate capitalism at home and in Chile. As Seattle NICH put it: "It is central to our work to educate the people in the U.S. to the issues of 1) how did the repression in Chile come about? and 2) how is the Chilean experience relevant to the people of the U.S.?"[12]

Diplomatic historians may doubt the significance of this solidarity organizing by the "far" Left, far out of the political mainstream. But the tendency to disparage radicalism as removed from what happens on Capitol Hill reflects a myopia about who actually generates letters and phone calls and visits to congressional offices. The business of radicals is to make life uncomfortable for those who are not radical, and the combined forces of Chile Solidarity proved they could do that on many occasions, as when a Chilean Navy sailing ship, the *Esmerelda,* was invited to participate in "Operation Sail" during the 1976 Bicentennial. It was alleged that the schooner had served as a torture center after the coup, and the storm of protest reached all the way into the august New York Yacht Club. Moreover, these gadfly campaigns to annoy the Pinochet junta occurred in a larger global context of condemnation, reflecting the United States' general loss of authority after the debacle of Vietnam. A July 1974 Pan-European Conference for Solidarity with Chile attracted leaders of both Communist and historically anticommunist social democratic parties and was keynoted by François Mitterand, the future president of France. A hemispheric conference in Mexico City was addressed by President Luis Echavarría, and Representative Michael Harrington, a Massachusetts Democrat and antagonist of the CIA, served as one of the U.S. delegates. Closer to home, in September 1974, the newly formed Center for National Security Studies, a left-leaning think tank, organized a "congressional conference" on Capitol Hill sponsored by Michigan senator Philip Hart, where CIA director William Colby answered questions from panelists like Richard Barnet of the Institute for Policy Studies and was booed for his insistence that there was no policy of deliberate assassination in the Phoenix Program he had directed in Vietnam.[13] Solidarity with Chile, like opposition to the U.S. war in Vietnam, was ultimately a worldwide phenomenon, and those who carried that banner in the United States had powerful allies abroad.

A world removed from the Marxist Left was the surge in church activism catalyzed by the coup in Chile. From the first day, the junta had targeted U.S. missionaries in Chile, and for good reason, since the Chilean group Christians for Socialism had attracted numerous North American supporters. Two Maryknoll priests, Francis Flynn and Joseph Dougherty, were expelled in the first days, as well as a Methodist volunteer, Carol Nezzo, and the Reverend Charles Welch of the Holy Cross Missioners. In late October 1973, St. George's College, an elite school run by U.S. priests that was opened to the poor during the Allende years, was taken over by a Chilean Air Force officer because it was "infiltrated by Marxism." The key figure in founding the Washington Office on Latin America, the main hemispheric human rights lobby in the past quarter century, was the Reverend Joseph Eldridge, another Methodist who was expelled after the coup. This pattern did not abate. In September 1974, the superior of the Holy Cross order, Father Robert Plasker, was put on a plane, and in late 1975, three U.S. nuns were expelled for allegedly hiding guerrillas of the MIR.[14]

What is most striking is the Catholic hierarchy's declaring its open opposition to U.S. policy in Latin America. This was a watershed moment in the evolution of post-Vietnam politics. From the Cold War's beginning, the Catholic Church was a pillar of anticommunism, at home and abroad. But North American Catholic perspectives had been changing since the 1960s, in response to epochal shifts in the Latin American Church. A new doctrine and practice called "Liberation Theology," intended to align the church with the vast poverty-stricken majority of its communicants rather than elites, began germinating in Brazil in the 1950s. In the 1960s, it swept across the Americas, stimulated by the Vatican II reforms of Popes John XXIII and Paul VI, and culminating in the 1968 Medellin Conference, where the assembled Latin American bishops declared a "preferential option for the poor."[15] The North American Church was not immune to these influences. During these years, thousands of priests, religious men and women, and lay volunteers went south as Papal Volunteers for Latin America (the *National Catholic Reporter* claimed four thousand from U.S. dioceses by 1966), and many of them came home radicalized, committed to spreading a new gospel of solidarity. The example of the Columbian priest Camilo Torres, killed in 1966 while fighting with a guerrilla group, attracted considerable attention in the United States (he was eulogized by Dorothy Day, among others), and in a case famous among the U.S. religious, a group of Maryknoll men and women were expelled from Guatemala in late 1967 as they were about to form their own Christian guerrilla front.[16] Similar processes of "reverse mission" affected numerous Protestant missionaries, like the Reverend Philip Wheaton, an Episcopal priest who left the death squad–ridden Dominican Republic to found the Ecumenical Program for Inter-American Communication and Action, the first church-based organization dealing with Latin America, in 1968.

A good example of the deep changes among North American Christians, affecting even the institutional structure of the Catholic Church, can be found in the 1970 conference of the Catholic Inter-American Cooperation Program. Initiated in 1964 by the Latin America Division of the U.S. Catholic Conference (USCC), by 1970 an openly radical message was preached to the four-hundred-odd participants in Washington, D.C. The theme was "Conscientization for Liberation," and speakers included Gustavo Gutierrez, the Peruvian theologian later silenced by Pope John Paul II; James Petras, the best-known Marxist scholar on Latin America in the United States; Paolo Freire, the eminent theorist of radical pedagogy; the Reverend Philip Wheaton; and Senator Frank Church.[17]

The Chilean coup was a catalyst in this emerging process of "conscientization" within the U.S. Church and its hierarchy. In October 1973, the Reverend Frederick McGuire, director of the USCC's Latin America Division, went to Santiago to investigate the human rights situation. His first-person report in the November 30 *National Catholic Reporter* was headlined "Freedoms Snuffed Out in Chile." It was unambiguously pro-Allende and condemned unnamed figures in the Chilean Catholic hierarchy that had lent official sanction to the military junta. By itself, this report and subsequent calls for action on human rights in Chile by McGuire's office would indicate merely that there were substantial liberal elements in the Church who were permitted to speak out. However, the requirements of what both radicals and prelates called "Christian solidarity" soon extended all the way to the top. The twenty-eight bishops sitting on the Administrative Board of the USCC—the highest-ranking body in U.S. Catholicism—voted unanimously on February 13, 1974, to denounce abuses of human rights by the governments of Chile and Brazil, and to urge the U.S. government to consider ending aid to these countries. They were led in this action by John Cardinal Krol of Philadelphia, the USCC president, who underlined his commitment a few months later by sending a telegram of "solidarity" to Cardinal Raul Silva of Chile, under fierce attack by Pinochet and his supporters for speaking out against torture.

The USCC's action, which committed the church offices in Washington to lobby against the junta and sanctioned action by hundreds of bishops and tens of thousands of priests and religious, is only a glimpse into the world of U.S. Catholic politics around Latin America during the 1970s and 1980s. It was largely church people, for instance, that bedeviled ITT's annual meetings for years, picketing in the hundreds and using their pension-fund holdings to make impertinent suggestions inside, such as the nomination of Charles Horman's widow, Joyce, as a corporate director.[18] However, it is a good place to end this outline of the anti-interventionist, even anti-imperialist, coalition that mobilized opposition to U.S. government policies in Chile, and later on a much larger scale when Central America became a battleground of the "new Cold War" in the 1980s.

Religious activism in the Chile Solidarity Movement, at the grassroots and the highest institutional levels, forces us to rethink the character of the New Left and the antiwar movement, and the results of the Sixties. The mobilization of radical Christians, more precisely the radicalization of mobilized Christians (like that of a section of the professional-intellectual elite described earlier), underlines that the "New Left" of white college students was only one part of the larger Left that cohered during the Sixties. Here, as elsewhere, I argue that an amorphous bloc that spanned the distance between polite liberalism and unalloyed radicalism came together originally in opposition to U.S. policies in the Third World, most importantly the war in Indochina, and that rather than falling apart, this broad foreign policy opposition consolidated and advanced in the Seventies.[19] This is the only way we can explain Jimmy Carter, who positioned himself in the dead center of the Democratic Party to win its 1976 nomination, turning to Gerald Ford during a presidential debate on October 6, 1976, and saying: "I notice that Mr. Ford did not comment on the prisons in Chile. This is a typical example, maybe of others, that this administration overthrew an elected government and helped establish a military dictatorship." In politics, opportunism is the most sincere form of flattery, and at that moment Carter certified that the "Vietnam syndrome," or opposition to Cold War interventionism, had become an underlying fact in U.S. political life. Though well understood in Washington, D.C., policy circles and by right-wing strategists, among scholars this is the least recognized legacy of the Sixties, though fully as significant as the "culture wars" that conservatives have publicized. It suggests that the "New Left," if we appreciate the breadth of what that term implies, never was defeated or dissolved. Rather, it melded into the fabric of our political institutions and habits, and by doing so, changed them profoundly.

Notes

1. Charles DeBenedetti with Charles Chatfield, *An American Ordeal: The Antiwar Movement of the Vietnam Era* (Syracuse, N.Y.: Syracuse University Press, 1990), esp. chap. 11, "Normalizing Dissent"; Melvin Small, *Johnson, Nixon, and the Doves* (New Brunswick, N.J.: Rutgers University Press, 1988).

2. Lars Schoultz, *Human Rights and United States Policy toward Latin America* (Princeton: Princeton University Press, 1981), 75, 371.

3. Sigmund offers only a general explanation for what he four times calls the "sense of culpability which many Americans felt after the coup." He stresses that "this sense of culpability had an important effect on U.S. policy, since the U.S. role in Chile was probably the single most influential case leading the American public and policy makers to make important changes in their view of the goals of American foreign policy." He quotes Senator J. William Fulbright to the effect that an "unprecedented number of telegrams, letters, and phone calls" expressing opposition to the junta flooded Congress after the coup, but he attributes public disapproval to a single event: "The most important medium through which the American public was persuaded of U.S. involvement was the book *The Execution of Charles Horman: An American Sacrifice* by Thomas Hauser . . . and the film based on the book, *Missing,* starring Jack Lemmon and Sissy Spacek." How a 1978 book and a 1982 film could spur a two-year debate leading to an aid cutoff in 1976 is never explained (Paul E. Sigmund, *The United States and Democracy in Chile* [Baltimore: Johns Hopkins University Press, 1993], 80, 85, 80).

4. Schoultz, *Human Rights,* 364, 370. Schoultz identifies five factors, culminating in Jimmy Carter's championing of human rights combined with the lack of any major security threat in Latin America in the mid- and late 1970s.

5. *Nation,* October 22, 1973.

6. For an in-depth study of the politics of Latin American studies in the United States, see Mark T. Berger, *Under Northern Eyes: Latin American Studies and U.S. Hegemony in the Americas, 1898–1990* (Bloomington: Indiana University Press, 1995). However, Berger misses the significance of both the North American Congress on Latin America, founded in 1966 and still going strong at the present with its widely read political-scholarly journal, the *NACLA Report,* and the more short-lived Union of Radical Latin Americanists (URLA), which from 1970 on mounted an aggressive campaign to force LASA to debate and denounce U.S. policy in the hemisphere.

7. *Nation,* October 29, 1973.

8. *New York Times,* April 14, 1974.

9. Schoultz, *Human Rights,* 53.

10. *Guardian,* September 26 and October 3 and 10, 1973.

11. See Max Elbaum, *Revolution in the Air: Sixties Radicals Turn to Lenin, Mao, and Che* (London: Verso, 2002), for a meticulous critical history of this stage of the New Left.

12. A proposed amendment in "Response to the Proposed Definition of the Anti-Imperialist Caucas (AIC) of the National Coordinating Center in Solidarity

with Chile (NCCSC),quoted in Van Gosse, "'El Salvador Is Spanish for Vietnam': The Politics of Solidarity and the New Immigrant Left, 1955–1993," in Paul Buhle and Dan Georgakas, eds., *The Immigrant Left* (Albany: SUNY Press, 1996), 312, 324.

13. *New York Times,* July 8 and September 14, 1974; February 23, 1975.

14. *National Catholic Reporter,* September 27, 1974; *New York Times,* November 6, 7, 8, 12, and 16, 1975.

15. The best histories of this shift and its relation to U.S. hemispheric policy are by Penny Lernoux: *Cry of the People: United States Involvement in the Rise of Fascism, Torture, and Murder and the Persecution of the Catholic Church in Latin America* (Garden City, N.Y.: Doubleday, 1980) and *People of God: The Struggle for World Catholicism* (New York: Viking, 1989).

16. See Thomas and Marjorie Melville, *Whose Heaven? Whose Earth?* (New York: Knopf, 1970). The Melvilles, who married after they left their orders, were two of the Catonsville Nine, a group of Catholic activists led by the priests Daniel and Philip Berrigan, who invaded a draft board in Catonsville, Maryland, in May 1968, burned hundreds of files of young men awaiting induction, and then waited for arrest. This celebrated case inspired dozens of similar raids by a so-called Catholic Left.

17. See the proceedings in Louis M. Colonnese, ed., *Conscientization for Liberation: New Dimensions in Hemispheric Realities* (Washington, D.C.: Division for Latin America, U.S. Catholic Conference, 1971); also Thomas E. Quigley, ed., *Freedom and Unfreedom in the Americas: Towards a Theology of Liberation* (New York: IDOC-North America, 1971). From the late 1960s through the century's end, Quigley was the key policy adviser on Latin America at USCC, part of a larger Washington, D.C., leadership that had considerable impact on policy making.

18. New York Times, May 9, 1974.

19. Van Gosse, *Where the Boys Are: Cuba, Cold War America, and the Making of a New Left* (London: Verso, 1993); "Active Engagement: The Legacy of Central America Solidarity," *NACLA Report,* 28, 5 (March/April 1995), 22–29; "A Movement of Movements: The Definition and Periodization of the New Left," in Roy Rosenzweig and Jean-Christophe Agnew, eds., *Blackwell Companion to Post-1945 America* (London: Blackwell, 2002), 277–302; *The American New Left: A History* (New York: Bedford/St. Martin's, forthcoming).

ANDREW SCHROEDER

4   The Movement Inside

BBS Films and the Cultural Left in the New Hollywood

> From the standpoint of the traditional "political" segments of the U.S. movements of the 1960s, the various forms of cultural experimentation that blossomed with a vengeance during that period all appeared as a kind of distraction from the "real" political and economic struggles, but what they failed to see was that *the "merely cultural" experimentation had very profound political and economic effects.*
>
> —Michael Hardt and Antonio Negri, *Empire*

DURING THE 1960s, every U.S. cultural industry experienced some sort of relationship to the upheaval that we understand in retrospect as that decade's distinctive "cultural revolution." The tales have gained a mythic glow over time, the major figures made to seem larger than life, but they still contain essential grains of truth. Hollywood's own mythic transformation tale began in 1969 with the emergence of the young auteur directors, the unexpected success of *Easy Rider,* and the remarkable rise of the BBS company (Bert Schneider, Bob Rafelson, and Steve Blauner).[1]

As with most political myths, this one contains elements of truth and fiction. Although founded on the idea of empowering individual directors, BBS was a collective, even sometimes cooperative, enterprise. Its unusual level of funded independence was a result of careful intention and a contingent event, an unforeseen result of the financial crisis of the former studios between 1966 and 1973. Coming apart as vertical units, the former studios became increasingly willing to let others take the blame for their production decisions. More and more, they preferred to act as absentee financiers.[2] That unexpected window of opportunity allowed BBS the time to set up a base of operations, accumulate talent, forge industrial alliances, and launch an attack on ossified forms of Hollywood filmmaking and their outdated social values.

What was BBS? Ultimately, nothing too substantial. BBS was a corporate subunit, a concentration of cultural workers, a handful of contracts, a distribution agreement, a lease on a building in Los Angeles, and a collective spirit bound up with the general atmosphere of late-Sixties social ferment.[3] It was a network enterprise. Business plans, budgets, themes, character types, visual styles, and political projects developed from one film to the next regardless of the exact constellation of authors involved. Over the course of eight films and eight years, BBS also represented some of the basic fault lines of its cultural moment as linked parts of a network. Doing so, it cleared vital space for a new wave of progressive U.S. cinema distributed through the still-powerful post-studio Hollywood.

Reading BBS as a network enterprise, semi-autonomous from its funding sources while intricately engaged with its historical moment, also opens up new possibilities for a critical reading of the 1970s New Hollywood. As the scholarship on the New Hollywood makes abundantly clear, many young filmmakers viewed BBS as the single best example of a workable break with studio orthodoxies and the dominant U.S. culture. For these figures, corporate institutions, cinematic content, and progressive politics were distinct but linked forces. In response to that tension, organizations of the 1970s New Hollywood (including such small, entrepreneurial firms as Francis Coppola's American Zoetrope Studios and Robert Altman's Lion's Gate Films) took on new political responsibilities through the lens of popular film. These organizations were neither dependent on the rigid command system of the vertical studios nor disaffiliated from the interests of the dominant system. They functioned somewhere in between these options. New "independents" and ministudios like BBS attacked the point of production through precision maneuvers of capital, narrative, celebrity, and ideology. While BBS did not succeed on its own in undermining the distribution structure that held (and still holds) studio-based power intact, BBS's point-of-production politics proved so influential among young executives and creative professionals in Hollywood that it helped to shift the center of Hollywood significantly to the left of most mainstream U.S. cultural politics. That shift has held up surprisingly well since the late Sixties, in a way that defies conventional descriptions of Hollywood as a purely retrograde ideological arm of corporate capitalism.

BBS's production strategy developed during the fluid formation of a new cultural and political regime in the West, in the wake of the disintegration of Fordism as a broad social formation. The New Holly-wood's blend of pop spectacle, high profits, flexible accumulation, coun-tercultural values, and progressive cultural politics—a blend strongly influenced by BBS—became a permanent, if often contradictory, part of dominant U.S. culture. The New Right, formed at the same time in a parallel set of developments, refers to the development odiously as the "cultural elite," arguing with surprising precision that the elites in the U.S. culture industries do in fact represent a generation formed by the political and cultural radicalism of their moment. In those terms, BBS de-cisively advanced a new cultural "common sense" for the post-Vietnam, post-Sixties period. In many ways we still inhabit the contradictions of the world made during those years, but the last frame of the story has yet to run. Our world remains unfinished. To move beyond the impasse of our times, stuck as we are between fears of co-optation and desires for political power, we need to understand the genuine ambivalence of Hollywood's position since the Sixties while responding flexibly to per-sistent questions of inequality raised ever more insistently by the in-creasing centralization and globalization of the corporate media.

Hey, Hey, We're Subversive: The Politics of BBS

Of the three founding members of BBS, Bert Schneider was the most influential and normally retained final cut on all BBS features. It was, af-ter all, his family connection to Columbia executive Harold Schneider that brought him and fellow Ivy League malcontent Rafelson to Hol-lywood in the first place. Schneider worked his way up through the ranks of Columbia's Screen Gems, beginning in the early 1950s. Rafelson slipped into the international film industry through the Japanese com-pany Shochiku while stationed in Tokyo by the U.S. Army. Meeting in New York, they quickly formed a fertile creative partnership.

In 1965, Schneider and Rafelson became the cocreators of *The Mon-kees* show for Screen Gems. *The Monkees* ran for three full seasons and produced high ratings among teenagers and preteens. The group and the show made Schneider and Rafelson rich men with moderate influ-ence in Columbia's TV division. By the end of their tenure in late 1967, Schneider and Rafelson were in a position to call most of the shots on their next project. So they formed the Raybert corporation (the direct precursor to BBS) and moved as fast as possible into commercial feature film production.

Late in 1967, they got the green light from Columbia on a film version of *The Monkees*, to be modeled on Richard Lester's films of the Beatles. The timing was less than perfect. The show's popularity was on the downslide and it had little or no currency at the cutting edges of the youth culture. The Monkees, in 1968, were not hip. However, the Raybert company would have full creative control, a $1 million budget, and a substantial profit stake, as well as the support of Columbia's distribution network. Schneider would produce, Rafelson would direct, and the Monkees would star. Everything above the line was in place almost from the get-go, except for the writer. That problem was solved with the addition of then B-grade character actor Jack Nicholson, whom they met through the L.A. countercultural party circuit. Nicholson's work on *Head* was a way for him merely to stay afloat in a Hollywood that had not yet learned to value his talents.

Nicholson also proved instrumental in convincing Rafelson and Schneider that their film had to expose the commercial mechanics of the Monkees if it was to have any shot at countercultural cachet. Schooled in Jean Luc Godard's critique of cinematic spectacle, Schneider and Rafelson were well prepared to receive this strategic advice. In practically no time, Nicholson was signed as the principal writer for the Monkees' movie, still ambiguously named "Untitled." Through the Nicholson connection and the endless party circuit, Henry Jaglom came into their orbit, as did such ex-Corman refugees and studio marginalia as Dennis Hopper, Peter Fonda, Laszlo Kovacs, Monte Hellman, Carole Eastman, Terry Southern, Karen Black, Toni Basil, Peter Bogdanovich, Ellen Barkin, Buck Henry, Mike Nichols, Martin Scorsese, and the widely revered but practically exiled Orson Welles.[4] BBS consolidated a crucial network of cultural workers and creative resources for the emergent New Hollywood Left.

Sometime in the early months of 1968, "Untitled" became *Head.* Legends of *Head*'s origin are still conflicting and may never be fully sorted out. One story puts it at a weekend drug orgy at a golf resort in Ojai, California. Another puts it at a marathon Santa Monica beachfront LSD session between Nicholson and Rafelson.[5] Each probably contains its own grain of truth, but the legends also pass a critical judgment, passed down through a generation of reviews, that *Head* was utterly incoherent. The drug stories wrote off stylistic surreality, offbeat humor, and narrative nonlinearity as self-indulgent myopia, or even worse, mere intoxication. To the contrary, *Head* was a consistent critical exercise right from the start, a hybrid of fun and politics.

Its antiauthoritarian playfulness took on political significance in light of the film's critique of the Monkees as commercial spectacle. At one point early on, for example, the full-screen image shrank to a tiny picture cropped in the shape of a TV and confined to the corner of a huge black background. While a succession of similar shapes playing a succession of switching channels repeated down and across the background, a cynical rendition of *The Monkees* TV theme song played on the soundtrack. By framing the Monkees as a "manufactured image," using techniques derived from Brecht and Godard, *Head* played directly to the audience's feeling of betrayal over revelations of the group's inauthenticity.[6] Pleasures of sound and image were interrupted by staccato bursts that directed the audience's anger away from the Monkees as a single instance of "false" imagery, and toward TV as a system of industrial reproduction. In that way, *Head* positioned *The Monkees* as the *rule*, not the *exception*, to the world-making capacities of TV. Unfortunately, its young audience wasn't ready for such a challenging work. *Head* miscalculated commercially and flopped badly at the box office.

The next BBS project built upon *Head*'s basic ideas while turning directly to face the growing counterculture. Late in 1968, while *Head* was nearing the close of its production schedule, Bert Schneider used $335,000 of the BBS budget to purchase the rights to a biker movie starring Dennis Hopper and Peter Fonda. The screenplay was written by those two, plus the camp-modernist writer Terry Southern. In all likelihood, Schneider expected the film would turn a respectable profit that might allow them to stay in business, based on the take from Fonda's last biker role, *The Wild Angels,* in 1966. Yet by 1969, that biker film, now called *Easy Rider,* turned out to be the greatest cost-to-profit blockbuster in the history of Hollywood movies up till then. BBS was immediately flush with cash and the envy of every small film company on both coasts. Studio heads started pouring money into a range of "countercultural" projects and BBS-style companies, while hiring all the young film hands they could gather in pursuit of the next big thing.[7] *Easy Rider* became not only an amazing profit machine but also one of the most widely recognized images of the late-Sixties counterculture, a sign of utopian idealism doubled with capital investment and mainstream circulation. Its evident contradictions between "underground style" and Hollywood marketing, memorably laid bare by Paul Schrader's lacerating review in the *L.A. Free Press,* opened the door to a possible fulfillment of the BBS project by securing a momentary financial shield and an aura among Hollywood executives as a field report on the desires of the "unreachable" countercultural youth audience.[8]

After their amazing success with *Easy Rider,* BBS was in a position to advance its collective project directly into mainstream U.S. culture. It was of course not the only radical film collective, but it was the most prominent. The difference between BBS and the more locally based, ideologically rigorous "underground" and Newsreel collectives is a crucial distinction. BBS did not intend to become politically pure yet culturally marginal. While keeping an eye on the alliance of aesthetics and radical politics that defined the Movement at its early-1970s height, BBS believed it was also possible to take over the most central areas of ideology formation directly, thereby making the countercultural margins into the new mainstream center.

Easy Rider became the symbol par excellence of this subversive "crossover" potential. During the wave of *Easy Rider* hype, Hopper turned up the rhetoric another notch by claiming publicly: "The studios are a thing of the past. They are very smart if they just concentrate on being distribution companies for independent producers." The seizure of power would be led by not just any "independent" producers, however, but by companies that tried in one way or another to challenge the standard division of labor in Hollywood. Henry Jaglom recounted it this way to Peter Biskind: "The original idea of BBS was that we were all hyphenates. We were all writers, directors and actors, and we would work on each others' movies, giving people points, making movies inexpensively, with everybody working at scale, everybody participating."[9] The New Left overtones are unmistakable and undifferentiated in spirit from other culturally and politically avant-garde collectives of the period. Likewise, the attack on the division of labor emblematized the new junction between progressive cultural interests and the financial decomposition of the studios. But the greatest gamble that the success of *Easy Rider* made imaginable was for such experimentation not to remain marginal at all. If a committed few with strategic positions played their cards right, they might reconstruct the division of labor at the point of production and anticipate a permanent reconstruction of the balance of power in Hollywood, if not the national popular culture.

The story of *Easy Rider* involved two bikers, played by Dennis Hopper and Peter Fonda, who seal a cocaine deal between Mexico and L.A., then set off together across the country to live the easy life in Florida. Along the way, they encounter a number of strange characters, including a hippie who takes them to a commune in the desert and an alcoholic southern civil rights attorney, played by Jack Nicholson. Nicholson's character bails them out of jail, then joins them on the leg of their journey to the Mardi Gras celebration in New Orleans. Along the way, the group is harassed and hunted by bigoted rural whites who sneak up on them in the night and beat Nicholson's character to death. Undaunted, the bikers carry on to New Orleans, where they drop acid in a graveyard with two prostitutes. Upon leaving the city, though, they are haunted by the earlier violence, and Peter Fonda's character apocryphally declares that they "blew it." In the end, they too are hunted down and killed by a similar group of rural whites with a shotgun blast from a passing truck.

Easy Rider was the first Hollywood studio production to engage fully with the counterculture, incorporating a rock-and-roll soundtrack and a filming style pulled directly from the New York underground. For that reason alone it stands as testimony to the widespread cultural changes going on within Hollywood in 1969. It fused the commercially successful cult formula of the Roger Corman biker movies with an up-to-the-minute countercultural sensibility that struck many audience members as an authentic image of cultural radicalism. Many critics at the time also took note of that stylistic change but dismissed the film as a superficial turn toward culture, away from the politics of the New Left. In retrospect, and with the advantage of additional research, we now see that this is a mistaken view. *Easy Rider* was a film deeply engaged in the political debates of its time, furthering in a different way the cultural politics developed in *Head*.

To fully appreciate the political meaning of *Easy Rider*, we need to look at not only what made it to screen, but also the design and story concepts that did not. In the original opening scripted by Terry Southern and actually filmed on Columbia back lots, Billy and Wyatt were freelance cultural laborers, carnival showmen doing motorcycle stunts at county fairs. After one of their shows, a promoter tried to rip them off. A bitter argument ensued, sparking their interest in getting out of the wage labor game altogether. They headed south to cut a massive cocaine deal in Mexico. Evading the border patrol, they set up the deal and returned to Los Angeles International Airport to make the sale to a record producer played by Phil Spector, himself an actual record producer. This was more or less where the released version began. None of the consequences of their decision to quit the carnival were altered, yet without that opening scene their characters seemed dislocated and al- most purely allegorical, without psychology or even personal history to match their obvious national-mythic symbolism (as Billy the Kid and Captain America). Taking the other opening into account changes our possible understanding of the film's ending in fundamental ways and locates *Easy Rider* squarely in line with major strategic arguments be- tween the New Left and the counterculture.

Among the significant contexts for this other *Easy Rider* was the no- tion of social refusal, or the construction of a space of authentic cultural politics set apart from the corrupted realm of commodities. This idea re- ceived its most famous treatment in Herbert Marcuse's formulation of the "Great Refusal."[10] According to Marcuse, while advanced commod- ity capitalism tirelessly excreted social groups and forces that it found useless for the production of value—the young, the *Lumpenproletariat,* some cultural avant-gardes, and many of the Third World revolutionary movements—these groups and forces retained a distinct and innova- tive form of revolutionary agency by virtue of their enforced marginal- ity from the logic of capitalist commodity value. Their agency was un- like, say, the industrial unions, which had already been boxed into negotiations with the cultural dominant, for it relied on rejecting en- tirely the social relations of capital and forming a new society in its margins as an eventual basis for the total revolutionary upheaval. Billy and Wyatt, in either version of *Easy Rider,* were members of the *Lumpen- proletariat.* In Marcuse's terms, they were ripe for refusal. Yet without the original opening, audiences did not get a sense of their tactical decision making, or the stakes in their plan to head across the continent and re- tire. Refusal became mythic. The images of the hippie and the biker (not to mention their outlaw namesakes) almost entirely replaced the signs of cultural work and strategic debate. This substitution all but divorced their voyage from its politics in favor of a more diffuse identification with the counterculture.

Reading *Easy Rider* in the context of cultural labor and the "great re- fusal" allows us to make sense of the film's apocalyptic ending. Wyatt's famous "we blew it" comment came right on the heels of Billy's insis- tence that they would soon be retiring in Florida. "Retirement" was one possible popular version of utopian refusal, yet one that retained an un- fortunate association with the social relations of capital. In its utopian form, retirement signified the possibility that ordinary people might one day experience the freedom traditionally associated with an ascendant bourgeois class. At a certain age, they would move into a social space unfettered by the necessities of wage labor. Yet retirement was unavoidably bound to an economy of necessity and labor, having been purchased only by years of "socially useful" labor, deferred gratification, and careful saving. Thus it supported wage relations by locating a space internal to those relations that appeared on the surface as their negation. Far from a gift or a right, retirement signified the exhaustion of the socially useless, the aged, and the infirm, who could no longer maintain capital's ever-increasing demands for productivity. Billy's expression of utopian hope was circumscribed not only by exchange value (i.e., the "big score") but also by capitalist labor relations. His death was the price of his strategic failure

Further complicating matters, the film posed for the viewer an alternative utopia—the freedom of endless movement. While the bikers did locate an end point from the outset (Florida), they discovered along the way another form of liberation in perpetual motion. This might have been part of the meaning of all those long sequences where nothing seemed to happen except empty travel down open roads. The Western landscape was constantly observed yet only as a landscape in motion. In that unfurling nothingness lay the projection of a limitless selfhood, unbounded by the claims of social life and politics. Yet their freedom of motion could base itself only on the intersection of several contradictions: between liberal self-determination, social investment (in the building of the interstate highway system), and the ubiquity of corporate capital in the guise of the automobile industry. In *Easy Rider,* these contradictions seemed to resolve into a kind of freedom in motion—a radically democratic, cosmopolitan selfhood relieved of the ordinary commitments of locality and the constraints of the flesh through the mechanical body of the motorcycle. Billy and Wyatt found release from the drudgery of self-definition and deferred gratification, and as their trip unfolded, motion itself became a utopian space where decisions about one's true identity and final destination might be infinitely postponed.

This utopia of perpetual motion and mechanical fetishism also failed. In some sense, it had to. It sustained itself only on the basis of exclusions.[11] Their illusion was that that they could keep moving through social space indefinitely without purpose. The trouble with that illusion is made manifest in the film by the unavoidable tension with locality. All during their travels, Billy and Wyatt encountered examples of local and possibly noncommodified forms of selfhood—an isolated horse farm, a desert commune, a local civic celebration, and even Mardi Gras itself. In the end though, bigoted rednecks returned the repressed locality as antirational nightmare and arbitrarily cut short Billy and Wyatt's freedom, leaving them dying by the side of a lonely Louisiana road. Locality, the film claimed, cannot be both encountered and neutralized. The political and cultural contradictions of the film were symptomatic of the contradictions BBS struggled with throughout the period of its rapid growth.

In 1971, BBS went into production on a follow-up for Rafelson and Jack Nicholson, who had emerged from *Easy Rider* as a major star waiting to happen. Called *Five Easy Pieces*, it quickly became one of the most often referenced period allegories of identity and cultural politics. *Five Easy Pieces* was an eminently political movie that purported not to be about politics at all. To unpack its meanings, we could do worse than begin with its map of cultural space: low cultures and high cultures divided roughly between the L.A. oilfields and Bobby Dupea's island home off the coast of Washington State. Likewise, Bobby's character split between the banal and the transcendent—one part tied to the blue-collar world of bowling alleys, trailer homes, and Tammy Wynette, the other stumbling through the effete luxuries of the bourgeois family and art for art's sake. Bobby himself never authentically occupied either of these worlds. His character was always out of joint with his surroundings. His available models of class, gender, and racial identity failed to allow him any meaningful alternatives to the high-low divide. Bobby Dupea thus occupied a prepolitical space where individual rebellion, not solidarity or communal commitment, appeared to be his only way out of the bourgeois family.

Five Easy Pieces was preoccupied with the inauthenticity (even impossibility) of social identity. Bobby, divided at heart, also divided for the audience right before its eyes. His character completely changed from one class to another midway. This created a jarring narrative effect, as if the audience was watching two movies stitched together instead of just one. When Bobby was first introduced, all of the viewer's available information indicated that he was a member of the white working class. He spoke with a working-class accent; he wore a hard hat; he worked at a blue-collar job; he participated in working-class leisure activities. When he left L.A. to visit his family, the audience discovered that he was actually of an upper-middle-class background. His pattern of speech

changed; he put on a suit and tie; he played Chopin on the piano; he socialized freely with people of an evidently bourgeois background. He
believed in none of it, adopting the alienated pose of the outsider even
in his own domestic space. His attitude was one of ironic distance and
disaffection. Bobby's choice to leave his family and move south, in essence to refuse his class privileges, cast him as a middle-class rebel
in flight from the privileges of his birthright. In other words, Bobby Dupea embodied one of the primary splits within the New Left at large—
between alienated, educated, white middle-class youth and the white
working class. Splitting Bobby this way, the film placed the politics of
white middle-class alienation into fundamental doubt as a viable social
strategy.

How successful was Bobby Dupea's image of rebellion? Many critics
claimed that his final choice to abandon Rayette pinned him to older
models of the antihero and condemned him to drift in alienation. Were
this actually the case, *Five Easy Pieces* would certainly have been guilty
of representing a failed revolution against fixed identities. Bobby would
have nothing left, no other option, but the refusal of his past. He would
likewise condemn cultural unrest to something like mere restlessness.
There are good reasons to believe large parts of this reading. For one,
Bobby's final escape appeared distinctly as a loss. The hum of tires on
blacktop, held through an extended closing shot, sounded a lament for
his banishment from society. Rather than admiring his rootlessness, the
viewer was urged feel sorry for Rayette and all but hopeless for Bobby.
The ending's absences negated the presence of all available models of
identification: the roles of son, husband and, crucially, the antiheroic
rebel. Yet the film's basic open-endedness blocked all hope for a return
to the reassurances of a past that from that point on would be available
only as nostalgia. Although Bobby's fragments never came together
again, he nonetheless retained certain possibilities for agency in and
through the act of negation itself. *Five Easy Pieces* artfully frustrated narrative closure in order to inhibit identification and stimulate further critical negation on the part of its audience. The loss of identity was also a
gain in new horizons of social possibility.

Bobby Dupea's identity position was directly analogous to the position of the BBS group itself as a fragmentary industrial form working
unevenly toward the ideals of commercial artistry and communitarian
individualism. Indeed, the practice of critical negation seems key to an
understanding of the politics of *Five Easy Pieces* and of BBS at the time.

By "critical negation," I mean the act of presenting social alternatives by indirection, negating social relations to clear a space within the viewer for the imagination of social alternatives. In negating what actually exists, it clears the way for unrealized social forms. The meaning of critical negation therefore resides not in the film alone, but also in the way it refers back to its own unresolved or incomplete moments in order to allow the viewer somehow to squirm through into other meanings not indicated on the surface of the film itself. In this way, *Five Easy Pieces* opened vital room for progressive cultural politics to maneuver in the new industrial environment of the New Hollywood without necessarily positing a precise alternative.

It is important to bear in mind that negation in *Five Easy Pieces* did not mean nihilism, nor did it pave the way for closure into fatalism. Instead, the film offered the audience social hope in the form of flashes of insight, where genuine social alternatives to a life lived in the prison of identity might be glimpsed. These moments recognized that the institutions that tried to enforce the necessity of identity were really nothing more than surfaces barely concealing the depths of their own arbitrariness and irrationality. *Five Easy Pieces,* like *Head* before it, imagined that a psychic split between surface and depth at the level of consumer subjectivity was the ascendant condition of its historical moment. It is no coincidence that two of the film's brightest moments became Nicholson signatures, moments that encapsulated the narrative pleasures of freedom represented by his character from that period. In one, Bobby leapt to the back of a truck containing a piano and played it furiously as the truck wheeled out of rush-hour traffic onto an unexpected freeway exit. In the other, Bobby told a truck-stop waitress how she might fulfill her own fruitless rules and still bring him a side order of toast. The former was a denser field of meanings, for as Bobby pounded melody from the borrowed instrument, the cars all around him sounded their frustration in a cacophony of honking horns. The car horns played a screeching accompaniment to his piece and by their dissonance brought into focus Bobby's struggle to squeeze rhythm and harmony from his recalcitrant surroundings. Both his initial act (leaping to the back of a truck) and his music defied the pettiness of urban capitalism signified by one of its most enduring symbols: the traffic jam. For just a moment, the viewer could glimpse what a certain kind of freedom might actually look and feel like, where defiance becomes as "easy" as leaping out of traffic to a waiting piano, as magical as the unimagined possibility that one did not need to remain exactly where one was, and that there was a place beyond the traffic where one is never sure where one will end up once the choice to pursue it is been made. Once performed, the freedom embodied there looks "easy"—a new possibility ushered into the world for Bobby and for the viewers urged to collective identification with the star.

The BBS project from this period of gathering cultural energy was not ideologically based in the narrow sense of putting forth programmatic images, to be adopted and followed slavishly by their audiences. The BBS project was not propagandistic. Instead, BBS films negated ossified social forms (the masculine hero, classical Hollywood narrative, the studio production unit) without necessarily fixing what would come afterward. In that sense, the negation of values and narratives was made possible by the negation of conventional Hollywood industrial forms. One might say that even if BBS did not have a good idea of what would come next in narrative terms, it did have a pretty good idea about industrial succession: namely BBS itself. All indications are that BBS understood itself to be a temporary phenomenon, even if certain members did not. The fact remains that BBS was never able to challenge the hegemony of the studios at the point of distribution, and thus its revolution always remained an anticipatory one at the point of production. Independent American cinema has referenced BBS constantly ever since, with good reason. BBS was a crucial negation of the actually existing Hollywood. This was no small feat, but it was nothing like a permanent replacement for the studios, made evident by the dispersal of BBS's talent through the studios themselves during the 1970s.

Dissemination: BBS after BBS

At its apex, BBS was marked by apparently irresolvable contradictions. On the one hand, it produced its third critical and commercial hit in a row with *The Last Picture Show*. Directed by Peter Bogdanovich and starring Cybil Sheppard, Jeff Daniels, and a cast of soon-to-be-famous young actors, the story of absent fathers and Old Hollywood nostalgia was certainly youth oriented and socially liberal, yet anything but politically radical. On the other hand, Schneider began moving further into the orbit of the radical political Left, particularly the antiwar movement and the Black Panther Party. He was a key supporter of Daniel Ellsberg in the Pentagon Papers case and was placed on the Nixon enemies list while being subjected to intense FBI surveillance. By 1971, he was perhaps the single largest funding source for the Black Panther Party as it fought to stave off a vicious legal and paramilitary counter-offensive. He played a direct role in aiding Huey Newton's flight from the United States to Cuba. Although never proven, rumors abounded of his support for the Weather Underground. He opened his home to Abbie Hoffman when Hoffman went underground in the wake of his conviction on drug charges. He almost single-handedly masterminded the return to Hollywood of radical auteur Charlie Chaplin. And in 1972, he and his partner, Candice Bergen, made a highly publicized trip to China that had Schneider, upon returning to the States, loudly touting the merits of Mao's Cultural Revolution and even importing the term "cultural worker" into his everyday business vocabulary.[12]

The pairing of the liberal Bogdanovich and the radical Schneider within the organization seemed to be a contradiction in ideological terms. Yet it was far more complex. Schneider insisted on maintaining ties with the left wing of the Democratic Party throughout his radical period and refused to cave in to suggestions from militants that partic-ipation in so-called mainstream political venues somehow precluded support for more avant-garde social forces. A similar position was gain-ing currency within the Black Panther Party at a moment when the party was trying to recoup its ranks by broadening contacts with inter-national revolutionary movements and focusing on Oakland city poli-tics as the gestation point for a legitimate popular base. Likewise, a number of ex–New Left activists, such as Tom Hayden, veered toward political opportunities that seemed to be opening up on the state and lo-cal levels, as well as in mainstream entertainment and journalism. Schneider's desire was that BBS occupy an institutional space within the main currents of Hollywood, thereby guarding against a counteroffen-sive within studio system while offering as much aid as possible to rad-ical forces outside.[13]

But calls from the Left for direct engagement between BBS films and radical movements were growing louder. Many on the Left thought that it was not enough simply to produce films with countercultural values. BBS ought to represent and engage the movements directly. Doing that in any consistent way was made difficult by the internal composition of the company. BBS was hardly unified ideologically. Its first foray into direct political articulation, the student radical film *Drive He Said*, proved to be a muddled failure that caused Schneider great public embarrassment. The director, Jack Nicholson, was empowered by the philosophy of directorial control to represent in *Drive He Said* his beliefs on psychosexual liberation and the mentally confining powers of cultural institutions—ideas linked in many ways to main currents of progressive thought at the time. However, his film was not unambiguously in support of the student movement. Nicholson's main character was a student radical driven mad by the demands of the institution, and martyred by the psychiatric profession. His ideas were complicated and often sophisticated, but their reception in 1971 provoked a furor among student radicals and the antiwar movement, both of whom saw *Drive He Said* as a slanderous betrayal of their interests.

As the Sixties turned to the Seventies, BBS was also starting to feel some heat from the Right and more centrist studio elites within Hollywood. After the follow-ups to *Drive He Said*—Henry Jaglom's *A Safe Place* and Bob Rafelson's *King of Marvin Gardens*—also failed to perform at the box office, Columbia Pictures began legal proceedings to dissolve its financial commitment to the BBS company. BBS wasn't alone. Most of the studio-financed counterculture films came in well under profit. BBS' failure was exceptional though, given the high profile of the organization. All of a sudden, BBS felt the sting of real independence. The company fell apart. The idea of maintaining BBS as an institutional axis of the Left in Hollywood fell prey to emerging concerns over changing audience tastes and cost controls.

By 1975, BBS was for all intents and purposes institutionally dead. Its distribution contract was terminated and the rights to its ancillary profits were tied up in the courts until 1979. Schneider, motivated by his involvement in the antiwar movement and his friendship with Daniel Ellsberg, initiated on his own a controversial long-term documentary project in 1971. It was just approaching completion in 1975.[14] *Hearts and Minds,* while not labeled a BBS product, overlapped sufficiently in its planning and production schedule with the last moments of BBS that it can reasonably be called a BBS film. It was also the first documentary released by a major studio about the causes and consequences of the Vietnam War. *Hearts and Minds* was perhaps the clearest expression of Schneider's mediation between liberalism and radicalism. Released to wide public controversy, *Hearts and Minds* won an Academy Award for best documentary and afforded Schneider his most memorable public political moment when he used his acceptance speech to read a statement from the provisional government of postrevolutionary Vietnam.

Still, not everyone on the Left was overjoyed with *Hearts and Minds*. Emile de Antonio, for one, wrote to his friends and associates throughout 1973 that *Hearts and Minds* was far inferior politically to his own work, *Vietnam in the Year of the Pig*. In a letter to Jane Fonda, he claimed: "I reviewed *Hearts and Minds* and was as hard on it as I could be. It's a contemptible work—quite literally. It has no politics, it has no structure and above all it is filled with contempt, the contempt of CBS-Beverly Hills liberals for all the Americans in it. And it ignores the Vietnamese." Jane Fonda, embroiled in work with the Indochina Peace Campaign since the failure of Nixon to end the bombing of the North after the so-called official end of the war in Vietnam, wrote back saying that although she agreed with de Antonio in principle about the film's politics, "it is a progressive film which can have a very powerful impact on some people who have never given much thought to the issue."[15] Once again, the issues were always more complicated than the name calling.

The crux of the debate between them, and ultimately with Schneider, was the relationship between liberals and radicals in the movement. De Antonio believed that the film dismissed the Vietnamese revolutionary movement altogether and therefore failed at the level of accurate and responsible political representation. Fonda, like Schneider, was committed to branching her own efforts out from the core of movement radicals and disagreed on the grounds that the important thing about *Hearts and Minds* was not the absence of the most radical line, but the way it reached popular audiences and encouraged a critical perspective on the war and its roots that many still hadn't approached as late as the mid-1970s. Actually, the film vacillated between the two. It did not fully encourage identification with the National Liberation Front (NLF), but it did argue that ordinary Americans steeped in the traditions of U.S. liberalism were morally complicit in the Vietnam War.

The most compelling scenes in *Hearts and Minds* showed Revolutionary War reenactors juxtaposed with Ho Chi Minh's early statements on conciliation with the United States. Revolutionary republicanism and anticolonialism were constructed as visual analogues. The implication was that opposition to the NLF, from the policy makers on down to popular rituals, was based on a willful blindness to the radical elements within the U.S. political tradition. That message demanded nothing like hatred of the United States or outright identification with the Vietnamese, only the assertion of what the film describes as a subterranean strain in U.S. history, the Revolutionary republicanism of the citizen soldier and opposition to institutional tyranny. On those terms, *Hearts and Minds* was simultaneously a radical and a liberal film, grounding itself on the radicalism inherent but submerged within U.S. liberalism.

Schneider's and Peter Davis's sense of the simultaneous culpability and possibility of U.S. liberalism was a much more complicated strategic standpoint than many interpretations of 1970s U.S. politics have been willing to allow. After Watergate and the final U.S. pullout from Vietnam, at least two things changed fundamentally in terms of the potential for a radical critique of the state. The first is the emergence of a broad sense of disillusionment with the government that seemed to mark the beginning of a trend toward popular disengagement from electoral politics. Many take this tendency to be the only relevant outcome of the scandal. Stephen Paul Miller argues that the Ford administration used the sense of public distrust of government brought on by revelations of Nixon-era excesses to cement trends toward limitations on government activism that Nixon had cannily undertaken in his attempts to co-opt the Great Society policies of Lyndon Johnson.[16] In 1976, although he didn't win the Republican nomination, Ronald Reagan was already setting the agenda for the emergence of a post-Nixon electoral mandate. By this reasoning, the outcome of Watergate was to undermine confidence in any political regime whatsoever, enabling an increasing drift toward privacy and personal self-involvement (the "me decade"), and finally paving the way for the rise of New Right variants of personalism and antistatism undertaken by Ronald Reagan and George Bush. This, however, was not the only outcome of Watergate. To claim that it was merely exaggerates a retrospective sense of defeatism from the perspective of newly marginalized or exhausted movement radicals.

In the wake of Watergate, a new round of political initiatives began under the aegis of the Carter administration and various local or regional political campaigns—Tom Hayden's in California for instance—that sought to re-instate many of the victories and values of the Sixties movements as normal features of U.S. political life. Through such underappreciated paths as the alternative energy and antinuclear movements during the latter stages of the oil crisis, the late 1970s witnessed a minirevival of genuine interest in liberal policy activism prompted by interaction with a range of increasingly powerful social movements including ecology and a prebacklash feminism. Had Carter not lost the 1980 election, those social movements that grew substantially throughout the 1980s even under harsh conditions of legislative and executive hostility might have been even more influential. As it was, the energies of the post-Sixties Left were mostly diverted to blocking the actions of an aggressive executive branch determined to revive Cold War bipolarism and militaristic investment priorities, rather than to aggressively initiate new progressive policies.

Just as the liberal state experienced a brief revival of interest on the Left in its progressive possibilities, so too did critical realism in Hollywood film. The year of the Carter presidential election, 1976, was in many ways the key year for considering what became of the New Hollywood Left, as well as the BBS project, after BBS broke up. At precisely the moment when Biskind and others have noted the movement's imminent demise, we can detect an amazing proliferation of forces.[17] This was, for instance, the year that Paramount Pictures released Bernardo Bertolucci's three-hour Marxist epic, *1900*, dedicated to the Italian Communist Party during the "historic compromise" of that year. Jack Nicholson's antiheroic character reached its peak of articulation and cultural influence with Milos Forman's *One Flew over the Cuckoo's Nest*, the antiauthoritarian dramatic comedy which long-time liberal Kirk Douglas had been trying to realize on film since he bought the rights to Ken Kesey's novel in 1963. Nicholon's performance, notably, came right on the heels of another collaboration with a great Italian Communist filmmaker in Michelangelo Antonioni's *The Passenger* (the final installment in his MGM trilogy, which also included *Blow Up* and *Zabriskie Point*)— a pop monument if there ever was one to the closure of formal European decolonization in the mid-1970s. The same year, Alan Pakula released *All the President's Men*. Robert Altman released *Nashville*. Martin Ritt and Woody Allen reconsidered the blacklist in *The Front*, a film that seemed to signal a new public awareness of Nixon-era surveillance politics. Hal Ashby, Jane Fonda, and Vanessa Redgrave returned to the Popular Front as a relevant stock of popular imagery, Ashby through his Woody Guthrie biopic *Bound for Glory*, Fonda and Redgrave through their anti-Fascist Lillian Hellman adaptation, *Julia*. Emile de Antonio and Haskell Wexler became cause célèbres once again in Hollywood after an unsuccessful move by the FBI to ban their film *Underground* on the Weather Underground—a victory won in no small part by the active lobbying efforts of people like Bert Schneider and Warren Beatty. Martin Scorsese, Robert de Niro, Karel Reisz, and Nick Nolte all made important, pre-*Rambo* contributions to the returning Vietnam veteran subgenre with

Taxi Driver and *Who'll Stop the Rain?*[18] Bert Schneider, Henry Jaglom, and Dennis Hopper did likewise on the small-budget film *Tracks.* And Bob Rafelson finally returned to directing in a Hollywood studio–backed project, after the debacle of *The King of Marvin Gardens,* three years of frustration over the collapse of BBS as an alternative funding source, and the hesitation of conservative executives to hire him on their own. In 1976, the New Hollywood Left reached full flower within the studios, even as many of the most important "independent" companies of the 1960s went under financially.

Rafelson's *Stay Hungry,* remembered today mostly for being the film that brought Arnold Schwarzenegger to Hollywood, was an underappreciated milestone in the late-Seventies turn toward the progressive potential of the liberal state and of mainstream Hollywood. Much like Warren Beatty's *Shampoo,* also released in 1976, *Stay Hungry* was an allegory of political corruption doubled with an appearance of excessive personalism and the muddle of class, race, and gender categories. The plot revolved around an ambivalent young real-estate broker working for a corrupt southern firm that specialized in underpaying tenants for their buildings, then building office towers in their place. The company purchased tangible assets merely to translate them once again into money at exploitative rates of profit. The body builders were likewise symbols of masculine muscle power made purely spectacular and exchangeable rather than productive. By the same token, the most vibrant and active character of the film was Sally Field's, whose task it was in the end to enable the young broker, played by Jeff Daniels, to overcome his identity-based limitations and do the right thing by refusing to participate in the company's scheme. Daniels's character, the son of wealthy southerners, had the job of buying up a local, working-class gymnasium run by a corrupt old miser using imported body-building talent at exploitative rates to make the profits that his gym may no longer provided during the recessionary Seventies. Along the way, Daniels, much like Bobby Dupea, is tortured by his own class prejudices until he finally rejects his vocation and decides to buy the gym by selling off his family's ancestral southern mansion, keeping it off the market and returning the tangibility of the gym's assets to ensure the possibility of a continued livelihood for the body builders.

The politics of *Stay Hungry* were basically reformist liberal. Yet its liberalism retained genuine social hope that the economic excesses of a postindustrializing capitalism could be controlled by the efforts of committed self-critical insiders and locally based active communities. This transaction echoed the desire for a revived social liberalism in the wake of the Carter election and belied the general sense of malaise stereotypically portrayed as the pervasive sentiment of the time. Unlike Bobby Dupea's escape into negation, Daniels decided not to flee and instead pursued the potential, however limited, for specific changes in the cultural and economic prerogatives of his moment. The late-Sixties radical rejection of class identity, privilege, and the welfare/warfare state was thus brought full circle into renewed social possibilities on the basis of more complex social identities and affiliations.

Schneider's work in the late Seventies covered related ground. His last producing job before retreating into more-or-less self-imposed isolation came in 1978 with the much-celebrated *Days of Heaven*, the Oscar-winning final project by director Terrence Malick before his own return to Hollywood filmmaking with *The Thin Red Line* in the late 1990s. *Days of Heaven* was the story of a working-class couple from Chicago in the early twentieth century. Tiring of urban labor, they headed to the Midwestern wheat fields to work in the harvesting crews of a wealthy landowner. At first, the land itself seemed to improve their working conditions, yet agricultural labor was just another form of class exploitation. Meanwhile, the couple pretended to be siblings rather than lovers in order to fend off inquiries into their private life. Deceit and masking became primary themes. The landowner, stricken with a fatal disease and told his death was imminent, became infatuated with the woman. She refused his advances at first, but her lover urged her to give in so they could deceive the owner and steal from him. The plan worked, until the landowner lived longer than expected. In time, the woman fell in love with him, and the landowner (now her husband) became suspicious of her unusually close relationship with her "brother." To ease her psychic burdens and keep their scheme alive, the brother left them. When he returned, the farm faced an almost biblical descent of a swarm of grasshoppers that ate up the crop, forcing the landowner to burn the remainder to prevent their spread. The conflagration erupted into a violent confrontation between the two men that ended in the stabbing death of the landowner. At that point, the film shifted into virtually a reprise of Malick's early-1970s neo-noir masterpiece, *Badlands*, where antihero Martin Sheen killed his teenage bride's father, then led her into a darkly comic killing spree across the northern United States. However, in that movie the father merely signified an abstract authority figure, the stoic face of tradition against the delirium of freedom. In *Days of Heaven,* on the other hand, the death of authority was figured specifically as the death of class constraints, the end of authority that bound the two lovers to a succession of fatal rebellious choices. While each film ended badly for the main characters, with their apprehension or death at the hands of authority, *Days of Heaven* avoided the nihilistic irony of *Badlands* by portraying its antihero's capture as a tragedy brought on by a failure to account for the closure of the repressive state. Freedom purchased by the death of patriarch came attached to the larger constraint of capital's regulation by the repressive state.

The tragedy of *Days of Heaven* was not that of transcendent fate but of the ignorance and impotence of individual rebellion against the state. Such individualist rebellion was guaranteed to fail insofar as it could not, in and of itself, outgun the law. The possibilities of liberalism returned at the moment the film recognized that its rebellion against terms of legality (the capitalist father) was doomed from the start by its overdetermination within a system of authorized violence under the law, that is, the state. The antihero's death at the end of *Days of Heaven* became a virtual call for return to a form of state authority capable of mitigating the excesses of capitalist accumulation and providing a legal foil for the possible procurement of a postcapitalist freedom.

This notion of the liberal state as a defensive instrument against the unmitigated excess of capitalist authority in turn becomes a very useful concept for understanding the role and position of the New Hollywood Left during the Reagan Revolution and New Right backlash of the 1980s. For many, Hollywood in the 1980s returned to being what it ought to be under classical theories of ideology, namely an expression of the dominant priorities of ruling elites. The rise of the blockbuster and the emergence of the first-weekend gross as the prime measure of cinematic success are both routinely cited as examples of a return to business as usual in Hollywood. This is not entirely wrong. New Hollywood progressives, then and now, persistently disparage the increasing velocity of these tendencies within a globalizing Hollywood apparatus. Still, they don't come close to telling the whole story, nor do they give full credence to the important defensive work performed by progressives in Hollywood during the Reagan period.

The notion of political defense is crucial here, for it indicates much of the difficulty faced by progressive culture workers in a system of dominance during a period when the state seemed almost to drop out altogether as a viable institutional means of opposition. In these terms, per-haps we can understand something more about the strategic stakes in the so-called culture wars. As Stuart Hall has pointed out, the so-called culture wars were generally initiated by the New Right in the 1980s as a way to use culture to unify a Republican Party coalition of business-people and backwoods types that did not make sense even at the time. The 1980s New Right therefore conducted the backlash against femi-nism and the rollback of the welfare state in *cultural* as well as in leg-islative terms. Each required the other. The response of the 1980s Holly-wood Left, deprived of many of its legislative resources by a succession of incompetent liberal congressional majorities, the complete absence of third-party alternatives, and the inability of the national Democratic Party to function effectively at all on the presidential level until the ad-vent of Bill Clinton, was thus primarily cultural and aimed at blunting the effects of New Right attacks by revaluing antiauthoritarianism, non-dominant political subjects, and basic democratic values as the objects of political desire. They did this through positional institutional action on their most favored ideological terrain. By the same token, as Gramsci long ago asserted, we ought to bear in mind that the "war of position" concept was always intended as a strategic supplement, not a replace-ment, for the "war of movement." In that precise sense, the Hollywood Left's positional politics kept resistance alive during a period when the configuration of dominant power blunted direct confrontations.

NOTES

Epigraph: Michael Hardt and Antonio Negri, *Empire* (Cambridge: Harvard Uni-versity Press, 2000), 276.

1. For the "auteurist" position on 1970s Hollywood see Diane Jacobs, *Holly-wood Renaissance* (South Brunswick, N.J.: A.S. Barnes, 1977); Michael Pye and Lynda Myles, *The Movie Brats: How the Film Generation Took Over Hollywood* (New York: Holt, Reinhardt & Winston, 1979); and Robert Kolker, *A Cinema of Loneliness* (New York: Oxford University Press, 1980).

2. For information on the postwar studio breakup and its aftermath see Jon Lewis, ed., *The New American Cinema* (Durham, N.C.: Duke University Press, 1998); Robert Ray, *A Certain Tendency of the Hollywood Cinema, 1930–1980* (Prince-ton: Princeton University Press, 1986); Thomas Patrick Doherty, *Teenagers and Teenpics: The Juvenilization of American Movies in the 1950s* (Boston: Unwin Hy-man, 1988); Robert Sklar, *Movie-Made America: A Cultural History of American Movies* (New York: Vintage Books, 1994); Richard Maltby, *Hollywood Cinema: An Introduction* (Cambridge, Mass.: Blackwell, 1995); Thomas Schatz, *Boom and*

Bust: The American Cinema in the 1940s (New York: Scribner, 1997); John Izod, *Hollywood and the Box Office, 1895–1986* (New York: Columbia University Press, 1988).

3. On the BBS production deals see the special BBS issue of the Canadian film journal *Movie*, August 1986.

4. On the relationship between Orson Welles and BBS see Frank Brady, *Citizen Welles: A Biography of Orson Welles* (New York: Scribner, 1989); David Thomson, *Rosebud: The Story of Orson Welles* (New York: Knopf, 1996); Simon Callow, *Orson Welles: The Road to Xanadu* (New York: Viking, 1996); Peter Bogdanovich, ed., *This Is Orson Welles* (New York: Da Capo Press, 1998).

5. On *Head* and the drug myth see Jay Boyer, *Bob Rafelson: Hollywood Maverick* (New York: Twayne, 1996); Peter Biskind, *Easy Riders, Raging Bulls: How the Sex-Drugs-and-Rock-'n'-Roll Generation Saved Hollywood* (New York: Simon & Schuster, 1998).

6. Martin Walsh, *The Brechtian Aspect of Radical Cinema* (London: BFI, 1981); George Lellis, *Bertolt Brecht, Cahiers du Cinema, and Contemporary Film Theory* (Ann Arbor, Mich.: UMI Research Press, 1982); Roswitha Mueller, *Bertolt Brecht and the Theory of Media* (Lincoln: University of Nebraska Press, 1989); Sylvia Harvey, *May '68 and Film Culture* (London: BFI, 1980); Fredric Jameson, *Brecht and Method* (London: Verso, 1998).

7. The late-Sixties wave of "countercultural" Hollywood movies included *Alice's Restaurant* (1969), *The Strawberry Statement* (1970), *The Revolutionary* (1972), *Billy Jack* (1971), and *Little Big Man* (1970). David Cook captures the mood of the industry well during that moment when he writes that the success of *Easy Rider* "convinced producers that inexpensive films could be made specifically for the youth market and that they could become blockbusters overnight. This delusion led to a spate of low-budget 'youth culture' movies and the founding of many short-lived independent companies modeled on BBS. But it also drove the studios to actively recruit a new generation of writers, producers and directors from the ranks of film schools like USC, UCLA and NYU where the auteur theory had become institutionalized as part of the curriculum" (David Cook, "Auteur Cinema and the 'Film Generation' in 1970s Hollywood," in Jon Lewis, ed., *The New American Cinema* [Durham, N.C.: Duke University Press, 1997], 11–37). George Lucas corroborated this view with regard to the conceptual foundations of Francis Coppola's American Zoetrope Studios: "Francis saw Zoetrope as a sort of alternative *Easy Rider* studio where he could do the same thing: get a lot of young talent for nothing, make movies, hope that one of them would be a hit, and eventually build a studio that way" (quoted in Biskind, *Easy Riders, Raging Bulls*, 91).

8. Cited from Kevin Jackson, ed., *Schrader on Schrader* (Boston: Faber and Faber, 1990).

9. Biskind, *Easy Riders, Raging Bulls*, 78.

10. Herbert Marcuse, *Eros and Civilization: A Philosophical Inquiry into Freud* (New York: Vintage Books, 1955) and *One-Dimensional Man: Studies in the Ideology of Advanced Industrial Society* (Boston: Beacon Press, 1964); Paul A Robinson, *The Sexual Radicals: Wilhelm Reich, Geza Roheim, and Herbert Marcuse* (London:

Maurice Temple Smith, 1970); Ben Agger, *The Discourse of Domination: From the Frankfurt School to Postmodernism* (Evanston, Ill.: Northwestern University Press, 1992). Also on the currency of the "great refusal" on the Left see Wini Breines, *Community and Organization in the New Left, 1962–1968: The Great Refusal* (New Brunswick, N.J.: Rutgers University Press, 1989), and Richard King, *The Party of Eros: Radical Social Thought and the Realm of Freedom* (Chapel Hill: University of North Carolina Press, 1972).

11. Stephen Kern, *The Culture of Time and Space, 1880–1918* (Cambridge: Harvard University Press, 1983); Paul Virilio, *Speed and Politics* (New York: Autonomedia Press, 1978),

12. Biskind, *Easy Riders, Raging Bulls*, 82.

13. On the relationship between Schneider and the Panthers, and on Panther strategies, see Huey Newton, *Revolutionary Suicide* (New York: Harcourt, Brace Jovanovich, 1973); Hugh Pearson, *The Shadow of the Panther: Huey Newton and the Price of Black Power in America* (Reading, Mass.: Addison-Wesley, 1994); Jennifer B. Smith, *An International History of the Black Panther Party* (New York: Garland, 1999); Charles E. Jones, ed., *The Black Panther Party (Reconsidered)* (Baltimore: Black Classic Press, 1998); David Hilliard, *This Side of Glory: The Autobiography of David Hilliard and the Story of the Black Panther Party* (Boston: Little, Brown, 1993); Elaine Brown, *A Taste of Power: A Black Woman's Story* (New York: Anchor Books, 1994); and Biskind, *Easy Riders, Raging Bulls*, 55–140.

14. On the history of the Daniel Ellsberg and the Pentagon Papers case see David Rudenstine, *The Day the Presses Stopped: A History of the Pentagon Papers Case* (Berkeley: University of California Press, 1996).

15. Emile de Antonio to Jane Fonda, November 5, 1974, and Jane Fonda to Emile de Antonio, November 22, 1974, Emile de Antonio Papers, Wisconsin State Historical Society, Madison.

16. Stephen Paul Miller, *The Seventies Now: Culture as Surveillance* (Durham, N.C.: Duke University Press 1999).

17. Symptomatic of this erasure is Glen Man's otherwise excellent book *Radical Visions: American Film Renaissance* (Westport, Conn.: Greenwood Press, 1994), which ends in 1976 and argues that afterward we find little more than declension.

18. It is interesting to note in this regard that as of 1976, the rights to the story that became the *Rambo* movies were held by the leftist film director Martin Ritt. Although Ritt only decided against making the *Rambo* movies by as late as 1979, it was by no means a given that Stallone's character should have become such a New Right icon. We could probably say the same for the *Star Wars* films—movies that at the time clearly signaled their complicity with a number of progressive motifs but were recoded later in more ideologically confining terms by their association with the neo–Cold War missile defense system.

Natasha Zaretsky

5   In the Name of Austerity

Middle-Class Consumption and the
OPEC Oil Embargo of 1973–1974

Since the events of September 11, 2001, we have heard over and over again that, in the course of one morning, the entire world changed—unequivocally, irreparably, and forever. And while at one level, it may be tempting to dismiss these declarations as hyperbolic, there is an element of truth to them; it is hard to imagine that September 11 will not be a historical watershed of incalculable proportions. But what may be less obvious is that we have heard these sorts of declarations before, and not all that long ago. Less than thirty years ago, during the Organization of Arab Petroleum Exporting Countries' (OPEC) oil embargo of 1973, media pundits and policy makers made very similar kinds of claims: namely, that an act of aggression emanating from the Middle East posed a grave challenge to the American way of life; that this Middle Eastern threat could somehow "hit people where they live" in a way that was unprecedented for U.S. citizens, who saw themselves as somehow immune from global conflict; and finally, that this act of aggression threatened to permanently unmake the world.

Historians have tended to cite the OPEC oil embargo as evidence of America's waning hegemony during the early years of the 1970s, and, to some extent, this essay draws on that interpretation. There is much evidence to support this view. Energy policy analysts, politicians, and commentators at the time portrayed the oil embargo as a profound national crisis, one that revealed that the nation had lapsed from a state of independence into one of dependency (in this case, dependency on Middle Eastern oil). And opinion polls suggested that, even as the public remained skeptical and divided over the causes of the embargo, they agreed that it constituted evidence of national decline in the immediate wake of the Vietnam War and as revelations about the Watergate scandal moved higher and higher up the chain of command.

While this essay relies on this standard interpretation, it also seeks to complicate it. As a significant cultural watershed of the early 1970s, the oil embargo contained meanings that were complex and sometimes immanently contradictory. For example, even as some claimed that the oil embargo, almost overnight, had transformed the United States into what one newscaster called "an enfeebled giant,"[1] a second public debate was taking shape that condemned the excesses of postwar consumer culture and predicted that the embargo would initiate a much-needed return to austerity, particularly among the American middle class. This discourse begat strange bedfellows, bringing together, however fleetingly, ecologists and oil company representatives, advertising executives and public intellectuals, scientists and theologians, and conservatives and the counterculture. These critics were divided in countless ways, but they were provisionally in agreement on one point: America's postwar prosperity had produced a bloated and profligate middle-class family that, in its consuming frenzy, had lost sight of the virtues of doing without.

This debate suggests that the oil embargo was a significant turning point not just within the realm of international politics, but within domestic politics as well. The embargo raised a host of questions about the future of the American middle class in an age of diminishing resources and economic dislocation. How would families modify their behavior in light of future energy shortages? Who within the family would be assigned primary responsibility for energy conservation? What forms of moral and economic readjustment would be required? Would the social movements of the 1970s be forced to modify their demands for greater social and economic entitlement in light of this new politics of austerity? How would the need for family sacrifice be reconciled with contemporary political challenges to traditional family forms, embodied most clearly in the women's liberation movement? And, finally, could material privation prove to be morally cleansing for middle-class Americans?

If these questions imply that the oil embargo was a moment of conservative retrenchment in a new era of economic austerity, then this is only part of the story. This cultural conversation also drew on left critiques of the affluent society and reflected the profound impact of these critiques on the wider culture. This was particularly true of the ecology and environmentalist movements, which were gaining considerable momentum and far-reaching support over the course of the 1970s. The oil embargo initiated a widespread public debate about themes that had long motivated the activists within these social movements: the implications of American energy consumption both for the environment and for other people throughout the globe; the alarming depletion of the earth's natural resources; and the need to develop alternative energy sources. This public debate—one that would come to encompass many people who identified with neither the counterculture nor modern environmentalism—surely would have looked very different had it not been for the social activism of the decade.

"Having Another Fix": The United States as Petroleum Junkie

Although the term "energy crisis" first appeared in 1970, it became instantly ubiquitous in the autumn of 1973 when OPEC declared an oil embargo against the United States. The embargo was motivated by both political and economic objectives: It was an act of retaliation for U.S. support of Israel in the Yom Kippur War, and it was also an attempt to recoup profit losses that had accompanied the devaluation of the U.S. dollar in 1971. The effects of the embargo were felt immediately. From May 1973 to June 1974, the retail price of gasoline rose from 38.5 cents to 55.1 cents per gallon. Some states implemented gas rationing, and long lines at gas stations became typical. In a televised address on November 7, 1973, President Nixon ordered a lowering of household thermostats to sixty-eight degrees, a reduction of air travel by 10 percent, increased carpooling efforts, and a lowering of highway speed limits.[2]

These material effects, however inconvenient, paled in comparison to the profound psychological impact of the embargo. In order to understand this subjective aspect of the crisis, one must emphasize the extent to which postwar economic growth had been predicated on access to cheap and plentiful petroleum. Between 1950 and 1974, oil consumption in the United States had doubled. Furthermore, between 1947 and 1974, the United States went from importing only 8 percent of its total petroleum to importing 38 percent, with much of this oil coming from the Middle East.[3] Many of the defining features of the postwar economic boom—from the thriving steel and automobile industries to the explosion in home and highway construction—were premised on the assumption that the United States would always have access to affordable oil petroleum. But by the late 1960s, oil policy experts recognized that the era of cheap and plentiful oil was drawing to a close, and by the winter of 1972, the rising costs and restricted availability of energy resources began to receive sustained, widespread public attention. But it was the OPEC oil embargo, which lasted from October 17, 1973, to March 18, 1974, that inaugurated the energy crisis of the 1970s. In the words of one historian: "America's energy crisis began symbolically in the third week of October 1973."[4]

The effects varied considerably from region to region, with some areas, such as the Northeast, experiencing high energy costs much more dramatically than others. Yet regardless of the regional differences, the embargo captured the imagination of the national public, which began searching for the explanation for this new challenge. Throughout the press, commentators routinely cast the oil embargo as a national crisis and, above all, as a crisis of biological survival.[5] Oil was not simply one aspect of advanced industrial society, but its "blood supply," "an integral part of the nation's life support system," and the "life's blood of American civilization."[6] These sanguinary metaphors contributed to the belief that, through becoming increasingly reliant on foreign oil, the nation had degenerated from a state of independence to one of dependency. Independence was America's birthright, proclaimed an editorial in *Reader's Digest*, and "it's up to us that we don't sell that birthright for a barrel of oil."[7]

Oil was also described as a potent drug that had now brought the nation to its knees. One well-known psychiatrist, Thomas Szasz, bitterly reflected on America's compromised position in the oil embargo: "Having betrayed our commitment to dignity and liberty, we now whimper and whine, a whole nation in the grips of auto petroleum withdrawal pains."[8] As with drug and alcohol addiction, America's lapse into this state of petroleum dependency appeared to constitute a failure of will. "We have become literally and figuratively fat," proclaimed William C. Westmoreland, the former commanding general of U.S. forces in Vietnam. "Perhaps the crisis will bring us back to some of the virtues that made this country great, like thrift and the belief that waste is sinful."[9]

This identification of petroleum as a habit-forming drug informed popular representations of OPEC as well. In editorial cartoons, oil suppliers from the Middle East were depicted as drug pushers, replete with intravenous needles, feeding tubes, and syringes. One cartoon showed a haggard Uncle Sam, outstretching a bare pockmarked arm to an Arab sheik who reassured him, "We're gonna let you have another fix."[10]

Another cartoon was set in a casbah where the bottle labels read "raw crude" and "diesel." As he pours a drink for a dejected Western businessman, the Arab bartender observes, "That's a terrible habit you've got there."[11]

These editorial cartoons drew on the discourse of drug addiction to suggest that the OPEC cartel had inappropriately gained the upper hand and was wielding power against the United States in ways that were not simply unfair, but even criminal and psychologically sadistic. But what is also revealing about these cartoons is that, by mobilizing the figures of the junkie and the alcoholic as signifiers of the nation, they convey a sense of abjection and shame in the 1970s about the newly compromised position of the United States itself and, more specifically, about the out-of-control nature of American consumption. That the embargo provoked a groundswell of rage against OPEC (which was often falsely equated with "the Arab world" or "the Middle East" writ large) is not particularly surprising. What *is* surprising is the extent to which a range of opinion makers seized on the embargo as an occasion to take angry aim at the American middle class, to condemn the excesses of postwar consumer culture, and to predict that a new era of material scarcity would somehow prove to be morally cleansing for Americans.

Before taking a closer look at this discourse, it is important to point out that these sorts of diatribes against consumer culture were not new. On the contrary, they were a standard feature of postwar social criticism. As historian Howard Brick points out, the discourse of abundance that emerged in the late 1950s was itself "more a criticism of conventional thought and practice than an endorsement of it."[12] Throughout the 1950s, novels such as Sloan Wilson's *Man in the Gray Flannel Suit* and sociological studies such as David Riesman's *Lonely Crowd* suggested that widespread affluence created a culture of conformity and threatened to undermine individuality. When economist John Kenneth Galbraith coined the term "affluent society" in 1958, he was not heralding the triumphs of this society, but pointing to the disjuncture between "private opulence and public squalor" that typified it.[13]

But even as postwar social critics expressed concern about the damaging effects of consumer culture, consumer goods themselves continued to function as potent symbols of what *Life* magazine editor Henry Luce had dubbed the American Century. In the 1950s, *Life* reported triumphantly that U.S. supermarket shoppers could choose from "thousands of items on the high-piled shelves . . . until their carts became cornucopias filled with an abundance that no other country in the world has ever known."[14] And in the famous "kitchen debate" of 1959 between Richard Nixon and Nikita Khrushchev, the U.S. vice president had marshaled energy-intensive consumer appliances as evidence of American capitalism's moral, political, and economic superiority over Soviet communism.[15] The shining kitchen appliances on display at the Moscow trade show were, according to the *New York Times*, "lavish testimonial(s) to abundance."[16] More than offering a privileged glimpse into an idealized domestic sphere, they seemed to constitute irrefutable proof of America's unlimited economic potential on the world stage.

Now, with the embargo, the symbolism of these consumer goods was turned on its head as these same appliances became symptomatic of pathological and addictive behaviors. "What we have here is a prosperity psychosis," declared one historian.[17] Only fourteen years after the kitchen debate, America's energy consumption habits no longer embodied national strength, but instead were endemic of a "binge," a "disease," an "orgy," and "insatiable appetites."[18] "We are being punished for our past sins of conspicuous consumption and planned obsolescence," reflected one clergyman.[19] "Our society has suffered from mental and physical atrophy," commented a Manhattan social worker. "This crisis could be a really good thing."[20]

Nowhere was this symbolic reversal more pronounced than in the case of the American automobile. More than any other consumer good, the car had emerged as a powerful symbol of postwar mobility—both literal mobility across space, and upward social mobility. Indeed, the American automobile had functioned as a metonym for many of the promises of the affluent society: the Fordist compromise, which claimed to enable workers to buy the same goods that they had produced; the spread of the suburbs; and a widening sphere of leisure that would enable more and more Americans to hit the open road. Only a few years before the oil embargo, the marketing objective of the American Petroleum Institute's advertising campaign had been simple. Targeting "virtually every owner of an automobile," the campaign sought to "increase the consumption of gasoline."[21] To that end, API advertisements in local newspapers showed detailed maps of close-to-home vacations and weekend getaways that could bring American families face-to-face with scenic, recreational, and historical attractions.[22] "Get to know your state (and your family) better—on this close to home tour," read one advertisement that suggested a loop driving tour from Los Angeles to San

Diego. "How about a family auto tour this weekend—just for a change?" beckoned another advertisement that included a detailed map of Virginia's historical attractions.[23]

With the embargo, however, the once simple objective of the API advertising campaign became infinitely more complicated as the major oil companies fended off accusations that they had contrived the oil crisis in order to amass unprecedented profits.[24] And the roomy American family automobile was deemed by one angry *New York Times* reader to be a "gas gulper, pandering to the gross tastes of a depraved consuming public."[25] Indeed, when you ask people today what they remember about the oil embargo, their memories almost always revolve around auto petroleum: the two-hour lines at gas stations, the rationing that occurred in some states, and the media spectacle of irate and panicky drivers committing acts of violence against each other, all in their frantic pursuit of gasoline.

But, significantly, energy waste within the private sphere of the home would also need to be redressed, and it was middle-class women, as consumers par excellence, who would need to be on the front lines of the nation's new war against energy excess. Newspapers and magazines assumed an overtly pedagogical role as they schooled readers in the rules of household energy conservation. "What's Your Energy IQ?" queried a writer from *Shell News,* who proceeded to administer a true/false test on thermostat settings, insulation, and indoor lighting.[26] "Where Does All the Energy Go?" read another headline for an article that went on to divulge the silent but voracious energy appetites of the space heater, the air conditioner, and the refrigerator.[27] Appearing in periodicals such as *Better Homes and Gardens, Good Housekeeping,* and *House Beautiful,* these how-to guides for household conservation were directed to women readers, who were seen as ultimately bearing responsibility for household energy waste.[28]

Advertisers also took up the cause as they attempted to inculcate a conservation ethic into consumers. Modern advertising had always entailed not simply the selling of products but the prescription of behaviors.[29] Historically, these prescriptions had sought to maximize consumption, but now advertisers found themselves in the anomalous position of having to curtail rather than stimulate consumer desire. The president of Standard Oil Company of Indiana conceded that this reversal was a shock to the oil industry, observing that the switch to a conservation message was "quite a change for us after training our people to go out there and sell. Suddenly, we are saying: 'Please don't come in and ask for so much.'"[30] A Mobil Oil advertisement urging customers to use less fuel called attention to the irony: "That may seem funny to you, coming from an oil company; but we simply think it's the right thing to do in the circumstances."[31] The anomalous task of advocating less rather than more fuel consumption was compounded by public skepticism about the severity of the energy crisis. The situation required, in the words of one advertiser, "a very delicate communication."[32]

Beyond the world of advertising and journalism, this new attention to conservation throughout the public sphere also represented an extraordinary moment in the history of the ecology and environmentalist movements, albeit one that had historical roots in the postwar period. Since the 1950s, these movements had worked to call public attention to the nation's wasteful energy habits and to promote a conservation ethic, one that would encourage more energy-efficient ways of living.[33] The publication of Rachel Carson's *Silent Spring*, an exposé on the harmful effects of DDT and other commonly used pesticides, had provoked a public outcry in 1962. By the early 1970s, the ecology and environmentalist movements had gained considerable momentum. The first Earth Day was held in April 1970, and opinion polling at the time suggested that environmental concerns were at the top of the public agenda. Meanwhile, longstanding groups like the Sierra Club grew in membership over the course of the decade, and new organizations like Greenpeace were founded. This activism profoundly changed the face of the national government, as well; the most obvious example of this was the establishment of the Environmental Protection Agency in 1970. In addition, books like Frances Moore Lappe's *Diet for a Small Planet* and Barry Commoner's *A Closing Circle*, both published in 1971, urged readers to reflect on the dire implications of a deeply troubling statistic: Americans comprised only 6 percent of the world population, but they were consuming one-third of the world's available energy sources.

Remarkably, the oil embargo brought this disturbing news home to a much wider public. Throughout the mainstream press, this alarming statistic about U.S. consumption was quoted over and over again, and readers who identified with neither the counterculture nor the ecology movement were now urged to consider the nation's energy consumption habits in a new light: as part of a globally interdependent ecological system.[34] Clinging to the logic that had undergirded the kitchen debate, President Nixon assured Americans that this statistic should inspire pride rather than embarrassment, proclaiming in the autumn of 1973: "That isn't bad; that is good. That means we are the richest, strongest people in the world, and that we have the highest standard of living in the world. That is why we need so much energy, and may it always be that way."[35] But in the final months of 1973, Nixon's assurances rang hollow and the logic of the kitchen debate appeared anachronistic. The revelation that the United States was consuming one-third of the world's available energy sources was now seen as evidence of American recklessness. "We have been on an energy binge and the hangover could be protracted and painful," predicted Arizona representative Morris K. Udall.[36]

Although the public discourse surrounding the oil embargo vividly captured the ecology and environmentalist movements' growing influence throughout the wider culture during these years, it also constituted only a partial victory for these movements for a number of reasons. Despite the rhetorical attention being paid to conservation, research at the time showed that the energy crisis was having only a marginal effect on household energy consumption. Furthermore, once the oil crisis had passed, rates of household energy consumption continued to climb, supporting historian David Nye's claim that Americans actually increased their energy use throughout the 1970s.[37] But most importantly, the emphasis on conservation presented the energy crisis as primarily one that afflicted middle-class families, which had the power and means to consume, and which now had the opportunity to mend their energy-dependent ways. This emphasis on consumption obscured the impact of the energy crisis on the nation's low-income families, disproportionately comprised of the elderly and minority groups. For them, the central drama of the crisis did not revolve around energy waste, but instead around a poverty that at times compelled them to choose between food and heat.[38] But this emphasis did more than simply obscure the impact of energy shortages on people living at or below the poverty line. It also assigned disproportionate blame to the middle-class family for energy waste, suggesting that energy reform could best be achieved through private restraint within the home rather than through wider structural change throughout the society. In truth, domestic households consumed a relatively small percentage of the nation's energy resources when compared with large corporations and industries.

"Learning to Love the Energy Crisis": Scarcity and Family Redemption

By focusing on the energy excesses of the middle-class family, the conservation message also converged with a broader discussion about family decline and alienation, and it is here that its Janus-faced dimensions come into full view. With its lexicon of dependency, self-sufficiency, and waste, the discourse surrounding the oil crisis quickly became about much more than thermostat settings, speed limits, and gasoline prices. On the contrary, the embargo inspired both somber meditations on the compromised state of the American family, and gleeful predictions of the family's regeneration in a new era of energy scarcity.

Meditations and predictions about energy scarcity were premised on a number of enduring claims about the American family in crisis. One of these claims was that individuals within the modern family had grown alienated from one another, and household technology was largely to blame. One *Newsweek* editorial appropriately entitled "Learning to Love the Energy Crisis" speculated on the redemptive features of the energy crisis, predicting that the crisis could rescue the family from its current state of alienation. "Cutting back on our use of fossil fuels will have the incidental effect of forcing us inside ourselves for human resources long dormant, and on each other," author Ralph Keyes wrote. "In the process families may revive as working units." Attributing the demise of family conversation to the discord produced by household appliances, Keyes continued: "Since normal conversation is hard against background noise exceeding 55 decibels, the din of fuel consuming appliances may be one reason family members seem not to talk so much, or at least not to listen."[39] Surveying the compromised state of the American family, Keyes appeared to have identified his culprit: the cacophonous dishwasher.

A second related claim was that energy scarcity would compel people to return their attentions to long-neglected communitarian and familial ties. The embargo promised to strengthen families, affirm religious commitments, and inspire neighborhood loyalties. The gas shortage was "the greatest thing for Christianity since World War II," exalted one minister, who insisted that church attendance was now on the rise thanks to the oil embargo's incursion on Sunday driving trips.[40] Shortages could lead to a "rediscovery of friends . . . and families because it will be harder to run away," predicted a sociologist.[41] As people stay home more, they're becoming "more neighborly," proclaimed one article celebrating the resurrection of the neighborhood block party.[42] One Connecticut housewife expressed frustration at an overloaded schedule that constantly had her chauffeuring her children from school to ballet classes to birthday parties and concluded: "I'm glad the energy crisis happened . . . if I spend less time chauffeuring, I can go back to painting and get to know my kids better." This woman expressed her hope that the fuel shortage would not only improve her relations with her children, but also afford her more time to pursue her own creative aspirations.[43] Finally, one commentator celebrated the embargo for the nostalgia that it would one day evoke, imagining that "[s]ome day, Americans may look back nostalgically at this cold comfort winter as a time when tightly knit families triumphed over adversity." Reflecting further on its sentimental potential, he conjectured that "[e]ventually, the energy crisis may even end up like the other crises, wars and upheavals in American history—as the setting for a warmhearted TV series."[44]

A third claim was that a commitment to self-sufficiency or "simplicity" would no longer be embraced solely by groups outside the mainstream, but would now become part of conventional familial existence. Scarce energy resources meant that now anyone could be a survivalist. A forty-three-year-old divorced mother of five children from Portland, Oregon, who routinely got up before dawn to get gasoline before coming home to cook breakfast for her children, described herself as "a hunter who has gone out and gotten his supplies for the week."[45] A married couple who embarked on a "no energy weekend experiment" were able to summon the survivalist spirit without ever leaving their suburban home. "Edie looked like a true pioneer heating the soup over the open fire," William Hoffer, her husband, reminisced in *House Beautiful.* "Later, Edie and I sat together in the den. Warm candlelight flickered off our faces. It had been a good day. We had found a source of new energy within ourselves that was not dependent on oil, gas or coal," Hoffer concluded, never revealing what had become of this new energy source once the weekend experiment had come to a close.[46]

Given that no one actually believed that the vast majority of families would suddenly start living like hunters, survivalists, and pioneers, we must ask about the symbolic meaning of these sorts of accounts. What kind of cultural and ideological work was being performed here? At the most obvious level, these accounts were drawing on a long tradition of social criticism that constructed mass consumption as a threat to the integrity and purity of the traditional family unit. But ultimately, the indictments of middle-class consumption that came to the fore during the embargo—like the fantasies of redemptive scarcity that accompanied them—must also be situated within the context of a much broader economic and ideological assault on the middle class during the 1970s. Both a Keynesian-Fordist economic regime and an expansive New Deal welfare state had fostered the unprecedented expansion of a the middle class during the postwar years. Federal housing, education, and training programs like the GI Bill had done a great deal to stimulate consumer spending. As historian Stephanie Coontz has argued, despite the trappings of independence, the nuclear family of the 1950s was one of the most heavily subsidized in U.S. history.[47] Thus the attack on middle-class consumption that emerged within the context of the embargo was never simply about consumption alone: It was also about the entire structure of social provision that that had enabled the expansion of the middle class throughout the postwar years, a "golden age" that, by the early 1970s, was drawing to a dramatic close.

WORKING WOMEN AND THE DANGERS OF CONVENIENCE

While these critiques of the middle-class family's excessive dependency on gadgetry, appliances, and convenience often targeted the family as a unit, they were in fact highly gendered. As I have already suggested, middle-class women were identified as the primary consumers (and hence wasters) of energy-intensive household goods, and they were assigned a pivotal role in the nation's new war against dependency on foreign oil. But women's work outside the home also assumed importance here, since women's employment earnings had been closely linked to the explosive growth of consumer spending during the postwar years. As the embargo provisionally redefined middle-class consumption as a kind of national emergency, women's roles as both consumers and workers came under increased scrutiny in a variety of ways. And women's liberation and the oil embargo—two themes that historians have rarely addressed together—became intertwined.

While conservation guidelines openly appealed to women as energy consumers within the home, the link between energy waste and women's work outside the home was subtler. This link often functioned as a tacit assumption within discussions of the energy crisis, and nowhere more so than in discussions of convenience. It was not only blenders, freezers, and television sets that were deemed guilty of energy waste, but also frozen foods and convenience supermarkets. The use of convenience foods had grown dramatically in the postwar period, and this trend accelerated in the 1970s.[48] "Housewives, especially younger ones, are either too lazy, too busy, or don't know how to cook," declared one food retailer as he offered an explanation for the boom in convenience foods. This explanation, according to a commentary in advertising agency J. Walter Thompson's company newsletter, "might well cause a militant feminist to explode faster than an overheated boil-in-the-bag pouch," but sales confirmed that the boom itself was unmistakable.[49] Like the spread of the dishwasher, the blender, and the television set, the proliferation of frozen foods was endemic to two related afflictions: national energy waste and family alienation. Cheerfully predicting the return of the family meal in the wake of the energy crisis, one editorial decried the "individual boil-pac servings," "TV dinners," and "Del Monte pudding cups" that had not only wrecked home-cooked meals, but also drained families of their originality.[50] What was never mentioned, of course, was that historically, the elaborate home-cooked meal had been prepared by either an unremunerated homemaker, a paid domestic worker, or some combination thereof.

These critiques of U.S. reliance on convenience often went hand in hand with implicit appeals to "Old World" tradition and values. For example, one Federal Energy Administration study compared energy consumption patterns in the United States with those of "other wealthy Western countries." Never actually defining the category of the household, the study was comprised of elaborate tables that showed the energy profligacy of U.S. households when compared to those of Europe and Japan, which remained conflated throughout the study. U.S. households relied on frozen and convenience foods, while European and Japanese households were more likely to use fresh foods. U.S. households shopped for groceries at large, dispersed shopping facilities, while European and Japanese households relied on small grocery stores and local neighborhood specialty shops. Large refrigerators meant that American families made weekly shopping trips, while European and Japanese families shopped daily for perishables. When asked to explain the underlying reason for European and Japanese consumption practices, the study repeatedly invoked a vague and hopelessly elusive term:

"tradition." It was tradition that compelled European and Japanese households to buy fresh foods at local specialty shops, and presumably it was an American repudiation of tradition that had set the stage for energy excess. Most importantly, the use of the term "household," itself vague and undifferentiated, dodged a crucial question: *Who* within the household was making the daily trip to the neighborhood specialty shop to buy the perishable foods to cook the family meal?[51]

It is important to note that this proliferation of "TV dinners" and "Del Monte pudding cups" did not signal the demise of the female homemaker or mean that women were spending less time on housework. On the contrary, historians of women and technology have persuasively argued that technological innovations actually engender new household responsibilities and duties for women, even as they claim to save time and promise less drudgery.[52] Nonetheless, the *perception* is significant here: The emancipatory promises of frozen foods and convenience stores—even if they went unrealized—took on more cultural significance, not less, as middle-class women with children entered the paid labor force in ever increasing numbers.

This perceived connection between frozen foods and working women was clearly visible in 1970s advertising. Never challenging the assumption that women bore primary responsibility for housework, advertisers now had to take account of women's ongoing efforts to balance domestic duties with labor outside the home. By the early 1970s, advertisements expressed sympathy for women as they encountered the same dilemma over and over again: There was never enough time. "General Electric knows your time is as important as ours," the company reassured women customers in an advertisement depicting a harried mother standing in her kitchen and talking on the telephone, surrounded by unfinished ironing, unfolded laundry, a bucket of cleaning supplies, a young boy, a hungry toddler, and a family dog urgently in need of a walk.[53] "Because you've got plenty to do, Mrs. Paul's makes Onion Rings," read an advertisement for frozen foods that included a collage of photographs of a woman shopping at the supermarket, playing tennis, seeing her son off to school, and sitting in front of a typewriter while talking on the telephone at a secretary's desk.[54] Another frozen-food advertisement celebrated the ways in which men were successfully adapting themselves to the new gender order and suggested that a dinner of Stouffer's lasagna was a fitting reward: "It isn't every girl who can work and run a home. And luckily you've got an understanding husband. Tonight, you're going to thank him for all the times he could've grumped and didn't. It's a good day for Stouffer's."[55]

These advertisements reified women's domestic roles, but they also revealed the extent to which, within print media, the proliferation of frozen foods had become associated with women's work outside the home and the double burden that it entailed. Thus when magazine editorials and advertising campaigns urged the middle-class family to adopt a more tempered and restrained approach to convenience foods and electrical appliances, they were not only envisaging a family that would "discover more gas for America" but also simultaneously calling for a nostalgic return to a simpler and more traditional model of family life, one that was somehow free of all the pressures presumably bearing down on the middle-class family, including those pressures posed by the "working woman."

Thus far, my discussion has proceeded from the premise that the conservation message surrounding the oil embargo was essentially shaped by gender conservatism. In an age of feminism, this message reified women's domestic duties and subtly constructed women's work outside the home as a drain on the energy reserves of both the nation and the family. In addition, the conservation message made it clear that it was primarily through domesticity that women could contribute to the nation. But it would be wrong to interpret this message solely through the lens of gender conservatism. Critiques of middle-class consumption—so pervasive throughout the embargo—also resonated with the politics of the women's liberation movement in complex ways. After all, just as the energy crisis was emerging as a national challenge, an ascendant women's liberation movement was also taking aim at the middle-class family, albeit for a different reason: to indict this family as a primary locus of women's subordination. To be sure, the conservation message linked women to the domestic sphere at the precise moment that many women were questioning this link. But the conservation message also dovetailed with feminism, both in its condemnation of certain family forms and in its critique of consumer culture. As a cultural watershed of the early 1970s, the oil embargo simultaneously reflected feminism's growing influence *and* the persistence of gender conservatism throughout the dominant culture.

Betty Friedan's classic, *The Feminine Mystique,* offers an illustrative case in point. Friedan's screed against middle-class suburban domesticity demands scrutiny not because it accurately reflected the lived experiences of most women (a presumption that has long since been dispelled), but rather because of its canonical status within liberal feminism. For our purposes, what warrants attention is the way that Friedan invoked images of appliances and gadgetry in order to expose the banality of the life of the suburban housewife. Indeed, Friedan focuses less on interpersonal relations and more on the housewife's vapid relationship to consumer goods. The suburban housewife, according to Friedan, "made the beds, shopped for groceries, matched slipcover material," all the while afraid to ask herself, "Is this all?" This housewife, presumably liberated by labor-saving appliances, was free to choose "automobiles, clothes, appliances, supermarkets." Yet despite the purported freedom and the endless choices accorded her by the consumer culture, this woman, according to Friedan, felt profoundly unfulfilled by her lot in life. Within discussions of the oil crisis, energy-intensive consumer appliances connoted consumer excess and waste. Similarly, for Friedan, consumer goods functioned as a kind of shorthand for the emptiness, indeed the "waste," she associated with the lived experiences of the women of her socioeconomic class and cultural milieu.[56]

But the ultimate aim of Friedan's attack on consumer goods also deserves attention here. When feminists like Friedan surveyed the middle-class family of postwar America, they saw a family that undervalued women's domestic labor and undermined women's creative and professional aspirations outside the home. They perceived an oppressive normative ideal that persisted in spite of the fact that women—and women with young children in particular—were entering the paid labor force in ever-increasing numbers. They punctured the mythology surrounding the suburban housewife, arguing that behind the sunny facade there was profound isolation, deep discontent, and thwarted dreams. They attacked consumer culture as sexist and reevaluated their prescribed role as consumers. While some feminists called for its reformation and others for its abolition, there was consensus that the nuclear family, specifically in its postwar incarnation, was a linchpin of women's oppression.

Bridging the divide between liberalism and conservatism, critics of the so-called affluent society writing during the oil embargo also cast aspersions on this family, but this time in order to serve very different political ends. For them, ever-widening prosperity had set the stage for energy excess, which in turn led to a compromised condition of national dependency on foreign oil. Energy excess and the excesses associated with women's liberation captured the same problem: Postwar affluence had produced unrealistic expectations, and these expectations would now need tempering. Feminists saw household appliances as empty symbols of an idealized home that aimed to keep women in their place, but critics of consumer culture came up with an opposing interpretation: These same appliances were symptomatic of family dissolution and the erosion of traditional roles. In an age of feminism, was it really surprising that the oil crisis inspired a nostalgic evocation of earlier ideals of family life, including those of the pioneer and the survivalist? Driven by scarcity instead of indulged by prosperity, unified by necessity rather than estranged by leisure, such families had presumably adhered to a clear division of labor and a traditional gender order. Above all, according to this nostalgic fantasy, these families all prized self-sufficiency, individualism, and autonomy over dependency.

CONCLUSION

Historians have tended to interpret the OPEC oil embargo in one of two ways. First, as I have suggested, they have cited the embargo, along with the Vietnam War and Watergate, as clear evidence of America's waning hegemony during the early 1970s.[57] They have argued that the embargo was one of several indicators of national decline and "malaise" during this period. While there is merit to this interpretation, it is problematic in a number of different ways. Significantly, even at the level of geopolitics, the embargo was not solely a blow to U.S. power; it also confirmed the nation's continued dominance within the West and among advanced industrialized states. For however painful the effects of the embargo in the United States, they were minor when compared to the impact of energy shortfalls on Europe and Japan.

Likewise, when examining the oil embargo's significance as a cultural watershed, as I have attempted to do, the filter of national decline can be misleading. If the energy crisis succeeded in forcing the nation to become less reckless and wasteful, then, according to John Kenneth Galbraith, "one can only assume that the Arab nations and the big oil companies have united to save the American Republic."[58] Just as the middle-class family functioned as both symbol of and antidote for national energy dependency, so the oil crisis was a harbinger at once of national decline *and* of potential regeneration. For critics of "the affluent society" like Galbraith, the embargo clearly represented an opportunity to reinstate earlier ethics of self-sufficiency, industry, and thrift. These mores, according to a long tradition of social criticism, had dissipated within a postwar economy driven by ever-rising levels of consumption. At first glance, it may appear that the shift from a discourse of abundance to a discourse of limits constituted a purely pessimistic vision of America's future. But the profound nostalgia inspired by the oil crisis suggests that a new era of tempered expectations was also tied to both national and familial redemption, and to an imaginary return to a pristine historical moment dictated by scarcity rather than by abundance.

Such redemptive calls for a "return to austerity" were premised on a profound gender conservatism, even as they superficially echoed certain feminist critiques of postwar consumer culture. At a time when women were questioning their identification with the domestic sphere and exploring alternatives to the nuclear family, demands for a privatized form of national sacrifice made it clear that women could make their most valuable contributions to the nation from the confines of the home. Debates about energy consumption and conservation did not speak solely to the international politics of oil; they also reflected domestic anxieties about family decline, women's labor outside the home, and feminism's potential threat to family and nation.

The second way historians have described the oil crisis, and the energy crisis of the 1970s more generally, is as a kind of lost opportunity—as a moment when Americans were made aware of the need for energy conservation and ecological sacrifice, only to quickly forget the lesson. They have argued that despite a new rhetorical attention to conservation and limits, consumer behavior in the United States did not change.[59] This interpretation of the energy crisis, while not incorrect, is too literal. Rather than simply bemoaning Americans' failure to change their consumption habits, we must also ask what the new awareness of limits actually accomplished, culturally and politically.

The cultural response to the embargo—and the amount of self-scrutiny about energy consumption that it inspired within the public sphere—was not simply a story of lost opportunity. It was also a testament to the enduring legacy of left critiques of American affluence, and to the growing vitality of the environmentalist message during these years. Indeed, the explosion of public interest in conservation that accompanied the oil embargo did not come out of thin air but was in fact many years in the making. The widespread condemnation of U.S. energy waste that accompanied the embargo is impossible to imagine without the vibrant environmental activism of the 1970s. This is not to overlook or diminish the obvious: with the growing rates of energy consumption over the course of the decade, the ecology and environmentalist movements would face an uphill battle in a culture that defined consumption as a national pastime.[60]

Ultimately, the embargo of 1973 also captured a moment of conservative retrenchment in the midst of economic turmoil and dislocation. As the Keynesian-Fordist economic regime came apart, middle-class families found themselves without a social safety net. By identifying the home as a locus of excess, oil company executives, advertisers, and public intellectuals all seemed to imply that, if American families were now hurting, they had only themselves to blame. If this indictment of the middle-class family constituted a form of victim blaming, then the tendency to spin out fantasies of familial regeneration in a new era of energy scarcity was an example of making a virtue out of necessity. Just as advertisers had tried to morally elevate consumption during the postwar years, now material privation would be invested with morally redemptive features.[61] Implicit in the imaginary return of the survivalist and the pioneer, then, was the illusion that all of the social and cultural transformations born by postwar prosperity could somehow be undone. In this way, the cultural work of the oil crisis entailed much more than a simple call for conservation. It also bound utopian dreams of plenty and helped pave the way for a leaner, meaner economic order.

NOTES

Acknowledgments: Material on J. Walter Thompson Company reprinted by permission of The Rare Book, Manuscript, and Special Collections Library, Duke University, Durham, N.C., from Louis H. Roddis Papers and from the following collections in the J. Walter Thompson Archives, Hartman Center for Sales, Advertising, and Marketing History: Review Board Records, Domestic Advertisements, Competitive Advertisements, Writings and Speeches, and Newletter Collection.

1. *CBS Evening News*, March 25, 1974, Vanderbilt Television News Archive, Vanderbilt University, Nashville, Tenn.

2. For the oil embargo's domestic impact and the Nixon administration's response, see Allen J. Matusow, *Nixon's Economy: Booms, Busts, Dollars, and Votes*

(Lawrence: University Press of Kansas, 1998), 241–75; and Richard H. K. Vietor, *Energy Policy in America since 1945* (Cambridge: Cambridge University Press, 1984), 193–271.

3. For overviews of U.S. oil policy during the postwar period, see Peter Odell, *Oil and World Power* (Harmondsworth, Middlesex: Penguin Books, 1986), 30; and Robert Stobaugh and Daniel Yergin, eds., *Energy Future: Report of the Energy Project of the Harvard Business School* (New York: Random House, 1979), 3–55. On the relationship between business and government in energy policy after World War II, see Vietor, *Energy Policy in America*, 91–145, and Daniel Yergin, *The Prize: The Epic Quest for Oil, Money, and Power* (New York: Simon & Schuster, 1991), 409–49. For a history of oil that focuses on the period from 1941 through 1954 specifically, see David S. Painter, *Oil and the American Century: The Political Economy of U.S. Foreign Oil Policy, 1941–1954* (Baltimore: Johns Hopkins University Press, 1986).

4. Vietor, *Energy Policy in America*, 193. For one of the most widely read policy predictions of future oil shortages, see James E. Akins, "The Oil Crisis: This Time the Wolf Is Here," *Foreign Affairs* 51, 3 (1973): 462–90. For overviews of the oil embargo of 1973–74, see Vietor, *Energy Policy in America*, 193–235, and Yergin, *The Prize*, 588–652.

5. On the ways in which the embargo's effects varied regionally, as well as the ways in which the embargo inspired regionalism, see James Reston, "Even Texas Is Running Short," *New York Times*, November 14, 1973; "U.S. Energy Crisis Stirs Self Interest of Regions," *New York Times*, December 20, 1973; Walter Isard and Phyllis Kaniss, "On Fuel Shortages and Damages to Regions," *New York Times*, February 2, 1974; "Oil Is a National Problem, but Seriousness Varies," *New York Times*, February 3, 1974.

6. *ABC Nightly News*, February 22, 1974, Vanderbilt Television News Archive; Energy Policy Project of the Ford Foundation, *A Time to Choose: America's Energy Future* (Cambridge, Mass.: Ballinger, 1974), 1; "Energy Crisis: Paradox of Shortage Amid Plenty," *New York Times*, April 17, 1973.

7. Walter J. Hickel, "The Energy War II: What We Must Do at Home," *Reader's Digest*, February 1974, 102.

8. Thomas S. Szasz, "When History Comes Home to Roost," *New York Times*, March 6, 1974.

9. "Cold Comfort for a Long, Hard Winter," *Time*, December 10, 1973, 34.

10. "Syria's Stake in Peace," *Houston Post*, April 22, 1974, Baylor Collections of Political Materials, Cartoons, box 57, file 1589, Baylor University, Waco, Texas.

11. "The Casbah," *The Chicago Sun-Times*, 1973, Baylor Collections, box 57, file 1588.

12. Howard Brick, *The Age of Contradiction: American Thought and Culture in the 1960s* (New York: Twayne, 1998), 2.

13. Sloan Wilson, *The Man in the Gray Flannel Suit* (New York: Simon & Schuster, 1955); David Riesman, *The Lonely Crowd: A Study of the Changing American Character* (Garden City, N.Y.: Doubleday, 1953); and John Kenneth Galbraith, *The Affluent Society* (Boston: Houghton Mifflin, 1958).

14. Quoted in Christopher Lasch, "The Culture of Consumption," in Mary Kupiec Cayton, Elliot J. Gorn, and Peter W. Williams, eds., *Encyclopedia of American Social History II* (New York: Scribner, 1993), 1381.

15. On the kitchen debate, see Walter Hixson, *Parting the Curtain: Propaganda, Culture, and the Cold War, 1945–1961* (New York: St. Martin's Press, 1997), 179–80; and Elaine Tyler May, *Homeward Bound: American Families in the Cold War Era* (New York: Basic Books, 1988), 16–20.

16. Quoted in James Patterson, *Grand Expectations: The United States, 1945–1974* (New York: Oxford University Press, 1996), 317.

17. Eric F. Goldman, "What We Have Here Is a Prosperity Psychosis," *New York Times*, January 11, 1974.

18. Morris Udall, "Ending the Energy Binge," *New Republic*, June 16, 1973, 12; Edward Teller, "The Energy Disease," *Harper's Magazine*, March, 1975, 16; Kenneth E. F. Watt, "The End of an Energy Orgy," *Natural History*, February 1974, 16; and Herbert Meredith Orrell, "More Does Not Always Mean Better," *America*, March 2, 1974, 148.

19. Reverend Dennis G. Ruby, letter to the editor, *New York Times*, December 18, 1973.

20. "Cold Comfort for a Long, Hard Winter," *Time*, December 10, 1973, 34.

21. "Meetings, American Petroleum Institute, Summaries, 1963–1970" file, box 5, Review Board Records, J. Walter Thompson Company Archives (hereafter JWTC Archives), John W. Hartman Center for Sales, Advertising, and Marketing Collection, Duke University Rare Book, Manuscript, and Special Collections Library, Durham, N.C. For a brief history of the American Petroleum Institute, see Painter, *Oil and the American Century*, 3.

22. "Meetings, American Petroleum Institute."

23. "American Petroleum Institute Tour Advertisements, 1968" file, Miscellaneous, box 3, Domestic Advertising Collections, JWTC Archives. On the centrality of the automobile to postwar consumer society, see William Chafe, *Unfinished Journey: America since World War II* (New York: Oxford University Press, 1999), 117–19; and Ronald Edsforth, *Class Conflict and Cultural Consensus: The Making of a Mass Consumer Society in Flint, Michigan* (New Brunswick, N.J.: Rutgers University Press, 1987), 13–69.

24. Suspicions of both the oil industry and the government were ubiquitous and came from any number of different directions. For some examples, see "The Gas Shortage—How Real Is It?" *U.S. News and World Report*, June 25, 1973, 34; "No Shortage of Skepticism," *Time*, January 28, 1974, 30; "Energy: Many Skeptical on Reasons for Crisis," *New York Times*, December 12, 1973; "'Energy Crisis': Second Look," *Nation*, February 19, 1973, 229; "The Energy Crisis: Fact or Fiction?" *Senior Scholastic*, March 26, 1973, 6; and M. A. Adelman, "Is the Oil Shortage Real? Oil Companies as OPEC Tax-Collectors," *Foreign Policy* 9 (winter 1972–73): 69–107. Two books in this skeptical vein are Christopher T. Rand, *Making Democracy Safe for Oil: Oilmen and the Islamic East* (Boston: Little, Brown, 1975); and Robert Sherrill, *The Oil Follies of 1970–1980* (Garden City, N.Y.: Doubleday, 1983).

25. Letters to the Editor, "Energy: A Crisis of Negligence," *New York Times*, November 15, 1973.

26. James A. Cox, "What's Your Energy IQ?" *Reader's Digest*, November 1974, 157–59.

27. "Your Home: Where Does All the Energy Go?" *American Home*, February 1974, 18.

28. Other examples include "Coping: How Women across the Country Solve the Energy Problem," *Vogue*, February 1974, 166; "Eight Steps You Can Take to Conserve Household Energy," *House & Garden*, January 1974, 24; "50 Ways to Save Fuel and Keep Warm," *McCall's*, February 1974, 36; "46 Ways to Conserve Energy in Your Home," *Better Homes and Gardens*, November 1973, 36; "How to Heat and Cool Your Home with Less Fuel," *Good Housekeeping*, March 1974, 139; and "What Every Family Should Know—and Do—to Solve the Energy Crisis," *Parents* 49 (June 1974), 22.

29. On the ways in which an increasing attention to the consumer over the product came to define modern advertising, see Roland Marchand, *Advertising the American Dream: Making Way for Modernity, 1920–1940* (Berkeley: University of California Press, 1985), 52–83, 164–205, 335–63. On advertising's role in the rise of a therapeutic ethos of self-realization, see T. J. Jackson Lears, "From Salvation to Self-Realization: Advertising and the Therapeutic Roots of the Consumer Culture," in Richard Wightman Fox and T. J. Jackson Lears, eds., *The Culture of Consumption: Critical Essays in American History, 1880–1980* (New York: Pantheon Books, 1983), 3–38.

30. "We Can Squeak By, If—," *U.S. News and World Report*, June 4, 1973, 26.

31. *New York Daily News*, May 17, 1973. "Mobilgas and Mobil Oil, 1973," file 5, box 25, Competitive Advertising Collection, JWTC Archives.

32. Henry Schachte, President, J. Walter Thompson Company, "Communication with the Consumer in Today's Gas Climate," Southern Gas Executive Management Conference, Ponte Vedra, Florida, November 20, 1972, "Henry M. Schachte, 1968–1977" file, box 31, Writings and Speeches Collection, JWTC Archives.

33. The literature on the environmental movement is vast. For an overview of the environmental movement during the postwar period and a history of conservation, see Hal K. Rothman, *The Greening of a Nation? Environmentalism in the United States since 1945* (New York: Harcourt Brace, 1998).

34. Comments on this statistic include Morris K. Udall, "Ending the Energy Binge," *New Republic*, June 16, 1973, 13; Ford Foundation, *A Time to Choose*, 6; Talk of the Town, *New Yorker*, December 10, 1973, 37; Margaret Mead, "The Energy Crisis—Why Our World Will Never Be the Same Again," *Redbook Magazine*, April 1974, 54; "An Age of Scarcity," *New York Times*, April 7, 1974.

35. "Remarks at the Seafarer's International Union Biennial Convention," *Papers of the Presidents of the United States: Richard Nixon, 1973* (Washington, D.C.: U.S. Government Printing Office, 1975), 980. For a commentary on this speech, see Talk of the Town, *New Yorker*, December 10, 1973, 37.

36. Udall, "Ending the Energy Binge," 13–14.

37. See David Nye, *Consuming Power: A Social History of American Energies* (Cambridge: MIT Press, 1998), 217–46. For studies that look at the effect of oil shortages on household energy consumption, see Bertrand Chateau and Bruno Lapillone, "Energy Consumption in the Residential Sector since 1973," in Eric

Monnier, George Gaskell, Peter Ester, Bernward Joerges, Bruno LaPillonne, Cees Midden, and Louis Puiseux, eds., *Consumer Behavior and Energy Policy: An International Perspective* (New York: Praeger, 1984); and Robert Perlman and Roland L. Warren, *Families in the Energy Crisis: Impacts and Implications for Theory and Practice* (Cambridge, Mass.: Ballinger, 1977), 79–116. Also see "Will Energy Plan Work? Recent Study of Family Attitude Hints at Rough Going," *New York Times*, October 10, 1974.

38. On the heightened vulnerability of the poor to energy shortages, see Perlman and Warren, *Families in the Energy Crisis*, 117–42. For the adverse effects of the energy crisis on African Americans, see "Crisis Said to Hurt Blacks the Most," *New York Times*, February 22, 1974; and "The Energy Crisis: For Blacks, A Disproportionate Burden," *New York Times*, February 9, 1974. On the impact of the crisis on the elderly, see "Fuel Crisis Impact on Low-Income and Elderly," Congressional Committee on Federal Food Programs, January 22–23, 1974 (Washington, D.C.: Government Printing Office).

39. Ralph Keyes, "Learning to Love the Energy Crisis," *Newsweek*, December 3, 1973, 17.

40. "The Coldest Winter?" *Newsweek*, December 31, 1973, 8.

41. "Cold Comfort," 34.

42. "Energy: How Bad Now? Painful Changes in Life Styles," *U.S. News and World Report*, February 11, 1974, 19.

43. "The Coldest Winter?" 8.

44. Ibid.

45. "Gasoline Shortages Are Forcing Exurbanites to Readjust Their Life-Style," *New York Times*, February 7, 1974.

46. William Hoffer, "No Energy Weekend Experiment," *House Beautiful*, May 1974, 16.

47. William Chafe, *Unfinished Journey: America since World War II*, 4th ed. (New York: Oxford University Press, 1999), 112–13; and Stephanie Coontz, *The Way We Never Were: American Families and the Nostalgia Trap* (New York: Basic Books, 1992).

48. On the history of frozen foods, see Harvey Levenstein, *Paradox of Plenty: A Social History of Eating in Modern America* (New York: Oxford University Press, 1993); Harvey Levenstein, *Revolution at the Table: The Transformation of the American Diet* (New York: Oxford University Press, 1988), 207–8; and Elaine N. McIntosh, *American Food Habits in Historical Perspective* (Westport, Conn.: Praeger, 1995), 119–20.

49. "Information Center Flash," J. Walter Thompson Chicago, January 6, 1970, "1970, January 6–August 10, Information Center Flash" file, box 2, J. Walter Thompson Newsletter Collection, Domestic Series, Chicago Office, JWTC Archives,

50. Ralph Keyes, "Learning to Love the Energy Crisis," *Newsweek*, December 3, 1973, 17.

51. Federal Energy Administration, "Per Capita Energy Consumption and Per Capita Income: A Comparison of the United States with Other Wealthy Western Countries," Energy Conservation, box 14, file 9-72, Conservation, vol.

1, 1973–74, Louis H. Roddis Papers, Duke University Special Collections, Durham, N.C. For an introductory look at consumption and gender in Europe, see Jennifer A. Loehlin, *From Rugs to Riches: Housework, Consumption, and Modernity in Germany* (Oxford: Berg, 1999).

52. On the paradoxical impact of technological innovation on women's domestic labor, see Ruth Schwartz Cowan, *More Work for Mother: The Ironies of Household Technology from the Open Hearth to the Microwave* (New York: Basic Books, 1983); and Susan Strasser, *Never Done: A History of American Housework* (New York: Pantheon Books, 1982).

53. File 8, 1972, box 6, Competitive Advertising Collection, JWTC Archives.

54. *Good Housekeeping,* November 1972, "Misc. Frozen Foods," file 23, box 16, Competitive Advertising Collection, 1972, JWTC Archives.

55. *Sunset,* April 1972, ibid. For an in-depth look at how the J. Walter Thompson Company was assessing the impact of women's changing roles on advertising during this period, see "The Moving Target" file, box 15, Company Publications Collection, JWTC Archives.

56. See Betty Friedan, "The Problem That Has No Name," reprinted in Wini Breines and Alexander Bloom, eds., *Takin' It to the Streets: A Sixties Reader* (New York: Oxford University Press, 1995), 461–67.

57. See, for example, Bruce J. Schulman, *The Seventies: The Great Shift in American Culture, Society, and Politics* (New York: Free Press, 2001).

58. "The Coldest Winter?" 9.

59. See, for example, David E. Nye, *Consuming Power: A Social History of American Energies* (Cambridge: MIT Press, 1998); and Jackson Lears, "Reconsidering Abundance: A Plea for Ambiguity," in Susan Strasser, Charles McGovern, and Matthias Judt, eds., *Getting and Spending: European and American Consumer Societies in the Twentieth Century* (Washington, D.C.: Cambridge University Press, 1998), 449–66.

60. On consumption as a national pastime, see Lawrence B. Glickman, ed., *Consumer Society in American History: A Reader* (Ithaca: Cornell University Press, 1999).

61. Stephanie Coontz points to this earlier attempt to endow consumption with moral purchase when she quotes motivational researcher Ernest Dichter explaining the aim of advertising: "We are now confronted with the problem of permitting the average American to feel moral . . . even when he is taking two vacations a year and buying a second or third car. One of the basic problems of prosperity, then, is to demonstrate that the hedonistic approach to life is a moral, not an immoral one" (*The Way We Never Were: American Families and the Nostalgia Trap* [New York: Basic Books, 1992], 171).

ANNE ENKE

6   Taking Over Domestic Space

The Battered Women's Movement and Public Protest

> When we finally went to the "dirty money" [corporate] sources to help fund shelter space, they told us we needed a director, governing board and this whole hierarchy to run it. Well we had *already* provided shelter for over 1,200 women, for two years, from *our* homes. . . . So . . . the first thing we did was to make the governing board identical to—*composed of*—the whole *membership*, and the membership consisted of everyone who *stayed* at or worked for Women's Advocates.
>
> —Sharon Rice Vaughan

WOMEN'S ADVOCATES in St. Paul, Minnesota, is one of the most well-known and longest-lasting battered-women's shelters in the country.[1] Though evidencing the lasting and far-reaching impact of women's movements of the 1970s, it is rarely included in the history of radical social movements. In 1972, the year of Women's Advocates' founding, an international movement against domestic violence against women was in its fledgling stage, lacking even a name for itself, but based in part on a perceived need for "a place" that offered temporary residence and resources for women trying to get away from violent partners. Critiquing the structural conditions that made women economically and socially vulnerable to male violence, the battered-women's movement shared roots, analyses, and strategies with women's movements that addressed rape, welfare, and homelessness, and similarly gained strength by building broad-based coalitions with other activist groups and public agencies. By the end of the 1970s, activists in the United States had created hundreds of housing facilities for battered women in both urban and rural locations, making "shelter" the signature stamp of the battered-women's movement.[2] During the 1980s and 1990s, women of color especially elaborated movement networks and strategies to take advantage of the particular resources available to specific Indian, Latina, African American, and Asian communities, and in the process have shown that "shelter" and "advocacy" for battered women can and must take on a vast array of forms.[3]

In the historiography and memory of the 1960s and 1970s, militant, direct action—sit-ins, takeovers—and mass protests have been so valorized that it is difficult to recognize radicalism in other forms and contexts. The battered-women's movement and much of the feminist and gay and lesbian liberation movements have been represented as concerns about personal, private, or "lifestyle" issues.[4] However, those movements not only are continuous with radical movements of the 1960s, but also have expanded radical critiques and strategies. Many of the founders of Women's Advocates first came together years earlier, through their involvement in the antiwar movement. There, they developed a critique of a violent society, a critique that meshed well with their budding feminist consciousness. Another thing that those white women brought with them from the antiwar movement was a feeling of constant emergency and the need to act *now*—taking risks, creating protests, and taking over spaces—to save people's lives. I argue here that one of the most important strategies of the battered-women's movement involved nothing less than a radical takeover, not of a government office for a few hours, but of *domestic space,* to create a place in which a woman could rightly demand public protection, privacy, and the inviolability of her own body at all times. Doing so required coalitional action and outreach to thousands of people beyond the existing feminist movement.

Feminists have argued that domestic space, far from being a woman's place, has taken shape firmly within male-dominated social structures.[5] In the United States, ideals originating in the early nineteenth century suggest that the privacy of domestic space is a (white, middle- or upper-class, heterosexual) male right, based on the inviolability of his property, including his domicile, his wife, and his progeny; as owner, he protects his wife's social and sexual status and the purity of his bloodline.[6] In the post–World War II years (largely in response to women's actual departure from the home), popular representations of domesticity as a private—yet nationalist—endeavor further painted a vision of the white, middle-class, nuclear-family "home" as the unassailable space essential to individual and national security.[7] Deviations from dominant domestic ideals made those ideals no less potent in their ability to privatize and support men's violence against women "in their own homes."[8] The women's movement, perhaps more than any other post-1960 social movement, not only condemned the lingering nineteenth-century liberal ideal of separate private and public realms, but also showed that personal and political realms were inseparable or even indistinguishable.

Women's Advocates' mission was not simply to add to or reform social services for women; instead, women in that grassroots organization launched a deep critique of society's division into public and private, and they organized to transform it by creating a domestic space that was intensely political. They argued that the notion of dichotomous public and private realms functioned to privilege white, middle- and upper-class, heterosexual men. The privatization of domestic space, in particular, isolated and confined women, reinforced men's "property rights" over them, and condoned violence as a private matter not subject to public intervention.[9] Neither social services nor legal practices had challenged the privatization of battering; indeed, many argued, existing services even contributed to the isolation of women who experienced domestic battering.[10] Normative conceptions of "home" as an apolitical space furthered women's invisibility. While women's liberation in general challenged this conception by asserting that "the personal is political,"[11] the battered-women's movement in particular went further, both critiquing domestic norms and creating an alternative homelike space that women embraced as a site of protection, politicization, and political resistance.

Women's Advocates battered-women's shelter entailed three important aspects of social change. First, it generated a politicized and politicizing "domestic" space. Second, Women's Advocates demanded that "public" institutions such as law enforcement agencies change to accommodate and support that new space. Third, Women's Advocates deepened their own social critique and vision by developing coalitions to address problems of race and class that emerged in the process of running a shelter. Far from cutting themselves off from people who did not share their feminist or leftist analyses, leaders in the battered-women's movement engaged state agencies and capitalist funding sources to create a lasting network of institutions that addressed domestic violence. Most importantly, as the Women's Advocates case reveals, the movement began with the ideas and needs of battered women themselves, and over the years a diversity of shelter residents and advocates innovated strategies to increase resources for women in violent relationships, decrease domestic violence, and sustain the movement.

POLITICIZING DOMESTIC SPACE

The founders of Women's Advocates emerged from one of many eclectic consciousness-raising collectives in the Twin Cities. They were "ten or so" white women in their midtwenties to late thirties, of working- and middle-class backgrounds, and had in common prior work with the Honeywell Project, which sought to prevent Honeywell's production of cluster bombs used in Vietnam. Sharon Vaughan of St. Paul had gained local prominence through her activism in the Honeywell Project; she had also been active in the local Catholic Left, but, recently divorced and with three children, she chafed at "St. Paul's Catholic values," which denied women accurate legal information related to marriage and divorce.[12] Minnesotans Monica Erler and Bernice Sisson each had years of traditional civic volunteer work behind them and a growing frustration with the lack of emergency services for women. Susan Ryan, a young VISTA volunteer originally from New York, was perhaps least tolerant of the establishment and demanded nothing less than community-based devotion to ending violence and hierarchies of gender, race, and class.

Upon learning that most female clients of the county legal assistance offices lacked basic legal rights information, especially regarding divorce and custody issues, the collective first created a divorce-rights booklet for women and worked to distribute information about custody, support, and name changes. Drawing on Ryan's VISTA program grants, they also established a telephone hotline, housed in an office donated by the legal assistance office.[13] Countless women throughout Minnesota called the phone service, alerting workers to a shocking reality: So many women were battered in their homes, but most had no place to go and no financial resources. While there were thirty-seven emergency shelters for men in the Twin Cities, the only place that a woman with children could receive emergency shelter—for one night only—was in a motel booked through Emergency Social Services. Lack of safe shelter and legal recourse led this first group of activists to found Women's Advocates in March 1972, a nonprofit group of volun-

teers who provided legal advocacy for women in abusive relationships.[14] As contact with women increased, advocates began to develop
a vision of "a place" for "women who 'need to get away right now.'"[15]

Women seeking Women's Advocates' services almost invariably came
from situations of extreme isolation, the result of domineering partners
and a society that did not acknowledge battering. While long-enduring
peace and civil rights movements strengthened critiques of all kinds
of violence, even they did not focus on violence in the home. Few battered women had been touched by the social upheavals of the 1960s.[16]
Activists offered clients shelter in their own homes and apartments.
Women and children crowded onto floors and couches, an experience
that was indeed politicizing for many, but it was a short-term solution
that was politically weakened by its relatively privatized nature. Thus
arose the idea of a formal shelter; it would be "like home" but collectively run, and not one person's property.

In part, it was the opposition Women's Advocates faced that prompted
activists to envision wide-reaching, almost utopian, change. Their early
efforts to help battered women—such as housing women in their own
homes and later building a formal shelter—were policed with neighborhood suspicion, evictions, and threats of lawsuits by actors concerned
with "men's rights." From the outset, therefore, advocates adopted a
role as "protector" of women, usurping a prerogative traditionally belonging to fathers and husbands. But advocates also demanded a "response from the whole public community."[17] They envisioned "a house
on every block" in which the whole neighborhood would be involved,
"like McGruff houses for kids, only they would be shelters for women."[18]
Such houses would not only act as discreet zones of safety for women,
but would also signal neighborly intervention in battering, making visible a formerly privatized issue. Women's Advocates, then, offered a vision of a dramatically changed public landscape that would support an
alternative domestic space.

In challenging normative notions of domesticity, and in nurturing
the politicization of residents and staff, Women's Advocates shelter itself
represented a concerted challenge to the boundary between public and
private. This was another kind of takeover, one which—in keeping with
feminist ideologies—also challenged the boundaries between the movement and the mainstream. Like other social movements, it incorporated
dramatic and at times militant acts aimed at radical social transformation. Unlike others, it aimed to take over the home, usurping it from a

public order that supported male violence within it, and reappropriating it as a space safe for women.[19]

Most accounts of the battered-women's movement narrate the movement's engagement with "the public" through a shift from grassroots funding to public and private funding sources. This exclusive focus on funding generates a familiar narrative of declining control over resources and discourses.[20] A very different story can be told, however, by tracing the process through which Women's Advocates laid claim to a new kind of space and insisted that existing social entities change to support it. Initially, Women's Advocates activists seemed to believe that the protection of women depended on constructing impenetrable walls between the shelter and the public world. But Women's Advocates constantly renegotiated those boundaries, forging new relationships with local police departments, batterers, the neighborhood, and the larger metropolitan community.

For the energetic founders of Women's Advocates, sheltering women was a logical and necessary extension of social movements that protested institutionalized racism, class stratification, and U.S. colonization of other countries. By 1972, advocates with homes took on an increasing number of women needing shelter. While their homes functioned as a sort of underground shelter system, advocates and residents caught their first glimpse of alternative domesticity: "Women and children slept in spare beds and on our living room floors, sharing our food and belongings. Our children met a succession of new friends."[21] Through opening their homes to a diversity of women and children, advocates, along with clients, further "realized the importance of women being together in one house, sharing their experiences and getting support from one another."[22] This experience, along with a feminist belief in democracy, shared authority, and female empowerment, prompted Women's Advocates to insist on a governing structure in which all residents, as well as advocates, were members of the board of directors, and all members had voting rights.[23] It was this moment—critical to the movement—during which formerly privatized individuals experienced, as a group, a shift from perceiving the world from within a nuclear-family framework to strategizing about the world as a community under one roof. This shift in perception also encouraged a coalitional approach—seeking involvement from a diversity of politicized groups—that would become an inherent and far-reaching aspect of the battered-women's movement.

Advocates saw their actions as radical challenges to society. Many advocates opened up their homes to women facing all manner of crises, convinced that such direct action "was part of working there and being an advocate." Their work as shelterers and advocates thus took place in the space of their own "private" lives, giving them their first taste of danger (e.g., men armed with knives or guns) intruding into their homes. As activists had for the civil rights and antiwar movements, many advocates believed that "taking risks and chances" was also "what you did for Women's Advocates."[24] More importantly, doing so convinced advocates that U.S. domestic norms and the privatization of nuclear households allowed, rather than protected women from, domestic violence. As Bernice Sisson, Women's Advocates volunteer for twenty-six years, explained, battering depended on "private homes" since "most batterers do not batter in front of others."[25] Equally important, this led to an intense focus on the boundary between outside and inside, as advocates tried to convert the exterior walls of their homes (and later the shelter) from barriers that hide violence within to barriers that keep violence out. Advocates at that time interpreted violence explicitly in gendered terms. They determined that the most important thing was that women be able to get to a space "free of violence," where they could "keep the man out" long enough for women to envision a further solution.

As if to confirm that Women's Advocates was challenging the public order and the hierarchies that supported it, backlash came from many fronts. After only a few months, one advocate got evicted from her apartment because neighbors complained that she was bringing too many women and children into what was supposed to be an adults-only property.[26] Sharon Vaughan, Women's Advocates' first director, explained that it helped that early activists tended not to have male partners. "I had kids, but I don't think I could have done any of [Women's Advocates work] with [my former husband]. . . . I didn't have to check in with anybody, to see if it was okay to have somebody sleep in my house."[27] But it was not long before advocates discovered that even their own private homes were under a tangible net of public surveillance. Vaughan eventually stopped housing women and children in the home she owned due to pressure from several sources: In her "homogenously white" neighborhood, neighbors noticed the many women and children of color coming and going at all times of the day and night, and they pressured local legislators to find out and put an end to "what is going on in there." At the same time, a men's rights group threatened to sue Vaughan for housing only women and children. She recalled: "I was really scared of them, because when all you have is a house, you know that's what you'll lose."[28] It was the "public"—neighbors, civic groups, legislators, and so on—who seemed to secure (or deny) privacy in accordance with gendered and racist norms about the use of space. Housing only women and children, Vaughan broke neighborhood and social codes about the gender, as well as the number and ethnicity, of residents and thereby forfeited her "right" to the privacy of the home she owned.

The challenge of housing women in their own homes prompted Women's Advocates to transfer to a new location their ideals of communal living and their challenge to the links between domesticity and violence. By July 1974, Women's Advocates had raised enough funds through public agencies and private donors to purchase a large Victorian house on Grand Avenue, a short bus ride from downtown St. Paul.[29] Vaughan explained that "one of the best things about [the neighborhood] was that it wasn't really a neighborhood. There was a big apartment building next to us, and a rooming house on the other side. . . . That makes it a great place for a shelter: because it's very visible and public, but it's not right in the middle of a residential neighborhood."[30] As shelters opened in other areas over the years, neighborhood acceptance proved to be critical to a shelter's survival. The battered-women's movement narrates countless incidents of local shelters being pushed out of their neighborhoods by angry neighbors, primarily in white or upper-class neighborhoods in which residents espouse homogeneity and longevity of property owners and occupants. Women's Advocates chose its block so well that, within a decade, they owned and occupied three adjacent houses on the block and thereby gained an unchallenged presence in and influence over an area otherwise on its way to gentrification.

Central to the advocates' vision was the desire to make the shelter feel like home, albeit a temporary one, rather than like a treatment facility. In the 1970s, that meant "scrounging" for "castoff" furniture, "covering the tatters with brightly colored throws," and finding things "to help create a homey atmosphere."[31] They sanded wood floors, stripped off old paint, installed louvered shades and drapes over all the windows, and filled the house with plants. While many commented on the beauty of the shelter, Pat Murphy's affectionate comment points even more to the meaning of the space: "We made do. It was *never* a *showplace*, it was a *home*. . . . It was ticky-tacky right from the start."[32] The shelter implied that battered women could and should make a public claim on their right to home. In the words of one former volunteer: "*Women* were not the ones who were crazy or needed to be institutionalized."[33]

Staff often felt ambivalent about changes that seemed institutional, and such measures became points of conflict. For example, finding that residents often took house bedsheets with them when they left, Women's Advocates eventually built locks on the cupboards. Vaughan recalled that the locked sheets were "the thing that made me totally wild with anger. You know, putting sheets behind these cages, and it was like putting women in cages so they wouldn't take them. There would be that kind of feeling."[34] To mitigate against this hierarchy, Women's Advocates instituted nightly meetings in which residents and staff would collectively develop house policy, forming and reforming rules usually through consensus and as need arose.

To keep women safe in this new, politicized domesticity, advocates attempted to create a shelter that was impervious to intrusion by emphasizing a commitment to house security. In the first year or two of the shelter's operation, there were a number of incidents in which violent men broke into the shelter, endangering the well-being of residents and staff.[35] Other scares included telephone bomb threats, and angry men pounding on doors and throwing rocks to break windows.[36] The sense of ever-present threat led advocates to take two actions: One involved building an elaborate security system around the house; the other involved pressuring the local police department to change its policies. Both measures reveal some of the ways that the movement perceived and analyzed patterns of violence against women, as well as their strategies for taking over domestic space and introducing it to the realm of public protest.

The house security system signaled Women's Advocates' determination to keep women inside safe even without public support. The system received a great deal of attention in local papers. A 1976 *Minneapolis Tribune* article subtitled "Battered: Security Is Essential" began its description of the shelter: "Women's Advocates looks like most of the large old houses on Grand Avenue in St. Paul, except for the wire mesh over the door and the highly visible alarm system across every window."[37] The reporter implied that security systems were not typical—indeed, they were newsworthy—on residential houses in that neighborhood. Attention to the security system disrupted the normative images of domestic space in which men protect women inside from threats outside; Women's Advocates painted a counterimage of violent men intruding into (an all-female) domestic space.

Advocates also attempted to control all the permeable elements of the house's boundary with the neighborhood outside. Not only did they cover windows with heavy-duty mesh wiring and alarm systems, but also they kept heavy drapes and shutters pulled across all windows at all times. The front door was kept closed and women constantly checked to see that locks were secured. Because of the electronic alarm system, residents were required to notify a staff person before opening any outside door or changing the position of any window.[38] At the time, advocates saw no alternative to maintaining this system, which sealed off the shelter from any relationship to its neighbors, as well as from the rest of the outside world. The darkness of the house, the rules against touching windows, and the surveillance of passersby were all intended to create security. Unwelcome intrusions only reinforced advocates' sense of dependence on a barrier that even the sun could not penetrate.

Women's Advocates did not intend, however, to reproduce the centuries-old image of the cloister as an impermeable, safe, and even chaste space. Ultimately, rules and alarm systems smacked of institutions and were thus at odds with advocates' vision of the shelter as home and private residence. Security rules implied that staff held exclusive power to draw the defining boundaries between inside and outside the shelter. Staff mediation, further, implied that residents bore a problematic relationship between inside and outside the shelter—indeed, that residents were vulnerably situated somewhere near that boundary, poised either to fall off to the exterior, or to add threatening potential to the interior. This element of an institutional relationship between residents and staff could be dispensed with only when Women's Advocates figured out how to create a shelter that was not cut off from the world, but that was part of it.

In the summer of 1976, advocate Pat Murphy visited a working shelter in Toronto. Murphy returned to Women's Advocates with a new vision of how a shelter could feel more like a safe home, and she still vividly recalls how her trip to Toronto altered her perspective on security.[39] The Toronto shelter, in Murphy's opinion, was staffed by women "just like the women at Women's Advocates—collective, smart, great politics, great women," and the "very big, old house" itself was "very like Women's Advocates' house." Residents similarly came from all walks of life and included children of all ages. But the "feeling" of the house, compared to Women's Advocates, was like day compared to night:

> There was such a sense of openness! The light! It was so light! . . . his place was wide open and the light was there and the doors were open and the windows were open. . . . There was clearly no sense of crisis going on. . . . And there was a foyer where men could come visit their girlfriends or visit with the kids . . . there were no rules like we had about "you can't tell him we're here" and all that kind of stuff. And the feeling in that house was so much better . . . the staff weren't fearful, the women in that house were not fearful. They and their kids went outside, played outside, came and went and were not fearful. It was just like a home.

Suddenly, to Murphy, the "feeling" at Women's Advocates stood in stark contrast: She saw Women's Advocates "all holed up against the fearful men out there . . . it was like a fortress, a fortress holding women in, imprisoning them here, we have them in this little prison, and we're going to get the walls high enough and nobody's going to hurt us or them."[40]

Murphy's visit to the Toronto women's shelter prompted a reevaluation of the effects of Women's Advocates' security measures, as well as a decision to open the house by publishing the address, opening the drapes, and letting in the light.[41] To Murphy, it was apparent that living in a "fortress" where the walls can never be quite high enough actually contributed to a feeling of fear. Murphy blamed advocates and staff for setting the fearful tone of the house: "*We* projected the need for that fear, with our rules: Don't tell him you're here, don't give out the phone number. . . . *We* projected that fear." Others agreed that the symbolism of an "open" house was crucial, and wanted to project a message that "women are not here to hide, and that women can be here and do not need to be afraid, that this is safe, this is a good place."[42] Most residents, most of the time, did experience Women's Advocates as a safe and good, even life-saving, place. But to go from "hiding behind a fortress" to being "open" required renegotiating Women's Advocates' relationship with the public, and reconceptualizing the relationship between gender, space, and power. Women's Advocates transformed normative ideologies about "private" domestic space as they discovered that to create a private and impenetrable domesticity was, in practice, to create a fortress or even a prison. Residents and advocates alike had much to celebrate: "Letting in the light" was an act that irrefutably politicized a domestic space by opening it up to engagement with the public world.

Residents' representations of the shelter revolved around a slightly different set of spatial images than those of many advocates.[43] Generally, residents represented the shelter neither as an institution nor as a home. They were not typically critical of house rules that governed women's manipulation of shelter boundaries; locked doors meant greater security, not entrapment. As one resident put it: "There's safety and emotional support here. Just having the door closed behind you and knowing you're safe is half of it."[44] For residents, inside/outside and public/private did not define a stable dichotomy between essentially different spaces. Abusive partners took over even the privacy of women's own bodies and at the same time walled women in to a space of extreme isolation. Domestic violence proved the contingency and malleability of the relationship between women's security and *all* spaces. While they preferred a place that felt "open," residents struggled more with a critical set of concepts: "leaving," for them, could imply banishment, exile, failure, danger, being alone or the end of being alone, escape, resistance, and liberation.

"Reaching Out, Looking In"

While advocates tried to create a place that felt like home, their initial representation of violence as perpetrated by males outside and something that could be kept out crumbled in the face of their experience. At the shelter, women encountered violence among each other and in disciplining children. A simple gender analysis proved inadequate, as all women at the shelter were forced to grapple with complex and ubiquitous dynamics of violence and power. Residents, some of whom became advocates, helped Women's Advocates shape itself around the difference that race and class made in uses of space and in experimental solutions to domestic violence. Through practice, Women's Advocates gradually exposed and redressed the white, middle-class bias of the shelter's policies. As soon as advocates acknowledged the multiple ways that hierarchy shaped the interior, as well as exterior, of the house, they brought the meaning of violence and nonviolence under closer scrutiny.

Advocates, most of whom had cut their political teeth in the antiwar movement, created and posted a set of house rules named "House Pol-

icy" to "protect everyone's safety." Initially, rules on house security focused only on the risk of violence from outside. And yet advocates became aware of women's own violent potential early on, through a few
incidents in which clients verbally or physically attacked staff members. To address this, advocates reiterated their ability to keep it out: As
one advocate told the *Milwaukee Journal* in 1976, "violence in the house
is simply not tolerated."[45] Rules portrayed violence within the house as
a very simple matter with a simple and workable solution, and rules
granted staff the right to evict anyone acting in a "violent or threatening" way. Staff thereby implied that they had the power to keep the
shelter free of violence.[46]

"House Policy" did not initially elaborate what would constitute
"violent or threatening" behavior among women, nor did advocates
see any need to explain why there was a code against violence among
women in the house. The definition of, and reason for prohibiting, violent behavior among adults was self-evident to advocates, at least in
the early years of operation. Initially, advocates put forth their lengthi-
est interpretation and discussion of violence *within* the house not under
the "House Security" section, but rather under the section called "House
Policy Regarding Children":

> It is important that Women's Advocates be a safe and secure place for the
> children who stay here as well as the women. For this reason we have
> general rules concerning care and behavior of children.
>   Violence is frequently a learned behavior. Children who grow up with
> it as part of family life and discipline may well incorporate it into their
> adult lifestyle. This is one of the reasons there is no violent discipline of
> children allowed during the time they are here. This includes spanking
> and slapping hands. The staff, especially the child care staff, are willing to
> work with women to find workable alternatives.

Vaughan retrospectively explained the "Regarding Children" policy
as an instance in which staff imposed white, middle-class values on residents.

> We had a rule that you couldn't spank children because that was a form of
> violence. And there wasn't any question in our minds that this was just. I
> remember [intervening when] a woman was whopping her kid, a woman
> of color who came from a really tough situation in her neighborhood, and
> she turned around and looked at me, and in this calm voice said, "It's
> normal to spank." Just like that. I never forgot that, because I thought,
> "Well, what *is* normal?" So even the radical philosophy [about violence]
> was up for grabs. . . . She said, "I teach her to whip anybody who comes

up to her, because otherwise she's going to get whipped." And I thought, . . . "I have a daughter too, and why would this not be the way I raise my kids?" I thought a lot about the social context of violence and nonviolence, and how . . . we did a lot of things that . . . came from our own context, not necessarily from the women we served.[47]

It was the very definition of violence that was suddenly "up for grabs" for Vaughan. "Violence" and "nonviolence" proved not to be self-explanatory or essential categories; rather, the terms were culturally and spatially specific.

Initially, advocates put forth a philosophy about child rearing that explicitly equated spanking and hand slapping with violence, assumed that those practices would make Women's Advocates space unsafe for children, and implicitly held parents responsible for normalizing battering as a form of violent control over others. Advocates thus acknowledged—and attempted to reform—one kind of women's behavior that they interpreted as "violence." In keeping with much of the feminist movement of the time, they defined power and violence so that, stereotypically, men were physically, economically, and socially more powerful than women, and adults more powerful than children. As women in the shelter discovered that hierarchy, control, and violence were part of the internal dynamics shaping the shelter space, they revised their simple gender analysis and definition of violence to one that recognized hierarchies of class, ethnicity, race, and sexuality. The experience of living in the shelter thus launched this idealistic, if initially naïve, group of activists into the forefront of emerging feminist theory and critique of the multiple dimensions of social hierarchies.

Revising definitions of gender and violence opened up Women's Advocates by the late 1970s to the reality of violence in lesbian relationships. Until then, advocates presumed males to be the perpetrators of violence, and sheltered women to be in heterosexual relationships. As Women's Advocates wrestled against their preconceived notions, lesbian clients increasingly demanded that Women's Advocates develop awareness of the particular needs and resources of lesbians. During the 1980s, lesbians then built on the battered-women's movement to develop a movement that would specifically challenge the multiple social roots of lesbian battering.

In addition to definitions of violence, the first group of shelter workers discovered that their own assumptions about food and waste disposal actually created class distinctions between residents and staff.

While many staff members came from working-class backgrounds and did not identify with the shelter's initial consumption plans, residents experienced the emphasis on whole grains, alfalfa and bean sprouts, and recycling as an imposition of values that they themselves had neither the leisure nor interest to pursue. Advocate Pat Murphy described this as a huge "culture clash" between women for whom "brown rice" was "real big" (many staff), and women who were "making it just living" or who were on public assistance or who simply preferred meat, sweet potato pie, chips, and pop (many residents). In distinction from social services that operated out of offices, Women's Advocates took the opportunity for transforming their own assumptions because, as Murphy put it, "you're not in an office seeing people for an hour. You're *living together*. So *all* of your cultural patterns and behaviors are there.[48] Staff conceded that consumption practices were one of the most tangible markers of class and ethnic hierarchy at the shelter and accordingly reprioritized around residents' preferences.

Claiming public space for a shelter included more than creating a functional house; it also meant transforming the existing social landscape. All residents had experienced the ways that existing public institutions kept them in violent relationships. Vaughan recalled the "image" that prevailed in her mind as she staffed the shelter: "Women would come into Women's Advocates, and it would be this shelter, and our back door was a cliff, and we'd push 'em out the back door and they'd fall off the edge." Under one roof, women developed a picture of systemic violence against women—a system supported by norms about gender, privacy, and domesticity. Beyond a roof, Women's Advocates addressed a long list of residents' needs: school arrangements for their children; visits to hospital emergency rooms; support from welfare, police, and courts; the search for affordable long-term housing; and retrieval of women's possessions from their former homes.[49] Meeting those needs involved intervention in all manner of public agencies and institutions.

Advocates' struggle to gain police protection revealed the ways that law enforcement was organized to protect established hierarchies. From the moment Women's Advocates opened, activists demanded that the St. Paul Police Department change its practices in order to protect women against abusive men. Thirty to forty residents and advocates marched down the mile-long hill to the state Capitol to confront the mayor about Women's Advocates relationship with the police. They also showed up as a group at the police department, demanding attention.[50] Direct action had been an inherent part of Women's Advocates from the beginning; protests at the Capitol flowed naturally from their basic goal to change the public landscape into one that supported a violence-free domesticity.

The struggle between Women's Advocates and the police department shows the influence that the battered-women's movement had on common notions of acceptable and unacceptable violence. Women's Advocates records show that during Women's Advocates' first year of operation, police response to emergency calls was slow at best. Officers were generally dismissive of women's demands for protection and treated calls from Women's Advocates as routine "domestics"—the term police used in cases of violence between heterosexual couples. They were reluctant to intervene in what they defined to be private matters or, worse, arrived on the scene with statements such as, "My job is to protect marriage."[51]

Women's Advocates insisted that women have a right to be protected even from private violence. But police department responses as late as September 1975 indicate that any such rights were yet to be won. Chief of Police R. H. Rowan recorded an incident in which an officer dispatched to Women's Advocates found a man aggressively demanding "visiting privileges" with his children at the shelter. The officer, rather than removing the man or intervening in the escalating tension, referred the couple to court arbitration and told the advocate on duty: "You're a woman's advocate, I'm a man's advocate." Notably, Chief Rowan found no fault with the officer's behavior and concluded that "[Women's Advocates'] complaint can not be sustained."[52] Advocates, familiar with this outcome, insisted that "public servants" such as police officers have "no right" to be "partial" in their protection of any citizens.[53]

Women's Advocates began submitting formal complaints to the police department in May 1975. The department initially responded to complaints with arguments about "legal procedure." In instances of armed break-in to Women's Advocates, officers sometimes dismissed Women's Advocates' request for intervention, arguing that they could only arrest a man if his wife explicitly demands his arrest at the time of his initial break-in, or if she demands his arrest in the event of future violent contact.[54] In response, Women's Advocates emphasized that their own primary function was to shelter and protect women, and that the police department should similarly bear *public* responsibility for ensuring the safety of everyone at Women's Advocates.[55]

Normative assumptions about (male) property ownership made police unwilling to recognize Women's Advocates as a private property against which men could be considered trespassers; police assumed that even when women owned a property, men retained a right of access to "their" women and children on that property. In mid-September 1975, Women's Advocates voiced their criticisms of the police department at a formal meeting with the department and Mayor Cohen of St. Paul. Their protests did change the department's practices to the increased satisfaction of Women's Advocates.[56] But their success depended to a large extent on subsequent legal confirmation that Women's Advocates shelter was, in fact, private property. During the meeting itself, Chief Rowan was "very concerned about the legal rights of men who wished access to their wives and children." Only after a representative from the city attorney's office determined that men do *not* have a "right" to "self-help" in seeking access to women or children, and that a man may be considered "at the very least a trespasser on Women's Advocates' property," did the police department begin to take seriously their role in protecting the shelter.[57] Before this legal clarification, common notions of private property were essentially gendered. Not only did privacy protect male property owners from social surveillance, but also it granted men the right to access "their" women on *any* property. Women, though they might become property owners, would gain privacy against social surveillance and protection against intruders and trespassers only through protracted struggle with public agencies.

By August 1976, the police department had adopted new policies to "relieve some of the difficulties," including "to give calls to your facility [Women's Advocates] a high priority designation."[58] Women's Advocates thereby successfully instituted an unprecedented relationship with the St. Paul Police Department, which included the presence and input of advocates at officer training sessions to educate officers on domestic violence and the options available and unavailable to women. Women's Advocates saw to it that officers would not treat the cases as "private" matters and therefore inappropriate for police intervention.

LIVING THE COALITION, 1975–1980

Women's Advocates was a politicizing space for both advocates and residents. Many shelter residents did not consider themselves feminists, nor even about to become feminists. But Women's Advocates was "a place to go" where individuals suddenly became part of a broad-based movement. After isolation and demoralization, Women's Advocates was a space that was both radicalizing and empowering for battered women across race and class differences. In early 1976, while talking with other residents and staff after her first day at the shelter, Lois remarked: "This is the first time I've felt like a human being. I've kept quiet for so long."[59] Being with other battered women at the shelter helped women begin to transform the meaning of leaving into a positive act that affirmed that they had the right to run their own lives. Most residents experienced life-changing moments of community and support, such as the celebration parties they held whenever a woman found an apartment after a long search. Among their liberating actions were en masse marches to the St. Paul Police Department or down the hill to the Capitol, where they interrupted legislative sessions to demand laws and programs that would meet women's needs for safe domestic space.

Women's Advocates was a specifically politicizing space that gave many women their first consciousness-raising experience not segregated according to race and class. One resident wrote of her arrival at Women's Advocates in fall 1975:

> I was given a bed the first chance I got I lay down to rest. . . . [Later] I went downstairs and found that a woman named Manuella had prepared a fried chicken and potato dinner. There were ten or so women sitting around the table eating. . . . I felt pleased and part of the pleasure came from the fact that here were women from several different racial groups all sitting together and sharing. . . . Often one hears, "Really, that sounds just like my husband/boyfriend." The revelation is quick in coming that the woman is not alone in her situation.[60]

Consciousness-raising came in the context of crisis and the first successful mobilization for change in these women's lives. By 1978, residents had also helped increase public awareness of battering and of the movement created to stop battering. In that year, Minnesotan Ellen Pence, a leader in linking the battered-women's movement with other movements, reflected: "Most people think there's more wife-beating than before. I don't think that's true. They also think because of women's liberation, women are getting more uppity so they're getting beaten up more. But it's just the opposite. Most of the women in shelters are not feminists. . . . They've just never had a place to go before."[61] Shelters like Women's Advocates became one place in which feminism extended beyond the lives of self-named activists to become a broader movement.

The shelter also created an unparalleled opportunity for experiencing, confronting, analyzing, and changing racist dynamics within its own walls and within feminist activism. Changes did not happen overnight; in the words of one advocate: "It wasn't like we just opened the doors and in came women of color and we figured it out. It was a long, three-year process."[62] Women at the shelter functioned as an unnamed coalition, learning about the ways that race, class, and (later) homophobia shaped battered-women's experience. As former resident Eileen Hudon put it: "It was in shelters that I first started talking about racism. What does that have to do with battering? Or what does homophobia have to do with battering? Well, it all has to do with a woman's safety, that's all. If you can't say the word 'homophobia' or 'lesbian,' if you don't understand a woman's community, how're you going to help? If you don't know what resources or powers are there, or what particular kind of dangers or isolation she has to deal with, then you're not doing your job."[63] This accomplishment of the movement, too often overlooked in histories of radicalism, was based on innovative responses to difference and power; not without struggle, Women's Advocates became one place that gave concrete meaning to the idea of coalition.

Early residents of the shelter—particularly women of color—felt they were largely on their own to deal with racism without the support and understanding of the (virtually all white) staff.[64] Indeed, according to Hudon, they thought that the staff "had no idea of the racism going on" among residents or between residents and staff. At least initially, some residents actively hid from the staff their perception of conflict between white women and women of color at the shelter. They perceived racism at the shelter to function similarly to racism in the wider society, but with one crucial difference: Whereas most urban space was defined by racial segregation, the shelter brought otherwise segregated women together under the same roof. Hudon recalled an escalating argument between a black woman, a Chicana woman, and a white woman in the second year of the shelter's operation. Hudon believed that "[the advocate] was instrumental in creating a division between white women and women of color at the shelter." Ultimately, the argument came to physical threat: "You had two women, a white woman and a black woman, facing off in the kitchen with knives." Hudon (an Indian woman) and a Chicana woman were actively but not physically involved. Before an assault occurred, "an advocate comes walking in. Everybody immediately acted like nothing happened. She asked what was going on, and everyone was just, 'Oh, we're just talking about what we're going to have for dinner.' Which was an absolute lie. She fortunately walked in at the right time, otherwise somebody probably would have been injured. But they [staff] did not know about this fight; I don't know if anybody [staff] knows—ha ha ha!"[65]

Being together under one roof allowed residents to share, for the first time, the trials of being battered women and simultaneously facing the racism and classism of social services, and therefore to foster a movement for radical change that incorporated race, class, gender, and sexuality. Through their activism, advocates learned about and responded to race and class conflict by devising tools to undermine the tendency toward hierarchies between staff and residents. From the moment advocates began sheltering women in their own homes, residents impressed upon them that "battered women are *all* women."[66] Residents also revealed that every woman came for shelter with her own specific resources and challenges; for the shelter to be a safe space, advocates needed to understand the cultural contexts that shaped residents' needs. Some residents, like Beatrice during the shelter's second month of operation, quite vocally criticized staff for being "do-gooders," "liberals" who were separated from and "better than" residents.[67] Women's Advocates began to keep a residents' notebook in which residents could anonymously evaluate staff as well as bring up conflicts they wanted addressed. Activists throughout the country—including former shelter residents—expanded this innovative strategy over the next decade by incorporating battered-women's needs assessments, service evaluations, and ideas for solutions to design increasingly effective shelter and advocacy programs.

Staff perceptions of racism led to two critical policy changes by 1978. Women's Advocates created a statement against racism and prominently posted that statement alone on the kitchen wall: "As a reminder to the staff, residents, and visitors: Racism is a form of violence which will not be tolerated at the shelter." Racism incurred the same consequences as violence toward others in the shelter, namely, eviction. The introduction of this policy reveals an acknowledgment of racist conflict at the shelter, due entirely to residents' increasing willingness to discuss or write about their perceptions of racist dynamics.

Even more significant, after several grueling house meetings and staff retreats, Women's Advocates made a decision to hire and maintain a staff that proportionally matched the ethnic and racial composition of the residents—at that time, 35 percent women of color.[68] Women's Advocates' insistence on maintaining a staff that was ethnically representative of residents arose initially out of the understanding that many women of color did not receive enough support or "safety" at the shelter; the original white staff, by themselves, were not aware of the specific challenges that faced battered Indian, Latina, or black women or the resources available to them. The meetings that resulted in Women's Advocates' new hiring policy did not simplistically envision that a black woman would best be served by a black advocate, or an Indian by an Indian. Rather, the policy, hinting at the value of coalition, was instated to draw *more* resources to the shelter, and to hold everyone accountable for being aware of the specific "intersectional" issues facing women of color.[69]

CONCLUSION

In the early 1970s, advocates focused on creating a shelter, a place for women to get away from their batterers long enough to make longer-term plans. This became the focus of the movement through the 1970s. As Pat Murphy told the *Minneapolis Tribune* in 1976: "The reason women who are battered continue to be battered is that they have no place to go. At least one or two or three or five or ten houses like this are needed in every town in the country."[70] By 1978, having received unprecedented state and national recognition of battering, advocates were critical of all the bills and programs that provided only for more shelters and counseling. "The shelter thing is really a stop-gap remedy. We have to get to the point where women and children are safe in their homes and are not forced to leave," Marlene Travis, chair of the State Task Force on Battering, told the *Minneapolis Star*.[71] Each of several shelters in the cities received four to seven times more requests for shelter than they could provide, turning away hundreds each month.

But, while shelters may be a stopgap, the process of creating one of the first shelters, as a resident or staff-member, was a radicalizing experience and generated far-reaching changes in the social landscape. As Lisbet Wolf, current director of Women's Advocates, recalled of her work with Women's Advocates in the 1970s: "It was absolutely the most transforming thing in my life, absolutely unique. We had nothing to model ourselves after. We did things right and we made devastating mistakes."[72] Many residents' lives were transformed too, as they collectively experienced "the power of women in crisis trying to make changes."[73] The act of creating and maintaining a space that is safe for women challenged normative gender-, class-, and race-laden conceptions of domesticity and privacy. Alone of all exclusively women's spaces in Minnesota during the 1970s, Women's Advocates was not just open to, but *did* serve, *all* women; to best advocate for and shelter—and ensure the safety of—a diversity of women, Women's Advocates became a space defined by coalition.

The battered-women's movement was similar to earlier social movements in that it arose through community organizing that originated in spaces not usually represented as political, in this case, women's private homes. The collective nature of southern civil rights organizing, for example, depended on spaces such as churches and kitchens not only because that was where black people *could* gather, but also because those spaces were normatively imagined and represented as apolitical spaces. During the 1950s and 1960s, ironically, dominant media representations of civil rights organizing both reinforced a norm of domestic security and masked the community-based nature of the movement by dwelling excessively on private, nuclear-family (i.e., specifically depoliticized) scenes in activists' homes, to the exclusion of formal and informal meetings in churches and the importance of extended kin and community networks.[74] A decade and a half later, the battered-women's movement was uniquely constructive because collective political alliances were realized not only within, but also about, domestic space. Thus from its inception, the battered-women's movement necessarily *resisted* a definition of "home" as a privatized, nuclear-family space that masks both the politics of security (national or personal) and the power relations inherent in domestic norms. Instead, the act of turning a private house into a shelter created a home built of collective action, a place that directly intersected with the public and political world.

As Women's Advocates created specifically politicizing shelters, it generated a social movement that was successfully built through the involvement of a broad range of people—self-identified feminists, women who distanced themselves from feminism, Indian women, black women, Latina women, and white women across all classes. The movement, thanks largely to the involvement of formerly battered women, has proven itself to be highly flexible, adapting to (and surviving) the vicissitudes of federal and state funding, and also imaginatively tapping community resources to minimize violence against women in disparate contexts, from Indian reservations throughout the country (each with unique financial and political resources) to multiethnic or homogeneously white neighborhoods in urban and suburban settings. While Women's Advocates' early vision of a neighbor-run "house on every block" has not been realized, the persistence and success of the battered-women's movement can in fact be measured by increased community involvement, networks, and coalitions at local, regional, national, and international levels. The movement thus achieved a goal fundamental to most progressive movements that arose in the 1960s, in that it radically challenged the relationship between the personal and the public, political world. While nineteenth-century ideals about the separation of domestic and political realms lingered well into the twentieth century, the women's movement proved that such separation was no longer viable. The battered-women's movement did not shelter itself from the rough and tumble real world. Rather, the movement learned to create shelters that served a diversity of women across political, ideological, and cultural differences and also engaged the larger social world in the interest of radical change.

Notes

Acknowledgments: Epigraph: Sharon Rice Vaughan, interview by the author, October 24, 1996, St. Paul, Minn. Quotations from the manuscript collection of Women's Advocates (St. Paul) Shelter reprinted courtesy of Women's Advocates Collection, Minnesota Historical Society, St. Paul, Minn.

1. Most literature on the battered-women's movement credits Women's Advocates (in the United States) and Chiswick Women's Aid (in London, since 1971) with being "the first" and getting the movement rolling. But there were battered-women's shelters before them: Haven House in Pasadena (1965–72); Ingraham Volunteers in Maine (1967–69); Transition House in Boston, which began virtually concurrently with Women's Advocates, and, though it may have been less influential nationally, raised awareness of the problem and the movement in New England and the mid-Atlantic states.

2. The battered-women's movements in England, New Zealand, and Australia also created shelters, though the structural and philosophical underpinnings of shelters varied a great deal from place to place. The meaning of "shelter" thus also varies. For example, in New Zealand, shelters receive enough government funding to shelter women for six months—the length of time (according to social workers' calculations) it takes for a woman to rebuild economic and social stability for herself and her children. In the United States, most shelters are limited by government funds that stipulate that women may reside in a shelter for a maximum of two weeks (Eileen Hudon, interview by the

author, September 22, 1997, Minneapolis, Minn.; Sharon Rice Vaughan, interview by the author, October 24, 1996, St. Paul, Minn.; and Lisbet Wolf, interview by the author, April 15, 1998, St. Paul, Minn.). See J. Hanmer and M. Maynard, eds., *Women, Violence, and Social Control* (London: Macmillan, 1987); and R. Emerson Dobash and Russell P. Dobash, *Women, Violence, and Social Change* (London: Routledge, 1992).

3. Women have created shelters on a neighborhood basis (intentionally serving various ethnic communities), such as Casa D'esperanza in St. Paul, Casa Myrna Vazquez in Boston, and White Buffalo Calf shelter on the Rosebud Reservation, South Dakota. Women also formed coalitions and networks addressing needs of women of color, such as the Women of Color Task Force of the National Coalition Against Domestic Violence (1980); the Sacred Circle National Resource Center in Rapid City, South Dakota; and the Indian Women Grant Program, which innovatively works with individual Indian communities' specific configuration of resources (Hudon interview).

4. Todd Gitlin has represented the view that radical activism ended before the advent of women's liberation and gay and lesbian liberation. While Terry Anderson's generous volume is "about the Sixties" and does include brief mention of women's liberation, in it he suggests that "scars" are the most notable legacy of "the movement," which for him ended with Wounded Knee in 1973. Others repeat this view even when focusing on often overlooked movements, as in John Sayer's claim that the standoff at Wounded Knee in 1973 was the last breath of militant, radical activism (Todd Gitlin, *The Sixties: Years of Hope, Days of Rage* [New York: Bantam, 1987]; Terry Anderson, *The Movement and the Sixties: Protest in America from Greensboro to Wounded Knee* [New York: Oxford University Press, 1995], preface and passim; John Sayer, *Ghost Dancing the Law: The Wounded Knee Trials* [Cambridge: Harvard University Press, 1997]).

5. Linda Gordon, *Heroes of Their Own Lives: The Politics and History of Family Violence, Boston, 1880–1960* (New York: Viking, 1988); Elizabeth M. Schneider, "The Violence of Privacy," in Martha Fineman and Roxanne Mykituik, eds., *The Public Nature of Private Violence: The Discovery of Domestic Abuse* (Routledge: London, 1994), 36–58; Wendy Kozol, "Media, Nationalism, and the Question of Feminist Influence," *Signs*, spring 1995: 646–67. Challenging the *historiographical* reification of "separate spheres" and the dichotomy between "public" and "private," see Linda Kerber, "Separate Spheres, Female Worlds, Women's Place: The Rhetoric of Women's History," *Journal of American History* 75, 1 (1988): 9–39.

6. See Gordon, *Heroes*, 293–99. On the systems that accord property and privacy to males and not females, see R. Emerson Dobash and Russell P. Dobash, *Violence Against Wives: The Case Against Patriarchy* (New York: Free Press, 1979), and Carol Karlsen, *The Devil in the Shape of a Woman: Witchcraft in Colonial New England* (New York: W. W. Norton, 1998).

7. Kozol, "Media, Nationalism." Also see Elaine May, *Homeward Bound: American Families in the Cold War Era* (New York: Basic Books, 1988).

8. "The ideal of domesticity has grown only more powerful as it has become less a matter of fact and more a matter of fiction. . . . It begins to exert power on our lives the moment we begin to learn what normal behavior is supposed to be.

. . . In this respect, the most powerful household is the one we carry around in our heads" (Nancy Armstrong, *Desire and Domestic Fiction: A Political History of the Novel* [New York: Oxford University Press, 1987]).

9. Also see Gordon, *Heroes;* Schneider, "The Violence of Privacy." With respect to legal definitions, Elizabeth Schneider argues that "the interrelationship between what is understood and experienced as private and public is particularly complex in the area of gender where the rhetoric of privacy has masked inequality and subordination. The decision about what we protect as private is a political decision that always has important public ramifications" ("Commentary: The Affirmative Dimensions of Douglas's Privacy," in S. Wasby, ed., *He Shall Not Pass This Way Again: The Legacy of Justice William O. Douglas* [Pittsburgh: University of Pittsburgh Press, 1991], 978).

10. See Ellen Pence and Melanie Shepard, "Integrating Feminist Theory and Practice: The Challenge of the Battered Women's Movement," in Kersti Yllö and Michele Bograd, eds., *Feminist Perspectives on Wife Abuse* (London: Sage, 1988), 282–98.

11. On the relationship of this idea to women's liberation see Sara Evans, *Personal Politics: The Roots of Women's Liberation in the Civil Rights Movement and the New Left* (New York: Vintage, 1980).

12. Vaughan interview.

13. Early forms of antirape organizations were similar in their reliance on borrowed minimal space (see Nancy Matthews, *Confronting a Rape Culture: The Feminist Anti-Rape Movement and the State* [New York: Routledge, 1994]).

14. Women's Advocates received two VISTA volunteer positions to help staff the operation.

15. Women's Advocates to "Friends," letter seeking support for a "Women's House," March 11, 1973, Women's Advocates Collection, Minnesota Historical Society, St. Paul, Minn.

16. Hudon interview; Wolf interview; Bernice Sisson and Pat Murphy, interviews by the author, January 22, 1998, St. Paul, Minn.; Joan [no last name], *Women's Advocates* newsletter; Diane Nelson, "Battered Women Statistics Minimize Problem," *Minneapolis Elliot Park Surveyor*, August 1978. The pattern is also described in Del Martin, *Battered Wives* (New York: Pocket Books, 1977), and Dobash and Dobash, *Women, Violence, and Social Change.*

17. Bernice Sisson to subscribers to *Women's Advocates* newsletter, November 1976. A study released by the Community Planning Organization, Inc., similarly concluded that "physical abuse to women is a serious problem affecting not only the individual woman, but the entire community in which she lives. The problem needs to be acknowledged as a public rather than a private problem" (quoted in *Women's Advocates* newsletter, November 1976).

18. Susan Ryan, interview by the author, September 8, 1997. Women's Advocates developed this ideal while advocates were housing women in their own homes, beginning in 1972. See Sharon Vaughan, "Where It All Began," in NOW's national newsletter, *Do It NOW* 9, 5 (June 1976); and Women's Advocates, *Women's Advocates: The Story of A Shelter* (St. Paul: Women's Advocates, 1980). "McGruff houses" are houses that occupants designate as safe for kids should a child be lost or threatened. Occupants designate the house by posting

a McGruff sign in the window, and schools familiarize children with the Mc-Gruff logo.

19. Women Strike for Peace was another, earlier movement that confronted the U.S. political and military machinery based on the desires of "housewives" to raise healthy children. That movement was similar in that it rooted its very radical politics in values much upheld as traditional. In contrast, that movement "believed in" traditional domesticity and did not challenge the fabric of home itself, nor the behaviors socially permitted in domestic spaces (Amy Swerdlow, *Women Strike for Peace: Traditional Motherhood and Radical Politics in the 1960s* [Chicago: University of Chicago, 1993]).

20. The narrative runs thus: Dependence on public and private money caused the movement to lose control of the discourse about battering, the systemic analysis was lost, and public investment consisted of Band-Aid solutions addressed to individuals, including building more shelters (see Wini Breines and Linda Gordon, "The New Scholarship on Family Violence," *Signs* 8, 3 [1983]: 490–531; S. Schechter, *Women and Male Violence: The Visions and Struggles of the Battered Women's Movement* [Boston: South End, 1982]). Also see Nancy Fraser, "Struggle over Needs: Outcome of Socialist-Feminist Critical Theory of Late-Capitalist Political Structure," in Linda Gordon, ed., *Women, the State, and Welfare* (Madison: University of Wisconsin Press, 1990). This narrative is not foreign to Women's Advocates. Some former advocates credit the decision to seek public and private funding with causing the most radical activists to leave Women's Advocates before the shelter formally opened. Though Women's Advocates decided in June 1973 to seek funding from corporations to help pay for a house, Women's Advocates intended to maintain a commitment to community involvement: In May 1974, *Women's Advocates* newsletter argued: "Time is still being spent talking to foundations and funding bodies, and there is just so much of paneled rooms with benevolent ancestors staring from the walls that a humble applicant can take. The men with the button-down shirts will never be a substitute for the checks that come in far smaller amounts from you" (*Women's Advocates* newsletter, May 1974).

21. Women's Advocates, *Women's Advocates*, 5; Vaughan and Murphy interviews.

22. Women's Advocates, *Women's Advocates*, 6; Murphy and Sisson interviews; Lois Severson, interview by the author, June 15, 1998, Schafer, Minn.

23. Women's Advocates created bylaws in 1972 that granted voting rights to paid staff, volunteers, and "any adult who is being or has been housed by Women's Advocates." Amended June 6, 1975, article 3 of the bylaws stated: "There is but one class of member, and all members have voting rights. The membership equals the Board of Directors, and the Board of Directors equals the membership. An adult achieves and maintains membership status by participating in an on-going work group, and by indicating acceptance of membership status" ("Notes on By-laws meeting," January 9, 1973; March 19, 1975; June 6, 1975, Women's Advocates Collection, box 1).

24. Murphy interview. Lisbet Wolf (formerly Lisbeth Levy), while downplaying the number of advocates who sheltered women in their homes, recalled mainly that "the bigger and more complex a woman's problems were, the more

Women's Advocates wanted to work with her, and so invited all kinds of issues into their own lives" (Wolf interview).

25. Murphy and Sisson interviews.

26. Women's Advocates was at that time housing its phone line, as well as women, in that apartment (Vaughan, Ryan, and Severson interviews; *Women's Advocates* newsletter, August 1973).

27. Vaughan interview.

28. Ibid.

29. *Women's Advocates* newsletter, March 1974. While still using their own homes as shelters, advocates received requests for thirty to forty women and as many children each month, and generally could fill requests for fifteen to twenty women and the same number of children, who occasionally arrived with a cat or dog and her new litter (*Women's Advocates* newsletter, July 1974).

30. Vaughan interview.

31. *Women's Advocates* newsletter, August 1974.

32. Murphy interview.

33. Sisson interview. Despite advocates' best efforts, institutional trappings encroached on the home through physical alterations and policy. Sheltering twenty women plus children and occasional pets took a toll on the quaint, less durable furnishings. Advocates conceded that linoleum, institutional bedroom furniture, and commercial-grade appliances would "last" and ultimately keep the house in good repair (Murphy interview; Women's Advocates, *Women's Advocates*, 13.

34. Vaughan believed that Women's Advocates should have solicited donations for sheets so that women could freely take them: "Then we could keep sheets coming in, and keep 'em going out" (Vaughan interview).

35. In a six-week phone log for fall 1974, advocates entered more than twenty notes about men threatening residents and former residents. Entries included descriptions of men who tried to find specific women at Women's Advocates by following other residents to social venues such as bars and harassing them there, a man repeatedly threatening to kill one resident, and men breaking in to former residents' new apartments, causing those women to change locks regularly. Still, entries on male violence comprised only about 2 percent of all phone-log entries (Women's Advocates Collection, box 1).

36. Paula Brookmire, "Haven for the Battered," *Milwaukee Journal*, August 8, 1976; Linda Picone, "Battered Women: Haven Is a Help," *Minneapolis Tribune*, February 1, 1976; *Women's Advocates* report to R.H. Rowan, Chief of Police, City of St. Paul, September 30, 1975; *Women's Advocates* newsletter, September 1975 and October 1975; Vaughan, "Where It All Began"; Wolf and Murphy interviews.

37. Picone, "Battered Women." Also see Paula Brookmire, "Haven for the Battered," *Milwaukee Journal*, August 8, 1976.

38. Women's Advocates "House Policy," August 1975 (Women's Advocates Collection, box 1).

39. *Women's Advocates* newsletter, September 1976.

40. Murphy and Sisson interviews.

41. *Women's Advocates* newsletter, September 1976.

42. Murphy and Sisson interviews.

43. Residents' sentiments are drawn from the Hudon interview; Joan, *Women's Advocates* newsletter, January 1976; Brookmire, "Haven for the Battered"; an anonymous resident, "The Eye of the Storm . . . Thoughts of a Resident," *Women's Advocates* newsletter, November 1975; and Lois, quoted in staff diary, January 1976 (Women's Advocates Collection, box 1).

44. Joan, *Women's Advocates* newsletter, January 1976.

45. Brookmire, "Haven for the Battered."

46. Women's Advocates, "House Policy."

47. Vaughan interview. Bernice Sisson recounted a very similar experience that caused her to question the cultural context of discipline and violence (Sisson interview).

48. Murphy interview.

49. *Women's Advocates* newsletter, November 1976; Murphy and Sisson interviews.

50. Murphy, Sisson, and Vaughan interviews. First documented report of joint resident/staff efforts, *Women's Advocates* newsletter, June/July 1975.

51. *Women's Advocates* newsletter, September/October 1975.

52. R. H. Rowan, Chief of Police, and Wilfred E. DuGas, Captain, to Maryann Hruby, September 3, 1975, Women's Advocates Collection, box 2.

53. Maryann Hruby to Internal Affairs Department, St. Paul Police Department, September 14, 1975, Women's Advocates Collection, box 2.

54. R. H. Rowan, Chief of Police, and Sergeant L. T. Benson to Sharon Vaughan, May 16, 1975; Sharon Vaughan to the Department of Police, City of St. Paul, June 5, 1975, Women's Advocates Collection, box 2.

55. Women's Advocates to R. H. Rowan, Chief of Police, City of St. Paul, September 30, 1975; see also Women's Advocates to Department of Police, June 5, 1975, Women's Advocates Collection, box 2.

56. Yearlong report of Monica Erler, September 29, 1975, Women's Advocates Collection, box 1.

57. *Women's Advocates* Newsletter, October 1975. Indeed, it seems that the department held such "responsibility" within a notion of male protection and "permissible violence" in which officers newly adopted the use of force and threats against batterers who disturbed Women's Advocates. For example, a letter from Chief Rowan to Women's Advocates on September 20, 1975, mentions that Rowan talked to the parole officer of one of the men who had been repeatedly and sometimes violently harassing Women's Advocates without police intervention. Rowan explained that the parole officer "had a discussion with [the harasser] as a result of my request, and has informed me that he felt he had created enough of a threat that [the harasser] would curtail his previous activities" (Women's Advocates Collection, box 1).

58. In a September 30, 1975, letter to R. H. Rowan, Women's Advocates demanded "that any call from Women's Advocates regarding threatened violence be given *top priority*, and the response be *fast* and *considerate*. That the Grand Avenue Squad check [Women's Advocates] . . . throughout the night on an ongoing

basis, and . . . the foot patrolman's beat [is] to include Women's Advocates. That there be greater availability of police records and reports made by Women's Advocates. That Women's Advocates be allowed input into the next scheduled in-service training programs for the St. Paul Police Department, in order to make all the police officers aware of what we are trying to do." Also discussed a yeat later in St. Paul Police Department to Dorothea Scott of Women's Advocates, August 26, 1976.

59. Quoted in staff diary, selection reprinted in *Women's Advocates* newsletter, February/March 1976.

60. "Eye of the Storm."

61. Suzanne Perry, "Beaten Women Reach for Shelter But Little is Left," *Minneapolis Star*, September 19, 1978.

62. Murphy interview.

63. Hudon interview.

64. There was one woman of color—a former client—on Women's Advocates staff when the shelter opened. Residents of color, however, retrospectively represent shelter staff as "white," either because they had no contact with the shelter's only African American staff member, or because they experienced the shelter as a place that, nonetheless, felt "white."

65. Hudon interview.

66. Hudon, Vaughan, and Sisson interviews.

67. House log, Pat Murphy's notes, November 13, 1974.

68. During 1978, Women's Advocates records show adult residents: 64 percent white (193), 36 percent minority (108), with 24 percent African American, 6 percent Indian, and 6 percent Latina (Women's Advocates Personnel Committee notes, July 25, 1978, Women's Advocates Collection, box 1).

69. "Intersectionality" is Kimberle Williams Crenshaw's term; see, for example, her "Mapping the Margins: Intersectionality, Identity Politics, and Violence against Women of Color," in Kimberle Williams Crenshaw, ed., *Critical Race Theory: The Key Writings That Formed the Movement* (New York: New Press, 1995).

70. Linda Picone, "Battered Women: Haven Is on Help," *Minneapolis Tribune*, February 1, 1976.

71. Perry, "Beaten Women," *Minneapolis Star*, September 19, 1978.

72. Wolf interview.

73. Hudon interview. See also Carol Petkiw, a former resident creating a resident support group, advertisement in *Women's Advocates* newsletter, January/February 1976; anonymous resident letter to Women's Advocates, 1975 (Women's Advocates Collection, box 4); Kathy, *Women's Advocates* newsletter, November 1975; anonymous resident, *Women's Advocates* newsletter, April/May 1975.

74. On *Life* magazine's coverage, see Kozol, "Media, Nationalism," 151–53. On the spaces of civil rights organizing, see Charles M. Payne, *I've Got the Light of Freedom: The Organizing Tradition and the Mississippi Freedom Struggle* (Berkeley: University of California Press, 1995).

Jeffrey Escoffier

7   Fabulous Politics

Gay, Lesbian, and Queer Movements, 1969–1999

We're here, we're queer, we're fabulous.

—Queer Nation chant

[A]bout fabulousness . . . there's an issue of investiture, that you become powerful because you believe yourself to be.

—Tony Kushner

Perhaps the far horizon of lesbian and gay politics is a socialism of the skin. Our task is to confront the political problematics of desire and repression.

—Tony Kushner

IT IS one of the clichés of "the Sixties" that innumerable new subcultures and movements—black power, the student antiwar movement, the New Left, hippie communes, pop art and minimalism, experimental theater and dance, rock music, and the counterculture—emerged in opposition to the mainstream U.S. society. One of the most notable developments is the emergence of openly gay and lesbian communities, which have continued to grow and thrive up to the present. The political movement that both grew out of and recreated these communities is one of the most significant to emerge from the political turmoil of the Sixties.

In the 1980s, political analysts labeled the gay movement, along with the women's movement, the black civil rights movement, and other race-based and ethnic movements, a form of identity politics. Though it shared many characteristics with these other "identity" movements, it was also distinctive in a number of important ways. First, it was a political movement whose initial project was the legitimation of particular forms of sexual desire. Second, it was a form of identity politics in a particularly unique way—it was rooted in a shared identity that lesbians

191

and gay men were socialized into only as adults, but it also helped to shape both individual identities and the group identities that it represented politically. Formation of both personal and collective identities was central to the movement's political process, and they were forged jointly.[1] The "fabulousness" of lesbian and gay politics refers to this creative process, a process of "confabulation"—of empowerment and representation, of imagination and institution.[2]

The testimony of historians and anthropologists has shown that homosexual behavior has existed in every historical period and in most human societies. However, in most cases, men and women who engaged in homosexual activity rarely saw themselves as a particular kind of person distinguished by their sexual desire. Nevertheless, in certain historical periods and in some societies, certain individuals did identify their sexual desires for those of the same sex as their primary emotional-erotic preference.[3]

During World War II, many American men and women, away from their families and communities and amassed in wartime same-sex environments, discovered their sexual desires for those of their own sex. After the war, the first efforts to organize homosexuals were undertaken—in Los Angeles, Chicago, and New York—by war veterans and by members, acting privately, of the Communist Party.[4] In 1951, Donald Webster Cory published his groundbreaking book *The Homosexual in America*, in which he declared that "homosexuals constitute what can be termed the unrecognized minority. . . . Our minority status is similar, in a variety of respects, to that of national, religious, and other ethnic groups: in the denial of civil liberties; in the legal, extra-legal, and quasi-legal discrimination; in the assignment of an inferior social position; in the exclusion from the mainstream of life and culture."[5] The homophile movement that emerged from these efforts did not attempt to promote a coherent homosexual culture, but instead, it worked within the postwar liberal consensus to educate the U.S. public that homosexuals were neither criminals nor mentally ill degenerates.

In 1969, a police raid on a Greenwich Village bar called the Stonewall Inn provoked a series of riots that mobilized drag queens, street hustlers, lesbians, and gay men, many of whom had been politicized by the movement against the war in Vietnam.[6] There were already many signs that homosexuals were in the process of creating a civil rights movement, inspired, in part, by the black struggles of the Sixties, but the Stonewall riots of 1969 crystallized a broad grassroots mobilization across the country.[7]

The movement that emerged after Stonewall resulted from a clash of two cultures and two generations—the underground homosexual sub-culture of the 1950s and 1960s and the New Left counterculture of 1960s youth.[8] The gay culture of the Fifties and early Sixties reflected its bitter consciousness of the oppressive stigma against homosexuality in its flamboyant, irony-charged camp humor, but it was not political. Fifties gay culture was invested in protecting the "secret" of an individual's homosexuality and expressing it only in a symbolic or heavily coded way. Cultural resistance to hetero-normativity was expressed through cross-gender performances and sex role-playing. The new gay libera-tionists, however, had little appreciation of traditional gay and lesbian life of the 1950s and 1960s. Instead of protecting "secrecy" as the right to privacy, gay liberationists gave political meaning to "coming out" by ex-tending the psychological-personal process into public life. To "come out of the closet" was to do the very thing most feared in the gay and lesbian culture of the 1950s. By putting coming out at the center of its political strategy, the gay liberation movement tended to mobilize those people who felt more emotionally committed to living a full-time life as homosexuals rather than those who experienced homosexual desire only sporadically, or who experienced desire for both men and women.[9]

Gay activists believed that gay liberation had "ramifications and im-portance," as Dennis Altman, author of the pioneering *Homosexual Op-pression and Liberation* (published in 1971) suggested, "not only for those of us who are homosexuals, who are finding the courage and self-as-surance to come out in public, but indeed . . . for everyone else." Les-bians and gay men also saw the connection between sexual preferences and gender norms. In a forum on sexual liberation, Altman went on to comment how "our society denies the inherent bi-sexuality of all hu-mans. . . . [A]mong most people who identity themselves as heterosex-ual there is a very determined and calculated attempt to deny their ho-mosexual component and this leads to the quite grotesque cults of masculinity and femininity."[10]

In the period immediately after the Stonewall riots, the gay and les-bian movement did not at first focus on the question of identity, or even strictly on civil rights—though black civil rights was, most certainly, on the political horizon—but on sexual liberation. The sexual revolution had been underway since the early Sixties and that—along with the student antiwar movement, which had mobilized millions of Ameri-cans against the war in Vietnam—influenced how gay activists framed their political struggles.

The first political organization formed in the wake of the Stonewall riots was the Gay Liberation Front (GLF), named in honor of the National Liberation Front, the Vietnamese resistance movement, and as a gesture toward the unity of the struggles of blacks, the poor, the colonized in the Third World, and women. One early flyer, distributed in the Bay Area in January 1970, announced: "The Gay Liberation Front is a nation-wide coalition of revolutionary homosexual organizations creating a radical Counter Culture within the homosexual lifestyles. Politically it's part of the radical 'Movement' working to suppress and eliminate discrimination and oppression against homosexuals in industry, the mass media, government, schools and churches."[11] The political analysis that informed GLF's politics was often developed by those who had been active in the New Left. Many of the early documents of the gay liberation were modeled on the Port Huron Statement, Martin Luther King's speeches, and Herbert Marcuse's theories. In 1970, former Students for a Democratic Society activist Carl Wittman wrote "A Gay Manifesto," one of the founding documents of the nascent gay liberation movement. "By the tens of thousands," Wittman announced, "we fled small towns where to be ourselves would endanger our jobs and any hope of decent life; we have fled from blackmailing cops, from families who disowned or tolerated us; we have been drummed out of the armed services, thrown out schools, fired from jobs, beaten by punks and policemen."[12] The universality of homosexual desire was assumed throughout these early documents and underlay the gay movement's gestures of cultural resistance. GLF activist Martha Shelley warned heterosexuals that "the function of a homosexual is to make you uneasy. . . . We will never go straight until you go gay. . . . We will no longer allow you drop . . . the homosexuals in yourselves."[13] Sexuality was political. The Red Butterfly, GLF's "cell" of Marxist intellectuals, invoked Herbert Marcuse: "Today the fight for Eros, the fight for life, is the political fight."[14]

Embroiled in the bitter and highly charged atmosphere arising from consciousness-raising groups, from political battles over the support of the Black Panthers, the antiwar movement, and debates about primacy of homosexual civil liberties, and from an explosion of gay male sexual activity, GLF barely survived two years before completely falling apart and splintering into many other groups focused on more narrowly defined goals, such as newspaper publication, cultural projects, transvestite support groups, effeminism, radical lesbian feminism, gay Marxism, and civil liberties.[15]

SEXUAL REVOLUTION AND THE POLITICS OF DESIRE

The sexual revolution as it emerged in the Sixties was the historical culmination of processes begun long before World War II. The term "revolution" usually implies something that occurs rapidly and dramatically.
However, the time frame of the sexual revolution is much longer (it resembles the time frame of the "industrial revolution"). It is an immense
and contradictory process, often not very obvious, stretching out over
the life span of two generations.[16] The post–World War II sexual revolution radically altered the sex/gender system, as anthropologist Gayle
Rubin has called the system that organizes the biological capacities of
sex and gender differences into the cultural and social patterns that
constitute our lives as gendered and sexual human beings.[17]

The sexual revolution that followed World War II was primarily fed
by changes in the social forms that organize sexuality and gender relations—for example, invention of the birth control pill, large-scale entry
of married women into the labor force, decline of the family wage, increased divorced rates, or the emergence of a new consumerism. In addition, three major political-cultural shifts spurred many of the changes
in U.S. sexual mores: first, the explosion of youth culture (and the student political movements), which reinforced the thirst of young men
and women for sexual experience before marriage; second, the emergence of feminism and the women's movement at the end of the Sixties;
and third, the gay liberation movement's dramatic Stonewall rebellion
in 1969. Each of these developments spurred new forms of nonreproductive (i.e., perverse) sexual relations. In time, the sexual revolution
also provoked a profound and powerful counterrevolution—the religious fundamentalist Right—that continues to wage a battle against the
forces and over the issues (homosexuality, abortion, sex education, and
nonmarital sexuality) that ignited the revolution.

New permutations of sexual desire and gender behavior generated
what Jonathan Dollimore calls *the perverse dynamic* (similarly, Michel
Foucault spoke of the "perverse implantation").[18] Freud argued that
perverse sexual desires (i.e., all nonreproductive forms of sexual behavior, such as kissing or oral sex) were incompatible with a stable social order; instead, they must be transformed, through repression and
sublimation, into forms of energy more compatible with "civilized society." Freud believed that sublimated sexuality put extraordinarily
large amounts of energy at the disposal of social activities.[19] In *Eros and
Civilization*, published in 1955, Marxist theorist Herbert Marcuse devel-

oped the emancipatory potential of Freud's theories. He argued for the possibility of "non-repressive sublimation" which would allow for new forms of work based on nonalienated labor as well as the creation of new kinds of libidinal communities.[20] However, by 1964, Marcuse was increasingly concerned that advanced industrial society had made sexual liberation impossible—not through intensified repression, but by harnessing "de-sublimated" energies through increased productivity and mass consumption. Instead, the desublimated sexuality released by the sexual revolution was channeled into commercialized forms of advertising and entertainment, and institutionalized forms of aggression, and it was isolated from broader forms of erotic life.[21]

Both Freud and Marcuse assumed that society governed perverse sexual energies primarily through repression and sublimation. However, Michel Foucault argued that the proliferation of discourses on sex—through the exercise of power/knowledge—stimulates the development of certain sexualities. In the *History of Sexuality: An Introduction,* Foucault showed that late-eighteenth-century and nineteenth-century discourses (such as medicine and psychiatry) promoted certain types of sexual persons: the masturbating child, the hysterical woman, the Malthusian couple (who practiced birth control), and the homosexual.[22] Through the construction of the discourses about these "identities," the society is able to govern what would otherwise be an uncontrolled underground sexuality. Thus, sexual revolution and its discourses of sexual liberation, in Foucault's theory, both emancipate those who are stigmatized for their sexuality and facilitate the governing of the newly emancipated identities.[23]

For the last thirty years, there has been a long-standing contradiction at the heart of contemporary conceptions of homosexuality—between (a) notions of behavior or sexual acts and (b) categories of persons, social roles, or identities. This contradiction functions like a true antinomy: two equally reasonable but inconsistent conceptions of homosexuality. In the late Sixties and early Seventies, the political-cultural basis for organizing homosexual liberation vacillated between a "universalistic" conception of homosexuality founded on everyone's presumed bisexuality (what Herbert Marcuse and Norman O. Brown characterized as "polymorphous sexuality"), and an identitarian conception of homosexuals as a category of persons organized around homosexual orientation.[24] In contemporary society, sexual orientation or identity (hetero-, homo-, or bi-) has achieved a certain degree of self-consciousness; today many people "choose" their social identifications ("lifestyles"), if not their sexual desires. Because the perverse dynamic stimulates and disperses new sexual desires across the population without regard for already accepted sexual identities, those identities may fail to adequately represent certain people's sexual behavior.

These two perspectives had originally surfaced in the political differences between a "liberationist" ideology (e.g., Gay Liberation Front) and a "gay rights" strategy (e.g., Gay Activist Alliance, which split off from GLF) during the early years of the gay movement. In 1969, most gay liberationists believed that homosexuality was a form of sexuality of which everyone was potentially capable. Leading social theorists of sexuality like Freud, Herbert Marcuse, Norman O. Brown, and Paul Goodman all argued that human sexuality was polymorphous.[25] One barrier to the "universalist" perspective was that the stigmatization of homosexual desire and other "deviant" sexualities made it extremely difficult to mobilize those people politically just because they experienced such desires—largely because they infrequently acted on them and were often not comfortable with them or in many cases not even conscious of them. Thus the liberationist perspective was not able to provide a framework that could effectively facilitate the organization of "an interest group" among those who shared similar sexual desires. Finally, many lesbians and gay men, in addition to many heterosexuals, believed neither in bisexuality nor the reality of polymorphous desire. The gay rights or identitarian approach emerged as the dominant political-intellectual perspective because it was compatible with the U.S. emphasis on civil rights, and also because it provided a viable basis for community organizing and development in the tradition of ethnic group politics.[26]

The Identitarian Moment

Up until 1977, gay politics was a mélange of sexual liberation, civil rights activism, alternative social activities, and feminist conscious-raising groups.[27] Thus the lesbian and gay movement possessed a double consciousness of being a sexual liberation movement, as well as a civil rights movement for those whose primary erotic orientation was homosexual. Almost immediately after Stonewall and into the mid-Seventies, the gay movement was organized around the political act of coming out—of making a full disclosure of one's homosexuality. Coming out was the praxis, the basis for mobilizing collective action, but it exerted an enormous emotional pull because it was a form of both political praxis and personal revelation. It produced a profound and emotionally charged political/cultural "catharsis" (to use Antonio Gramsci's formulation) among lesbians and gay men as they made the transition from passive acceptance of the stigma to an active attack on it.[28] The movement's first years were organized almost completely around efforts to establish a supportive social environment to come out into—all sorts of community institutions were established to reinforce and nurture those who came out. Inevitably, such a stress on public disclosure had a historically significant and ironic effect because it gave political priority to the sexual identity of the person disclosing their homosexuality.

Almost from the beginning of the movement—during the tempestuous days of GLF—tensions emerged between women and men. Gay men were often no less misogynists than most heterosexual men. Lesbians were critical of the hothouse sexual atmosphere that soon surfaced in meetings and social events; gay men often remained indifferent to consciousness-raising exercises and criticism. Very early in the 1970s, impatient with gay men's lack of interest in women's issues, many lesbians left the gay organizations to focus on feminist politics.[29] Thereafter, at least until the early Eighties, there remained a certain separate and parallel development between lesbian social/political activities and those of gay men. Lesbian feminism was the most thoroughly developed political philosophy to emerge from the heady days of early feminism and gay liberation—it was both a theory and a politics of lesbian identity. It was first publicly articulated in 1970 in the pamphlet "The Woman-Identified Woman" published by Radicalwomen (some of whom had been active in early GLF) and elaborated more fully in Jill Johnston's *Lesbian Nation*.[30] Through a series of popular and provocative essays and books, lesbian feminist writers created an intellectual and political framework that offered bold and vigorous interpretations of feminist politics, pornography, rape, lesbian culture, and history.[31] Despite their ideological differences and social separatism, lesbians and gay men developed coalitions at several key historical junctures to respond to political attacks from political actors outside the lesbian and gay male communities.

The identitarian paradigm emerged triumphant as the dominant form of homosexual praxis when religious conservatives in Dade County, Florida, organized to rescind a recently passed gay civil rights ordinance in the Dade Country Metro Commission. Under the banner of Save Our Children, Anita Bryant, a popular singer, organized a campaign in May and June 1977 to put a referendum on the ballot to repeal the civil rights law in a specially held election. Save Our Children, as its name suggests, organized a campaign around the idea of homosexuals as sexual predators and seducers of children. "Homosexuals acts are not only illegal," Bryant proclaimed, "they are immoral. And through the power of the ballot box, I believe the parents and straight-thinking normal majority will soundly reject the attempt to legitimize homosexuals and their recruitment plans for our children."[32] Lesbians and gay men across the United States mobilized to helped Dade County gay and lesbian activists fight the Save Our Children ballot referendum. When the gay rights ordinance was overturned, activists in the major gay centers across the country organized the first in a series of candlelight marches that brought out thousands of lesbians and gay men.

In the footsteps of Bryant's Miami triumph, similar ballot referendums were organized by religious conservatives in St. Paul, Minnesota (April 1978); Eugene, Oregon (May 1978); and California (the Briggs Initiative, November 1978) that mobilized ever larger numbers of gay men and lesbians.[33] The tumultuous year and a half of lesbian and gay mobilizations finally led to a victory against the Briggs Initiative in California. The years 1977 and 1978 were watershed years for the gay movement, analogous to 1968 on the Left. The mobilization that ensued helped to institutionalize identity politics (à la ethnic identity) as the homosexual political paradigm in the United States. And for the first time, nationally recognized leaders appeared in the gay and lesbian movement. San Francisco's Harvey Milk, a member of the city's board of supervisors, emerged from these civil rights battles as the best-known gay political leader in the country.[34] In addition, gay Democratic Clubs (within the Democratic Party) became the primary political vehicles of the movement. However, the political struggles of 1977–78 also installed the religious Right as the gay movement's evil twin over the next decade and a half.[35]

In the period between 1977 and 1988, the theory and politics of "homosexual identity" emerged as an explanatory framework on the vernacular as well as the academic level. The 1970s saw the growth of fully articulated gay and lesbian communities—they consisted of a range of institutions from bars, bookstores, bathhouses, community centers, counseling centers, choirs and musical groups, small businesses, and concentrated real-estate developments to Chambers of Commerce—all of which helped foster the institutionalization of lesbian and gay identities.[36] During the Eighties, particularly among intellectuals, the primary debates on homosexual identity focused on whether a homosexual identity was socially and historically constructed or was, in some way, biological and transcended historical time period and cultural differences.

Although the Stonewall riots had originally involved black and Latino homosexuals and transvestites, as well as working-class gay men and lesbians, the movement that emerged to confront the backlash of 1977–78 took on an increasingly specific racial and class character—primarily white, college educated, and often middle class.[37] Gay and lesbian communities in the major gay centers—New York, San Francisco, Boston, and Los Angeles—consisted most often of young white men and women who were willing to leave their families and the places where they had grown up to settle in a large city where they would be able to lead an open and predominantly gay lifestyle. Discrimination and racism directed toward people of color existed throughout the gay community. Many blacks and other racial minorities might wish to participate in the life of the community, but they often found themselves excluded from the commercial establishments that grew up within the newly liberated gay communities emerging in the wake of Stonewall. Occasionally, gay activist groups would demonstrate outside a bar, a bathhouse, or some other commercial establishment that discriminated against people of color, but many gay men in particular failed to observe the picket lines (lesbians were generally more responsive).

Gay men and lesbians of color also faced racial discrimination in housing and employment and therefore did not have the same opportunities that white homosexuals did to live in the newly emerging gay neighborhoods. They often continued to live in the communities where they had grown up. "Sheer economic necessity and fierce white racism, as well as the joy of being there with black folks known and loved, compelled many gay blacks," bell hooks observes, "to live close to home and family. That meant however that gay people created a way to live out sexual preferences within the boundaries of circumstances that were rarely ideal no matter how affirming."[38] These circumstances discouraged lesbians and gay men of color from coming out—they never received the kind of political "protection" that white gay men and lesbians did. In addition, many people of color were unwilling to come out if that meant breaking with their families and communities.[39] "By separating, as we often do, race from class, gender and local community, we deracinate the very foundations of identity," Framji Minwalla has observed, thereby "removing the analysis and judgment of an individual's behavior from the specific understanding provided by cultural memories and heritages."[40] Without the political inclusion of race in the gay movement's agenda, coming out as the centerpiece of gay praxis ultimately failed to promote the politics of civil rights for all those who value their homosexual desires.

The lesbian and gay movement's identitarian project, in conjunction with its racial politics, created a dilemma that has beset the movement throughout its history—the identity's coherence requires *difference* in order to define itself and to establish its boundaries, but every attempt to regulate the identity's homogeneity provokes new differences within it that will be excluded. "Identity norms breed deviations," observed Erving Goffman.[41] Thus the lesbian and gay movements have generated an endless series of separatist groups and disgruntled claimants who clamor for inclusion in the "lesbian and gay community." From, approximately 1973 until 1981, lesbians and gay men created parallel but separate homosexual emancipation movements. Bisexuals, sadomasochists, queers, man-boy-loving, fetishists, drag queens, transvestites, and transgendered people were excluded, as they fought for inclusion, from the hegemonic definition of homosexual identity or community. At the same time, the implicit racial politics of gay identitarianism marginalized women and men of color. These struggles over the definition of identity and its historically contingent character made it almost impossible for nationally recognized leaders and organizations to emerge. Each fluctuation in the meaning of "homosexual" and in the membership of the community undermined leaders and political organizations modeled on earlier or different definitions.[42]

The interplay between culturally defined identities and the political struggles of groups included or excluded by the definitions make identity politics a form of cultural politics. The lesbian and gay movement of the 1970s had taken upon itself the immense historical task of helping to create, many times over, both socially and politically, forms of homosexual identity that had not existed before the movement emerged in the wake of the Stonewall riots. New formulations of the identities central to "homosexual emancipation" have proliferated throughout the last thirty years. Like all identity movements, it has experienced significant debates around the politics of naming (for example, colored, Negro, black, or African American), and since the fifties it has been identified politically as homophile, gay, gay and lesbian, lesbian feminist, queer and LGBT (Lesbian, Gay, Bisexual, and Transgendered). In addition to the more traditional forms of politics, the movement created the social context—through social and cultural institutions such as dances, consciousness-raising groups, hotlines, bookstores, newspapers and magazines, and publishing collectives—for individuals to organize their personal identities around sexuality.

THE RISE OF HOMOPHOBIC POPULISM

The rise of the religious Right was a reaction, in part, to the dramatic social changes of the Fifties and Sixties. Since the black civil rights struggles of the Fifties, the United States has experienced successive waves of paranoid politics focused on blacks, liberals, women, and, most recently, homosexuals—only the most recent examples of what Richard Hofstader has called the paranoid style in U.S. politics.[43]

The religious Right's mobilization against homosexuality had its intellectual origins in the antihomosexual interpretation of biblical texts, but its political mobilization arose in response to its belief that homosexuality contributes to the breakdown of the family. Open homosexuality is disapproved of, not only because it implies a nonreproductive sexuality, but also because young women and men coming out as lesbians, gay men, or bisexuals demonstrate that the family's control over youthful sexuality is threatened. Homosexuality is thus interpreted in "moral" terms—as a moral choice on the part of men and woman who fail to see the necessity of keeping religious laws. In addition, the religious Right's belief that homosexuality is a moral choice necessarily implied for many on the Right that reproductive sexuality, as the basis of the family, was also being rejected. Of course, most lesbians and gay men do not experience homosexual desire as a choice, and the belief of many religious conservatives that homosexuality is morally evil has been psychologically devastating to young homosexuals growing up in those families.

These intellectual/ethical beliefs might not have any political significance if the religious Right was not using widely felt homophobia as the basis for making their beliefs about homosexuality into law and public policy. There are two basic approaches that the religious Right has adopted to achieve its goals. Many of the most bitterly fought campaigns against lesbians and gay men grew out the religious Right's strategy to make it illegal to "promote" the tolerance or acceptance of homosexuality. The Right's appeal is ironic precisely because its argument actually violates a basic American political belief. Any campaign that targets tolerance of homosexuality on the basis of religious beliefs is a violation of *the separation of church and state.* The religious Right is attempting to turn the religious beliefs of fundamentalist Christian denominations into law.

The other strategy of the religious Right is to argue that homosexuals do not need civil protections and that lesbian and gay demands for civil rights are pleading for "special" legal protections that are unnecessary. Antigay conservatives do not believe that society discriminates against homosexuals. Usually a populist or class element supplements this argument, which suggests that gay men and lesbians are wealthier and better educated than most Americans and therefore do not need "special" protections. Both of these political strategies appeal to the large preexisting reservoir of homophobia among Americans.[44] Beyond the homophobia, these strategies also appeal to other populist sentiments: the distrust of "proselytizing" (the belief that lesbians and gays "recruit" young people), and the resentment against underground or "invisible" minorities that have economic power—attitudes resembling the anti-Semitic beliefs held by paranoid and reactionary political movements in the past.

Fundamentalist campaigns that stress the belief that homosexuals are asking for "special rights" obscure the fact that openly gay men and women actually suffer discrimination and denigration. As economist Lee Badgett has shown, lesbians and gay men usually earn less than their comparable (by age, occupation, and race) counterparts. Ironically, it is the religious Right with its conservative allies that has dramatically shifted the distribution of wealth so that less than 10 percent of the population controls almost 70 percent of the wealth.[45] These more general public issues are related to the political interests of the lesbian and gay communities in the same way that AIDS activism relates to national health insurance—these issues cut across a broad spectrum of Americans. They are not unique to lesbians, gay men, or other sexual and gender nonconformists. "Americans will have to recognize their gay family, friends, and neighbors as fellow citizens," Michael Nava and Robert Dawidoff have argued in their eloquent and forceful broadside, just to "protect their own individual freedom, not to mention traditional American democratic pluralism."[46]

Homophobic varieties of populism had gained increasing legitimacy through a series of political and legal battles since Anita Bryant's victory in 1977—the proliferation of antigay legislation at local levels, the 1986 Supreme Court decision in *Bowers v. Hardwick,* the enforcement of the closet in the military through the policy of "Don't ask, don't tell."[47] However, the Right's juggernaut slowed in May 1996, when the U. S. Supreme Court in *Romer v. Evans* struck down an amendment to the state constitution of Colorado that nullified any existing antidiscrimination ordinances in the state but also barred the passage of any gay and lesbian civil rights laws in Colorado. The decision by the U.S. Supreme Court to overturn Amendment 2 of the Colorado constitution marked a turning point in the history of homosexuality in the United States. The decision represents a subtle shift in public discourse—away from the acceptance that homosexuality is a category defined by traditional religious doctrine as an evil against which society is justified in adopting the severest forms of repression (which the Court had upheld in *Bowers v. Hardwick* just ten years before) to a definition of homosexuality as a quotidian trait or characteristic of human behavior to be treated in a socially responsible manner by lawmakers, judges, and citizens—a transition that takes lesbians and gay from the status of sexual outlaw to citizen.

U.S. society, which had for so long exhibited the complex historical intertwining of homoeroticism and homophobia, now has an explicit public discourse dedicated to the status of homosexuality in U.S. life. The public discourse links the conversations of ordinary men and women, gay or straight, to the institutional discourses of churches, to the legislatures of cities, states, and Congress, and to the Supreme Court—debating issues ranging from the rights of gay men and lesbians to serve in the military to the right of privacy (*Bowers v. Hardwick*), from the legitimacy of civil rights legislation (the Colorado decision) to the right of same-sex marriages. The public discourse is highly contested, defined by sexual latitudinarism as well as homophobic populism, but it is no longer a taboo subject of public conversation.[48]

The 1996 majority opinion in *Romer v. Evans,* written by Justice Anthony Kennedy, argued that the provision under consideration, which singled out Colorado's homosexuals, violates the U.S. Constitution's equal-protection guarantee that "[a] state cannot so deem a class of persons stranger to its laws," thus establishing a legal disability so sweeping that the majority of the Court concluded that it was otherwise inexplicable except for simple hatred—"animus," in the Court's language. As the Court implicitly noted, such language resembled that used to characterize the laws passed by the Nazis to disenfranchise German Jews.[49] The parallel was reenforced by the opening of Justice Antony Scalia's dissenting opinion: "The Court has mistaken a Kulturkampf for a fit of spite. The constitutional amendment before us here is not the manifestation of a 'bare . . . desire to harm homosexuals,' . . . but rather a modest attempt by seemingly tolerant Coloradans to preserve traditional sexual mores against the efforts of a politically powerful minority to revise those mores through the use of laws." Scalia's use of the ominous German term "Kulturkampf" suggests the long German history, from Bismarck to Hitler, of state-initiated "culture wars" against minority religious and cultural groups.[50] Both opinions acknowledge, in different ways, the ongoing culture wars that have placed homosexuality at the center of U.S. political life.[51]

The Supreme Court's Colorado decision of 1996 is one of the more recent episodes in the culture wars over homosexuality that have been waged continuously since 1977—before then erupting only intermittently, such as during the McCarthy scare in the Fifties. Together with the political effect of the AIDS epidemic that provided an entree into the governing process, homosexuality represents a historically complex intertwining of religion, politics, and culture. Gay and lesbian identity politics are only in part about the social status of self-identified homosexuals; they are also about the meaning of sexuality, gender, the family, and even community in our society.

AIDS AND THE CONTRADICTIONS OF IDENTITY POLITICS

The tumultuous Seventies showed almost unbelievable political and social gains for gay men and lesbians, but the decade also revealed enormous obstacles. Nevertheless, the gay community's most staggering setback was yet to appear. The complex syndrome of diseases that goes by the name AIDS was first discovered among gay men in 1981.[52] However, from the moment that the gay male community became aware of AIDS (it was first called GRID—"gay-related immune deficiency"), it triggered strong political responses both inside and outside the gay community. Gay activists realized immediately that an epidemic of a fatal sexually transmitted disease originating in the gay male community was politically explosive. It provided the potential for drastic political action against the gay community. It would allow homophobic conservatives to demonize homosexuals and offer the grounds for promulgating an antisexual morality.

As the number of deaths in the gay community grew exponentially, the inadequate response of federal and local authorities provoked increasing despair and anger. Soon gay men banded together to try to deal with the problems of the epidemic more effectively. In addition, it soon became apparent that the public health authorities were less than responsive to the epidemic than to previous fatal outbreaks, such as Legionnaire's Disease in Philadelphia in 1975. In late summer 1981, a group of gay men met at author Larry Kramer's apartment in New York City and established the Gay Men's Health Crisis (GMHC)—today one of the largest AIDS organizations in the country—to organize a medical–social service response to AIDS.[53]

Even before the human immunodeficiency virus (HIV) itself was discovered, the epidemiological evidence suggested that the disease was probably transmitted through blood and sperm. Doctors initially advised gay men to stop having sex. However, groups of activists in New York and San Francisco focused on education as a way to limit the growth of the epidemic. Safe-sex guidelines were developed, and organizations were set up to disseminate information about the epidemic and counsel worried people who feared exposure.[54]

The dimensions of the epidemic seemed to expand enormously—other communities were affected—Haitians, African Americans, hemophiliacs and other recipients of blood transfusions, and IV drug users; the incubation period seemed to be growing longer. The gay community's own organizing efforts, important and valuable though they were, were far short of the effort required to deal with an epidemic of such huge proportions.

By the mid-Eighties, gay and lesbian politics, though nurtured by an ethnic-like model of community, was increasingly unable to cope with the devastating impact of AIDS among gay men. It became clear that a more forceful political response was needed. In the fall of 1987, GMHC founder Larry Kramer invited a group of friends to create ACT UP (AIDS Coalition to Unleash Power) and launch a direct-action campaign against the federal government and the medical-industrial complex. Soon after, chapters of ACT UP sprang up in cities across the country. ACT UP revitalized a style of radical political activity that had flourished in the early days of the gay liberation movement—it was grass roots and confrontational and possessed a flair for imaginative tactics that captured media attention. It targeted the FDA to speed up the approval of drugs that combat opportunistic infections, pharmaceutical firms to lower the prices of drugs, the National Institutes of Health to expand its research on AIDS, and public indifference that hindered AIDS education and encouraged discrimination against people with AIDS from employers, landlords, and insurance companies.

The growing impact of AIDS in the African American and Latino communities forced activists to broaden the definition of their constituency. While ACT UP groups around the country primarily consisted of gay white men, the need to reflect the epidemiology of AIDS and to build alliances with other communities affected by the epidemic led to a politics that strove to be more inclusive and more open to coalition building. It was never a smooth process. Various groups and communities affected by AIDS sometimes had little else in common, or were also socially stigmatized groups with even fewer resources than the gay community, or consisted of vocal segments uneasy toward or disapproving of homosexuality. Strategically, AIDS activism increasingly experienced tensions with identity-based gay and lesbian political elites and their political agendas.

The politics of AIDS activism forced gay and lesbian activists into coalitions with activists from other communities and increased interaction with the federal, state, and local governments. AIDS activism transformed the relation between the lesbian/gay community and the state. Lesbian and gay community organizations dealing with AIDS got government funding and participated in policy making to a much greater extent than ever before. The AIDS movement has had a significant impact on AIDS research, public health policies, and the funding of treatment, care, and education.[55] In addition, AIDS funding created large-scale institutions with jobs and career possibilities that had not existed in the lesbian and gay communities before the AIDS crisis.

These economic and institutional developments had two major effects on the gay and lesbian communities. First, they encouraged lesbian and gay political institutions to engage to a greater extent than ever before with other communities, with governmental agencies, and with mainstream institutions. Second, they transformed the class structure of gay and lesbian leadership. The new jobs and career possibilities attracted a new generation of leaders who were upwardly mobile and educated at elite universities and colleges. This new leadership was often drawn from among those directly affected by AIDS, who in the past might have pursued careers along more conventional lines but took up AIDS activism to fight for their lives. The older generation of gay leaders had chosen gay political life as an alternative to mainstream career possibilities. But very early on in the epidemic, they were both physically and emotionally devastated by AIDS and were soon displaced by the new generation.

AIDS seriously decimated the gay male community but also forced it to reach out to other overlapping communities and social groups. The epidemic also seriously undermined the self-sufficiency of the community's cultural and economic institutions, so painstakingly constructed in the 1970s. As AIDS spread to black and Latino communities, the limitations of gay identity politics became ever more problematic. Almost from the beginning, the devastation of AIDS in the black and Latino communities grew exponentially. The countervailing demands of gay and lesbian identity politics and of AIDS activism produced a political situation that required a new political perspective—one that recognized a stable conception of identity, as well as the diversity and kinship of all sexual minorities, and the range of possible gender roles and of ethnic and racial identities. One response was the development of Queer Nation and a "politics of difference" that sought to build bridges with other marginalized communities.[56] But Queer Nation was short-lived and never really succeeded in building coalitions with communities of color. The other response was the development of an AIDS politics that dealt with HIV/AIDS in a generic way within communities of color—that is, without distinguishing between people with AIDS who became infected through IV drug use or men who were infected by having sex with other men.[57]

One historical irony is that the AIDS epidemic has facilitated the open participation of homosexuals in the process of government—primarily through the formation of policies dealing with medical and epidemiological research on HIV, in the development of HIV prevention, and in the treatment and care of people with AIDS. Once representatives of gay men and women were included in the formulation of policies, and perhaps even more significantly, once the details of homosexual sexual practices became the subject of epidemiological and prevention discourses, it also became increasingly difficult for political leaders to avoid confronting other issues raised by the gay and lesbian communities.

Queer and Present Dangers:
Sexual Politics in the Clinton Years

By 1990, the lesbian and gay movement had achieved a visible, though still somewhat marginal, presence in U.S. public life. The AIDS crisis in the previous decade had profoundly challenged the community, but ironically, it had also created political opportunities. Nevertheless, the persistence and changing character of homophobia remained a fact of life. The AIDS crisis had tremendous impact on a whole generation of gay men, many of whom had never been politically active or even interested in the gay movement. Many of those men and their friends joined ACT UP and the AIDS movement to fight for medical and social services for those dying of AIDS. The AIDS crisis and the rise of the religious Right's homophobic politics intensified gay men's experience of sexual stigmatization and thus provoked divergent political responses.

The New Right's homophobic populism had also created a crisis for those men and women on the Right who were themselves homosexual. Under attack from the end of the political spectrum where they had made their political homes, they resented the gay and lesbian community's insistence on coming out as an ethical-political act, its direct action tactics, the prominence of its sexuality (which AIDS had only heightened), and its flamboyant public displays (nudity, leather, and drag) at gay parades and other events.

The gay conservative strategy was a response, in part, to attacks on gay civil rights and AIDS policy from the religious Right. Nevertheless, gay conservatives have failed to understand how the religious Right's political project deliberately employs false and misleading representations and violates basic political guarantees like the separation of church and state. Instead, journalists Bruce Bawer and Andrew Sullivan, and political consultants Marshall Kirk and Hunter Madsen, proposed mounting an educational and public relations campaign—partly to undo the negative effects of what they saw as the gay subculture's radicalism and flamboyance. They wanted to focus on "the ignorance that makes straight people fear homosexuality and consider it a threat to American society." The gay conservative agenda would require a major reconstruction of gay/lesbian politics, in particular a rejection of identity politics in favor of assimilation into U.S. middle-class society.[58] Ironically, the gay conservatives sought to eschew the identity politics that created the enabling conditions for their own political emergence and their strategy of assimilation.

The election of Bill Clinton to the presidency in 1992 dramatically transformed the political terrain on which homosexuals fought for their civil rights and recognition for their relationships, and against social stigma and discrimination. The Clinton administration had come to Washington offering the most extensive social reform program since Lyndon Johnson's Great Society programs in the Sixties—an activist economic policy, national health insurance, and most significantly for the lesbian and gay community, a proposal to remove the ban against allowing openly gay men and lesbians to serve in the military.

During the election, Clinton had campaigned widely in gay and lesbian communities throughout the United States. Lesbians and gay men had voted for him and had contributed significantly to his election.[59] Thus when he came to office, he appointed openly gay men and lesbians to cabinet-level positions and the White House staff. Within weeks of his inauguration, Clinton had announced that he was going to lift the ban on homosexuals serving in the armed services.[60] The debate on homosexuals in the military was his administration's first major political battle. The adoption of the "Don't ask, don't tell" policy in 1993 was a major defeat—a defeat that hindered the Clinton administration in its conduct of defense and foreign policy, over and over again.[61] Few if any of Clinton's policies in support of gay and lesbian civil rights were successful or have endured. In the end, it appeared that Clinton was almost more dangerous as a friend than the religious Right had been as an enemy.

Despite the setbacks of the Clinton years, homosexual communities continued to develop—both politically and socially—and continued to find increasing acceptance and visibility in U.S. society. Yet, as legal scholar William Eskridge notes, "there are today more antigay laws than ever before." While direct action along the lines of ACT UP and Queer Nation has declined, political action increasingly focuses on lobbying and legal challenges. Organizations like the Human Rights Campaign, a lobbying organization based in Washington, D.C.; National Gay and Lesbian Task Force, also based in Washington; Lambda Legal Defense Fund, a public interest law firm; and the Gay and Lesbian Rights arm of the ACLU have become more prominent. In the 1990s, gay and lesbian political efforts—part of the unfinished business of U.S. democracy, as philosopher Morris Kaplan noted—were predominately preoccupied by three related issues—decriminalization of private, consensual homosexual acts between adults; protection of lesbian and gay men from discrimination; and recognition of lesbian and gay relationships and families.[62] It is the last of these—the civil union or marriage of same-sex couples—that has become the central political issue for gay and lesbian political and legal institutions, although the rights of lesbian and gay parents, co-parents, and foster parents is also a significant issue in terms of public visibility.

William Eskridge has argued that recognition of civil union and marriage for same-sex couples is the strategic centerpiece of gay and lesbian politics—not only will these social forms secure the tax benefits, health insurance, property rights, and parental arrangements that heterosexual couples enjoy, but also the politics of marriage will help create the political conditions under which lesbians and gay men will be able to achieve social equality.[63] It is the marriage issue that has brought about a fusion of lesbians and gay men who are political liberals (e.g. supporters of Clinton and Gore) and gay and lesbian conservatives.

Making same-sex marriage the political priority, Michael Warner has warned, is a grave political mistake. By making marriage the centerpiece, gay politics has abandoned its "historic fight against the stigmatization of sex."[64] Cleaning up the gay image in order to blend in, to be "normal," separates "sex" from "identity." It implies that homosexual erotic acts are not good. The political danger of separating sex from identity creates the opportunity for oppressive measures like the conservative Defense of Marriage Act that has been introduced into Congress, along with other policies built on a politics of sexual shame.[65] The military's "Don't ask, don't tell" policy, HIV prevention efforts, and urban zoning policies (openly gay or sex-oriented business) have been shaped by the politics of sexual shame that underwrites the separation. Since the adoption of "Don't ask, don't tell"—ostensibly intended to liberalize treatment of homosexuals in the military—record numbers of gay men and lesbians have been discharged.[66] Michael Warner, Michael Bronski, and David Nimmons have shown that the gay, lesbian, and queer communities have developed "an alternative ethical culture" that is ignored, unfortunately, all too frequently by mainstream and conservative analysts.[67] In many ways, the marriage debate resembles the tensions reflected at the beginning of the movement between liberationist sexual politics and identitarian civil rights, as they now resurface in a new configuration as political differences between a radical sexual politics and a liberal-conservative civil rights focus on marriage and assimilation.

Sexuality, Citizenship, and Democracy

The trajectory of homosexual politics from the defense of the sexual outlaw in 1969 to the well-behaved queer citizen of 2002 who wants to marry, have children, and serve in the military is one of the most remarkable social transformations in the period after World War II.[68] In the homophobic days before the Stonewall riots, lesbians and gay men were pariahs—stigmatized and excluded from open participation in civic and social life. However, in their capacity to pass as "straight," lesbians and gay men pay taxes, fight in wars, and vote in elections—they are citizens.[69] However, they lose, in effect, some of the rights of citizenship when they engage in homosexual acts.

In the late Eighties and early Nineties, "queer politics" celebrated the significance of the homosexual as the other, the different, or the marginal—reinforced by the tremendous influence of queer theory in the academy—and currently defines the community as LGBT (lesbian, gay, bisexual, transgendered). However, mainstream contemporary gay and lesbian politics has increasingly focused on the political recognition of citizenship—based primarily in the public interest law firms and electoral political organizations—and acknowledges the power of conforming and of passing, and the satisfactions of belonging and acceptance.[70] Inside the lesbian and gay communities there is, nevertheless, considerable ambivalence toward the campaign for citizenship, because the outlaw status of homosexuals is historically very significant. It originally spurred the creation of the gay and lesbian movement, stimulated cultural creativity, and helped to mobilize the building of lesbian and gay communities across the nation.

There is, however, yet another more fundamental and riskier irony in the increased participation of lesbians and gay men in politics and in the governing process. This increased political participation is enabled by, while at the same time masking, those disciplinary mechanisms and normative processes already in place in U.S. society.[71] Lesbians, gay men, and bisexuals continue to be shaped by the stigma on homosexuality—for example, shame of the body, the restricted psychological horizons, the corrosive secrecy, the performative skills of passing, fear of homophobic violence, unsanctioned relationships, truncated political rights—while using these disabilities as resources for resistance. Even the corporate effort to expand the lesbian and gay market that resulted from the growth of urban homosexual communities has a "regulatory" or "disciplinary" effect through the economic structuring of the psy-chological and physical needs that are satisfied by goods and services available in the "gay" market. In addition, social acceptance and the recognition of these political rights may well ensure the spread of vari-ous normalizing and regulatory practices. Certainly, it was one of Fou-cault's most bitter truths that every institutionalized form of political rights also enabled various disciplinary and normalizing processes. Yet it is only the active exercise of our democratic rights that allows us to re-sist, modify, or restructure disciplinary and normalizing mechanisms.[72] It is this complicated and double-edged process that has been charac-terized as "mainstreaming" by lesbian and gay activists. Like a struggle in quicksand, the effort to define political rights may result only in sink-ing further into a morass of normalizing discipline.

It is not possible to escape completely this messy and contradictory conception of civil life. No one can ever step totally outside the society in which one is raised—not even by emigrating can one escape com-pletely from one's socialization and language—nor is it necessary to ac-quiesce in society's gender and sexual norms and the stigmatization of homosexuality to endorse the social contract of one's community. Social life is riven by all sorts of crosscutting cleavages. There are no transcen-dent solutions to the ambivalence of identity—only the social structures of friendship, love, and solidarity, nurtured among the sexual minorities (homosexual and other) by the dialectic between perversity and com-munity.

In our society, political and cultural inclusion must be negotiated by complicated maneuvers linking the *building of communities* with *direct political action* in the context of *political alliances* with other social groups and movements. This triangular strategy of community building, direct action, and political alliance was conceptualized by the Italian political theorist Antonio Gramsci, who argued that, in the highly developed civil societies of European and North American market societies, oppo-sitional political movements must wage both a "war of position" (i.e., building communities) and a "war of maneuver" (direct action plus po-litical alliances) in order to resist hegemonic institutions and ideologies (challenging the heterosexual, male-centered, and pronatalist cultural norms and institutions that stigmatize homosexuality).[73] Building les-bian, gay, and queer communities to include the full range of economic, cultural, and political institutions will by itself never achieve political inclusion. It will probably always be necessary to resort periodically to grassroots politics to mobilize the lesbian, gay, and queer communities on particular issues and specific enemies. And until a majority of the population sees itself as "queer"—that is, as sexually unique and different—homosexuals and other sexual minorities will have to rely on political allies for mutual political support. Until sexual citizenship is achieved, gay, lesbian, transgender, and bisexual communities will negotiate the Gramscian triangle in order to advance toward an affirmation of sexual variety.

NOTES

Acknowledgments: This essay has benefited enormously from my many conversations with Syd Peterson on gay, lesbian, queer, and postgay politics and life. I also want to thank Van Gosse, James N. Green, Amber Hollibaugh, Syd Peterson, and an anonymous reader for their comments on earlier versions of this essay.

Epigraphs: Queer Nation chant from Alex Chee, "A Queer Nationalism" *OUT/ LOOK*, Winter 1991; Tony Kushner interviewed by Michael Cunningham, "Thinking about Fabulousness," in Robert Vorlicky, ed., *Tony Kushner in Conversation* (Ann Arbor: University of Michigan Press, 1998), 74; Tony Kushner, "A Socialism of the Skin (Liberation, Honey!)," in *Thinking about the Longstanding Problems of Virtue and Happiness: Essays, a Play, Two Poems, and a Prayer* (New York: Theatre Communications Group, 1995), 32.

1. Jeffrey Escoffier, *American Homo: Perversity and Community* (Berkeley: University of California Press, 1998).

2. I want to thank James N. Green for suggesting the term "confabulation" for the process of creative action through empowerment and institutionalization. See Hans Joas, *The Creativity of Action* (Chicago: University of Chicago Press, 1996), 196–209; and Cornelius Castoriadis, *The Imaginary Institution of Society* (Cambridge: MIT Press, 1987), 115–32.

3. David M. Halperin, *One Hundred years of Homosexuality and Other Essays on Greek Love* (New York: Routledge, 1990), esp. chaps. 1 and 2.

4. Molly McGarry and Fred Wasserman, *Becoming Visible: An Illustrated History of Lesbian and Gay Life in Twentieth-Century America* (New York: NYPL/Penguin Studio, 1998), 139–57; also Allan Berube, *Coming Out under Fire: The History of Gay Men and Women in World War Two* (New York: Free Press, 1990).

5. Donald Webster Cory, *The Homosexual in America* (New York: Julian Press, 1950), 120–21.

6. Martin Duberman, *Stonewall* (New York: Dutton, 1993).

7. Eric Marcus, *Making History: The Struggle for Gay and Lesbian Rights, 1945–1990, An Oral History* (New York: HarperCollins, 1992); Dudley Clendinen and Adam Nagourney, *Out for Good: The Struggle to Build a Gay Rights Movement in America* (New York: Simon & Schuster, 1999).

8. Escoffier, *American Homo*, 33–64; John D'Emilio, *Sexual Politics, Sexual Communities: The Making of a Homosexual Minority in the United States, 1940–1970* (Chicago: University of Chicago Press, 1983).

9. Escoffier, *American Homo*, 33–64, 79–98.

10. Dennis Altman, *Coming Out in the Seventies* (Sydney, Aus.: Wild & Woolley, 1979), 16–17. See also Dennis Altman, *Homosexual Oppression and Liberation* (New York: Outerbridge & Dienstrey, 1971).

11. Arthur Marwick, *The Sixties* (Oxford: Oxford University Press, 1998), 726.

12. Carl Wittman, "A Gay Manifesto," in Mark Blasius and Shane Phelan, eds., *We Are Everywhere: A Historical Sourcebook of Gay and Lesbian Politics* (New York: Routledge, 1997), 380.

13. Martha Shelley, "Gay Is Good," in Blasius and Phelan, *We Are Everywhere*, 393.

14. The Red Butterfly, "Comments on Carl Wittman's 'A Gay Manifesto,'" in Blasius and Phelan, *We Are Everywhere*, 388.

15. Terence Kissack, "Freaking Fag Revolutionaries: New York's Gay Liberation Front, 1969–1971," *Radical History Review*, no. 62, spring 1995. See also some of the documents collected in Blasius and Phelan, *We Are Everywhere*, 380–412.

16. Escoffier, *American Homo*, 33–64.

17. Gayle Rubin, "The Traffic in Women," in Rayna R. Reiter, ed., *Toward an Anthropology of Women* (New York: Monthly Review Press, 1975).

18. Jonathan Dollimore, *Sexual Dissidence: Augustine to Wilde, Freud to Foucault* (Oxford: Clarendon Press, 1991), 103–30; Michel Foucault, *The History of Sexuality: Volume 1, An Introduction* (New York: Pantheon, 1978), 36–49.

19. Sigmund Freud, "'Civilized' Sexual Morality and Modern Nervousness," in Philip Rieff, ed., *Sexuality and the Psychology of Love* (New York: Simon & Schuster, 1963).

20. Herbert Marcuse, *Eros and Civilization: A Philosophical Inquiry into Freud* (Boston: Beacon Press, 1955).

21. Herbert Marcuse, *One-Dimensional Man: Studies in the Ideology of Advanced Industrial Society* (Boston: Beacon Press, 1964).

22. Foucault, *History of Sexuality*, 103–14.

23. Michel Foucault, "'Omnes et Singulatim': Toward a Critique of Political Reason," in *Power*, vol. 3 of *Essential Works of Foucault*, ed. James D. Faubion (New York: New Press, 2000), 298–325.

24. Eve Kosofsky Sedgwick, *Epistemology of the Closet* (Berkeley: University of California Press, 1990), esp. 1–66.

25. Richard King, *The Party of Eros: Radical Social Thought and the Realm of Freedom* (Durham, N.C.: University of North Carolina Press, 1972).

26. Escoffier, *American Homo*, 1–28.

27. Ibid. Also see selections from one of the first gay newspapers in *Come Out! Selections from the Radical Gay Liberation Newspaper* (New York: Times Change Press, 1970).

28. Escoffier, *American Homo*, 58.

29. Clendinen and Nagourney, *Out for Good*, 85–105, 164–73.

30. Blasius and Phelan, *We Are Everywhere*, 396–99.

31. Escoffier, *American Homo*, 130–33.

32. Clendinen and Nagourney, *Out for Good*, 299.

33. The Gay Rights Writer's Group, *It Could Happen to You . . . An Account of the Gay Civil Rights Campaign in Eugene, Oregon* (Eugene, Ore.: Gay Rights Writer's Group, 1989).

34. David Jernigan, "Why Gay Leaders Don't Last: The First Ten Years after Stonewall," *OUT/LOOK*, Summer 1988, 33–49.

35. Escoffier, *American Homo*, 205–22. See also Chris Bull and John Gallagher, *Perfect Enemies: The Religious Right, the Gay Movement, and the Politics of the 1990s* (New York: Crown, 1996).

36. Escoffier, *American Homo*, see chap. 2, "The Political Economy of the Closet," 65–78.

37. Duberman, *Stonewall*, 167–280.

38. bell hooks, *Talking Back: Thinking Feminist, Thinking Black* (Boston: South End Press, 1989), 120–21.

39. Jose Quiroga, *Tropics of Desire: Interventions from Queer Latino America* (New York: New York University Press, 2000), 1–29, 191–226.

40. Framji Minwalla, "When Girls Collide: Considering Race in *Angels in America*," in Deborah R. Geis and Steven F. Kruger, eds., *Approaching the Millennium: Essays on Angels in America* (Ann Arbor: University of Michigan Press, 1997), 104.

41. Erving Goffman, *Stigma: Notes on the Management of Spoiled Identity* (Engelwood Cliffs, N.J.: Prentice-Hall, 1963), 129.

42. Jernigan, "Why Gay Leaders Don't Last."

43. Richard Hofstader, *The Paranoid Style in American Politics and Other Essays* (New York: Knopf, 1964).

44. Lisa Duggan, "Queering the State," in Lisa Duggan and Nan D. Hunter, eds., *Sex Wars: Sexual Dissent and Political Culture* (New York: Routledge, 1995), 179–93.

45. Lee Badgett, "Beyond Biased Samples: Challenging the Myths on the Economic Status of Lesbians and Gay Men," in Amy Gluckman and Betsey Reed, eds., *Homo Economics: Capitalism, Community, and Lesbian and Gay Life* (New York: Routledge, 1997), 65–72; and M. V. Lee Badgett, *Money, Myths, and Change: The Economic Lives of Lesbians and Gay Men* (Chicago: University of Chicago Press, 2001).

46. Michael Nava and Robert Dawidoff, *Created Equal: Why Gay Rights Matter to America* (New York: St. Martin's Press, 1994).

47. William Eskridge notes that "there are today more antigay laws than ever before" (see William N. Eskridge Jr., *Gaylaw: Challenging the Apartheid of the Closet* [Cambridge, Harvard University Press, 1999], 205, 362–72, and on *Bowers v. Hardwick*, 149–73). On the military's antigay policies see also Janet E. Halley, *Don't: A Reader's Guide to the Military's Anti-Gay Policy* (Durham, N.C.: Duke University Press, 1999).

48. Escoffier, *American Homo*, 223–228.

49. Eskridge, *Gaylaw*, 205–11.

50. Ibid., 14, 80–82, 294–95.

51. "Gay Rights Laws Can't Be Banned, High Court Rules" and excerpts from the Court's decision, *New York Times*, May 21, 1996, sec. A.

52. Elizabeth Fee and Daniel M. Fox, eds., *AIDS: The Burden of History* (Berkeley: University of California Press, 1988); Elizabeth Fee and Daniel M. Fox, eds., *AIDS: The Making of a Chronic Disease* (Berkeley: University of California Press, 1992); Douglas Crimp, ed., *AIDS: Cultural Analysis, Cultural Activism* (Cambridge: MIT Press, 1988); John Manuel Andriote, *Victory Deferred: How AIDS Changed Gay Life in America* (Chicago: University of Chicago Press, 1999).

53. Larry Kramer, *Reports from the Holocaust: The Making of an AIDS Activist* (New York: St. Martin's Press, 1989).

54. Jeffrey Escoffier, "The Invention of Safer Sex: Vernacular Knowledge, Gay Politics, and HIV Prevention," *Berkeley Journal of Sociology* 43 (1998–99): 1–30.

55. Steven Epstein, *Impure Science: AIDS, Activism, and the Politics of Knowledge* (Berkeley: University of California Press, 1996).

56. Allan Berube and Jeffrey Escoffier, "Reflections on Queer Nation," reprinted in Escoffier, *American Homo*, 202–4.

57. Cathy J. Cohen, "Contested Membership: Black Gay Identities and the Politics of AIDS," in Steven Seidman, ed., *Queer Theory/Sociology* (Cambridge, Mass.: Blackwell, 1996), 362–94.

58. Bruce Bawer, *A Place at the Table: The Gay Individual in American Society* (New York: Poseidon Press, 1993); Andrew Sullivan, *Virtually Normal: An Argument about Homosexuality* (New York: Knopf, 1995); Marshall Kirk and Hunter Madsen, *After the Ball: Will America Conquer Its Fear and Hatred of Gays in the Nineties?* (New York: Doubleday, 1989). See also the gay conservative website, the Independent Gay Forum, at www.indegayforum.org

59. See Mark W. Hertzog, *The Lavender Vote: Lesbians, Gay Men, and Bisexuals in American Electoral Politics* (New York: New York University Press, 1996); and Robert W. Bailey, *Gay Politics, Urban Politics: Identity and Economics in an Urban Setting* (New York: Columbia University Press, 1999), 97–137, esp. 114.

60. Halley, *Don't*, 1–5.

61. On the impact of the gay question on Clinton's foreign and defense policies see David Halberstam, *War in a Time of Peace: Bush, Clinton, and the Generals* (New York: Scribner, 2001), 204–7.

62. See Morris B. Kaplan, *Sexual Justice: Democratic Citizenship and the Politics of Desire* (New York: Routledge, 1997), 3, 14–17.

63. William N. Eskridge Jr., *Equality Practice: Civil Unions and the Future of Gay Rights* (New York: Routledge, 2002).

64. Michael Warner, *The Trouble with Normal: Sex, Politics, and the Ethics of Queer Life* (New York: Free Press, 1999), viii.

65. Escoffier, *American Homo*, 186–228; Kushner, "A Socialism of the Skin," 19–32.

66. Between 1982 and 1994, there was a decline every year in the number of people discharged for homosexuality. However, since the '"Don't ask, don't tell" policy was instituted, such discharges have gone up dramatically (see Cass

218 JEFFREY ESCOFFIER

R. Sunstein, "At Ease," review of *Don't: A Reader's Guide to the Military's Anti-Gay Policy,* by Janet E. Halley, *New Republic,* September 6, 1999, 41–45).

67. Warner, *The Trouble with Normal,* 41–80; see also Michael Bronski, *The Pleasure Principle: Sex, Backlash, and the Struggle for Gay Freedom* (New York: St. Martin's Press, 1998); David Nimmons, *The Soul beneath the Skin: The Unseen Hearts and Habits of Gay Men* (New York: St. Martin's Press, 2002).

68. For an excellent exploration of the theoretical issues relating to sexuality and citizenship see Kaplan, *Sexual Justice,* 1–9, 207–38.

69. Sarah Schulman, *My American History: Lesbian and Gay Life during the Reagan/Bush Years* (New York: Routledge, 1994).

70. Escoffier, "Inside the Ivory Closet" and "Under the Sign of the Queer," reprinted in Escoffier, *American Homo,* 104–17, 173–85.

71. Foucault, in *The History of Sexuality,* repeatedly addresses this question. For another exploration of this theme in early Greek and Christian discourse see Foucault, "Omnes et Singulatim," and Michel Foucault, *Discipline and Punish: The Birth of the Prison* (New York: Vintage Books, 1979).

72. Foucault, "Omnes et Singulatim," 307–11.

73. Antonio Gramsci, *Selections from the Prison Notebooks* (New York: International Publishers, 1971), 229–40, 245–64.

Christopher Capozzola

8   A Very American Epidemic

*Memory Politics and Identity Politics
in the AIDS Memorial Quilt, 1985–1993*

DURING A gay protest march in San Francisco in November 1985, local activist Cleve Jones asked participants to carry placards bearing the names of people they knew who had died of AIDS. Protesters then posted the names on a wall of the San Francisco Federal Building, and in surveying them, Jones says he was reminded of a quilt. Soon thereafter, in grief over the death of a friend, Jones made the first panel of what was to become the AIDS Memorial Quilt, whose 44,000 panels now bear witness to the memories of some of the 468,000 people in the United States who have already died of AIDS.[1]

But in 1988, just three years after the AIDS Memorial Quilt was born at a political demonstration, Cleve Jones, then acting as the executive director of the Names Project Foundation, told reporters that "we're completely non-political; we have no political message at all." Jones's attempt to distance the Names Project from politics reveals the complexities of political culture and political activism in the 1980s, and encourages us to examine memory politics, cultural politics, and identity politics together with the issue-oriented, interest-group activism that is often assumed to encompass the full definition of politics. What kind of politics did the AIDS Quilt envision in its design, and what kind of politics did it embody in its practices?[2]

In its first decade, the AIDS epidemic disproportionately affected particular social groups that often found existing cultural forms for mourning unable—or unwilling—to represent the emerging crisis. In turn, communities responded to AIDS by developing new cultural products that could accommodate the urge to memorialize and mourn those who

Reprinted from Christopher Capozzola, "A Very American Epidemic: Memory Politics and Identity Politics in the AIDS Memorial Quilt, 1985–1993," *Radical History Review,* 82 (Winter 2002): 91–109. Copyright 2002 by MARHO: The Radical Historians Organization, Inc.

had died. These were particularly visible among urban gay men, then just emerging from the hotly contested battles of "personal politics" in the late 1960s and 1970s. Mourning that might have been private and cultural took place in the midst of an activism that had made personal issues into the stuff of politics. These categories worked as opposites at the same time that the boundaries between them were consistently blurred. Creations of cultural meaning, like the AIDS Memorial Quilt, intended as acts of personal memory and collective mourning, were drafted into political battles and affirmed as instances of militancy. Long before Cleve Jones stood in front of the San Francisco Federal Building, culture and memory were already bound up with the political in the public response to the AIDS epidemic.[3]

From its outset, the constituency of the AIDS Memorial Quilt was always an issue of controversy. The Names Project made extensive use of what its founders called "traditional American" symbolism in an effort to reach out to "mainstream" America's hearts and pocketbooks. Names Project founders sought to demonstrate that the disease was, indeed, as Jones claimed, "a very American epidemic," or to prove, as another Names Project document put it, that "America has AIDS."[4] The attempt to nationalize a global epidemic that had disproportionately struck segments of a national population embodied some obvious tensions, but it can best be understood within the overlapping contexts of nationalism and identity politics in the 1980s.

The Names Project voiced its claim to national inclusion at a moment in U.S. political culture when the power to define Americanism rested primarily with conservatives who were hostile to all people with AIDS and gay men in particular. The Names Project was one of many efforts to challenge that cultural power in the language of Americanism itself, insisting that active and caring national responses to AIDS and people who had the disease were not fundamental departures from U.S. traditions in the political and memorial realms.[5]

This reworking of U.S. national identity had a radical edge at a particular moment in history, but its limits quickly became apparent. Although Jones repeatedly acknowledged the Quilt's origin as a memorial and political tool "by gay men and for gay men," he and his supporters recognized early on that the demographics of the AIDS epidemic were more encompassing. Responding to activism by women with AIDS and in communities of color that were also hit hard by AIDS, the Names Project worked throughout the late 1980s to make the Quilt more inclusive of race, gender, class, and sexuality.[6]

But the AIDS Quilt was never just about culture and memory. It was also intended as a tool of political mobilization and a weapon in the battle for access to economic resources that could be used in the fight against AIDS. Its use of the language of Americanism and its claim on inclusion was most closely connected to activism in the early years of the epidemic, particularly around its first public display at the 1987 National March on Washington for Lesbian and Gay Rights. But from the very beginning, radical activists from groups such as Queer Nation and the AIDS Coalition to Unleash Power (ACT UP) raised questions about the Quilt's inclusiveness and the political limits of its focus on grief and memory.

There were many tensions: between the Quilt's private power and public voice; between its gay and its American identities; between cultural politics and the politics of economic distribution. Despite all its weaknesses, despite all its limits, during the years from 1985 to the mid-1990s, the Quilt managed to resolve those tensions in positive ways. The form of the memorial mattered a great deal: Its creation, display, and ultimate meaning were radically inclusive, and its framework of memory was consistently democratic in ways that could encompass its multiple constituencies and their varying definitions of politics.[7]

AIDS AND THE POLITICS OF MEMORY

In 1981, there were just over three hundred cases of AIDS reported worldwide. United Nations officials estimated in December 2002 that 27.9 million people have died of AIDS since that time, and more than 42 million people are currently infected with HIV. While AIDS had clearly reached global epidemic proportions by the mid-1980s, the initial pattern of its devastation in the United States and Western Europe seemed limited, most notably to gay men and people who used intravenous drugs. Existing social stigmatization of these groups combined with and was intensified by a lack of knowledge of the disease's causes and methods of transmission, creating a nationwide epidemic of fear in the early 1980s.[8]

In a culture of stigma, fear, and discrimination, people with AIDS often chose to be silent about their illness, contributing to difficulties in both personal and collective commemoration. Many early victims of AIDS refused to be identified as such in their obituaries, and gay friends and lovers were often excluded by the deceased's families from funeral services and burials. Even when conventional methods of mourning were available, they were often insufficient to cope with the epidemic nature of the disease. As one person put it, "Who the hell would think that you'd go to 15 funerals in 19 months?"[9]

The dispersal of recently urbanized gay men—in the return of many to spend their dying days with family and in the literal dispersal of ashes rather than interment in cemeteries—acted to obscure the collective nature of the epidemic even further. For Cleve Jones, this retreat into silence was dangerous. "I felt that we lived in this little ghetto on the West Coast which would be destroyed without anyone in the rest of the world even noticing. I knew we needed a memorial."[10] Jones was motivated to overcome the silence and willful forgetting of AIDS that characterized conventional frameworks of memory in the early years of the epidemic. "I was obsessed by the idea of evidence. . . . I felt that if there were a field of a thousand corpses, people would be compelled to act. . . . I wanted to create evidence [of AIDS deaths] and by extension create evidence of government failure."[11]

The origins story of the AIDS Memorial Quilt raises complex questions about the practice of cultural politics and the political nature of memory in the early years of the AIDS epidemic. Recent scholarship in history, anthropology, and cultural studies argues that the creation of memory as a social practice helps to shape the collective identities of groups. Nowhere is this process easier to examine than in the construction of monuments and memorials, deliberately conceived as public acts of memory.[12]

The process of memory formation in social contexts has two distinct yet interrelated elements: that of the commemorative and that of the monumental. The archetype of the commemorative in modern Western culture is the gravestone: It is directed primarily at the past and seeks to testify to, record, and document the loss of a person or the passing of an event. Its enactment is primarily, but never fully, private and individual. The monumental function of memory, whose analogous archetype is the monument, is aimed primarily at the future and seeks to interpret loss or passing and put it to contemporary or future political uses so that, in the words of Abraham Lincoln's Gettysburg Address, "these dead shall not have died in vain." While it speaks to individual and private concerns, this function is self-consciously public. All cultural memory work embodies both aspects, even when some attempt to deny or play down the presence of one of the two forms of memory. Like the Vietnam Veterans Memorial, to which it has often been compared, the AIDS Memorial Quilt represents a relatively unique memorializing tactic in which the commemorative and political functions of monuments are densely intertwined. This linkage holds the key to the Quilt's pluralist politics.

The AIDS Quilt performs the commemorative function of memorials through its creative design. Each cloth panel measures three feet by six feet. Eight panels, chosen for aesthetic considerations, theme, or common geographical origin, are then sewn together to make a larger panel that is attached to other groups of eight to fit the capacity requirements of a display space. There are currently more than 84,000 names recorded in the 44,000 panels of the Quilt, representing about 18 percent of AIDS deaths in the United States, albeit just a fraction of the estimated 29.7 million AIDS deaths worldwide. The creation of panels is highly egalitarian in nature. Anyone—family, friends, strangers, or even people with AIDS themselves—can make a panel; in fact, individuals can be memorialized in more than one panel. No panel that meets the necessary size specifications is rejected, emphasizing the AIDS Quilt's refusal to place limits on either the expressive content of the memorial or its eventual interpretation.[13]

The AIDS Quilt creates an alternative site of memory for many who have been excluded from traditional means of mourning. Understandably, then, it frequently resembles those forms, in particular the cemetery: Formal names and the record of birth and death dates often accompany religious symbols such as crosses, doves, Stars of David, and figures of Our Lady of Guadalupe. Elaborate rituals also accompany its display, which begins with an intricately choreographed unfolding conducted by white-clad Quilt volunteers, while others publicly read the names of those memorialized on the Quilt. The intonation of names is central to the AIDS Quilt's aim of breaking through the silences that surround people who have died of the disease. As one Quilt viewer has written: "Think of the personal engagement that such a rigorous, simultaneous structure evokes from all who participate [in the reading of names]. . . . At its end, I finally comprehend what the Names Project means, why names must be spoken."[14]

The AIDS Quilt gives a voice to the dead, but it also records the lives and emotions of the panelmakers as well. The Quilt's interactive atmosphere is furthered through the inclusion of blank "signature panels" and markers and pens, which allow viewers to write messages and responses to the Quilt. Here, the audience literally inscribes its interpretations onto the monument itself, and these inscriptions become part of the symbolic material that others ultimately use in interpreting the memorial. The blank panels contribute to the communal participation in the formation of meaning, especially when debates are triggered by condemnations of homosexuality or by provocative statements about the Quilt's relation to political activism.[15]

The AIDS Quilt's emphasis on the people who are commemorated in it—their lives and their deaths depicted in the Quilt itself—has made it difficult for the 14.5 million people who have viewed the Quilt to ignore it or make it into a nebulous abstraction. As one viewer has written: "There is no viewing distance from which viewers confront the monument in its entirety; the Quilt's relentless emphasis on the dead necessitates our interaction with individuals."[16] Instead of offering its viewers a symbolically empty screen upon which they project their individual interpretations and recollections, the AIDS Quilt provides a proliferation of symbolic material that onlookers themselves must make sense of by participating in the memorial. "No one tells the viewer where to start, finish, or pay particular attention. Nor does it require of the viewer anything like an 'appropriate' response. For despite the enormous grief that inspired and attends it, tackiness and camp also play their irrepressible roles—the carnival always interrupts the wake."[17]

What is missing is not interpretive material, but interpretive hierarchy. Rather than a monument that provides viewers with an answer to political problems, the AIDS Quilt simply poses the age-old question of politics—what is to be done? The inescapability of commemoration is used to make the AIDS Quilt's political function equally inescapable. Through the monument's cultural memory work, we become part of the memorial, and our enclosure within the AIDS Quilt implicates us in the events—both private and public—that it commemorates.

Here we must consider the relationship between individual and collective memory, for it is the formation of collective identity that is at the heart of the AIDS Quilt's radically inclusive and democratic take on the complexities of identity politics in the 1980s. While some individual panels make explicit reference to religious, racial, or ethnic identity or employ traditional U.S. symbols (such as the eagle or the flag), and others are explicit in their references to gay rights activism and sexual liberation, most of the panels in the Quilt resist reduction into social or political categories. More typically, they record each individual through unique representations of hobbies, family, and love relationships.

Through this process, the people memorialized in the Quilt are commemorated as unforgettable individuals embedded in social relationships rather than statistical representations of forgettable risk groups. As Quilt volunteer Jack Bier put it: "The quilt helps [viewers] to start putting a story together. People do not generally get a story when they are taught about AIDS; they just get the statistics. But the quilt brings out the stories."[18]

But this process, while highly individualized, also creates a collectivity, one which is then mobilized as a political body in a complex and contingent manner as the community created by the AIDS Quilt is called upon to confront the political structures that have made its formation necessary in the first place. The Quilt embodies a consciousness not just of the political *nature* of commemoration, but of the political *potential* of these acts as well. Individual memory itself is a political act in the cultural work of the AIDS Quilt, but in gathering a collectivity, the Quilt also creates political responsibilities.

BECOMING AMERICAN

Cleve Jones often tells of how he learned to quilt from his grandmother, evoking a heartwarming image of cross-generational bonding that could grace a Norman Rockwell cover of the *Saturday Evening Post*. Quilting in America has always been a cultural practice filled with divergent social meanings, from the calico quilts of travelers on the Oregon Trail to the freedom quilts that marked the way stations of the Underground Railroad. Quilts have played a role in American collective memory and in the nostalgia and romance of U.S. national mythology. But Jones's vision is largely an invented tradition. For most of U.S. history, quilting has been ignored as just one among the many chores of the nation's women. By the mid–twentieth century, with mass-produced household items like bedspreads cheaply available to all Americans, participation in quilting, particularly in group settings such as quilting bees, had drastically declined.[19]

The 1970s and 1980s saw a revival of quilting from two very different points of origin. Feminists and women's historians recovered the history of women's quilting work, while Reagan-era cultural nostalgia brought a new interest in U.S. traditions of domesticity. In a culture with rapidly shifting attitudes toward death, these developments were linked to changes in the use of cultural creativity in therapeutic and grieving situations. The odd convergence of these trends, and not solely the accidental arrangement of placards on a wall, ensured that the most famous memorial to AIDS took the form of a patchwork quilt.[20]

Jones and his colleagues have always acknowledged this and have often spoken of the Quilt's dialogue with U.S. symbolism. In the original design of the AIDS Quilt and in its accompanying literature, the Names Project deliberately attempted to cast the Quilt in specifically American terms in order to argue for the inclusion of AIDS into an arena of national concern. Cleve Jones explained that he fervently wished to "recapture traditional American values and apply them to [AIDS] too."[21] But what were those values? In a recent interview, Jones's reflections revealed both his hopes and his assumptions: "This is such a warm, comforting, middle-class, middle-American symbol. Every family has a quilt; it makes them think of their grandmothers. That's what we need: We need all these American grandmothers to want us to live, to be willing to say that our lives are worth defending."[22]

Jones's own frustration at many Americans' avoidance of the AIDS crisis motivated these claims for inclusion, but they were also based on his belief that the gay community was not capable of responding to AIDS on its own. In the political competition for the allocation of economic and cultural resources to battle AIDS, the relationships between Jones's grandmothers, their grandsons, and their political representatives would play a key role.

The attempt to describe AIDS activism and people with AIDS with an American cultural vocabulary at the historical moment of the mid-1980s may seem somewhat peculiar, given the ways that gay identity spanned national boundaries and the global nature of the AIDS epidemic, visible even then. Many criticized the Quilt for precisely these reasons, as well as for the "middle-class, middle-American" assumptions of its inventor. But we should think about these claims to nationhood not as rejections of gay identity politics or as evasions of the global implications of AIDS, but—with a sensitivity to the historical contexts out of which they arose—as challenges to a discourse of nation and family that was particularly prevalent in the 1980s.

Claims for national inclusion had radical implications, given the seemingly "un-American" nature of the disease in the cultural contexts of the early 1980s. The post-1960s counterculture and the sexual revolution had many opponents, but despite occasional victories like Anita Bryant's 1977 Save Our Children Campaign in Florida, members of

"family values" groups seemed to pose little threat to the gay libera-
tionists of San Francisco's Castro District and New York's Greenwich
Village. By 1981, conservatives were in control, and they had a friend in
the White House. It was against this cultural backdrop that the Quilt's
most public displays were set, and to great effect. Confrontations with
national symbols were drawn in the clearest strokes in AIDS Quilt displays on the Mall in Washington in October 1987, 1988, and 1992. Laid
out in the symbolic heart of U.S. political culture and cultural memory,
within view of the White House, the U.S. Capitol, and the Lincoln Memorial, the Quilt confronted the exclusions of U.S. political authority
and argued for the inclusion of people with AIDS into not just memorial
but political structures from which they had been left out. The connections between viewing the Quilt and participating in political protest
were also most direct at these moments, as activist Betty Berzon made
clear: "In the afternoon the sadness of the quilt experience gave way to
exhilaration as, under gray and overcast skies, the marchers stepped
off in an explosion of energy, shouting, singing, and chanting the rally-
ing cries of gay pride."[23]

The silence of the Reagan and Bush administrations about these public displays only solidified the community the Quilt created and the political stance it engendered. Whether or not the cultural history of the
1980s will be described as the Reagan era, the role of President Ronald
Reagan in the political, medical, and cultural history of the AIDS epidemic will always loom large. During the 1980s, many AIDS activists
condemned the Reagan administration for its silence on the issue of
AIDS; the president did not even mention the word "AIDS" publicly until more than 21,000 Americans had already died of the disease.[24]

In fact, the power of Ronald Reagan and national conservatism as
mobilizing symbols may very well have been more central to AIDS and
gay activism than participants realized at the time. Certainly greater
funding, tolerance, and compassion might have come out of a presidential administration led by Jimmy Carter, but in all likelihood not
much more, and the anger that catalyzed around the Reagan administration is palpable in a wide range of historical and cultural artifacts
produced by people with AIDS in the early 1980s.[25]

It was not merely Reagan the president but Reagan the cultural symbol to which AIDS activists responded. Following Reagan's lead, conservatives of the 1980s asserted cultural power through their claim on
the definition of family. This struck particularly at gay men, who were

often excluded from family structures or had rejected them in the midst of the sexual revolution. Furthermore, conservatives often described the nation in terms of the family, a connection that excluded those who were, for whatever reasons, not part of conventional families.

Understandably wary of this discourse of family and nation, many critics called into question the Names Project's attempt to include people with AIDS in the U.S. national imaginary. Marita Sturken feared that this form of accommodation would allow the continued marginalization of people with AIDS: "Notions of 'patriotism' and 'family heritage' implicit in the Quilt may simply backfire and act to rescript those memorialized into a discourse of Americana in a country that continues to view their deaths as less than tragic."[26] Yet this view underestimated the radical nature of Jones's project at a time when a claim to membership in the American nation seemed all but off-limits to people with AIDS. The makers and viewers of the Quilt challenged the hegemony of cultural meaning over the discourse of the family, insisting that people with AIDS were part of the national family and pointing out the contradictions of exclusion. As Elinor Fuchs noted: "The Quilt, without an ounce of apparent confrontation in its soft and comforting body, is a hugely visual riposte to official culture's fervent wish that AIDS would just disappear. . . . Its association of gay sexuality with Reaganite cultural mythology—the celebration of the rural American, family American, homemade American, nostalgic American—in effect forcing its spectators to embrace in a single image what to many is an impossible contradiction—this is no doubt the Quilt's most brilliant and far-reaching element of ironic masquerade."[27] The symbolic discourse surrounding the nation and the family was reshaped by the memorial work of the nation's actual families, who created meaningful panels and wrote touching letters showing that the connections of family could—and did—continue to include gay men, people who used intravenous drugs, and other people with AIDS whose lives and identities were stigmatized.[28]

Debates about the constituency of the AIDS Quilt and of AIDS activism also took place in a struggle over the relationship between the Quilt and the gay community. By the late 1980s and early 1990s, the changing demographics of AIDS were impossible to ignore: The disease was disproportionately ravaging poor communities of color at the same time that it continued to spread in overwhelmingly white, middle-class, urban, gay neighborhoods. Some white gay AIDS activists felt that their organizations needed to expand their services and their political mobilization efforts; others worried that attempting to reach everyone in the category of "people with AIDS" would strain organizational resources and efface both the special catastrophe that gay men lived with and the responses that they had developed. These tensions were aired nationwide in community papers, at City Council hearings, and at political meetings and protest rallies. They also appeared in the Names Project and raised challenges to the assumptions of many of the Quilt's founders.[29]

At times, in its search for national inclusion, Names Project staff consciously played down the fundamentally gay nature of the organization. In 1988, Cleve Jones stated publicly that "the Names Project is not a gay organization. . . . To say we are would be a disservice to the thousands of AIDS patients who are not gay, and it ignores the fact that during the past two years, the majority of new cases are from the heterosexual population."[30] Jones's disavowals of the Quilt's close relationship to the gay community were part of his larger aim of bringing the AIDS crisis to national attention through a symbolic language adapted to the mainstream. "We very deliberately adopted a symbol and a vocabulary that would not be threatening to nongay people," said Jones. This rhetoric made the Quilt's inclusion in the U.S. cultural landscape easier for some people to digest, a goal that Jones pursued at least in part for programmatic political reasons. "[We] needed a strategy that would affect the outside world, which clearly is going to decide whether we're going to survive."[31]

But there were dissenting voices. Many critics claimed that the Names Project's efforts at cultural inclusion "de-gayed" the AIDS Quilt, effectively erasing the contributions of the community out of which the Quilt had grown. Robin Hardy was angered that "the Names Project . . . has siphoned hundreds of thousands of dollars out of gay pockets, but omits the word 'gay' in its literature and puts a photograph of a mother and children on the cover of its commemorative booklet."[32] Activist Eric Rofes thought that "de-gaying AIDS might bring more funding, but isn't the cost too high?" and *Bay Windows,* a lesbian and gay newspaper in Boston, editorialized that "although . . . Cleve Jones is correct when he says that nobody could walk around the Quilt and not be struck by the gay community's losses, that doesn't mean that the current trend among AIDS organizations to put gay men at the bottom of the outreach heap is right."[33]

Jones and the leadership of the Names Project tried to balance several goals: to challenge political and cultural exclusion, to make inclusion possible, and to accommodate racial and sexual diversity. The use of the language of Americanism, broad enough to contain many different viewpoints, usually served Jones well. At other times, however, it did not, particularly in the Names Project's early encounters with African American and Latino communities dealing with epidemic use of intra-venous drugs as well as high rates of HIV-infection among gay men of color. Arguments for the application of "American values" to the AIDS crisis rang hollow in inner-city neighborhoods long ignored by white America and its government. The AIDS Quilt itself often appeared jar-ringly out of place, as the $3,000 cost of displaying the Quilt strained communities and activist organizations that could barely mobilize funds for AIDS education or health care. As one critic asked: "Is it a privilege to be able to mourn in the middle of an epidemic?"[34]

Ongoing arguments by Jones and his colleagues for inclusion into U.S. cultural mythology consistently ran up against the assumptions embedded in how Names Project organizers had defined U.S. identity and its possibilities. These difficulties were exacerbated as the Names Project extended its work beyond its founding and core constituency of white middle-class gay men to include the numerous other Americans affected by AIDS, Americans whose understanding of and relationship to myths of national identity were dramatically different from those of Cleve Jones. So long as that project was conducted through rhetorical manipulations by Names Project staff and other middle-class white ac-tivists, it was bound to get stuck on its multiple and contradictory as-sumptions. It succeeded in the democratic project of the Quilt itself, when people with AIDS, panelmakers, and their families spoke out for a broad definition of American identity, articulating thereby their place in, and their vision of, U.S. nationalism.[35]

WHAT KIND OF IDENTITY POLITICS?

Through its radically inclusive and democratic structure, the AIDS Quilt accommodated multiple identities at the same time that it created a collective one. In its earliest years, when AIDS was widely seen as a foreign phenomenon visited upon people beyond the pale of the imag-ined national community, the Quilt and its makers presented an argu-ment for inclusion within that community and created an identity not just as people affected by AIDS, but more specifically as Americans affected by AIDS. This form of identity politics—which was pursued not just in the cultural work of the Quilt but in many other arenas as well—had significant consequences for the political activism surrounding the AIDS epidemic.

Criticism of the Names Project extended to the tone of its political message. Viewers such as Douglas Crimp thought the AIDS Quilt didn't go far enough, and that it could create political passivity rather than consciousness. "Public mourning rituals may of course have their own political force, but often they seem, from an activist perspective, indulgent, sentimental, defeatist."[36] Activists accused the Names Project of failing to follow through on the more focused and didactic political potential of the AIDS Quilt. "Does the quilt itself educate those in need of information on how not to contract or spread HIV disease?" asked Rick Rose, who argued in 1992 that the AIDS Quilt was a poor allocation of already insufficient resources. "More than ten years into the epidemic, the Quilt has taken on a life of its own . . . weighing 30.7 tons. That's a lot of quilt and a lot of time, money, and resources, all of which could be spent in other ways. . . . To justify its tremendous costs, the quilt must be used in a more proactive role if it is to continue."[37] Rose would likely have preferred the approach of the radical AIDS activist group ACT UP, which petitioned the Names Project in 1992 to use Quilt panels for an act of civil disobedience; protesters had hoped to wrap George Bush's vacation home with the Quilt to draw attention to the AIDS crisis.[38]

Activist critics demanded that the memorial confront and speak to the U.S. public. But those who criticized the Quilt's political program were criticizing something that did not really exist. As Jones said in response to political criticisms, "No one ever said the Quilt was the answer." Instead of providing a political answer, as traditional monuments often do, the AIDS Quilt provided a political tool, enabling a politics that reflected its vision of pluralism and its accommodation, not merely of demographic difference, but of political diversity as well.[39]

Coming to terms with issues of activism and diversity in the Names Project sheds light on broader trends of political culture after the 1960s. The pursuit of identity politics in the United States in the 1980s must be seen within long-term shifts in the modern West toward the expression of political activism through what sociologists have called new social movements. These social forces, as defined by Jürgen Habermas, are thought to reflect new political conflicts which "no longer arise in areas of material reproduction. Rather, the new conflicts arise in areas of cultural reproduction, social integration, and socialization. . . . In short, the new conflicts are not sparked by problems of distribution, but concern the grammar of forms of life."[40] Often involving cultural creativity, theater, and performance, these movements' contests and struggles have concerned symbols and meanings more than issues of institutional access and economic resources. The gay liberation movement of the 1970s, which saw changes in lifestyle as fundamental challenges to the structure of power in society, clearly fits this model.

The movements formed by gay men in the 1980s in response to the AIDS crisis at once confirm and challenge our understanding of new social movements. For many in the Names Project, the ties to earlier movements were genealogical. Cleve Jones was himself a member of the Gay Liberation Front and also active in San Francisco electoral politics in the 1970s. "I got involved in 1980–81. . . . I had been an activist in the gay liberation movement and had worked with Harvey Milk. To me my activism was a natural outgrowth of my work in gay liberation, and the early days were very much grassroots, ad hoc. . . . We were just gay activists who were trying to alert our brothers."[41] Jones's story mirrors those of many other activists—particularly in New York and San Francisco—whose AIDS activism was of a piece with their ongoing commitment to a gay and lesbian identity politics that matches Habermas's definition.[42]

Cultural politics was never the point of AIDS activism in the early years of the epidemic. Funding, research, health care, and other questions about the allocation of scarce social resources headed the agenda. But the circumstances of history had created a unique intersection of interest-group politics and identity politics, of old and new social movements.

In the 1980s, most commentators, particularly gay men in the hardest-hit communities, felt that the marginality and stigmatization of sexual minorities allowed structures of government, health care, and the media to ignore the devastation of the disease without voicing any meaningful public response. But perhaps, in retrospect, another pattern comes into view. The relatively sophisticated political organization of segments of the gay community made it possible for AIDS to receive a great deal of funding and a quick response from the public sector. Dennis Altman noted that "among the groups most affected by AIDS, only the homosexuals have been able to mobilize and articulate political demands." Furthermore, suggests Altman, the disease also mobilized more gay men into activism—whether for narrowly tailored issues related to AIDS or to gay and lesbian rights more generally—than had ever been involved in such movements before.[43]

If we consider AIDS next to other major health crises of the modern era, the significance of already existing networks of gay politics is put into sharp relief. Arriving in the middle of an era of identity-based politics, the AIDS epidemic taught that diseases create identities, even when those identities overlap in the imagination of the so-called general public with existing social categories such as gay men or drug users. People with AIDS did not exist as a social category that could act in the arenas of interest-group politics before the disease. Gay people did. That there was a close correlation between the categories of gay men and people with AIDS in the early years of the disease in the United States meant that disease activism could take place at a much more rapid and better-organized pace than any other disease activism in U.S. (or world) history. Had gay men not already been organized as a political and cultural body around their identities, they would not have been able to mobilize politically and culturally specific responses to a crisis that disproportionately affected them as a group.[44]

Critics of identity politics often suggest that its practice has led to narrow, fragmented, and selfishly oriented communities. Those who make this suggestion should look seriously at the alliances formed in the 1980s in the realms of AIDS volunteer service, AIDS education, and AIDS activism. In the early days of the AIDS crisis, identity politics saved and prolonged lives, not merely of the gay men whose identity politics facilitated a quick response to the emerging epidemic, but of all those affected by AIDS who gained access to the institutions of medicine, politics, and culture established by gay men and their allies in the early 1980s.[45]

The AIDS Memorial Quilt was one of those institutions. Even as it disavowed its gay identity, it created a cultural space for gay men who were dealing with AIDS. Even as it spoke the language of power and nationalism, it drew from and mobilized large numbers of gay men, their families, and friends. But it was never "only" a gay project, so long as its panels gave voice to the diverse constituencies of AIDS. On the eve of the first Quilt display in New York City in 1988, Clarke Taylor, director of New York's Names Project chapter, expressed his hope that the Quilt could bring unity in the response to the AIDS crisis: "For the first time in eight years, the city is going to be together on AIDS. It will be physically together, representationally together and, in the long run, politically together." It was a utopian claim, more fantasy than reality. But it had an element of truth to it.[46]

The Quilt put its cultural space to work for the purpose of political mobilization. AIDS activism, particularly in the 1980s when research funds were not forthcoming, differed from the new social movements that Jürgen Habermas describes, in that debates did in fact concern problems of resource allocation. That these problems could at times be addressed by cultural products such as the AIDS Quilt, which has raised more than $3 million for local AIDS service organizations at the same time that it has addressed issues of cultural meaning and personal life, only shows that identity politics was always related to areas of struggle more traditionally defined as political in the case of AIDS activism.[47]

Thomas Yingling has suggested that AIDS "is the disease that announces the end of identity."[48] By this, he referred primarily to the universal experience of death even under highly differentiated experiences of life. But the AIDS Memorial Quilt also demonstrates a reworking of identity politics and resource politics. For a moment, the pursuit of a politics of respectability, inclusion, and nationalism achieved a great deal for people with AIDS, their families, and friends. Created in an era in which notions of nationality and the family were tinged in reactionary ways by the cultural conservatives who dominated politics and the media, the Quilt ultimately claimed some aspects of those very notions that supposedly excluded it. Did panelmakers do this out of acceptance of nationalist beliefs, as a self-conscious strategy of political activism and fund-raising, or out of some postmodern quest for ironic subterfuge? The Quilt panels, of course, in all the wild contradictions to which they give voice, prevent us from choosing any one of those conclusions but force us to reckon with a politics that might conceivably allow us to do all three.

POSTSCRIPT

If memory politics, identity politics, and resource politics were useful tools in the early response to AIDS, they were a mixed blessing. AIDS activism—dominated in the 1980s by white gay men raised in the Americanism of the 1950s, schooled in the politics of the 1960s, and liberated by the sexual cultures of the 1970s—was predetermined by earlier patterns of political organization, for better and for worse. Through its articulation of the AIDS crisis in a "nonthreatening" manner, the Names Project succeeded in bringing the disease before a wide range of Americans who might have avoided the issue in the 1980s. But now that Newt Gingrich and Miss America have appeared at Quilt displays and the Names Project has received a grant from the National Endowment for the Arts, it is perhaps time to rethink the relationship between nationalism and activism. In the year 2003, the Names Project is an actively international organization dedicated to incorporating worldwide cultural traditions of memory and quilting. With U.S. political and cultural institutions responding in at least a partial way to the concerns of American people with AIDS, a continued focus on U.S. national identity is now quite simply not that radical. Furthermore, as the disease's global impact rears its ever uglier head, it is the formation of transnational cultural and political responses that is desperately necessary now.[49]

The history of the formation and structure of the AIDS Memorial Quilt tells a complex story of public and private, personal and political, protest and acquiescence, inclusion and resistance. It also provides some lessons for those who seek to extend the cultural and political response to AIDS in the future. Any attempt to use the AIDS Quilt—and its communities—to form an identity and craft a political program has been made transparent by the panels themselves and the lives they remember. That is not a bad thing. On the contrary, that transparency is a fundamental precondition of a democratic political program. Only a recognition of the pluralism the Quilt embodies can allow its viewers a critical appropriation of multiple and ambiguous traditions, one that allows for and encourages collective identities that serve political ends, but that is incompatible with predetermined and exclusionary boundaries of politicized identities.[50]

The men and women who confronted the AIDS epidemic in its early years recognized these ambiguities. Sometimes they demanded inclusion of the disease within one or another tradition. Sometimes they resisted the assumptions of these traditions, or challenged their failures. And at moments, they carried out acts of critical appropriation—by making panels for the Quilt, by visiting it, and by opening their hearts, wallets, and political imaginations to the lessons its panels taught. The AIDS Memorial Quilt offers a valuable example of the reconciliation of memory and politics in a pluralist society. Memorials must never abandon their duties in either the commemorative or political realms, but they can never substitute for our own participation in commemoration and political action. In an era in which memory and identity are part and parcel of the practice of every kind of politics, we cannot let politicians—radical or conservative—decide what our memories mean. Nor can we let our memories do our politicking for us.

Notes

Acknowledgments: For their assistance in the preparation of this essay, I would like to thank Terry Aladjem, Eliza Byard, Jim Carr, Nora Connell, Jeffrey Escoffier, Robert Genter, Van Gosse, Cleve Jones, Pratap Mehta, Richard Moser, Roy Rosenzweig, and members of the Columbia University Queer Studies Group.

1. Cleve Jones, interview by the author, Cambridge, Mass., December 5, 1993; Jones, with Jeff Dawson, *Stitching a Revolution: The Making of an Activist* (San Francisco: Harper San Francisco, 2000), 103–9. Figures are current as of October 2001 or December 2001 and can be found in Names Project Foundation, "Quilt Facts," at http://www.aidsquilt.org, and U.S. Centers for Disease Control and Prevention (CDC), "Basic Statistics," at http://www.cdc.gov/hiv/pubs/facts.htm.

2. Cleve Jones, quoted in William Goldstein, "The Quilt: Stories from the Names Project," *Publishers Weekly*, February 19, 1988, 43.

3. Sara Evans, *Personal Politics: The Roots of Women's Liberation in the Civil Rights Movement and the New Left* (New York: Knopf, 1979); David Allyn, *Make Love, Not War: The Sexual Revolution, an Unfettered History* (Boston: Little, Brown, 2000). For surveys of gay activism in the 1970s see Dudley Clendinen and Adam Nagourney, *Out for Good: The Struggle to Build a Gay Rights Movement in America* (New York: Simon & Schuster, 1999); and Eric Marcus, *Making History: The Struggle for Gay and Lesbian Equal Rights, 1945–1990: An Oral History* (New York: HarperCollins, 1992).

4. Jones interview; also see Names Project Foundation, *The Names Project AIDS Memorial Quilt* (San Francisco: Names Project Foundation, 1993).

5. Jones interview.

6. Ibid.

7. In this essay, I confine my discussion to the years between 1981—when AIDS was first identified in the United States—through the early 1990s, ending with the inauguration of Bill Clinton. I choose the latter date not because it ushered in a new era in AIDS treatment, research, or funding (it certainly did not), but because the notable public silences of the Reagan and Bush administrations in the early years of the epidemic were significant organizational prompts for AIDS activists in general and the Names Project in particular. The terrain shifted again after 1995 and 1996, as multiple-drug therapies halted disease progress among many of the middle-class gay men in the United States who could afford treatment, while the disease's long-noted global dimensions became almost inconceivable in their devastation. The social history of AIDS has mutated as

quickly as the virus. The Names Project, which is now much more self-consciously multicultural and internationalist, is only beginning to catch up. What I have to say applies to a cultural and political moment that has already passed into history.

8. Figures are from CDC, "Basic Statistics," and Joint United Nations Programme on HIV/AIDS, "HIV Information and Data," at www.unaids.org/hivaidsinfo/index.html, and are current as of December 2002. The standard work on the early years of the AIDS epidemic is Randy Shilts, *And the Band Played On: Politics, People, and the AIDS Epidemic* (New York: Penguin, 1988), recently supplemented by John-Manuel Andriote, *Victory Deferred: How AIDS Changed Gay Life in America* (Chicago: University of Chicago Press, 1999), esp. 47–82.

9. Judy Spiersch, quoted in Cindy Ruskin, *The Quilt: Stories from the Names Project* (New York: Pocket, 1988), 11. A chilling catalog of restrictions on the mourning of people with AIDS can be found in Miriam Horn, "Grief Re-Examined," *U.S. News and World Report*, June 14, 1993, 81–84.

10. Cleve Jones, quoted in Dan Bellm, "And Sew It Goes," *Mother Jones* 14 (January 1989): 35.

11. Jones interview.

12. The discussion here is condensed from Christopher Capozzola, "The Monumental Moment: Recent Monument Design and the Search for Pluralist Frameworks of Memory" (A.B. honors thesis, Harvard College, 1994), on deposit at the Harvard University Archives and Pusey Library. Key works in the study of memory include Paul Connerton, *How Societies Remember* (New York: Cambridge University Press, 1989); Maurice Halbwachs, *The Collective Memory*, trans. Francis J. Ditter Jr. and Vida Yazdi Ditter (New York: Harper & Row, 1980); Michael G. Kammen, *Mystic Chords of Memory: The Transformation of Tradition in American Culture* (New York: Knopf, 1991); David Lowenthal, *The Past Is a Foreign Country* (New York: Cambridge University Press, 1985); Pierre Nora, *Realms of Memory: The Construction of the French Past*, ed. Lawrence D. Kritzman, trans. Arthur Goldhammer (New York: Columbia University Press, 1996); and the journal *History and Memory*.

13. Figures about the AIDS Memorial Quilt are from the Names Project Foundation, "Quilt Facts," and United Nations, "HIV Information and Data," and are current as of October 2001 and December 2002, respectively. See also Jeff Weinstein, "Names Carried into the Future: An AIDS Quilt Unfolds," in Arlene Raven, ed., *Art in the Public Interest* (Ann Arbor: University of Michigan Research Press, 1989), 48. For an illuminating study of people who have made panels to commemorate themselves, see Shoshana D. Kerewsky, "HIV+ Gay Men's Processes of Making Their Own AIDS Memorial Quilt Panels" (Ph.D. diss., Antioch New England Graduate School, 1997).

14. Weinstein, "Names," 50. See also Peter Hawkins, "Naming Names: The Art of Memory and the NAMES Project AIDS Quilt," *Critical Inquiry* 19 (summer 1993): 752–79. A wide variety of Quilt panels can be seen in Cindy Ruskin, *Quilt;* The NAMES Project AIDS Memorial Quilt, *Always Remember: A Selection of Panels Created by and for International Fashion Designers* (New York: Simon &

Schuster, 1996), and Names Project Foundation, "The Quilt Archive Project" and "Online Display," at http://www.aidsquilt.org.

15. Jim Carr, Names Project–Boston, interview by the author, Boston, March 22, 1994. Marita Sturken, however, notes that there is very little discussion of public issues in the signature panels (see Sturken, *Tangled Memories: The Vietnam War, the AIDS Epidemic, and the Politics of Remembering* [Berkeley: University of California Press, 1997], 199). At the first national display of the Quilt, viewers used the signature panels to inscribe the names of those they knew who were not yet memorialized in its panels ("Topics of the Times: The AIDS Memorial," *New York Times*, October 14, 1987).

16. Jonathan Weinberg, "The Quilt: Activism and Remembrance," *Art in America* 80 (December 1992): 37.

17. Hawkins, "Naming Names," 764. See also Paul Treichler, "AIDS, Homophobia, and Biomedical Discourse: An Epidemic of Signification," in Douglas Crimp, ed., *AIDS: Cultural Analysis/Cultural Activism* (Cambridge: MIT Press, 1988), 31–70.

18. The research of Shoshana Kerewsky confirms that "responses [of panel-makers] primarily centered on relational activities (individual, interpersonal, and community)" and "the meanings that they attributed to making their own panels were more local and personal than the available literature on the Quilt in general might suggest" (see Kerewsky, "HIV," 1). Jack Bier, quoted in Sandra Friedland, "Displaying the AIDS Quilt in the State," *New York Times*, May 27, 1990.

19. Elaine Hedges, *Hearts and Hands: Women, Quilts, and American Society* (Nashville, Tenn.: Rutledge Hill Press, 1996); Flavia Rando, "The Person with AIDS: The Body, the Feminine, and the NAMES Project Memorial Quilt," in Nancy L. Roth and Katie Hogan, eds., *Gendered Epidemic: Representations of Women in the Age of AIDS* (New York: Routledge, 1998), 196; David F. Shaw, "Women and the AIDS Memorial Quilt," in Nancy L. Roth and Linda K. Fuller, eds., *Women and AIDS: Negotiating Safer Practices, Care, and Representation* (New York: Haworth, 1998), 213–16.

20. Hedges, *Hearts and Hands*. For a literary instance of the feminist revival of quilting, see Alice Walker's 1973 story "Everyday Use," in Henry Louis Gates Jr. and Nellie Y. McKay, eds., *The Norton Anthology of African American Literature* (New York: Norton, 1997), 2387–94. Shaw's "Women and the AIDS Memorial Quilt" suggests that the appropriation of quilting as therapy could not have occurred without the transformations of religion and spirituality in the 1960s and 1970s often subsumed under the rubric "New Age." I would add to this the changes in the culture of grief and death following the publication of Elizabeth Kübler-Ross's *On Death and Dying* (New York: Macmillan, 1969). Another significant combination of these trends can be seen in the work of the Berkeley-based Shanti Project, which was one of the first organizations to respond to the outbreak of AIDS in the cultural realm (see Charles Garfield, *Sometimes My Heart Goes Numb: Love and Caregiving in a Time of AIDS* [San Francisco: Jossey-Bass, 1995]). Shilts demonstrates Cleve Jones's connections to the Shanti Project as early as 1982 in *And the Band Played On*, 123.

21. Jones interview.

22. Cleve Jones, quoted in Andriote, *Victory Deferred,* 366.

23. For a record of the 1987 Washington displays, see Ruskin, *Quilt;* "Denying AIDS Its Sting: A Quilt of Life," *New York Times,* October 5, 1987; "Memorial Quilt Rolled Out," *New York Times,* October 12, 1987; "200,000 March in Capital to Seek Gay Rights and Money for AIDS," *New York Times,* October 12, 1987; Betty Berzon, "Acting Up," in Mark Thompson, ed., *Long Road to Freedom: The Advocate History of the Gay and Lesbian Movement* (New York: St. Martin's Press, 1994), 308.

24. M. Murray Mayo, "A Cultural Analysis of the Meanings in the NAMES Project AIDS Memorial Quilt" (Ph.D. diss., Kent State University, 1995), 4. Ronald Reagan did not establish the Presidential Commission on the Human Immunodeficiency Virus Epidemic until 1987, but even then he chose to ignore the commission's 1988 report, as did President George Bush the report of the National Commission on AIDS in 1991 (Pierre André, *People, Sex, HIV, and AIDS: Social, Political, Philosophical, and Moral Implications* [Huntington, W. Va.: University Editions, 1995], 30). A great deal of work remains to be done in analyzing the cultural politics of the Reagan era. Some of this has been done in Kenneth MacKinnon, *The Politics of Popular Representation: Reagan, Thatcher, AIDS, and the Movies* (Cranbury, N.J.: Associated University Presses, 1992); Alan Nadel, *Flatlining on the Field of Dreams: Cultural Narratives in the Film of President Reagan's America* (New Brunswick, N.J.: Rutgers University Press, 1997); and Michael Paul Rogin, *Ronald Reagan, the Movie, and Other Episodes in Political Demonology* (Berkeley: University of California Press, 1987).

25. See Laurie Udesky, "Randy Shilts: 'For Me, Coming Out Was Very Political,'" *Progressive* 55 (May 1991): 30–34.

26. Sturken, "Conversations with the Dead: Bearing Witness in the AIDS Memorial Quilt," *Socialist Review* 22 (April–June 1992): 92. See also Sturken, *Tangled Memories,* 215–17. For a similar argument about developments in Margaret Thatcher's Britain, see Simon Watney, "The Spectacle of AIDS," in Crimp, *AIDS,* 82.

27. Elinor Fuchs, "The Performance of Mourning," *American Theatre* 9 (January 1993): 17.

28. Joe Brown, ed., *A Promise to Remember: The Names Project Book of Letters* (New York: Avon, 1992). See also Kath Weston, *Families We Choose: Lesbians, Gays, Kinship* (New York: Columbia University Press, 1991).

29. For just one example, in early 1989, a series of activists debated the relationship between gay groups and AIDS activism in response to a controversial article in the *Nation.* The original article and many of the responses are reprinted in Darrell Yates Rist, "AIDS as Apocalypse," *Christopher Street* 11 (February 1989): 11–20. See also Eric E. Rofes, "Gay Groups vs. AIDS Groups: Averting Civil War in the 1990s," *Out/Look* 2 (spring 1990): 8–17.

30. Cleve Jones, quoted in Marita Sturken, "Cultural Memory and Identity Politics: The Vietnam War, AIDS, and the Technologies of Memory" (Ph.D. diss., University of California at Santa Cruz, 1992), 267.

31. Cleve Jones, quoted in Sturken, "Conversations with the Dead," 85; Jones, quoted in Bellm, "And Sew It Goes," 35.

32. Robin Hardy, quoted in Sturken, *Tangled Memories,* 208.

33. Both in Rofes, "Gay Groups vs. AIDS Groups," 12–13.

34. Sturken, "Conversations," 88.

35. Sturken (*Tangled Memories,* 255–59) emphasizes the role of the AIDS Quilt in the formation of what she calls "counternational" discourses, but I believe they are less self-consciously resistant than Sturken describes them, and so I prefer the term "national."

36. Douglas Crimp, "Mourning and Militancy," *October,* no. 51 (winter 1989): 5.

37. Rick Rose, "Has AIDS Outgrown the Quilt?" *Advocate,* no. 617 (December 1, 1992): 6. The Quilt now weighs approximately fifty-three tons (see Names Project Foundation, "Quilt Facts"). Tom Schiller suggests the Quilt's possibilities for mobilizing family members of people with AIDS in a personal account in Garfield, *Sometimes My Heart,* 186, but Shaw suggests that there were limits to the Quilt's political mobilization in that most survivors were inspired by their Quilt experiences to continue political work they were already doing, rather than being politically mobilized in the classic sense ("Women and the AIDS Memorial Quilt," 224–29).

38. Jones interview.

39. Ibid.

40. Jürgen Habermas, "New Social Movements," *Telos,* no. 49 (fall 1981): 33. See also Mayo, "A Cultural Analysis," 9–15; and Josh Gamson, "Silence, Death, and the Invisible Enemy: AIDS Activism and Social Movement 'Newness,'" *Social Problems* 36 (October 1989): 351–67.

41. Jones, quoted in Nancy E. Stoller, *Lessons from the Damned: Queers, Whores, and Junkies Respond to AIDS* (New York: Routledge, 1998), 34–35. For more on Jones's 1970s activism, see Andriote, *Victory Deferred,* 75–76; Frank A. Conway, "People to Watch: Cleve Jones," *Christopher Street* 11 (May 1988): 36–39; Jones, *Stitching a Revolution,* 23–87; and Shilts, *And the Band Played On,* 16–17.

42. Gamson, "Silence"; Stoller, *Lessons,* 113–33; and Andriote, *Victory Deferred,* 83–122.

43. André, *People, Sex, HIV, and AIDS,* 33; Dennis Altman, "Legitimation through Disaster: AIDS and the Gay Movement," in Elizabeth Fee and Daniel M. Fox, eds., *AIDS: The Burdens of History* (Berkeley: University of California Press, 1988), 309. The contrasting interpretation emphasizes the ways in which powerful institutions of public health, government, and media narrowed and shaped the range of possible responses to the AIDS crisis, often acting against the interests of people with AIDS even while claiming to serve them (see Elinor Burkett, *The Gravest Show on Earth: America in the Age of AIDS* [Boston: Houghton Mifflin, 1995], and Michael A. Hallett, ed., *Activism and Marginalization in the AIDS Crisis* [New York: Haworth, 1997], esp. 1–16).

44. The deployment of the cultural symbols of Americana was certainly easier for middle-class white gay men, who were often raised in that cultural surround, moved easily in and out of it, and were able to subvert it from within in ways that other AIDS activists may not have been able to do. Gamson makes a similar point about activists from ACT UP in "Silence," 362.

45. Perhaps nothing demonstrates this better than the commitment of HIV-negative gay men to AIDS activism ever since the earliest days of the crisis. For

some personal accounts, see Andrew Sullivan, "Gay Life, Gay Death," *New Republic*, December 17, 1990, 19–25; and Lon G. Nungesser, *Epidemic of Courage: Facing AIDS in America* (New York: St. Martin's Press, 1986). Of course, not all persons with AIDS have had full access to the kinds of social networks that relatively powerful urban white gay men constructed, yet the work of these institutions and their ongoing if uneven commitment to servicing a global AIDS crisis demonstrates a remarkable level of cross-identity commitment. Consider also Dennis Altman's point that "the American irony is that groups such as [Gay Men's Health Crisis] or AIDS Project-Los Angeles are almost perfect examples of Reaganite volunteerism, but right-wing moralists have prevented the White House from acknowledging their roles" ("Legitimation through Disaster," 312). Sturken (*Tangled Memories*, 156–59) disagrees, arguing that women and people of color have been consistently underserved by AIDS organizations dominated by gay men.

46. David W. Dunlap, "Quilt Unfolds Painful Story of AIDS," *New York Times*, June 20, 1988. The Quilt also brought people together in the volunteer organizations that helped people make panels (see coverage of Metro New York Quilters in Elaine Louie, "Making a Panel for the AIDS Memorial Quilt," *New York Times*, October 1, 1992).

47. Figure from Names Project Foundation, "Quilt Facts."

48. Thomas E. Yingling, *AIDS and the National Body*, ed. Robyn Wiegman (Durham, N.C.: Duke University Press, 1997), 15.

49. This is all the more true as contributions to AIDS organizations in the United States have tumbled, including the Names Project, which cut its budget by 30 percent in 1997 (see Andriote, *Victory Deferred*, 381; Sam Whiting, "AIDS Quilt Has Become Her Banner," *San Francisco Chronicle*, December 12, 1997; Sturken, *Tangled Memories*, 181–82).

50. Jürgen Habermas, "A Kind of Settlement of Damages," trans. Jeremy Leaman, *Economy and Society* 17 (November 1988): 541. From a very different perspective, but with a remarkably similar conclusion, see Herbert Muschamp, "Labyrinth," *Artforum* 26 (December 1987): 12.

CAROLYN STRANGE AND TINA LOO

9   Holding the Rock
     The "Indianization" of Alcatraz Island, 1969–1999

IN THE 1960s, an era of political turbulence and social upheaval,
popular rock and folk musicians expressed their hope that life in America would never be the same. When Bob Dylan declared, "The times,
they are a-changin'," other musicians like the Chambers Brothers sang
about the need to act "today," lest the chance for change might "slip
away." Throughout the country, especially in hippie centers like San
Francisco, protest against the Vietnam War and calls for civil rights took
on an urgency that reached its peak in the late 1960s and early 1970s. In
the midst of those politically charged times, when radical transformation seemed imminent, American Indians also leapt into the limelight
by making their grievances known on an unlikely stage: Alcatraz, the
wind-swept island known as "the Rock," where the Bureau of Prisons
had locked up what it claimed were America's "toughest" criminals. Rejecting the old slogan that "Indians don't demonstrate," San Francisco
Bay Area Indians, many of them students, seized the island as "Indian
Land." For these Native activists, the time had come to reclaim and remake the Island after more than a century of government occupation.[1]

These were not the first protesters to use Alcatraz to press indigenous
land claims. In 1964, a small group of Indian people had occupied the island briefly to protest the official designation of the island as government "surplus" property, rather than native land. Although they managed to capture headlines, their occupation lasted only a few days, and
media attention quickly waned.[2] The 1969 seizure of the Rock was a different story. In the name of "Indians of All Tribes," protesters landed on
the abandoned island on November 20, 1969, and refused to leave. For
more than a year, occupiers drew mainstream media attention to the

Reprinted from Carolyn Strange and Tina Loo, "Holding the Rock: The Indianization
of Alcatraz Island, 1969–1999," *The Public Historian* 23/1 (Winter 2001): 55–74, by permission. © 2001 by The Regents of the University of California. Reprinted courtesy of the authors.

plight of Indian people: They made demands for Indian self-determination, set up housing, and ran a school and a health clinic. In short, they made Alcatraz their home. Their welcome mat was huge red-lettered graffiti on the landing dock: "INDIANS WELCOME" and "YOU ARE ON INDIAN LAND." Elsewhere on the island, political slogans and symbols were painted over buildings where prisoners and guards had eked out a tense and uneasy existence. Now vibrant messages and images of liberation and protest ("Red Power" and a gargantuan red fist) gave the site new meanings. Sarcastic graffiti above cells in the Main Cell Block announced that the real prisoners ought to be Nixon, Agnew, and Alioto, the San Francisco mayor who had provoked the protest after he cooked up a deal for the city to sell Alcatraz to a commercial developer. In the final days of the occupation in June 1971, numerous buildings were destroyed by fire, and many were torn down after the federal government reestablished control over the site.[3] Yet much of the graffiti survived. The Indians had been removed, but the words and pictures of their groundbreaking and ground-claiming protest remained, leaving both a tangible and symbolic resource for remembrance.

Thirty years after the occupation began, another remarkable event took place. This time, Indians, many of them veterans of the occupation, had the government's blessing to occupy the island. Native people struck an Anniversary Planning Committee in 1998 and worked with several other government agencies, commercial operators, and volunteers to hold a daylong celebration on Alcatraz Island in October 1999. Millie Ketcheshawno, the events coordinator, explained that the day was meant to "salute all of those brave, strong-hearted Warriors who stood together and held the Rock for nineteen months. Their fight for the rights of Native Peoples will be remembered."[4] The National Park Service (NPS), the official caretaker of the island, agreed and actively encouraged the committee's efforts and supported its objectives. Though NPS general superintendent Brian O'Neill had, as we will see, previously rejected a permanent monument to the occupation on the island, he embraced this one-day celebration: "This special cultural, musical and educational event will help keep alive the importance of Alcatraz to the Indian community, and to all people."[5]

Native activists and historians agree that the occupation of Alcatraz was a pivotal event in Indian political history. During the anniversary celebrations, veterans and political allies imagined Alcatraz's enduring relevance in terms of a spark that lit the flame, or a stone that sent off ripples in a pond. Using similar metaphors, historians of the occupation have underlined its importance. Troy Johnson describes the protest as a "catalyst for change" without which the government might not have rolled back the damaging "termination" policy.[6] Paul Chaat Smith and Robert Allen Warrior stress that Indian discontent and mobilization for change had been brewing for a decade before the occupation. They too, however, describe it as "a fulcrum, a turning point," in Indians' will toward self-determination and in Americans' consciousness of Indian grievances. Whatever the metaphor, the consensus is that the occupation was a place-making event that had made history.[7]

Looking back at a dramatic action and contextualizing it in relation to events that preceded and followed it is a routine means of historical explanation. Arguing, as many have, that the occupation of Alcatraz is important historically does not explain why or how it has come to be remembered today, however. Such an argument is circular and relies on a notion of inevitability, effectively side-stepping the necessity for critical inquiry. Explaining public remembrance requires that one ask why and how events are remembered. After all, it is always possible to forget, especially (as was the case with Alcatraz) if actions are unsanctioned or embarrassing to the government of the day. And even when disturbing events are later commemorated, sponsors may not present them in a positive light.[8]

The prospect of future government-sanctioned celebrations of the occupation in cooperation with Native people was unthinkable in its immediate aftermath. In federal authorities' eyes, the occupiers were lawless trespassers and vandals who had destroyed government property. By the end of the occupation, the Indians were not heroes or martyrs in the wider public's mind, but troublemakers. An atmosphere of distrust and suspicion descended over the two groups: one, the custodians and site interpreters, and the other, Indian activists struggling to marshal political gains out of apparent defeat. Once Alcatraz Island became a park in 1973, representatives of the federal government, not the protesters, presented the official storyline of Alcatraz, typically characterizing the occupation to tourists as a frivolous or destructive action.[9] Viewed in light of the legacy of political tension and continuing power imbalances between Indians and the federal government, the thirtieth-anniversary celebration on Alcatraz seems extraordinary, not inevitable.

Alcatraz's protest graffiti, now faded and peeling, visually signal how easily the memory of the occupation might have disappeared. Just as the natural forces of wind, rain, and saltwater have eroded the defiant images painted on buildings during the occupation, so too can time weaken memories of struggle. And as Holocaust scholars note, outright denial of the painful past is not uncommon.[10] In this case, however, the recollection of the occupation has become more, not less, vivid over the past decade, and noble struggle, not tragedy or defeat, has become the dominant motif in government-sanctioned commemorations. Indeed, these messages have been packaged and preserved in a variety of forms, including tours, videos, guidebooks, and, most recently, graffiti conservation and restoration projects. Troy Johnson suggests that such support for and general interest in Alcatraz's Indian history demonstrates how "time may heal all wounds, but sometimes time needs some help."[11]

His observation neatly summarizes public historians' wider argument that the past's interpretation at public historic sites is neither fixed nor pre-ordained.[12] Instilling public memory is possible only when "a shared need to remember what had not been remembered before" can be created.[13] In other words, key actors, making decisions and pressing demands in the context of broader policy changes and shifts in political, fiscal, and cultural climates, determine the possibility and character of commemoration.

How, then, did Alcatraz emerge as an Indian place? From the point of view of aboriginal people, particularly the Ohlone people who claim the Rock as ancestral land, Alcatraz is, was, and will always be Indian land. What we are tracing is not the true nature or legal status of Alcatraz, but the ways in which its public interpretation has changed over time, from the NPS's stance of ignoring the occupation or presenting it in a unfavorable light, to recent investments of time and resources into the preservation of its memory as a place-changing event.

NPS agents were important players in this process, but they did not act in isolation to bring about this change. In fact, two broad currents of commemoration have flowed around the island over the past thirty years, gathering the people, memories, and ideas that have shaped it symbolically. One, which we might think of as internal and official, originated with the NPS, both at the level of policy-making and grassroots interpretation initiatives. The other was external, the product of unofficial actions by nonstate institutions and actors, including Indian activists, occupation veterans, and academics. These two distinct currents converged around the Rock by the mid-1990s, leaving a more "Indianized" island in their wake.[14] Alcatraz visitors could thereafter encounter the island's aboriginal past much more directly, as a result of the systematic, concerted, and eventually joint efforts of the NPS and Native Americans to commemorate the Indian occupation of 1969–71.

Alcatraz's notoriety as a former prison site appealed to the fourteen Bay Area urban Indian college students who planned the invasion. They envisaged it as a kind of "street theatre"; as agitprop.[15] Their choice of place was symbolic as well as strategic. Claiming the site of America's most infamous prison guaranteed the occupiers national and international attention, allowing them to make the point that all federal lands and not just the Rock belonged to Native Americans. Moreover, for Indians of All Tribes, "America's Devil's Island" bore an uncanny resemblance to "the rez." According to their proclamation, the site of the former penitentiary was "more than suitable for an Indian reservation, as determined by the white man's own standards":

> It is isolated from modern facilities, and without adequate means of transportation.
> It has no fresh running water.
> It has inadequate sanitation facilities.
> There are no oil or mineral rights.
> There is no industry so unemployment is very great.
> There are no health care facilities.
> The soil is rocky and non-productive; and the land does not support game.
> There are no educational facilities.
> The population has always exceeded the land base.
> The population has always been held as prisoners and kept dependent upon others.[16]

From the outset, Alcatraz's preexisting reputation as a cruel place offered an opportunity for activists to dramatize the plight of Indian people; paradoxically it also presented the possibility to reimagine the place as the home for American Indian rebirth and self-determination.

Growing support from Native and non-Native Americans across the continent quickly transformed what began as a humorous and ironic critique of U.S. Indian policy into a concrete model of what aboriginal emancipation might look like. For many of the occupiers and their supporters, the regeneration of Indian people came to be tied, symbolically and actually, to a self-conscious remaking of Alcatraz Island. As one participant told a gathering of the Indians of All Tribes in late 1969: "We will not ever get anything till we make Alcatraz."[17] In that spirit, the island's inhabitants inscribed the Rock with more than two hundred pieces of graffiti. The occupiers also modified the Bureau of Prison's coat of arms above the entrance to the cell house so that the eagle sitting on the Stars and Stripes shield wore a sign that said, "This land is my land." Later, someone painted the word "FREE" into the vertical red and white stripes of the shield.[18] "What an ironic twist of fate for an old prison island with a grim and sadistic past," recalled occupation veteran Adam Fortunate Eagle. "In its heyday desperate men went to any extreme, even certain death, to escape the island; in 1969 Indian people were just as desperate to get onto the island to seek their freedom."[19]

The process of appropriating and Indianizing Alcatraz involved more than painting the island red.[20] Most ambitious of all were the plans for an All-Indian University and Cultural Complex on the site of the former prison, consisting of Thunderbird University, a cultural and ecological center, and (tongue-in-cheek) a Bureau of Caucasian Affairs. Thus, as central as the physical occupation of the island was to making their point, holding the Rock also depended on other tactics of place making, ranging from graffiti on the site itself to the proposed conversion of the penitentiary into a cultural center, and parts of the guards' quarters into classrooms.

In the face of overwhelming logistical, political, and economic odds, these ambitious plans failed to materialize. Instead, in June 1971, nineteen months after the occupation began, federal marshals escorted the last holdouts off the island and bulldozers were brought in. The destruction of burned-out buildings and the graffiti that adorned them sent an unmistakable message about the island's new identity. Having sat by and watched while protesters forged pan-Indian identity and a sense of collective protest against federal Indian policy, the government suddenly flexed its muscles to "render the area 'placeless.'"[21] Whether or not federal agents set fire to the buildings, as many Indians believed, the razing of structures festooned with antigovernment graffiti literally obliterated the occupiers' sense of place and prepared the ground for Alcatraz's new role as a national park. In geographer Robert Rundstrom's opinion, the bulldozers conveyed "an unambiguous reassertion of federal authority and an unmaking of place."[22]

Nonetheless, some of the graffiti remained, and destructiveness was not the only government agenda. New traditions were in the making as the site underwent its transition into a park, because NPS custodians were mindful of the occupation's political significance for Alcatraz's history. While one branch of the state was erasing the remnants of the occupation, another was taking the first tentative steps toward recording it. From this perspective, it is difficult to characterize government actions as the straight "invention" of hegemonic views of the past. If anything, the federal government's actions were contradictory and complex. Shortly after the last protesters left the island, the NPS sent in a team of historical conservators to photo-document the graffiti.[23] Though some in the federal government may have hoped that the conservators' photos could be used to build a legal case against the occupiers, the Park Service's involvement in this task (rather than that of the FBI or the San Francisco police, for instance) confirms that at least one state agency had a sense at the time of the occupation's historical importance. On this occasion, at least, the government's "memory work" produced a record of an illegal action that created a resource for possible future commemoration.

The NPS's concern about recording occupation graffiti grew out of its earlier move to establish a framework for Alcatraz's interpretation as a nationally significant site with a multifarious history. In preparation for its proposed takeover of the island, the NPS undertook a study of the island's potential as a park. Called "A New Look at Alcatraz," it was released shortly after the occupation began. Ironically, the document proposed that the Rock be made into a federal park that acknowledged the site's Indian history.[24] In March 1970, federal negotiators tried to use that concept of a park with "maximal Indian qualities" to convince Indians of All Tribes to end their protest.[25] Indian negotiators testily rejected the proposal, insulted at the idea of handing over Alcatraz only to see it turn into a tasteless Indian theme park. As the occupation wore on, the protesters' resolve hardened and NPS's early keenness to foreground native history at the site softened. Despite the agency's prompt action to document the graffiti, it did not follow through on its plan to interpret Alcatraz's Indian history once the island became part of the Golden Gate National Recreation Area (GGNRA) in 1973. By this point, public sympathy for the occupation had gone up in smoke, along with some of the island's buildings. The possibilities for presenting Alcatraz as Indian land seemed remote, as NPS policy makers defined the island's historical importance solely with reference to Spanish exploration as well as military, transportation, and prison history.[26]

Although a formal legislative framework for the recognition of Indian history at national historic sites was in place when Alcatraz opened as a park, it did not result automatically in the interpretation of the occupation. The original National Park Service Act of 1916 committed the federal government to acknowledge and preserve the aboriginal past on the lands under its jurisdiction, and the 1966 National Historic Preservation Act had reconfirmed that commitment. Despite these legislative imperatives, however, the NPS had a poor track record in this regard. For much of the twentieth century, the agency ignored aboriginal claims, treaties, and patterns of customary use in acquiring and administering park lands. Only active resistance on the part of a number of tribal groups in the 1960s and 1970s forced the NPS to revisit its policies regarding resident peoples in national parks and to adopt a more culturally sensitive approach to managing the land under its stewardship, including developing interpretive programming that would highlight the history of its first occupants.[27]

By the 1970s, the NPS began to take more seriously its responsibilities to present Indian history in its park interpretation at sites with historic tribal presence. But here, Alcatraz posed a problem. Because the occupiers were urban Indians, many of them relocatees from distant reservations, and because the event in question had occurred in the very recent past, the occupation did not square with the NPS's conception of authentic aboriginal history, that is, something that involved indigenous peoples engaging in activities tied to ancestral lands.[28] Furthermore, the very radicalism of the pan-Indian ethos at Alcatraz meant that there was no single tribal group with whom the NPS might have worked through official channels. Nevertheless, in incremental and informal ways, the climate of concern about aboriginal history on Alcatraz did begin to warm by the 1980s at a grassroots level.

The impetus to commemorate the occupation came from Alcatraz staff members, not as a result of concrete directives from on high. Although long-serving rangers note that the atmosphere for interpreting the island's aboriginal history became more favorable in the 1980s, they agree that it was individual rangers, working in an ad hoc fashion and operating under the freedom granted to them to develop programs, who took the first real steps.[29] Initially, rangers drew on their own knowledge of the event, supplemented by sporadic research undertaken in their spare time. Despite their best efforts, throughout the 1970s and early 1980s, a lack of resources and a reluctance on the part of Native Americans to help the NPS package that part of the island's history for public consumption meant that programming was slow to develop.

As the twentieth anniversary of the occupation approached, two factors internal to the NPS promoted the official Indianization of Alcatraz beyond what had been achieved informally. A new interpretive prospectus for Alcatraz, issued in 1987, emphasized the need to present the multiple histories of the island in a way that would better reflect the cultural diversity of the U.S. population. Programming that highlighted Alcatraz's aboriginal history would fit the bill perfectly and would also meet the NPS's new Native American Relationships Management Policy, promulgated the same year, which deemed that the agency would "actively promote tribal cultures as a component of the parks themselves."[30] Rangers found themselves with more time to develop just such initiatives, for 1987 also saw the inauguration of an audiotaped prison cell-house tour, something that freed them to engage in other interpretive activities. Interest among rangers to develop specialized programs was high, and research began in earnest. The result, twenty years after the occupation began, was the first specialized tour, provocatively titled "Alcatraz Is Indian Land."[31] Taking their cues from the graffiti that remained on the site, rangers illustrated how Indians had rendered Alcatraz into a place of hope, defiance, and struggle.

Still, barriers to a fuller interpretation of the occupation remained. The Bay Area Native community remained largely distrustful of the Park Service and continued to refuse overtures from Alcatraz staff to help expand interpretive programs. Their reluctance was understandable, as Ranger Craig Glassner recalls: "After all, we were the bad guys, the guys in uniform; we were the government."[32] Moreover, when Native Americans did organize to commemorate the occupation, their proposals received what might easily have been interpreted as a bureaucratic brush-off from the NPS's higher administration. Although he acknowledged the symbolic importance of the occupation, GGNRA general superintendent Brian O'Neill rejected a 1990 proposal of the Native American Alcatraz Indian Project to erect "The Spirit Keeper," a permanent monument to the events of 1969–71. As he told occupation veteran Adam Fortunate Eagle, as well as two non-Native supporters of the project, a "visual monument" would compromise the interpretive balance on the island. Not only did the NPS have to put forward an objective interpretation of Alcatraz's history, but also it had the responsibility to "present all aspects of the island's scenic and natural as well as historic qualities. We feel a statue or monument would overshadow the incredible diversity of the island's 22 acres." The Park Service did not, he insisted, "want to allow one theme to dominate the others."[33]

For O'Neill, achieving an interpretive equilibrium on the island also involved maintaining a balance of interpretive power. It was not just a question of what histories were told, but who got to tell them. The general superintendent noted that the agency already allowed one Native American group to commemorate the occupation independently. Each November, the International Indian Tribal Council conducted its annual UnThanksgiving sunrise ceremony without input from the NPS, and that, he intimated, was enough.[34] Any additional recognition of the 1969–71 period would have to be the result of a cooperative effort between the NPS and Native Americans.[35]

Equally disappointing for some rangers was the typical visitor's manifest lack of interest in the island's aboriginal history. Since its opening, the mystique of Alcatraz, carefully cultivated by J. Edgar Hoover in order to appear tough on crime, whetted visitors' appetite and lured them to walk in the footsteps of famous criminals.[36] As former ranger John A. Martini put it: "Many folks, if you try to talk to them about the Indian story, especially before you've told them about Al Capone, they'll tune you out completely."[37] Those who tuned in were frequently hostile, accusing Indians of All Tribes of being vandals who had destroyed and defaced government property. Ironically, the Indians' peaceful occupation inspired condemnation among non-Native visitors, whereas the exploits of notorious murderers and kidnappers who had been imprisoned in the cell house seemed unquestionably worthy of commemoration.[38] If the visiting public could have dictated the stories told at Alcatraz, the occupation would never have been placed in a positive light.

Peevish tourists did not halt efforts to Indianize the island's interpretation, however. Rangers committed to the ideal of public education felt sufficiently committed to continue their efforts to commemorate the occupation. In the meantime, Congress passed legislation that required the NPS to revise its thematic framework "to reflect current scholarship and represent the full diversity of America's past."[39] Small gestures signaled that park management was finally prepared to add Indian history, and the occupation in particular, to the palette of Alcatraz stories. In 1992, the Golden Gate National Park Association published Adam Fortunate Eagle's memoirs *Alcatraz! Alcatraz!* and made them available for purchase at the Alcatraz bookshop. Two years later, in 1994, NPS employees developed an official web site that identified and explored the occupation as one of the four major interpretive themes on the island (the others being its penitentiary, military, and natural histories).[40]

Working with professional historians, the NPS completed its revision of the thematic framework for historical interpretation in all national parks in 1994. Unlike the previous effort, in 1987, to diversify the interpretation of national parks, this thematic overhaul was touted as a radical reconception of the U.S. past. Academic historians and an NPS working group came up with its revisions at a time when Americans were engaged in a rancorous debate over the content and purpose of history. Precipitated by an attempt to set voluntary national standards for the teaching of the discipline in public schools, the 1994 "history wars" sent reverberations through the country's universities, galleries, museums, and parks, as well as its Senate chambers.[41] On one side was an influential group of academic historians who criticized the orthodox approach to U.S. history, in which the journey from the past to the present was a tale of progress marked by great events and great (white, more often than not) men. "American history has been remade," announced historian Eric Foner in 1991, because the social movements of the 1960s and 1970s had "shattered the consensus vision that had dominated historical writing."[42] On the other side were prominent conservative politicians, bureaucrats, and pundits like Pat Buchanan, Lynne Cheney, and Rush Limbaugh, who denounced such views as "political correctness," arguing that the principal role of history wherever it was taught was to preserve tradition and instill patriotism.[43]

Mindful of both Foner's critique and the conservative reaction to it, the working group determined that national park interpretation had to be "remade," albeit carefully. Alcatraz's identity as a place where one of America's protest movements had originated made it a prime site for the interpretation of one of the working group's new proposed subthemes: "creating social institutions and movements." Based on the understanding that "why people organize to transform their institutions is as important to understand as how they choose to do so," the occupation could be interpreted as a significant event, which "influenced American history but did not produce permanent institutions."[44] Thus, although Indians of All Tribes did not achieve its principal goal of reclaiming ownership of Alcatraz, the occupiers' bid for liberation and self-determination, a militant action once condemned by state authorities, could now be incorporated as an important incident in the nation's history.

In doing so, however, the NPS was careful to leaven the story of American Indian dispossession and oppression in a manner that would deflect charges from the Right of political correctness. That balancing act is evident in the Alcatraz curriculum guide developed by rangers working in the educational arm of the Park Service. *Unlocking Alcatraz* (1994) highlights how the Indian occupation can help students to understand Americans' "ongoing struggle to define freedom."[45] Successful implementation of the NPS's curriculum guide will not only incorporate the occupation into the politically palatable story of the struggle for American freedoms, but also transform students' sense of Alcatraz as a place without transforming the place per se, in the way a permanent monument or recognition of aboriginal sovereignty would.

In another of its bids to shake up historical conventions, the working group stressed that indigenous peoples not be relegated to the distant past. At the Golden Gate National Park, this concern, in conjunction with statutory imperatives, translated into greater efforts to involve aboriginal people in park interpretation. When NPS archaeologists discovered the remains of Bay Area Ohlone/Costanoan tribal groups during the 1998 excavations of Crissy Field (a part of the GGNRA on the shoreline close to Alcatraz), the NPS and local Indian people began to forge formal relationships.[46] As archaeologists described their efforts to consult with indigenous peoples on the project: "It wasn't all absolutely perfect but it is a developing and productive dialogue which never existed in the park before."[47] On a more casual basis, rangers also solicited Indian people's opinions on park policy. For instance, at a pow-wow held with NPS approval on Alcatraz in 1997, attendees learned that plans were underway to document and stabilize occupation graffiti on the site. As the survey form explained: "We need the help of individuals who participated in the occupation of Alcatraz in making decisions about how best to preserve the graffiti."[48] By the time the thirtieth anniversary of the occupation came around, the NPS was prepared not only to acknowledge Alcatraz's Indian history but also to encourage Indian people to participate in its retelling.

The NPS was neither the sole nor even the chief architect of Alcatraz's "Indianization," however. As it happened, rising academic interest in documenting the occupation's history, along with veterans' growing willingness to tell their stories publicly, added Indian voices to the site's interpretation. Site interpretation of the occupation could have proceeded without Indian involvement, but these complementary changes external to the agency lent NPS interpretive shifts greater legitimacy. Rather than orchestrating public memory of the event, the NPS operated largely in a reactive mode, allowing government outsiders and historical insiders the freedom to determine how and by whom the occupation story would be told on the island. The Indianization of Alcatraz, while buoyed by broader NPS policy objectives, became possible only after a series of separate, independent, and unofficial initiatives to remember the occupation occurred in its wake. It is to those that we now turn our attention.

Indian efforts to apply the lessons of the occupation began almost immediately after the last Native Americans were removed from the Rock in 1971. Although the American Indian Movement (AIM) had been formed in 1968, the spirit of the "Alcatraz–Red Power movement" shifted the organization's direction, transforming it into a more radical and nationally active organization.[49] It was only after AIM's leaders had spent time on the island that they "realized the possibilities available through demonstration and seizure of federal facilities."[50] Occupation veterans, among other AIM members, seized the Mayflower II in Plymouth, Massachusetts, in November 1970 and went on to occupy the Bureau of Indian Affairs Washington offices in 1971. As well, former Alcatraz "warriors" participated in the "Trail of Broken Treaties" March in 1972, the stand-off with the FBI at Wounded Knee on the Pine Ridge Reservation in 1973, and the Longest Walk on Washington in 1978. By the end of the decade, more than seventy Native demonstrations or occupations conducted to protest injustices and to demand redress had taken place across the country.[51] Although AIM captured more headlines over the decade, Indians of All Tribes had been the first to seize the nation's attention. While these other important actions were significant moments in the Red Power movement's history in the 1970s, the occupation's pioneering status, and Alcatraz Island itself, accrued unique significance in activists' memories.

Subtler forms of Native activism also helped to ensure that Indian people would honor the memory of Alcatraz as an Indian place. In an era of student radicalism and curriculum reform, Alcatraz veterans, many of whom had been students during the occupation, took up leadership roles as educators in the postoccupation era. In the spirit of the Indians of All Tribes' Proclamation, Native Americans renewed their demands for more culturally relevant and sensitive curricula and educational institutions to meet their needs. The decade between Alcatraz and the Longest Walk witnessed the establishment of American Indian studies centers at more than one hundred U.S. universities, as well as nearly two dozen reservation community colleges.[52] Thunderbird University may not have been built on Alcatraz, as Indians of All Tribes had wished, but many versions of it rose from the ashes of the occupation, its closest analogue being Denagawide-Quetzalcoatl University. "D-Q U" was established in 1971 on abandoned federal government lands near Davis, California, the result of a successful Indian occupation by Alcatraz veterans, among others. One of the first courses on offer was two-time occupation veteran Grace Thorpe's "Seminar in Surplus Land," a primer in "securing [federal] surplus land for educational and health purposes."[53] Commemorating the occupation became, in part, a matter of curriculum planning and collecting college credits, as well as constructing barricades.

At the same time, Indian people continued to visit Alcatraz to keep its memory alive. Without the approval of NPS personnel (and arousing the suspicion of FBI agents, according to one ranger), small groups of Native people began to commemorate the occupation in visitation rituals soon after the occupation ended.[54] In this unsanctioned fashion, memories gathered at the site, condensing on Alcatraz as successive ceremonies memorialized the event. Throughout the 1970s and 1980s, Native people privately marked UnThanksgiving Day, as they had in the early days of the occupation, while rangers and tourists looked on from a distance. In another ceremony, this one designed to garner public attention, AIM chose the island in 1978 as the starting point for the Longest Walk, a protest march to Washington that called attention to unanswered demands for fairness and justice toward American Indians. By that point, the NPS did not interfere with these unofficial commemorations but participated merely by having rangers escort Indians to and from their chosen ceremonial site. Meanwhile, from a distance, Park Police disguised as curious tourists still kept their eyes and telephoto lenses trained on the celebrants.[55] While Indians clearly remained committed to memorializing the occupation on the site where it occurred, the possibility of NPS-Indian cooperation remained remote well into the 1980s.[56]

Nevertheless, institutional and informal ritualistic frames for the reverential recollection of the occupation kindled Alcatraz's spirit in individuals who later became prominent figures in Native politics and protest. Occupation veteran Wilma Mankiller, who became the Cherokee Nation's first female chief, credits Alcatraz with renewing her commitment to her people. "Ironically," she recalls, "the occupation of Alcatraz, a former prison, was extremely liberating for me. As a result, I consciously took a path I still find myself on today as I continue to work for the revitalization of tribal communities."[57] Although jailed Indian activist Leonard Peltier was in Seattle at the time, laying claim to surplus federal lands, he points to it as one of the keys to his politicization.[58] Joseph Myers, a Bay Area student during the occupation, went on to become the director of the National Indian Justice Center. As he reflected: "Alcatraz encouraged young people to become themselves, as opposed to hiding their Indianness. Alcatraz changed things."[59]

More broadly and fundamentally, the occupation led many Native Americans, even those who had never set foot on Alcatraz, to embrace their identities as aboriginal peoples again. Navajo Lenny Foster recalls that Alcatraz "gave me back my dignity and gave Indian people back their dignity."[60] According to La Nada Boyer, who had been a student leader during the occupation, "Alcatraz was symbolic in the rebirth of Indian people. We were able to raise, not only the consciousness of other American people, but our own people as well."[61] The graffiti is the most visible evidence of both the occupation and its intangible inspirational qualities for Native people. In response to the Alcatraz survey question, "What significance did the graffiti have for you then, and in what ways is it meaningful to you now?" each of the veterans who responded mentioned its enduring capacity to instill pride. As one woman declared: "It shows and proves that the occupation is validated. It was and is an important part of history and should be maintained for future reference."[62]

These two distinct currents of remembrance—one bureaucratic and largely white, the other unofficial and mainly aboriginal—might have remained divided by distrust, or they may have drifted together over time. What did bridge the gulf of mutual suspicion was academic interest in the occupation. When Troy Johnson decided in 1991 to study the occupation for his Ph.D., his decision to rely largely on veterans' oral histories had profound repercussions for the Indianization of Alcatraz. Encouraging former occupiers to tell their stories reactivated individuals' memories and simultaneously helped to forge a sense of collective memory among those who had actually been there. By articulating private memories with public remembrance, Johnson's work reinvested Alcatraz with special meaning for Indian people.[63]

Motivated by a sense of the larger historical importance of what they had done on Alcatraz, many former occupiers were ready to reenter the public forum and remake Alcatraz by memorializing it. A generation after the occupation, they no longer used graffiti to convey their messages. Instead, a number wrote memoirs of the occupation, which were published, along with a number of academic papers, in a special issue of the *American Indian Culture and Research Journal* to mark the occupation's twenty-fifth anniversary in 1994. The same year also saw their participation in the first public celebration of the occupation, an event held in conjunction with the start of AIM's long walk for justice, a march on Washington inspired by the incarceration of Leonard Peltier. Every year since, the International Indian Treaty Council, a branch of AIM, has held public sunrise ceremonies and UnThanksgiving pow-wows to mark the occupation and its legacy, events that draw growing numbers of occupation veterans and indigenous peoples from around the world to Alcatraz.[64]

Recognizing that remembrance could be framed not just textually as written memoirs or seasonally in the annual UnThanksgivings, but also filmically, Native Americans harnessed the power of the documentary to their cause in the years after the twenty-fifth anniversary. Working with the National Park Association's Jon Plutte, independent Native filmmaker Jim Fortier and academic Troy Johnson, many occupation veterans recorded their remembrances of the events of 1969–71. The result was *We Hold the Rock,* a twenty-eight-minute video completed in 1998 and permanently installed on Alcatraz Island. With minimal narration, the film recounts the occupation from the perspective of those who participated in it and illustrates the story with contemporary photographs and news footage of the event. In many ways, *We Hold the Rock* perpetuates occupation and objectives: It is a direct outcome of the heightened consciousness and changed political landscape the occupiers helped forge, and it flags the enduring Indian identity of Alcatraz, something Indians of All Tribes was at pains to underscore. Moreover, the video continues the alternative educational work central to the occupiers' purpose, for *We Hold the Rock* has been adopted for use in the California school system.[65]

Building on the success of *We Hold the Rock,* Fortier, Plutte, Johnson, and occupation veteran Millie Ketcheshawno formed a private production company and produced a feature-length documentary independent of the National Park Service, released February 1999 to mark the thirtieth anniversary. Entitled *Alcatraz Is Not an Island,* the film explores the occupation's legacy, showing how its transformative powers touched all Native Americans and even pushed a reluctant government bureaucracy into action.[66] Producing both the video and the documentary gathered the memories of Native American occupiers and government officials around the site, just as watching it draws a new generation of people into an interpretive process that Indianizes Alcatraz. The filmmakers hope that, like the event thirty years ago, their version of the occupation gains national attention, showing non-Native Americans that for aboriginal peoples, Alcatraz stands as a "rock prison of liberation," testimony to the power of collective action.[67]

The occupation of Alcatraz might have turned out very differently. Native people could have interpreted it as a failure. The federal government might have obliterated all evidence that protesters had once made it Indian land. And the passage of time could have made it difficult to recall the event. As Paul Chaat Smith and Robert Warrior wrote in 1996: "For most of those who did not directly experience the surge of activism it has all but faded from memory. If it is recalled at all, it is as a series of photojournalistic images of Indians with bandannas and rifles."[68] Well-publicized and popular events like the thirtieth-anniversary celebration, featuring ceremonies to honor Alcatraz warriors and speeches from veterans about their experiences, are proving them wrong.[69] And so are NPS-led efforts to preserve the occupation's visible traces. In 1997, the documentation and assessment of all existing graffiti began, and by 1999, it was completed. That a fine art conservator was hired to help stabilize images that were slapped up in the heady moments of a political action confirms the reverential treatment that the occupation has come to receive on Alcatraz.[70] The expression of political beliefs on the Rock not only changed people's consciousness—first, Indians', and much later the NPS's—but also transformed the place itself. As Indians of All Tribes spokesperson Richard Oakes declared during the occupation: "Alcatraz is not an island."[71] His words proved to be prophetic. The ritualistic recollection of the occupation over the past thirty years has sanctified the island in the same way that memorials to fallen soldiers sanctify battle sites.[72] As sometimes happens in dynamic processes of public remembrance, yesterday's rebels can become today's martyrs and heroes.

In spite of these symbols and gestures of cooperation between the NPS and Native peoples, for most of the visiting public, Alcatraz's identity remains closely tied to its prison past. The persistent undertow of U.S. Penitentiary Alcatraz and its flamboyant Hollywood dramatizations draws visitors by the millions. While some may learn about the occupation during their visits, either by taking a special tour or by watching *We Hold the Rock*, public memory of the occupation and its ongoing political meanings continues to flicker in the shadows cast by gangsters and movie stars.

Even at the level of government policy, the NPS's recognition of the occupation's national significance and its commemoration has not translated into concrete action by other agencies on aboriginal issues. Indeed, many activists point out that despite the gains they have made with federal agencies like the NPS, Indian grievances are, in fact, much lower on the nation's political agenda today than they were in the early 1970s, even though Indians continue to struggle against racism and injustice.[73] As one respondent to the graffiti survey somberly defined the occupation's significance: "We stood united, it was our Declaration of Independence then and now. But nothing much has changed for us."[74]

For Ohlone leader Rosemary Cambra, the Indianization of Alcatraz is particularly bittersweet. Though supportive of events like the thirtieth-anniversary celebration and proud of what Alcatraz has come to mean for aboriginal peoples around the world, Cambra argues that Alcatraz is, fundamentally and above all else, an island. It is a part of Ohlone territory, not a symbol of either America's prison past or the power of pan–Indianism. Challenging both Native and non–Native American claims to Alcatraz at the thirtieth-anniversary celebration, Cambra clarified what the island meant to her. "I am considered an aboriginal leader," she stated. "This is my land. But I am homeless, landless. And I pose this question to all of you. Will you help me? Will you help me in my struggle of reclaiming my land?"[75] Pleas like these underline indigenous people's ongoing struggles for acts of restitution, not just moving ceremonies. The gap between reverential remembrance and reparation remains vast.

NOTES

Acknowledgments: Research funding for this article was provided by the Social Sciences and Humanities Research Council of Canada. The authors would like to acknowledge the following people for sharing their thoughtful views on the commemorative processes at work on Alcatraz Island: Craig Glassner, Steven Haller, John A. Martini, Paul Scolari, and Guy Washington; all of the U.S. National Park Service; and Jim Fortier, Jon Plutte, and Troy Johnson. We would also like to thank Mary Gentry and Susan Ewing-Haley of the Golden Gate National Recreation Area Archives, who made our work play and saved us from having too many MUNI adventures.

1. For accounts of the occupation see Paul Chaat Smith and Robert Allen Warrior, *Like a Hurricane: The Indian Movement from Alcatraz to Wounded Knee* (New York: New Press, 1996); Troy Johnson, *The Occupation of Alcatraz Island: Self-determination and the Rise of Indian Activism* (Urbana: University of Illinois Press, 1996); and Troy Johnson, Joanne Nagel, and Duane Champagne, eds., *American Indian Activism: Alcatraz to the Longest Walk* (Urbana: University of Illinois Press, 1997). "Indians don't demonstrate" was a slogan associated with the National Congress of American Indians.

2. Most accounts of the 1969 occupation credit the 1964 landing with inspiring the idea of using Alcatraz for a more extensive protest (see Smith and Warrior, *Like a Hurricane,* 11).

3. These events are recounted in greater detail in Smith and Warrior, *Like a Hurricane,* and Johnson, *The Occupation of Alcatraz.*

4. Millie Ketcheshawno, "Welcome to the Alcatraz Occupation Thirtieth Anniversary Celebration," *Alcatraz Thirtieth Anniversary, 1969–1999* (San Francisco: Alcatraz Thirtieth Anniversary Planning Committee, October 23, 1999), 3.

5. Brian O'Neill, open letter, October 14, 1999, reprinted in *Alcatraz Thirtieth Anniversary,* 2.

6. The termination policy of 1953 aimed to assimilate Indian people and gradually to terminate Indian residence on reservations. During the occupation in 1970, the federal government began to reverse the policy by instituting tribal self-government and land transfers back to Native people (Johnson, *The Occupation of Alcatraz,* 218).

7. Author's personal observations, Alcatraz Island, October 23, 1999; Johnson, *The Occupation of Alcatraz,* 217; Smith and Warrior, *Like a Hurricane,* 37.

8. On the memorial strategies associated with violent, disturbing, or rebellious events, see Kenneth Foote, *Shadowed Ground: America's Landscapes of Violence and Tragedy* (Austin: University of Texas Press, 1997).

9. John A. Martini, interview by Carolyn Strange, Toronto, July 1999, and Guy Washington, interview by Carolyn Strange, Toronto, October 1999. Martini and Washington served as park rangers during the 1970s.

10. Pierre Vidal-Naquet, *The Assassins of Memory: Essays on the Denial of the Holocaust,* trans. and foreword by Jeffrey Mehlman (New York: Columbia University Press, 1992).

11. Troy Johnson, interview by Carolyn Strange, Toronto, July 1999.

12. The literature in this area is vast. Seminal works include Eric Hobsbawm and Terence Ranger, eds., *The Invention of Tradition* (Cambridge: Cambridge University Press, 1983); Paul Connerton, *How Societies Remember* (Cambridge: Cambridge University Press, 1989); Maurice Halbwachs, *On Collective Memory,* trans. F. J. Ditter and V. Y. Ditter (New York: Harper & Row, 1980); and Pierre Nora, "Between Memory and History: Les Lieux de Memoire," *Representations* 26 (spring 1989): 7–25.

13. Iwona Irwin-Zarecka, *Frames of Remembrance: The Dynamics of Collective Memory* (New Brunswick, N.J.: Transaction, 1994), 126.

14. This idea comes from Edward Casey, "How to Get from Space to Place in a Fairly Short Stretch of Time: Phenomenological Prolegomena," in Steven Feld

and Keith H. Basso, eds., *Senses of Place* (Santa Fe, N.M.: School of American Research Press, 1996), 24. Here we wish to underline our central argument: There is no consensus over the meaning of the term "Indianization." Indeed, it remains a contentious issue that complicates efforts to interpret Alcatraz's history and future.

15. Martini interview. On the occupation itself see Johnson, *The Occupation of Alcatraz*. On the educational context from which the occupation emerged see Steve Talbot, "Indian Students and Reminiscences of Alcatraz," 104–12, and Edward D. Castillo, "A Reminiscence of the Alcatraz Occupation," 119–28, in Johnson, Nagel, and Champagne, *American Indian Activism*.

16. From the "Proclamation of Indians of All Tribes," reprinted in Peter Bluecloud, ed., *Alcatraz Is Not an Island* (Berkeley: Wingbow Press, 1972), 40–42.

17. Statement made by a participant in the Staff and Physical Operations roundtable discussion at the Indians of All Tribes National Conference on Alcatraz Island, December 23, 1969, cited in Robert A. Rundstrom, "American Indian Placemaking on Alcatraz, 1969–1971," *American Indian Culture and Research Journal* 18, 4 (1994): 189.

18. Rundstrom, "American Indian Placemaking," 193–95.

19. Adam (Nordwall) Fortunate Eagle, "Urban Indians and the Occupation of Alcatraz Island," in Johnson, Nagel, and Champagne, *American Indian Activism*, 73.

20. Rundstrom, "American Indian Placemaking," 199.

21. Ibid.

22. Ibid., 192.

23. Johnson interview.

24. John Garvey and Troy Johnson, "The Government and the Indians: The American Indian Occupation of Alcatraz Island, 1969–71," in Johnson, Nagel, and Champagne, *American Indian Activism*, 165.

25. That was how federal negotiator Robert Robertson described the park. The federal government made the offer for a park in response to the demand by Indians of All Tribes for a cultural center (see J. Campbell Bruce, "'Indianized' Alcatraz Park," *San Francisco Chronicle*, April 1, 1970, file 12 of 16, 2 of 3; and Austin, Director, Western Division, GSA, to Nicolai, July 2, 1970, file 14 of 16, 2 of 2, both documents in box 6, RG 269, National Archives Records Administration [NARA], San Bruno, Calif.). On the Indians' rejection of that proposal, see Dale Champion, "Indians Reject Park Plan," *San Francisco Chronicle*, April 8, 1970, "Alcatraz III," Box 16, RG 269, NARA.

26. The themes the NPS identified as pertinent to Alcatraz were Spanish exploration, transportation and communication (the Alcatraz lighthouse), the Mexican War, the Civil War, the Spanish-American War, political and military affairs concerning both the fortifications history and the military prison, and, finally, "society and social conscience: prison reform" (this despite the fact the penitentiary hardly exemplified reformist goals) (Erwin N. Thompson, *The Rock: A History of Alcatraz Island, 1847–1972, Historic Resource Study* [Denver: National Park Service, 1972], 510).

27. Robert H. Keller and Michael F. Turek, *American Indians and National Parks* (Tuscon: University of Arizona Press, 1998), 233–34.

28. Paul Scolari, interview by Carolyn Strange, Toronto, 6 July 1999 and 31 August 1999.

29. Martini interview; Steve Haller and Craig Glassner, interviews by Carolyn Strange, Toronto, July 1999. All served as rangers on the Rock.

30. Keller and Turek, *American Indians and National Parks*, 234.

31. "Alcatraz Is Indian Land" tour text, November 11, 1988, "Alcatraz Program Evaluation" file, box 65, Division of Interpretation Administration Files Ca. 1970–1993, Golden Gate National Recreation Area Archives, San Francisco (hereafter, GGNRA Archives). They could inform themselves further by reading a one-page mimeographed sheet containing an outline history of the occupation written by the Rock's first Native American ranger, Naomi Torres.

32. Glassner interview. Since the 1990s, Glassner has been the site's principal interpreter of the occupation.

33. Brian O'Neill to Adam Fortunate Eagle, March 8, 1990, "Alcatraz 1988–1993, Interpretive Activities," file K-18, box 48, Superintendent's Files, GGNRA Archives. See also O'Neill to Susan Brandt, January 29, 1990, ibid.; and O'Neill to Peg Bachmeier, June 13, 1990, file 12, box 84, Division of Interpretation Administration Files, GGNRA Archives.

34. O'Neill to Susan Brandt, 29 January 1990, "Alcatraz 1988–1993, Interpretive Activities," file K-18, box 48, Superintendent's Files, GGNRA Archives.

35. Ibid.; O'Neill reiterated this sentiment in his letter to Adam Fortunate Eagle and to Peg Bachmeier, both supporters of "The Spirit Keeper." See O'Neill to Adam Fortunate Eagle, March 8, 1990, "Alcatraz 1988–1993, Interpretive Activities," file K-18, box 48, Superintendent's Files, GGNRA Archives; and O'Neill to Peg Bachmeier, June 13, 1990, file 12, box 84, Division of Interpretation Administrative Files, GGNRA Archives.

36. We explore this in greater detail in our article "Rock Prison of Liberation: Alcatraz Island and the American Imagination," *Radical History Review*, 78 (fall 2000): 27–56.

37. Martini interview.

38. Glassner interview.

39. PL 101-628, sec. 1209 (1991).

40. See http://www.nps.gov/alcatraz. Ranger Craig Glassner, who conducts the "Alcatraz Is Indian Land" special tours, is the web site's chief architect.

41. There are a number of books and articles on various aspects of the "history wars," many of them dealing with specific controversies like the West as America exhibit at the Smithsonian's National Museum of American Art, or the cancellation of the National Air and Space Museum's exhibit on the dropping of the atomic bomb on Hiroshima. *History on Trial: Culture Wars and the Teaching of the Past* (New York: Alfred A. Knopf, 1998), by Gary B. Nash, Charlotte Crabtree, and Ross E. Dunn, deals with the debate over national history standards.

42. Eric Foner, *The New American History* (Philadelphia: Temple University Press, 1991), x. Although Foner was not listed among the working group participants, they cited his work in their preamble (see "Revision of the Na-

tional Park Service's Thematic Framework," http://www.cr.nps.gov/history/ thematic.html).

43. Nash, Crabtree, and Dunn, *History on Trial*, chap. 5, esp. 122–27, and chap. 8.

44. "Revision of the National Park Service's Thematic Framework." The Organization of American Historians, the National Coordinating Committee for the Promotion of History, and the American Historian Association participated with NPS professionals to devise the 1994 revisions.

45. *Unlocking Alcatraz: Curriculum Guide: Federal Penitentiary (1934–1963) and Native American Occupation (1969–1971)* (Fort Mason, San Francisco: U.S. Department of the Interior, National Park Service, and Golden Gate National Recreation Area, 1994), i.

46. The federal Native American Graves Protection and Repatriation Act of 1990 defined Native American ownership and control of Native cultural items and obliged the government to work with aboriginal peoples in repatriating human remains.

47. *Archaeology on Crissy Field: A Q & A Session with Mathew Clark, Richard Ambro, Lee Barker, and Paul Scolari* (San Francisco: Golden Gate National Recreation Area, c. 1998).

48. Paul Scolari, a ranger who acts as park Indian liaison and historian for the GGNRA, composed the survey and distributed it in October 1997. We are grateful to Paul for giving us a copy of the survey along with the twenty-seven veterans' responses.

49. "Alcatraz–Red Power Movement" is the term coined in Troy R. Johnson, "American Indian Activism and Transformation: Lessons from Alcatraz," in Johnson, Nagel, and Champagne, *American Indian Activism*, 9–44.

50. Johnson, *The Occupation of Alcatraz*, 219–20. John Trudell, an Alcatraz veteran, was chair of AIM from 1973 to 1979.

51. Johnson, *The Occupation of Alcatraz*, 223–40.

52. Alvin M. Josephy Jr., Joanne Nagel, and Troy Johnson, "Introduction: 'You Are on Indian Land,'" in their edited documents collection, *Red Power: the American Indians' Fight for Freedom*, 2d ed., (Lincoln: University of Nebraska Press, 1999), 3.

53. Cited in Josephy, Nagel, and Johnson, *Red Power*, 194. On D-Q U, also see Jack D. Forbes, "The Native Struggle for Liberation," in Johnson, Nagel, and Champagne, *American Indian Activism*, 129–35.

54. Washington interview. On the importance of ritual in fixing collective memories, see Foote, *Shadowed Ground*, 8.

55. Martini interview.

56. This is the consensus of the rangers we interviewed, including those who had been employees in the period as well as more recent hirees, such as Paul Scolari, who have studied the history of Indian-NPS relations at Alcatraz.

57. Wilma Mankiller and Michael Wallis, *Mankiller: A Chief and Her People* (New York: St. Martin's Press, 1993), 192.

58. Leonard Peltier, *Prison Writings: My Life Is My Sundance* (New York: St. Martin's Press, 1999), 93.

59. Troy R. Johnson, *We Hold the Rock: The Indian Occupation of Alcatraz, 1969–1971* (San Francisco: Golden Gate National Recreation Area, 1997), 51.

60. Cited in Josephy, Nagel, and Johnson, *Red Power,* 39–40.

61. Quoted in "Alcatraz Occupation Thirtieth Anniversary," 4.

62. Shirley Guevara (Mono), graffiti survey response, October 1997. She indicated that she had been on Alcatraz for "about one week after the occupation began."

63. Johnson interview. This concept of private and public memory comes from Irwin-Zarecka, *Frames of Remembrance,* 4.

64. Glassner interview.

65. Johnson interview.

66. Jim Fortier, interview by Carolyn Strange, Toronto, September 1, 1999. Screened at the American Indian Film Festival, *We Hold the Rock* won first prize in documentary film (see www.turtle-island.com/docu.html).

67. "Alcatraz, Symbol of Oppression, Rock Prison of Liberation," *Unlocking Alcatraz—Curriculum Guide* (San Francisco: Golden Gate National Recreation Area, 1994), iv.

68. Smith and Warrior, *Like a Hurricane,* vii.

69. The thirtieth anniversary was well publicized over the Internet, and it received extensive coverage in Bay Area newspapers and magazines. It was also a feature story in *Native Peoples;* see Ben Winton, "Taking Back 'the Rock,'" *Native Peoples* 13, 1 (fall 1999): 26–34.

70. Paul Scolari, interview by Carolyn Strange, Toronto, August 31, 1999.

71. Richard Oakes, "Alcatraz Is Not an Island," *Ramparts* 11, 6 (December 1972): 38, 40. This phrase was also chosen as the title of the Diamond Island film about the occupation.

72. Foote, *Shadowed Ground,* 8, 15.

73. "The Legacy of Alcatraz and Related Issues—Panel Forum, 23 October 1999." The speakers were Betty Cooper, Luwant Quitaquit Harrison, Ron Pinkham, and Rosemary Cambra.

74. Linda Whitewolf Sanchez (Chickasaw and Maori), graffiti survey response, October 1997.

75. Tribal chairwoman of the Ohlone Muwekma Tribe Rosemary Cambra, "The Legacy of Alcatraz."

Kitty Krupat

10 Out of Labor's Dark Age
Sexual Politics Comes to the Workplace

IN OCTOBER 1995, John Sweeney was elected to head the nation's labor federation. A coup engineered from within the AFL-CIO by an oppositionist cadre bent on ousting the administration of Lane Kirkland,[1] Sweeney's victory was widely regarded as a repudiation of forty years of conservative leadership under Kirkland and his predecessor, George Meany. To mark the first anniversary of this event, a group of historians organized a labor teach-in at Columbia University in October 1996. It drew nearly two thousand participants, a mixed crowd of leftist intellectuals and progressive trade unionists, coming together in a spirit of celebration and rapprochement. The teach-in was explicitly future oriented, but implicitly it was also an homage to an earlier moment in labor history, when factory workers and intellectual workers might meet at a union hall or on a picket line.

This is the period Michael Denning has called the "Age of the CIO." Breaking away from the American Federation of Labor, the Congress of Industrial Organizations undertook mass industrial organizing campaigns in the 1930s and 1940s that brought many thousands of immigrant workers, people of color, and women into unions. Along with auto workers and meat packers came professionals and semi-professionals in the burgeoning communications industries, such as film and radio. This intellectual and social mix was stirred not only by an activist cadre of socialists and communists within the CIO, but also by an alliance of intellectuals and cultural workers Denning defines as a cultural front.[2] In this atmosphere, a concept of social unionism developed that was still an ideal for many who joined the labor teach-in at Columbia. Distanced from labor in the Meany-Kirkland era, they now wished to reassert an alliance between labor and intellectuals. Timely as well as visionary, the Columbia teach-in gave voice to these ambitions.

The teach-in has justly earned its referential status. That said, it was not without its contradictions or its moments of historical amnesia. On opening night, an array of labor luminaries and academic celebrities sat front and center on the stage. Behind them, a group of clerical workers from Barnard College sat mutely, like so many actors in a tableau vivant. Members of the United Automobile Workers union, they had just won a bitter six-month strike against the college, a Columbia University affiliate. Midway through the proceedings, the philosopher Richard Rorty rose to deliver a stinging critique of New Left movements in the 1960s and 1970s. The failures of identity politics in this period, he maintained, were largely responsible for a vitiated Left in the following decades.[3] Rorty's remarks drew an audible hiss from some members of the audience. Silently, I took offense myself. In the presence of these Barnard workers, Rorty's remarks seemed incongruous, even rude.

In 1974, fresh from the antiwar movement, I had joined the organizing staff of District 65. The Barnard workers—a markedly diverse group, with women and people of color in the majority and a significant number of openly gay members—were already there. They had organized into District 65 in 1973, at the height of New Left social activism. They were not an anomaly but among thousands of office and professional workers in both public and private sectors—mainly women and people of color—who were unionizing on the heels of identity-based political movements. Many new union leaders who emerged from these organizing campaigns had been through basic training in New Left movements. Though we did not theorize it this way, we apprehended class as a category that had been reconfigured by identity politics of the Sixties and Seventies. From our shop-floor perspective, class appeared much as labor historian Daniel Walkowitz has argued that it is: an amalgam of identities, including race and gender along with economic position.[4]

I have begun with recollections of the Columbia teach-in because it was among the first public forums for a discussion about the future of U.S. labor at what many believed was an auspicious moment. This discussion, which continues to this day, turned out to be a retrospective analysis as well as a prognostication.[5] What emerged was a new discourse of pro-unionism, cast as a narrative whose historical analogues are the dark ages and the renaissance. It usually begins something like this: "Organized labor, awakening from its quarter-century 'era of stagnation,' finds itself, Rip Van Winkle–like, in a world transformed. While labor slept. . . ."[6]

This example is taken from "Labor's Day: The Challenge Ahead," an important essay by Jeremy Brecher and Tim Costello published—along with seven responses—in the September 1998 *Nation* magazine. For good reasons, the authors chose to discuss the industrial sector and the challenges John Sweeney continues to face as labor struggles to rebuild its traditional base in the new century. In that connection, the deep-sleep metaphor works. The service sector is another story, however, one that is missing from Brecher and Costello's account. Most likely, they omitted it in order to focus more sharply on their particular subject. Yet the service sector is where most Americans are employed and where unions have organized, even in the doldrums of a quarter century. Service workers in all their diversity and all their identities are left out when Brecher and Costello delineate a "reconfigured working class." They map this new working class along geographical and economic lines, with race factored in tangentially. Gender and sexuality are virtually absent from their argument.[7]

Social identity is present to some extent in contemporary debate about the future of organized labor. It is prominent, for example, in *State of the Union: A Century of American Labor,* the latest work of historian Nelson Lichtenstein.[8] Nevertheless, the subject is easily sidelined or muted. This can happen even in the most innovative analysis. Take, for example, a wonderful collection of essays entitled *A New Labor Movement for a New Century.* In the introduction, editor Gregory Mantsios asks the big question: "Why did a labor movement that was so vibrant, massive and capable of bringing about fundamental change in the 1930s and 1940s become virtually moribund in the 1980s and 1990s?"[9] Twenty-one commentators in this very excellent volume provide thoughtful answers to that question and offer prescriptions for a healthy labor movement in the twenty-first century. Four essays, focusing specifically on women and people of color, are grouped under the heading "Diversity and Inclusion." Segregating the topic in this way inadvertently implies that "diversity and inclusion" may be separated from the larger discussion of organizing strategies, union democracy, political action, and international affairs, which are the other topics in this book. More to the point, of the four essays on diversity, only one—"Getting Serious about Inclusion" by José La Luz and Paula Finn—suggests that social identity is a component of class.[10] And, despite a generous sprinkling of comments on racism and sexism throughout the anthology, not one essay even refers to homophobia or to sexual orientation as a factor in workplace struggle.

Despite overt antiworker and antiunion policies of the Bush administration, public intellectuals and journalists continue to offer a labor critique that is generous in spirit compared to the relentless negativity of labor reporting in previous decades. However, to the extent this critique glosses over questions of social identity, it tends to distort both the history and the meaning of John Sweeney's victory in 1995. It obscures the steady development of an identity-based class formation that I believe *created* the political space for labor reform in the first place. My argument rests on three interrelated points: First, while the institutional labor movement was moving rightward in the 1950s—and while it was in a period of drastic decline—workers themselves were laying the basis for progressive change in the 1990s. Seen in this light, the ouster of an old-guard leadership was not a mutiny engineered by a few union presidents at an AFL-CIO convention but an inevitable response to pressures from below. Second, identity-driven campaigns beginning in the late 1960s and continuing through the next two decades of labor's "dark age" were reshaping our conception of class struggle.[11] I hope to add something by my third claim: The beginnings of a gay and lesbian workers' movement can be traced through emerging forms of class struggle in this period.

If sexual identity is rarely defined as a component of class, it is brought into clear view by the documentary *Out at Work: Lesbians and Gay Men on the Job*.[12] This film, by Tami Gold and Kelly Anderson, follows three workers—two of them union members—who come out on their jobs and become leaders in the struggle for sexual rights and representation in the workplace. The class consciousness of their position is underscored by the nature of their demands: not simply issues of principle but economic rights as well—rights to job security and equality of benefits, among other things. Here, then, is a clear case in point, not just for the constitutive relationship between class and social identity, but also for the argument that social identity can be, and often is, the axis of class struggle. In this sense, it provides the inspiration for a revisionist history of working-class formation in the latter half of the twentieth century.

In his book *The Origins of Postmodernity*, Perry Anderson makes an almost offhand remark that sums up the context for a decline-and-fall narrative of labor since the 1950s. With the onset of the Cold War,

Anderson observes, "the labour movement was neutered and the left hounded."[13] His use of the term "neutered" is of some interest, suggesting, as it does, that "big labor" was emasculated. As I hope to show later in this essay, the masculinity of labor *was* compromised, but to more productive purposes than Anderson envisions. His point here is that conservative political forces and growing corporate power in the Cold War years conspired to undermine organized labor. Of that there is no doubt, and this idea is the bedrock upon which most accounts of recent labor history rest.

My attempt to reframe conventional accounts is not intended to dispute fundamental verities. Nor do I wish to downplay the importance of a change in institutional leadership. Early on, the Sweeney administration defined a progressive agenda for labor, designed to boost numbers and power. If Sweeney has not delivered on this promise, he has at least embraced a more progressive unionism. In December 1999, he led thirty-five thousand trade unionists through the streets of Seattle to protest antiworker policies of the World Trade Organization. In the old AFL-CIO, this thrilling display of labor militancy and solidarity with young activists of diverse political tendencies would have been unthinkable. Despite a dismal organizing record, there have been some bright spots. Innovations in campaign strategy brought 1.5 million new members to the AFL-CIO in the three-year period between 1997 and 1999. In addition, the Sweeney program has made some legislative gains, including an increase in the federal minimum wage.[14] Despite these fruits of change, I nevertheless want to offer a ground-floor perspective on the new labor order ushered in by John Sweeney and his administration. Mine is a counternarrative, or revisionist history, that foregrounds a wave of organizing and new class formation. Looking at our history this way suggests two things: that the "dark ages" of labor's decline were not so dark and that the "renaissance," heralded in 1995, was in the making decades earlier.

THE NARRATIVE OF DECLINE

Labor's right to organize, guaranteed under the National Labor Relations Act (NLRA) of 1937, was sharply curtailed by restrictive provisions of the Taft-Hartley Act passed in 1947. Bitterly opposed by organized labor from its inception, Taft-Hartley has never been overturned, nor has labor achieved ameliorating labor law reform. Throughout the Reagan-Bush era, new organizing was stymied by a series of probusiness changes in the NLRA, virtually transforming pro-union legislation into an instrument of corporate power. This combination of factors—coupled with deindustrialization and the flight of jobs to global markets—accounts for labor's sharp decline in the last forty years. In some respects, however, labor contributed to its own undoing. The decline-and-fall view of recent labor history relies heavily upon labor's "sins," starting with its turn from social to business unionism.

Class was the matrix of solidarity in CIO social unionism, the rubric that united working men and women of all races and social positions. At its most visionary, social unionism can be described as a culture of organizing: militant in its class consciousness; "holistic" in its attention to education and leisure activities;[15] ideological in its stance on a range of social justice issues, from civil rights to war and peace. One of social unionism's more utopian aims was the development of rank-and-file democracy and leadership. Ideally, rank-and-file democracy would lead to full representation on the basis of race, ethnicity, and gender. But this principle was honored in the breach more often than not. Though African Americans and women made strides during the Age of the CIO, they continued to be underrepresented in the union movement, both in membership numbers and leadership positions.[16]

By the end of World War II, social unionism was badly compromised. Organized labor had made its greatest gains during the New Deal administration of Franklin Roosevelt, but in this period it had also set a precedent for compromise. Linked to the Popular Front alliance by strong antifascist sentiment, the CIO joined forces with the administration, entering into a wartime compact with government and business.[17] Labor had a seat on the tripartite War Labor Board (WLB), for example. Often a reluctant partner, labor nevertheless helped to establish WLB policies that were adamantly opposed by its own constituency. These included wage restrictions and a "no-strike" pledge, fiercely resisted by wildcat strikers in auto, steel, and other industries.[18] If the cause of antifascism could be served by this form of cooperation—and if, into the bargain, labor might achieve favorable conditions for organizing—it would also lay the basis for concession bargaining and for a long-term marriage of convenience between labor and the Democratic Party.

The anti-red crusade that crippled the labor Left also had its origins in the New Deal period. The House Committee on Un-American Activities, headed by Martin Dies, held its first hearings in 1938, an ominous beginning to the witch hunt that would culminate in anticommunist affidavits, required of union leaders under provisions of Taft-Hartley. Persecuted from the outside, CIO unions battled internally. Communists and fellow travelers were purged. Between 1948 and 1950, eleven unions and a million members were drummed out of the CIO.[19] When the AFL and CIO merged in 1955, the labor movement had already begun its rightward turn.[20]

Despite the ravages of red-baiting and despite the increasing power of corporations, labor was still in a relatively strong position when George Meany was elected to head the new Federation in 1955. The AFL-CIO had good reason to be confident: America's postwar industrial economy was booming. With basic industry virtually organized by the late 1940s, total union membership reached an all-time high of 35 percent in 1954.[21] Attention shifted away from organizing the unorganized toward increasing benefits for an already established membership and strengthening the existing base of labor power. Not in all unions but on a fairly general scale, business unionism—a top-down, corporate style of union practice—replaced social unionism. The hallmark of business unionism was bureaucratization and professionalism, with attorneys and administrators negotiating contracts and managing sophisticated benefit plans. In this model of unionism, members became, in effect, clients. Vital energies of rank-and-file activism were sapped in the process.

Following the lead of successive administrations from Eisenhower onward, the AFL-CIO assimilated into the Cold War apparatus. After the Cuban Revolution of 1959, for example, the Federation established the American Institute for Free Labor Development (AIFLD). An affiliate of the AFL-CIO International Affairs Department, AIFLD was created to train and support anticommunist unions in Latin America. Though by 1980, AIFLD's board was composed entirely of union officials, its founding board had included executives of United Fruit, Pan American Airlines, and the W. R. Grace Company.[22] Though many unions within the Federation and thousands of individual union members were playing an exceptional role in the advancement of civil rights—and later in the antiwar and feminist movements—the Federation itself was drifting into the middle ground, opting for neutrality on controversial domestic issues such as abortion rights, and toeing the administration line on foreign policy, supporting the war in Vietnam even when the nation as a whole was divided on the question.

All along the way of this history, the industrial base of America was shrinking. Often the last hired, women and people of color were among the first factory workers to lose their jobs. Unprepared for this eventuality, the labor movement was slow to react. Continuing to place its faith in the Democratic Party, the Federation spent millions on electoral campaigns. But in 1980, some member unions—including the Teamsters and the air-traffic controllers union (PATCO)—were staunch supporters of Ronald Reagan. In 1981, less than a year after his election, Reagan betrayed his labor allies and fired more than eleven thousand striking air-traffic controllers. The labor movement suffered a particularly humiliating defeat. To complicate matters, unions were coming under ideological attack from both the Right and the Left. If the reactionary Right measured unionism on a scale of socialist evils, the Left took organized labor to task for accommodationist party politics, its support of U.S. foreign policy and neo-liberal economics, as well as for concession bargaining at home. Within the ranks of organized labor itself, many union members and some union leaders shared this left critique.

Throughout the Eighties and Nineties, union membership continued its steady decline. In an increasingly right-wing political environment, corporations had held the upper hand for quite some time and seemed to be running roughshod over unions. The percentage of organized workers had dropped to about 10 percent of the private sector when John Sweeney was elected to head the Federation in 1995.[23] In these circumstances, the ouster of an old-guard leadership was celebrated by union members and labor advocates across the country. The renaissance was at hand.

The boilerplate of many popular accounts, this truncated history is true enough. But it is a flat account. Reading between the lines, we get a fuller picture. Something was actually going on during the putative dark age of labor's decline. Indeed, a renaissance of sorts was in the making. To offer but one stunning example: In 1987, home health-care workers in Los Angeles began an eleven-year struggle to gain representation through the Service Employees International Union (SEIU), whose president at the time was John Sweeney. That struggle came to fruition in February 1999, when seventy-four thousand workers achieved what the New York Times described as labor's biggest win since 1937.[24] No doubt, victory in this long union struggle was facilitated in its final phase by the emergence of a new and progressive labor leadership in the mid-1990s. But the important point, here, is that this victory was the fruit of pioneering efforts in the service sector that had begun more than a decade before.

RETHINKING THE RENAISSANCE

In the 1960s, women and people of color—office workers, professionals, and paraprofessionals in both public and private sectors—began to unionize in significant numbers for the first time.[25] In the public sector alone, four million workers organized between 1959 and 1980.[26] Cultural workers were organizing alongside service employees and professionals. Writers and editors, journalists, graphic designers and museum workers, teachers and graduate students were adding their voices to an emergent class struggle, in some ways reminiscent of the Age of the CIO.[27] Though it is tempting to emphasize the grassroots nature of this groundswell in unionization, the truth is some unions spent huge sums to support white-collar organizing efforts. If a drive failed—and many did—these unions would never recoup a cent in dues income.[28]

Growth in white-collar sectors was never enough to offset losses in the industrial sector. Nevertheless, it brought new issues and new forms of organization into view. The language of class had already changed. No longer the fundamental distinction between workers and owners, class was also defined by education and skill, workplace hierarchies, taste and lifestyle. If many white-collar and professional workers had been raised in working-class families and neighborhoods, they now identified themselves as middle class.[29] Yet, to the extent they shared workplace conditions and concerns, to the extent they occupied a common position in the power relations between labor and management, they were also working class. While workplace inequities fueled their ambitions, the source of their solidarity often lay in the particularities of social identity rather than economic position. What emerges from these contradictions is a picture of class as a multiple identity, both complex and ambiguous. I believe that the ambiguities inherent in this class conception are productive, for they allow workers to struggle for rights and representation on many fronts simultaneously and to recognize profound connections between the politics of identity and the universality of class.

Affinities of race, gender, and sexuality have always been points of solidarity among workers. What distinguishes this period, however, is how these affinities were articulated as fundamental trade-union principles. New union members put their particular concerns on the bargaining table for the first time. These concerns had everything to do with identity politics: gender-based pay equity, comparable worth, child care, affirmative action, domestic-partner benefits, and expanded protections against discrimination. They introduced challenging ideas about democratic trade unionism, demanding representation at every level of union structure for women, people of color, differing age groups, and eventually sexual orientations. Negotiating for labor-management committees on issues such as health and safety, affirmative action and child care, union members began to formulate a notion of worker involvement in policy making at a higher level than traditional collective bargaining frameworks had allowed. For example, the Harvard Union of Clerical and Technical Workers (HUCTW) established an unorthodox (and still controversial) form of collective bargaining. Rather than assuming an adversarial position in negotiations, HUCTW emphasized consciousness raising through discussions between university administrators and clerical workers. It is tempting to suggest that there is a link between this modus operandi and the fact that HUCTW is a union of women workers and leaders. If so, they are a powerful sisterhood. Their first union contract included recognition in principle of the role support staff should play in university governance.[30]

The drive toward empowerment was a significant factor in bringing sexual identity into the workplace. Nevertheless, in the early years of white-collar organizing, questions of race and gender were paramount and sexuality was low on the order of priorities. Homophobia remained largely unexplored, despite preoccupations with other forms of social injustice. But in a disciplined union movement—by which I mean, quite simply, a movement schooled in the dialectic of right and wrong—homophobia could be presented and examined as a social injustice along with racism and sexism. If only grudgingly, most committed unionists would at least stand by the old maxim: "An injury to one is an injury to all.[31] In an identity-conscious milieu, gay workers could begin to test this principle. If nothing else, the atmosphere was conducive to a new struggle for representation. Even if they were not "out" in the political sense, many gay workers in the culture industries were more comfortably assimilated in their workplaces than gay workers in other industries. If straight unmarried couples and single parents could demand equality of union benefits, gay and lesbian workers might risk coming out of the closet to demand the same, starting with explicit protections against discrimination.

At first blush, the *Village Voice* is not a typical example of the unionized workplace. But in fact, the *Voice* is representative of an influential sector of organized professionals and cultural workers who have helped to define the current culture of organizing.[32] The *Voice* was founded in 1955 by a trio of "beat generation" devotees, including Norman Mailer. They conceived of the *Voice* as a neighborhood newspaper, a venue for writers and artists who congregated in Greenwich Village. In the next twenty-one years, the paper would go through several changes of ownership and management. Through it all, the *Voice* retained something of its alternative flavor. In the mid-1970s, it was still a polymorphous workplace, where a nine-to-five ad taker one day could be a reporter the next; where a former *New York Times* book reviewer, Eliot Fremont-Smith, wrote stately literary prose, while Jill Johnston, an open lesbian, talked about the ups and downs of her love life in a weekly column on dance.

Though faithful in some ways to its bohemian traditions, the *Voice* was nevertheless moving perceptibly toward the commercial mainstream and was a very profitable national enterprise by the time Rupert Murdoch bought it in 1977.[33] When the sale was announced, *Voice* workers went into a panic. Fearing that Murdoch would sweep the place clean in an effort to turn their paper into another of his commercial tabloids, they formed a wall-to-wall union over the weekend and presented themselves to District 65 on Sunday evening. I was assigned by the union to be their organizer. After an election in the spring of 1977, their union was certified by the National Labor Relations Board, and several months later, they began negotiations for a first contract. Early on, *Voice* then-publisher William Ryan committed to affirmative-action goals, mandating 10 percent minority representation in every department of the newspaper. Employees sought and won an affirmative-action committee to monitor progress. In many other ways, the first *Voice* contract was revolutionary. Besides providing benefits for freelance writers—unheard of in standard newspaper contracts—the first agreement also contained a broad equal-rights provision that laid the basis for redefining family to include same-sex relationships. At the time of these first negotiations, District 65's health plan was already covering unmarried straight couples as a matter of practice. Gay and lesbian couples were formally included through contract-renewal talks at the *Voice* in 1982. Jeff Weinstein, an openly gay staff writer, was a member of the negotiating committee. Backed by his straight colleagues, he bargained hard and won, despite the employer's determined defense: "We will not go beyond what the law requires." In the end, they did, and it was management's attorney, Bertrand Pogrebin, who coined the phrase "spousal equivalents" to include gay and lesbian couples for the first time in the District 65 Security Plan, as well as in the union's bereavement clause.[34]

The *Village Voice* example leads to an interesting comparison. Through a merger of District 65 and the United Auto Workers (UAW), *Voice* employees were represented by the same union that demanded protections for gay auto workers in 1996 contract talks with Chrysler. This demand was among the last issues to be resolved, and it went all the way to Chrysler's CEO, Bob Eaton. Jack Laskowksi, a UAW vice president, described this top-level meeting. There were two unresolved economic issues. Union president Stephen Yokich put them on the table, then turned to Laskowski and asked, "Is there anything else?" Laskowski tacked on the gay rights demand. Eaton wouldn't hear of it. Once all the economics were resolved, Laskowski explained, gay rights became a potential strike issue. UAW dropped the demand, believing the union could not mount a national strike over gay rights.[35] I think that is probably true. As an outsider and in hindsight, I am uneasy about questioning the wisdom of UAW leaders at that critical moment. Nevertheless, at the time, I had a lingering doubt. Did the union abandon the cause too readily? Short of a strike, were there other forms of public pressure that could have been applied?

At the point of decision, a rancorous argument took place between union delegate Ron Woods—a lone, gay holdout for the demand—and other UAW members. The question of how much crass homophobia figured in this hostile exchange is wide open. On the surface, however, it played out as a debate between class and identity politics. In the male-intensive auto industry with its culture of masculinity, a muscular vision of working-class solidarity prevailed. The "weaker" claims of social identity were abandoned. In this connection, the distinction that Laskowski made between economic and noneconomic issues is of interest. Chrysler (and its straight employees) did not perceive the demand for gay rights as an economic issue—not a cost factor, like wage increases or fringe benefits. Neither did the union, for that matter. But for lesbian and gay workers who face discrimination in hiring and promotional opportunities, protections against discrimination have everything to do with economic security.

While no one knows what percentage of auto workers are gay and lesbian, I think it is safe to say only a small minority of them are out at work. Thus the voices of gays and lesbians were muted in this class-identity debate and remain generally absent from the culture of organizing in this and other industrial sectors.[36] At the *Voice,* by comparison, the union dropped a number of its demands in the course of bargaining, but it was unthinkable in that workplace of ex-hippies, war *refusniks,* feminists, and queers to forsake rightful demands for equality of benefits and representation. This comparison between differing sectors within a single union points to the uneven and fluctuating development of an identity-based class culture. The class compact of an earlier, industrial era is encoded in the bone-crushing handshake between white and black laborers that is still the AFL-CIO's logo. This vision of class solidarity persists in many sectors of the workforce. But even in its strongholds, it has been challenged, and increasingly it is mediated by newer, fuller conceptions of class that acknowledge sexual identity along with gender and race.

An interesting sidelight to the *Village Voice* story is the process of education that went on, on *both* sides of the negotiating table. Zeke Cohen, the union's chief negotiator, was an old-style laborist with deep working-class roots. The son of poor Jewish immigrants, he had risen to union leadership from the ranks of a small quilting shop in Manhattan's garment center. His trade-union values were learned from class-conscious radicals in the 1940s. In some ways he was as ill prepared by his experience to bargain for same-sex domestic partner benefits as were the guys and gals in suits on the other side of the table. Yet, in short order, Zeke was not only held in high esteem by the *Voice* workers, he was loved.

Zeke was not comfortable with the lingo of identity politics. "What's this shit?" he said, when the *Voice* workers presented him with a "politically correct" preamble they wished to include in their first collective-bargaining agreement. Curiously, the *Voice* workers took irascible comments like this in stride. They seemed to trust Zeke's good instincts, and they were right. Zeke had the advantage of an experienced organizer, whose ear is attuned to what is *not* said. If only intuitively, he understood the terms of class solidarity among these workers and modulated his own rhetoric of class to inflect it with the language of identity politics. By the end, he had earned the right to speak in family terms. He could have called a dyke a dyke without being misunderstood.

On reflection, Zeke was not so much intuitive as well trained in daily exchanges with the "broads,"a group of young women organizers (including me), who worked under his supervision. We would rattle on to him about the ugly sexism of his male colleagues. He would listen seriously. "Yeah, that guy's a real putz. Tell him to go and *fuck* himself," he earnestly advised us on one occasion. Then, with transcendent self-irony, he said: "Now, you broads go into my office, take off your clothes, and lie down. I'll be right in." It was a moment of high parody. Zeke flashed an impudent smile, and we were overcome with laughter. On another occasion, Zeke barged into my office and stopped dead when he saw that a colleague of mine was there, nursing her infant daughter. He blushed to the roots of his slick black pompadour. "Sorry, wrong restaurant," he muttered and turned on his heel.

Like the *Voice* workers, the "broads" took Zeke Cohen for who he was—not a poor benighted fellow of his times, but someone blundering his way into the contemporary moment. Admittedly, my interpretation of "Cohen's rehabilitation" depends on a hunch I have: that radicals-for-life are distinguished by their capacity to change with the times—to stay tuned to the struggle, even when it appears in unfamiliar forms. All the same, it took a lot more than tolerance and humor to get us through the transition from class to identity politics. It was quite a battle, illustrated in another anecdote from my early union experience.

Among the most forward looking of union leaders, District 65 president David Livingston was an early champion of white-collar organizing. In the mid-1970s, he hired a group of women to lead campaigns in the female-intensive publishing and higher-education industries. With a history of civil rights activism going back to the Scottsboro case, District 65 was always race conscious and had had a Black Affairs Committee for some time.[37] Following this example, the new women leaders attempted to establish a committee as well. A radical of the old CIO, Livingston clung to his belief in the universality of class. He was irritated. "Why do you need a women's committee?" he asked. "A worker is a worker. We make no distinctions based on sex." "But what about the Black Affairs Committee?" we asked. In characteristic manner, Livingston brushed off the apparent contradiction and continued to resist our demand. He could not—or would not—see the logic in our effort to link gender to race in the politics of both class and identity.

Increasingly, however, the union was focusing its attention on offices and nonprofit institutions, where women employees were in the majority. As a consequence, male leaders of District 65 were drawn deeply into feminist struggles both inside and outside the workplace. An organization founded on the principles of social unionism, District 65 and its older leaders remained sensitive to rank-and-file aspirations. Though it may have been difficult to abandon old notions of class, it did not take a great leap of imagination to grasp the potential power of union-minded feminists. Eventually, we got our women's committee. By 1982, District 65 members at the *Village Voice* had formed one of the first gay union caucuses in New York.[38] Though this story is particular to one union, and a small one at that, I venture to say it suggests larger continuities between CIO social unionism and identity politics of a later time.

OUT AT WORK AND ON THE LINE

Of the seventy-four thousand home-health-care workers who won union representation in 1999, the majority were women, people of color, and immigrants. We have to assume that gays and lesbians were present in their number, as they are in every sector of the workforce. As organized labor struggles to rebound in the millennium, it has to target the many thousands of low-wage, exploited workers who have been left behind in the shuffle of deindustrialization. At the same time, it must organize a diverse population of workers in new sectors of the economy and in workplaces that have been traditionally nonunion. In fact, that is already happening. Since the 1980s, industrial unions like the UAW have been broadening their base to incorporate white-collar and professional units, including workers in the academy, for example. Together, at least four major unions—the American Federation of Teachers, the Communications Workers of America, the Hotel Employees and Restaurant Employees Union, and the UAW—have committed many millions to organizing teaching and research assistants, adjuncts, and in one case even undergraduates who work in residence halls. Demands made by university workers characteristically foreground identity-based claims, such as affirmative action and domestic-partner benefits for gay as well as straight couples. Another example: In 1992, the National Writers Union affiliated to the UAW. That year, it sent representatives to the union's national convention and lobbied successfully for an amendment to the UAW constitution, adding sexual orientation to the existing articles of nondiscrimination.

In 1996, after the setback at Chrysler, UAW vice president Jack Laskowski vowed that an antidiscrimination clause covering gay workers would be in the next Chrysler contract.[39] And it was. On September 25, 1999, UAW members at DaimlerChrysler set the pattern for Ford and

General Motors (GM), ratifying a contract that added sexual orientation to the "equal applications" clause. On June 8, 2000, the agreement was augmented to provide domestic-partner benefits to same-sex couples among the 466,000 employees of DaimlerChrysler, Ford, and GM. Although Chrysler workers in Canada have had these benefits since 1993, this U.S. agreement is the most sweeping of its kind in the North American industrial sector. The hope is that it will encourage more LGBT industrial workers to come out of the closet and take a forceful stand for workplace rights.[40] And the hope is too that Ron Woods will be recognized for the enormity of his contribution to this victory.

Gay workers (even in heavy industry) are taking their place at the table, and they are changing the language and culture of organizing in the process. It is a small sign, but the morally loaded term "sexual preference" has been replaced in many union contracts by "sexual orientation," the term of choice in gay communities. "We're queer, we're here," is not unheard of on the picket line. The concept of queer strategy has entered even the mainstream labor movement. Red days at Barney's department store—where the majority of employees are gay—is a good example.

Every Tuesday during contract negotiations in April 1996, employees—who are members of the apparel workers union UNITE—defied the all-black dress code. Men in bright lipstick and women in red waited on customers, to the chagrin of buyers and managers. The grand finale of this queer contract campaign was an alternative fashion show outside the store, featuring drag queens and dykes. As they strutted their stuff down a makeshift runway, they flashed UNITE picket signs. One of their demands was an end to excessive overtime. "He can't get his beauty sleep," the (straight) emcee said, as one especially flamboyant queen made his entrance. Garment workers from other UNITE shops stood in the street, cheering the queers on.[41]

If these seem like sporadic examples of gay activism, the national growth of gay union caucuses points to a developing, stable base of organization. Though there had been ad hoc alliances of gay union members since the Seventies, not until the Eighties did these take shape as effective coalitions.[42] The Gay Caucus at *Village Voice* was fundamental to an informal New York City coalition that had been meeting since the early 1980s. Similar groups, such as the Gay and Lesbian Labor Action Network (GALLAN) in Boston, developed in other union towns.[43] In October 1987, queers descended on Washington, D.C., for the second national gay pride march in the country's history. Gay union members marched as a bloc, union banners and signs held aloft among the other insignia of gay pride. On the eve of that demonstration, the AFL-CIO had opened its vast marble lobby for a premarch rally and reception. Among the speakers at that rally were the presidents of America's two largest public sector unions, Gerald McEntee of the American Federation of State, County, and Municipal Employees (AFSCME) and John Sweeney of SEIU. Not coincidentally, these unions had perhaps the largest and most active gay caucuses.[44] In 1998, three years after Sweeney was elected to head the AFL-CIO, Pride at Work—a national caucus of gay, lesbian, and transgendered trade unionists—was affiliated to the AFL-CIO, joining the Coalition of Labor Union Women, the Coalition of Black Trade Unionists, the Labor Council for Latin American Advancement, and the Asian-Pacific-American Alliance, all of which had affiliated during the Kirkland administration. The historical development of a new class conjuncture was symbolically complete. Will this symbolic gesture translate into something more tangible? In "Getting Serious about Inclusion," La Luz and Finn say no—not until the constituency groups are "re-defined as organizing groups."[45]

In his first public statements as president of the AFL-CIO, John Sweeney committed the Federation to a vigorous, new, and multicultural organizing effort. "The secret to our success and the greatest potential for organizing," he declared, "is among women, people of color, and young workers."[46] This comment, made the day of his election, has been augmented to include lesbian and gay workers. In "The Growing Alliance between Gay and Union Activists," an essay that appeared first in the winter 1999 edition of *Social Text,* Sweeney offered a very specific organizing agenda that begins with a mandate for leadership: "We must draw gay and lesbian union members into our programs for leadership development and provide opportunities . . . to become leaders in their workplaces and in their unions."[47]

This mandate has mostly been honored in the breach. Nevertheless, there is an emergent gay rights movement within the ranks of labor, and it is intimately connected to the growing power of a new identity-based class coalition. The history of this class formation was present, if unacknowledged, in the AFL-CIO leadership transition that took place in 1995. Some months before the AFL-CIO convention that year, the heads of several unions mounted an open campaign to oust Federation president Lane Kirkland. Leading the insurgents were—again—

McEntee and Sweeney. Built in the last thirty years—the "dark ages"— their public sector unions probably represent more women, people of color, and gays than any others. It is no accident that these unions were the advance troops for change in 1995. Nor was Sweeney's opposition slate constructed out of mere political expediency.[48] Sweeney's running mate was Richard Trumka, president of the United Mineworkers of America (UMWA), a union now so small it is barely viable. But Trumka was young, and he was an outspoken, even brash, critic of the old guard. His fiery speeches were laced with the rhetoric of class struggle. He had gained a reputation for charismatic leadership during the 1989 UMWA strike against the Pittston coal company and several other coal operators in Appalachia. Won against great odds, the strike represented a triumph of class solidarity over corporate power and government intervention.[49] With Linda Chavez Thompson of AFSCME, the Sweeney slate demonstrated more than progressive and potentially militant class struggle. It was also a recognition of the diversity principle in representation. The AFL-CIO Executive Council had included a few women since the 1980s, but no woman, and no person of color, had been elected by convention delegates to executive office before Chavez Thompson.[50] Anyone who knows the labor movement gets the message, but its basis in historical process may not be taken into full account.

Before the AFL-CIO convention in October 1995, black labor leaders had presented both presidential candidates with demands for greater representation by African Americans. A constitutional amendment passed at the convention provided for expansion of the Executive Council, with ten seats designated for women and people of color.[51] True, no openly gay woman or man holds office in the Federation, but the new emphasis on multiculturalism suggests that possibility is no longer inconceivable.

To bring this story full circle, I come back to the Columbia teach-in and its aftermath. In May 1997, teach-in founders met with John Sweeney to discuss the institutional potential of a labor-intellectual alliance. Sweeney agreed to support the establishment of Scholars, Artists, and Writers for Social Justice (SAWSJ), and an interim steering committee was developed. Although SAWSJ has since lapsed into inactivity, its origins offer an instructive tale. In the spring of 1997, the question of diversity was first and foremost on the minds of some new steering committee members. After heated discussion, a decision was made to delay formation of the organization until women and people of color, students, and other activists were fully represented in the group.[52] Within a year, the organization had made progress toward this goal. Scholars, Artists, and Writers for Social Justice held its first annual meeting in April 1998. In marked contrast to the teach-in of 1996, two rank-and-file union leaders shared the speakers' platform with intellectual and labor elites. Of eight keynoters, four were people of color and three were women. Though the question of sexual identity had slipped to the background of internal SAWSJ discussions, it was kept alive by a few members of the steering committee and surfaced at this founding convention with a screening and discussion of *Out at Work*. At the next SAWSJ meeting, a year later, one workshop was devoted to the subject of gay labor rights. It included Charisse Mitchell, transgendered herself and a public advocate for the rights of transgendered workers.

LIVING CLASS

Historian Robin Kelley has said that "class is lived through race and gender."[53] It is the word "lived" that captures my attention. To *live* class implies an engagement. At its most intense, this engagement is described rhetorically as class struggle. I like Kelley's maxim very much, precisely for the degree of agency it implies, but I have wondered why he did not include sexual identity. I tried it out: "Class is lived through race, gender, and sexual identity." Given the extent to which rights, privileges, and social position are determined by sexual identity, my reformulation feels right. More so, when I consider the history of workplace struggle for gay and lesbian rights. Much of that history is necessarily absent from this discussion.

While the account I have offered points to a few victories for those who have been historically underrepresented in the labor movement, it omits years of struggle and defeat. In 1970—even in San Francisco— gay firefighters and teachers were denounced by local union leaders for displaying affection on a picket line and carrying pro-gay signs. The San Francisco Central Labor Council later issued a condescending plea for tolerance, calling the group a "small, unschooled, and new" sector of the movement.[54] This is but one example in a dramatic history of struggle for sexual representation in the workplace and the labor movement. While historians and analysts of contemporary labor have increasingly focused on race and gender, in the main, they have failed to recognize the vital signs of class struggle in contemporary movements for gay and lesbian workplace rights.

At the risk of oversimplification, I would suggest that the mere fact that such movements have developed in the workplace—that they have been advanced through workplace struggle—demonstrates that sexual identity is intimately connected to class and to the ways class is asserted. This is made more obvious to the extent straight workers and union leaders have incorporated these struggles in the broad pursuit of workers' rights. This is not to say there is a single comprehensive agenda for workers' rights. Class is not monolithic and class struggle is not all embracing, all the time. Nevertheless, in the crossings and partings that mark the various ways workers identify themselves, points of solidarity emerge. Sexual identity is a lived experience for *all* workers. Of course, workers who identify as straight live it very differently. They live it in the comfort of social approbation and with all the rights and privileges that come from respectability. Never mind that straight workers routinely engage in sexual practices that might be considered deviant—promiscuity, homosexual affairs, sex-work-on-the-side. What straight folks do in bed is mostly nobody's business when it comes to workplace benefits. That is not the case for those who are openly gay, lesbian, bisexual, or transgendered. Straight workers and straight advocates for workers' rights may not be ready to abandon hetero-normative standards of sexual propriety, but they are becoming more conscious of inequities in this double standard. In that sense, the potential for solidarity across lines of difference is nowhere more evident than in the struggle for gay and lesbian workplace rights.

NOTES

Acknowledgments: In studying labor history, I have sought to understand my own experience. If I have understood anything, I owe it to my mentor in the union and my enduring comrade, Milton Reverby. This essay is dedicated to him with thanks and love. Many people contributed to the completion of this essay. My friend and colleague, Patrick McCreery, helped me understand the complexities of gender and sexual identity. My teacher Andrew Ross encouraged me to write. Finally, I am indebted to the scholarship of others, including Stanley Aronowitz, Liz Cohen, Michael Denning, Miriam Frank, Robin D. G. Kelley, Nelson Lichtenstein, and Daniel Walkowitz.

An earlier version of this essay appeared under the same title in Kitty Krupat and Patrick McCreery, eds., *Out at Work: Building a Gay-Labor Alliance* (Minneapolis: University of Minnesota Press, 2001).

1. Kirkland retired in August 1995. The AFL-CIO Executive Council elected Tom Donohue—secretary-treasurer of the Federation under Kirkland—to fill

out Kirkland's term. Thus, Donohue, not Kirkland, was actually Sweeney's opponent in the October 1995 election.

2. Michael Denning, *The Cultural Front: The Laboring of American Culture in the Twentieth Century* (London: Verso, 1996). For a general description of the period, see also Lizabeth Cohen, *Making a New Deal: Industrial Workers in Chicago, 1919–1939* (Cambridge: Cambridge University Press, 1990).

3. I attended the Columbia teach-in and base my comments on recollections of Rorty's speech and the audience reaction.

4. Daniel Walkowitz, *Working with Class: Social Workers and the Politics of Middle-Class Identity* (Chapel Hill: University of North Carolina Press, 1999). The "fluidity" of class identity is a central theme throughout this study.

5. A spate of news and journal articles on the future of U.S. labor followed in the wake of John Sweeney's election and has continued. Between its summer and winter issues of 1998–99, for example, *Dissent* magazine carried a debate on the subject of union democracy, sparked by Steve Fraser's article in the summer edition, "Is Democracy Good for Unions?" A qualified defense of bureaucratic decision making in labor organizations, Fraser's essay was critiqued in separate pieces by Stanley Aronowitz, Herman Benson, and Gordon K. Haskell. The series concluded with a rebuttal by Fraser. This debate continued in the Letters column of *New Labor Forum*, spring/summer 1999.

6. Jeremy Brecher and Tim Costello, "Labor's Day: The Challenge Ahead," *Nation*, September 21, 1998, 11.

7. See Brecher and Costello, "Labor's Day," 17 and throughout.

8. Nelson Lichtenstein, *State of the Union: A Century of American Labor* (Princeton: Princeton University Press, 2002.)

9. Gregory Mantsios, ed., *A New Labor Movement for the New Century* (New York: Monthly Review Press, 1998), xv.

10. José La Luz and Paula Finn, "Getting Serious about Inclusion: A Comprehensive Approach," in Mantsios, *A New Labor Movement*, 175.

11. Robin Kelley has argued these points with clarity and passion. See *Yo Mama's Disfunktional! Fighting the Culture Wars in Urban America* (Boston: Beacon Press, 1997), chaps. 4 and 5. Nelson Lichtenstein's comments on this subject are also instructive; see his essay "Falling in Love Again? Intellectuals and the Labor Movement in Post-War America," *New Labor Forum*, spring/summer 1999, 25–26.

12. *Out at Work: Lesbians and Gay Men on the Job* was released in 1997. A second version of this documentary, *Out at Work: America Undercover*, was produced for HBO and aired first in January 1999.

13. Perry Anderson, *The Origins of Postmodernity* (London: Verso, 1998), 89.

14. See Lichtenstein, "Falling in Love Again?" 19. In commending progress made by the Sweeney administration, Lichtenstein points not only to gains in the minimum wage but also to the defeat of fast-track legislation and to the AFL-CIO's Union Summer program, aimed at recruiting young organizers from campuses across the country. The figures on new organization between 1997 and 1999 were supplied by Mark Splain of the AFL-CIO organizing department.

15. In this regard, the International Ladies' Garment Workers Union is an obvious example. ILGWU was conducting educational and cultural programs within fifteen years of its founding in 1900. *Pins and Needles*—an ILGWU production with music by Harold Rome—is perhaps the best remembered of CIO theatrical productions. It was first performed in the summer of 1936.

16. For an analysis of workforce and union participation by blacks—and black women in particular—during this period, see Jacqueline Jones, *Labor of Love, Labor of Sorrow* (New York: Random House/Vintage Books, 1985), chaps. 6 and 7.

17. Michael Denning goes further to argue that CIO labor was "the base" of the Popular Front (see Denning, *The Cultural Front*, throughout).

18. Nelson Lichtenstein, *Labor's War at Home: The CIO in World War II* (New York: Cambridge University Press, 1982; new edition, Philadelphia: Temple University Press, 2003), throughout. The number of wildcat strikes between 1942, when the WLB was established, and 1945, when it was dismantled, is a measure of rank-and-file discontent. For a summary of strike activity, see Lichtenstein, *Labor's War at Home*, 133–35.

19. See Denning, *The Cultural Front*, 24.

20. In *Labor's War at Home*, Nelson Lichtenstein provides a full account of these debilitating effects on postwar unionism; for a summary, see the epilogue, 233–25.

21. "Basic industry" refers to the giant smokestack industries, such as steel and auto. Lichtenstein puts union density in these industries at 80 percent by the late 1940s (see *Labor's War at Home*, 233). See also Stanley Aronowitz, *From the Ashes of the Old! American Labor and America's Future* (New York: Houghton Mifflin, 1998). Aronowitz offers a variation. By the late 1940s, he, says, more than 40 percent of all U.S. factory workers were organized (*From the Ashes*, 27).

22. Daniel Cantor and Juliet Schor, *Tunnel Vision: Labor, the World Economy, and Central America* (Boston: South End Press, 1987), 41–47. AIFLD was implicated in a series of anticommunist intelligence activities in the Dominican Republic, Guyana, and Brazil. In 1964, AIFLD trained workers who participated in the coup that ousted Brazilian president João Goulart.

23. See Aronowitz, *From the Ashes*, 11.

24. See the front-page story by Steven Greenhouse, *New York Times*, February 26, 1999.

25. See Aronowitz, *From the Ashes*, chap. 2, "The Rise and Crisis of Public Sector Unions."

26. Ibid., 61.

27. In my union, District 65, the bulk of new organizing from 1974 onward took place among professionals and paraprofessionals, including cultural workers in publishing, museums, bookstores, and offices. (Perhaps the largest number of professionals in 65 were university employees, childcare workers, and lawyers.) The National Writers Union, which affiliated to the UAW in 1992, began organizing in the late Eighties, as did the Graphic Artists Guild, also affiliated to the UAW.

28. The American Federation of Teachers, American Federation of State, County, and Municipal Employees, and the Service Employees International

Union are obvious examples in the public sector. In the private sector, District 65 is one example. A costly campaign among major publishing companies—including Simon & Schuster, Random House, and Harcourt Brace—failed, despite organizing efforts over a five-year period. Victories at Boston and Columbia Universities came only after a ten-year campaign and several lost elections.

29. For a profound analysis of this class transformation, see Walkowitz, *Working with Class.*

30. See John Hoerr, *We Can't Eat Prestige: The Women Who Organized Harvard* (Philadelphia: Temple University Press, 1997), 227.

31. Yvette Herrera, director of mobilization and education for the Communications Workers of America, recounts a telling exchange: At a workshop on sexual diversity, a steward objected on religious grounds to the recognition of gay rights. Discussion later turned to the case of a gay worker, fired because he was HIV positive. This same steward took an aggressive position in defense of the gay worker. The union would not tolerate discrimination against any member, she said, and proceeded to describe how she handled a grievance in this case (see "Homophobia: Labor's Last Frontier?" in Krupat and McCreery, *Out at Work,* 198).

32. References to the *Village Voice* and to District 65, throughout, are based largely on my own experience as a 65 organizer between 1974 and 1989. I was the lead organizer of *Voice* employees in 1977 and remained the *Voice* contract administrator for several years.

33. For a history of the *Village Voice,* see Kevin Michael McAuliffe, *The Great American Newspaper: The Rise and fall of the Village Voice* (New York: Scribner, 1978). My account is also based on personal knowledge of *Voice* history, gained in the years I served as staff organizer for the union of *Voice* employees.

34. The *VV* contracts of 1979 and 1982—along with other documents pertaining to health coverage and affirmative action—are preserved in the files of UAW Local 2110.

35. Jack Laskowski described these final negotiations in the HBO film *Out at Work: America Undercover.* My account of these negotiations and the internal debate that ensued is based on two other sources: a January 3, 1999, interview with UAW *Solidarity* magazine staffer Michael Funke, and James B. Stewart, "Coming Out at Chrysler," *New Yorker,* July 1977.

36. See Herrera's discussion of this phenomenon in "Homophobia," 202–3.

37. The Scottsboro case began in 1931, when nine young black men were indicted for the alleged rape of two white women in Scottsboro, Alabama. The case dragged on through a lengthy appeals process, ending with convictions of four defendants in 1937. (A fifth was convicted of lesser assault charges.) The District 65 photo archive contains a picture of union leaders who had chained themselves to the pillars of a Washington, D.C., courthouse to protest the travesty of justice.

38. Miriam Frank, "Lesbian, Gay, and Bisexual Caucuses in the United States Labor Movement," typescript, 21. (Later published in Gerald Hunt, *Laboring for Rights: A Global Perspective on Union Response to Sexual Diversity* [Philadelphia: Temple University Press, 1999]).

39. See Laskowski's comments in the HBO version of *Out at Work.*

40. See Keith Bradsher, "Big Car Makers Extend Benefits to Gay Couples," *New York Times,* June 9, 2000, sec. C, 1.

41. See Andrew Ross, "Strike a Pose for Justice," in Krupat and McCreery, *Out at Work,* 78–91. The fashion show was videotaped. It was also covered by the *Village Voice* and *Women's Wear Daily.*

42. Teachers in New York and San Francisco were among the first to establish such groups in the Seventies. See Frank, "Lesbian, Gay, and Bisexual Caucuses," 2.

43. See ibid., 21.

44. See ibid., 8–19.

45. La Luz and Finn, "Getting Serious about Inclusion," 180.

46. Kelley, *Yo Mama,* 129, 206 n. 8.

47. John Sweeney, "The Growing Alliance between Gay and Union Activists," *Social Text,* winter 1999, 31–38. The essay later appeared in Krupat and McCreery, *Out at Work.*

48. Robin Kelley's investigation of this very point supports my claim (see *Yo Mama,* chap. 5). Citing the importance of what he calls "the changing face of labor," Kelley says that "the victory of John Sweeney (president), Richard Trumka (secretary-treasurer) and Linda Chavez Thompson (executive vice president) . . . depended to a large extent on their position vis-à-vis the so-called minority workers."

49. The strike lasted nine months and spread to ten states, with wildcat strikes erupting at several mining operations across the country. In the seventh month of the strike, ninety miners occupied a main coal-processing plant in Virginia and remained inside for several days, in defiance of a governor's order. I was among thousands of supporters, including UMWA members from other parts of the country, who converged on the scene, keeping vigil in front of the plant. State police, armed with rifles, stood at the ready outside the plant gates. Ultimately, the governor guaranteed amnesty, and the ninety miners ended their sit-in.

50. Interim officers, elected by the Executive Council after Kirkland's retirement, included Barbara Easterling of the Flight Attendants union.

51. See *New York Times,* July 15, 1995, 6. See also *AFL-CIO News,* November 5, 1995, 7.

52. I base this account on my own experience as a member of the SAWSJ Steering Committee.

53. See Kelley, *Yo Mama,* 109.

54. See Gaile Whittington, "Gay Labor Pain," *Berkeley Tribe,* January 30, 1970.

RICHARD MOSER

11   Autoworkers at Lordstown
Workplace Democracy and American Citizenship

As THE 1960s began, philosopher Hannah Arendt looked to the American Revolution as a way to understand what freedom might mean for her own time. Quoting Thomas Jefferson she wrote: "For political freedom means the right 'to be a participator in government' or it means nothing."[1] Arendt's admiration for the American Revolution was tempered by her criticism that the Constitution left citizens few means of direct political participation. Although her constitutional remedies were not adopted, millions of Americans embraced a similar understanding of freedom by creating powerful social movements that exercised political participation in the name of equality, justice, and peace.[2] The diverse and sometimes conflicting goals of the civil rights, women's, youth, labor, peace, environmental, gay, black power, and community movements shared one essential principle—participatory democracy.

The democratic movements and social conflicts of midcentury are perhaps best seen as a partial revolution that reshaped political constituencies, transformed public thinking, and left America deeply divided. We have lived in the stalemate ever since.

The history of Local 1112, an activist union of autoworkers in northeast Ohio, offers us a way to explore how some Americans lived the legacy of the Sixties through the changing domestic and international conditions of the subsequent decades. Perhaps the most daunting challenge to the movements in the post-Sixties era was a chilling sense of financial insecurity. Labor historians and social observers look back on those years as a time when America's unique economic arrangements, called the midcentury social contract or the labor/capital accord, underwent a historic revision.[3]

The history of Local 1112 suggests that some workers did more than merely survive these changes. They set to work on the new economic order and found that their material well-being, values, and sense of justice demanded an extension of their participation and power at work. The history of participatory democracy in the workplace holds profound, if unappreciated, implications for our notions of property ownership, for it suggests the possibility of establishing the concept of property rights in jobs. Given the centrality of property rights to the U.S. political tradition, these developments enable us to envision an important evolution in the theory of U.S. citizenship.

THE CONTEXT

In the wake of World War II, the United States enjoyed unrivaled power, and most Americans enjoyed a remarkable period of opportunity that encouraged faith in government and business leaders. Unions fought hard and won material benefits for millions of people. These struggles earned the labor movement a degree of power that was real but limited to a narrow sphere of workplace issues such as pay, benefits, and working conditions. Business leaders retained undisputed control over industry and upheld their end of the bargain by reluctantly tolerating unions and permitting a rising standard of living for workers.

By the late 1960s, however, this postwar social contract had begun to subvert itself as a result of the multiple crises that came to a head during the Vietnam War. Not only did the war lead to a crisis of faith in political and cultural institutions, but also it damaged the U.S. economy. America's vast military spending produced no marketable goods or services, resulted in relatively few jobs compared to other forms of capital investment, and diverted research money from more productive purposes. As the war dragged on, GNP slowed and prices rose.[4] In 1968, the economy tottered on the brink of disaster as a monetary crisis signaled the end of America's economic golden age.[5]

President Nixon responded to the economic crisis by ending the gold standard for U.S. currency in 1971 and instituting wage and price controls that spurred inflation, unemployment, and profits.[6] By the mid-1970s, the rate of economic growth declined and there began an almost unprecedented redistribution of wealth from the vast majority of working people to the very richest Americans.[7]

U.S. industry had thrived from a sheltered position in world markets because all major rivals were devastated by World War II. Combined with the relative lack of domestic competition, this comfortable supremacy allowed U.S. business leaders to ignore advances in industrial technology and focus narrowly on short-term profits.[8] The limitations of this approach were revealed when international competitors came on line during the 1970s.

The labor/capital accord collapsed in part because of this international competition but also because it treated U.S. workers as second-class citizens who lacked the right to engage in meaningful decision making. By concentrating all power over production in the hands of management, the United States forfeited the opportunity for countless shop-floor innovations.[9] This centralized authority also clashed head-on with a rising awareness of democratic rights inspired by the civil rights movement.

Young workers in particular longed for meaningful work and for less work altogether. Questions of health and safety, pace of work, and protection from arbitrary dismissal became prominent union issues early in the decade. Labor went to bat for basic political and human rights. Unions fought hard for the 1964 Civil Rights Act, the 1965 Voting Rights Act, and the 1971 Occupational Safety and Health Act, all of which benefited millions outside the union movement. The United Auto Workers (UAW) and other unions helped to fund the civil rights movement, and tens of thousands of union members bucked the prowar AFL-CIO leadership to oppose the Vietnam War. This new politics was also expressed in a wave of strikes and worker militancy, of which Lordstown became one of the most notorious. National strikes at General Electric and the U.S. Post Office and the coalminers' campaign against black-lung disease all emphasized issues of power rather than pay.[10]

Organizations of reform-minded workers fought for more democracy within unions and for a more aggressive approach toward management. Perhaps best known is the Teamsters for a Democratic Union (TDU). After twenty years of struggle, TDU won the right to democratic elections and in the early 1990s elected reform candidates to national leadership. Groups like the Dodge Revolutionary Union Movement, founded by autoworkers in 1968, attacked racial discrimination and advocated black nationalism.[11] In 1972, the Coalition of Black Trade Unionists was organized to promote the interests of African Americans and grew to fifty chapters by century's end. The Coalition of Labor Union Women, organized in 1974, advanced the women's movement into labor's ranks.[12] In the 1990s, gay, lesbian, and bisexual workers formed Pride at Work, a national caucus that was "out and organizing."

This new brand of post-1960s working-class politics, intertwined with varied social concerns, is sometimes called social movement unionism.

Social movement unionism sought to advance the interests of Americans regardless of union membership, and to build alliances with other movements. This more ambitious and political form of unionism upset the balance of power at the heart of the labor/capital accord.[13]

LORDSTOWN AND THE LABOR REVOLT

The General Motors assembly plant at Lordstown was built in 1966 in a rural part of the Mahoning Valley just a few miles from Youngstown, Ohio. The plant and GM's new model, the Vega, were touted as exemplars of technological innovation that would best international competitors.[14]

The new union struggled for the kind of work environment other UAW workers had already achieved. It resorted to the kinds of tactics workers used in the 1930s when industrial unions were just beginning. Members sat in, slowed down, or took extra time to enforce the highest-quality production standards. When serious conflicts arose, they walked off the job in unofficial wildcat strikes.[15] In 1970, a long and bitter national strike stopped production at Lordstown.

By 1969, Local 1112 and GM management had negotiated a generous version of the midcentury social contract. Union and management would agree to be adversaries on questions of pay, benefits, and workload. While the union exerted discretion over the details of work assignments and some workforce changes, production and hiring decisions and all the major investment, technological, and pricing matters were regarded as the unassailable right of management. An uneasy truce prevailed at Lordstown.

That labor peace ended abruptly when a new, aggressive management team, General Motors Assembly Division (GMAD), arrived on October 1, 1971.[16] The ensuing conflict would bring national media attention to Local 1112 and spur debate on worker alienation, or "the blue-collar blues."[17] In retrospect, GMAD's arrival signaled the beginning of the end of the labor/capital accord for the workers of the Mahoning Valley and inaugurated a time of intense struggle, searching, and experimentation.

GMAD practiced a highly confrontational management style aimed at total control.[18] In the name of efficiency, GMAD pushed back the perimeter of union power by targeting the number and nature of jobs. The crunch began when GMAD abruptly laid off hundreds of the 7,700 workers at Lordstown while still maintaining the fastest assembly line in the world. Whether it was the loss of 400 workers, according to GM, or 700, according to the union, the pace of work became unbearable to many.[19] This new regime, which allowed workers only thirty-six seconds to perform certain assembly line jobs, was enforced by strict discipline.[20] Supervisors were increased by fifty to a total of six hundred and bossed workers around with "direct orders." The harsh discipline provoked comparisons with prison or the military, particularly for the many Vietnam veterans working at Lordstown.[21] Workers called GMAD "the Gestapo," "Get Mad and Destroy," or "Gotta Make Another Dollar." "It was," in the words of one ex-foreman, "a tough crackdown."[22]

When the quality of the Vega declined abruptly, GM alleged sabotage, while Local 1112 alleged management by terror. At least nine hundred were punished with disciplinary layoffs for refusing or failing to keep up with the new pace or for sabotage. Workers were guilty until proven innocent and disciplined or discharged without due process. For the editor of the union's paper, *See Here,* GM now operated outside American values: "As we enter the General Motors complex, it puts you in mind of entering a foreign land consisting of a dictatorship that the 'General' rules or tries to rule with an iron hand."[23]

Many workers feared the worst: GMAD's behavior was not designed to increase efficiency, but to break the union itself.[24] Workers responded with a campaign of shop-floor struggles, wildcat strikes, and —in 1972 and 1974—official strikes.

Beginning in September 1971, workers attempted a kind of guerrilla warfare that slowed down production. The union insisted on working the "normal" pace that existed before GMAD. Workers hampered production by slowing down or simply following company rules to the letter. Some workers responded to the authoritarian discipline with youthful abandon typical of the hippie counterculture. The running joke at the time was: "Q. How come you only work three days a week? A. Because I can't live on two."[25] People celebrated their resistance, even their suspensions from work. "If people saw some guy with . . . a foreman walking down the aisle . . . they'd be yelling, . . . giving the power sign. Even if they ain't for the union, they want to show the company they're behind it."[26] GMAD's assault forced displays of unity otherwise unlikely: A number of older leaders began growing beards to pique management's dislike of hairy hippies.

Workers were accused of sabotage, and cars did show up with sides dented or keys broken off in the ignition. Workers and union leaders claimed that the accusation of sabotage was used to cover the work overload.[27] The work slowdown created a sense of collective power and proved the union could control working conditions. The battle in the plant lasted for almost six months before culminating in the March 1972 strike.

The strike brought a great deal of national publicity, and attention focused on the union's elected leadership. Gary Bryner, the union's twenty-nine-year-old president, was hailed as "a new breed" of union leader because of his support for a four-day workweek, racial justice, and an end to the war in Vietnam.[28]

With the backing of the national UAW leadership, workers turned out in large numbers to deliver an overwhelming 97 percent vote to support the strike.[29] Picket lines were strong, union meetings drew thousands, and the plant was sealed tight. For twenty-two days, production stopped.

Neither GMAD nor Local 1112 could win a clear-cut victory. All the workers punished for not keeping up were rehired with back pay. Most of those laid off by GMAD's restructuring were rehired and most of the five thousand grievances resolved. Work pace returned to something resembling normal, but tensions would remain.[30]

By summer 1973, GMAD had renewed its offensive and the workers once again resorted to direct action. There was a wildcat strike in the truck plant when a welder was sent home for refusing to work where a broken exhaust fan failed to remove toxic fumes. One thousand workers followed him out the door. Workers brought in their meals to boycott the unhealthy cafeteria food. When company guards prohibited large containers, hundreds of workers showed up carrying oversized coolers. One Puerto Rican worker, suspended for repeatedly bringing in food and drink, organized a hundred Latinos to protest in nearby Youngstown.

In 1974, management's failure to ensure quality production became a strike issue.[31] A worker from the paint shop chided G.M. management: "Lets face it . . . G.M. officials don't want educated thinking people to work for you . . . you might lose your own non-productive job. . . . You also lack the willingness to listen. The assembly line worker has much to offer toward the growth of G.M.; toward the quality of *our* product."[32]

The pressure from GMAD had once again unified Local 1112. Sporadic resistance flared, and some fourteen thousand grievances lay unresolved. Workers voted overwhelmingly to walk out. The 1974 strike stood up to the company's "terror" but could only sustain the stalemate.[33]

JOBS AND WORKPLACE DEMOCRACY

The various strikes and job actions were about more than narrow economic interests of pay and benefits. They raised the question of who should govern the world of work. In an appeal to what seemed simple fairness, Paul Cubellis, the union's shop chair, captured the essence of the struggle for workplace democracy: "All we are asking for at Lordstown . . . is what we already had. Nothing more. . . . We are not asking for any more than for our people who fight these production lines, to be treated like American workers, human beings, not as pieces of profit making machinery."[34] "American workers" and "human beings" are not mere economic instruments or second-class citizens, but political figures possessing the right to govern. Workers waged a defensive battle aimed at conserving the conditions of the past, but to do so, they advocated ideas and actions that pointed beyond the narrow political confines of the labor/capital accord. Most suggestive of change was the implicit link between job protection and workplace democracy.

In a comprehensive study of the Lordstown strike, David Moberg observed: "Workers wanted the power to keep their job. . . . Asked abstractly, workers often admitted that management had a right to hire and fire. In every other way, they saw the paramount issue for the union . . . as the protection of jobs for everyone."[35] To save their jobs, the workers had to win a share in the government of the enterprise.

A NEW GENERATION OF WORKERS?

The strikes and struggles of the 1970s brought nationwide media attention to Lordstown. Following a provocative front-page article in the *New York Times*, television crews from *Sixty Minutes* and CBS showed up. *Time, Harper's, Life, Business Week,* the *Wall Street Journal,* the *Christian Science Monitor, New York Review of Books, Motor Trend,* and *Rolling Stone* all covered Lordstown. *Newsweek* called the strike "an Industrial Woodstock," while *Commonweal* saw the "showdown" as "the most dramatic instance of worker resistance since the 1937 Flint sit-downs."[36]

Observers were drawn to Lordstown because its workforce, with an average age of twenty-four, seemed to represent the arrival of the counterculture at the gates of industry, and the wedding of youth rebellion to unionism. These observations were only half true, because they ignored important continuities with working-class culture and history. The Lordstown activists were drawn from an industrial working class long familiar with struggle and solidarity. The Mahoning Valley was a steel-workers' stronghold, and many at Lordstown were their kin. In the 1930s, the UAW itself was organized thanks to a nationwide worker revolt against speed-up issues similar to those facing Lordstown workers in the 1970s. Indeed, workers contested power and sought democracy throughout the twentieth century.[37]

Lordstown's connection to earlier labor history is particularly striking in light of the relationship between war and workers' movements. U.S. wars in the twentieth century tended to weaken managerial control, because labor demand was high and good profits were easily had without the need for excessive labor discipline. War spending and government regulation tended, however, to make workers restless, because they promoted inflation while limiting wage increases.

World War I provoked a massive strike wave in 1919 that was waged with direct-action tactics and made workers' rights a real issue in the United States. The economic conditions produced by World War II also emboldened demands for greater rights at work. The UAW's "open the books strike" of 1945 demanded that the car companies disclose their finances to the public to prove they could well afford wage raises without price increases. For a few years, the UAW struggled to exercise national policy and managerial responsibilities in the auto industry, until the Taft-Hartley Act passed by Congress in 1947 made it almost impossible for unions to gain workplace democracy. In the following year, the UAW accepted management's right to rule in the "Treaty of Detroit," and the political parameters of the labor/capital accord were set for the next two decades.[38]

While the laws continued to favor management in the Vietnam era, other aspects of the time provided new opportunities for organizing. Unlike previous conflicts, the Vietnam War occurred against a background of powerful protest movements that added new dimensions to the meaning of workers' rights.[39] Particularly within the UAW, the civil rights, peace, and to a lesser degree the environmental and women's movements were supported and recognized as coinciding with labor's interests. Despite some real shortsightedness in relation to racial issues, the UAW represented social movement unionism more than did other large unions of the period.[40]

The young workers at Lordstown held deep-seated antiauthoritarian and antiwar attitudes. Among these young workers were veterans radicalized by the Vietnam War and the GI and veteran peace movements.[41] Their status and experience made them weary of taking orders, sensitive to illegitimate authority, and powerful role models for other workers. The *Detroit Free Press* captured the link between veteran attitudes and worker unrest. Touring the plant, reporters saw "Vietnam returnees in Army Jackets. They grin and flash the peace sign to newsmen. . . . But they sometimes have another salute for the foreman whose back is turned."[42] When Vietnam Veterans Against the War leader John Kerry spoke at the 1972 UAW convention for peace, veteran benefits, and good jobs, many at Lordstown applauded.[43] Some veterans adopted alternative lifestyles, while others became class-conscious activists who led resistance in the plant and flirted with radical politics: "I could see a better way of running things. . . . The workers are getting more educated. . . . They will realize there's a better way of changing things than wars and taking over other countries for profits. . . . If the United States has all this money to fight wars, they have enough money to take care of things here at home. . . . You don't have some people with everything and people without anything."[44] While such ideas were hardly majoritarian views, David Moberg found that about 20 percent of those he interviewed expressed similar sentiments.[45]

UAW supported civil rights activities, and African Americans like Ray Lewis were a part of the local leadership from the early days of 1112. Nonetheless, blacks still found themselves working the hardest and dirtiest jobs disproportionately to their numbers (15 percent), and a union survey found that African Americans were dealt harsher punishments for breaking work rules.[46]

African Americans organized in 1971 when seven hundred showed up for work wearing shirts that bore the UAW symbol and the group's name—Du Du Ujamma. An African American leader described Du Du Ujamma as "a political caucus" that aimed at getting "two or three hundred . . . to come to a union meeting."[47] They fielded a slate for the union election but were roundly defeated by a white backlash. Leaders of Du Du Ujamma tried to calm white suspicions by appearing before a general membership meeting.[48] Du Du Ujamma based its appeal on a mix of black pride, African heritage, and class consciousness.

Lordstown suggested a growing affinity between campus activism and working-class sensibilities. Staughton Lynd, a well-known radical intellectual, took the story of Lordstown to the University of Wisconsin at Madison in 1972. Madison had been a center of student activism since the early days of the antiwar movement, and in the early 1970s, graduate students organized America's first graduate-employee union. Addressing an assembly of graduate students, Lynd drew potent parallels between Lordstown and Madison. When he evoked a "new kind of working-class militancy . . . led by young people your own age," Lordstown was hailed with a wild ovation.[49]

In a 1972 survey, Moberg found that 25 percent of the Lordstown labor force were "traditional union loyalists," defined as activists with strong ideological ties to unionism. Fifteen percent were "counter cultural unionists" who identified with students and rock and roll and felt "sympathetic to many politically or culturally radical currents ranging from ecology, peace, and women's movements to . . . yoga, vegetarianism, and craft work." Moberg claimed that another 5 percent were "factory radicals" who espoused leftist political views and were always ready to fight GM.[50] It has yet to be demonstrated that any campus or community, even at the height of the Sixties, had more than 45 percent of its population engaged in political action.

For Lordstown, as for much of the U.S. working class, the Sixties was mostly like our common image of the Fifties. It was not until the Seventies that Lordstown's workers initiated major cultural changes. It is worth considering that Woodstock, the most remembered single event symbolizing the counterculture, did not happen until the summer of 1969. It was also that summer that the riots at the Stonewall Inn in New York City initiated a large gay activist movement. Similarly, it was not until the early 1970s that a majority of Americans consistently thought the Vietnam War was wrong and the Vietnam Veterans against the War articulated working-class discontent with empire. The women's and environmental movements found their capacity to effect both legislation and the outlooks of millions of Americans in the Seventies as well.

The events at Lordstown formed one small part of a larger pattern inside and outside the labor movement. Wave after wave of activism and a disastrous war had, by the end of the 1970s, produced a new political constituency in the United States. Social movement unionism, of which Lordstown was but one example, emerged as an important and enduring expression of the new ways Americans thought and acted in the late twentieth century.

THE END OF THE LABOR/CAPITAL ACCORD AND LORDSTOWN IN THE 1980s

The history of Lordstown offers us a way to think about the 1980s not only as a period of conservatism but also as a time when democratic possibilities beyond the political confines of the labor/capital accord became visible. The most formidable challenge facing the new spirit of participation was the decline of the midcentury social contract. By the late 1970s, slower economic growth, global competition, government and corporate policy, and the drive to maximize profits brought an end to the period of rising material wealth for most Americans.[51] Some measure of wealth had helped enable Americans to voice expectations beyond mere material comfort and elevate their desires toward the improvement of their social, spiritual, and political lives.

A series of events shifted the costs and risks of economic stagnation to workers and consumers and altered the political terrain. Despite the Democratic Party's comfortable majority in Congress and control of the White House in the late 1970s, labor failed to win even moderate legislative victories that could have challenged the economic restructuring.[52] When the new Republican president, Ronald Reagan, fired striking air-traffic controllers and staffed the National Labor Relations Board with those hostile to workers' rights, he seemed to deny labor's role as a legitimate part of the social order.[53] Reagan also weakened the Occupational Safety and Health Administration. At the same time, Republicans and Democrats passed new tax, budget, money, and debt policies that accelerated the redistribution of wealth away from working people.[54]

Given the green light by government, business assaulted labor. More work at less pay was enforced through increased surveillance and supervision of employees.[55] Corporate America spent millions on new forms of union busting in an intensified legal and criminal assault against union-minded workers.[56] New business conditions made it possible to weaken unions by moving operations to rural or less-organized regions. Additionally, corporations sought to escape high wages and environmental regulations by going abroad to invest the profits they had made in the United States.[57] When companies could not run from the U.S. standard of living, they undermined it by hiring part-time and contingent workers without health care, decent compensation, or job security.

Throughout the late 1970s and 1980s, political and business leaders failed to promote the rates of economic growth typical of the 1943–70 period. When growth returned in the 1990s, the lion's share of new wealth went to the very top. Instead of pursuing the public good, workloads were intensified and wealth redistributed upward.

In the early 1980s, catastrophe hit the Mahoning Valley. In rapid succession, the steel industry deserted Youngstown, the auto industry suffered a wrenching decline, and the country was in the throes of the worst downturn since the Great Depression. Writing in *See Here,* John Russo warned Local 1112 that "all bets are off."[58]

After nearly a century of profitable operation, the steel industry threw thousands out of work. Steelworkers responded with a social innovation of enormous potential. Based upon their long association and reliance on the steel industry, workers, community activists, and legal scholars asserted community property rights over the abandoned factories. Although this approach failed in court, the concept of community property rights recognized that there was a compelling public interest in private property and that social relationships could define property ownership.[59] The idea of worker ownership persisted, and by the late 1990s, Ohio would lead the nation with some eighty worker-owned enterprises.[60]

As the 1982 recession choked off buying power and car sales, the UAW was confronted with aggressive demands for wage concession from the three big car companies. The union conceded, and GM received $2.5 billion back from workers in 1982.[61] Local 1112 sided with 48 percent of all UAW members and voted overwhelmingly against subsidizing some of the richest and most powerful corporations in history. GM's transfer of wealth proved successful indeed when it rebounded to a $3.7 billion profit in 1983.[62] The autoworkers had paid a high price for their jobs.

While workers became increasingly dependent upon GM for employment, GM became increasingly reliant on worker initiative to turn profits. To achieve quality production, GM had to begin to revise its political ideology based on management's exclusive right to organize and manage production. The crisis of the early 1980s made way for the rapid advance of participatory and cooperative work strategies.[63]

The origin of these cooperative programs, known as Quality of Working Life (QWL), is complex. As early as 1967, delegates to the UAW convention approved a resolution that called for a more humane work environment and worker participation in decision making. The UAW first brought such ideas to the bargaining table in 1970, and by 1973, GM began a modest implementation of QWL-style rhetoric and initiatives despite significant resistance from high-ranking GM officials.[64]

The 1972 Lordstown strike itself was a significant long-term cause of the shift toward worker participation. Like no other single effort, Lordstown forced the issues of worker alienation and managerial practice onto the agenda of U.S. business, labor, and governmental leaders.[65] By the mid-Eighties, the national agreement between GM and the UAW endorsed QWL programs.

Worker-participation programs, when the union is less than a co-equal partner, can subvert rather than promote democracy. Yet at their best, they can help humanize work according to democratic values that recognize mutual interdependence rather than the dictatorship of management. At Lordstown, the democratic side of worker participation showed real promise precisely because years of activism had created strong solidarity and good leadership. Al Alli, a militant and farsighted leader, was elected shop chair in 1976 and was returned to leadership for more than two decades.

By the mid-1980s, Lordstown's QWL programs, jointly designed by union and management consultants, allowed workers to volunteer for training that emphasized the value of cooperation and worker participation. Environmental committees raised awareness about hazardous chemicals, and ergonomics teams redesigned tools and workstations to make the job fit the person, not the person fit the job. Many of the programs focused on quality controls by reengineering production, reducing costs and embracing shop-floor innovations. One committee tried to reverse the loss of jobs through "insourcing" work currently done outside the plant.[66]

When jobs were cut in 1985 and 1986, members had the right to draw full pay from GM by enrolling in a jobs bank run by the union. Workers were creatively reassigned to other duties. "We were keeping the rolls. . . . So we took a chance . . . we sent two guys from our jobs bank to school."[67] When the union's experiment was discovered by management, the union prevailed on GM and paid tuition for 150 more to attend Youngstown State University, where they gained undergraduate and advanced degrees as full-time students. Another 400 workers were schooled in a variety of trade skills. Scores of volunteers went to Warren and Youngstown to work with senior citizens. Some worked at the union hall.

The union's claim on job ownership was also evident in the buyout programs. In August 1987, seventy-one workers agreed to leave the plant and sell their jobs back to GM. GM purchased the jobs at a sliding scale, with senior employees receiving up to $50,000 each, for a total of $2,595,000. Another fifty workers became eligible for buyouts later that year.[68]

When management shut down the truck line, almost two thousand jobs were threatened. Union leaders proposed a four-day workweek that eliminated overtime, increased leisure, and saved all the jobs.[69] The union further secured work by convincing management to update Lordstown's technology. After twenty years, *See Here* celebrated its anniversary with headlines claiming that the union's greatest achievement had been "saving jobs for the Valley workers."[70]

The failures of worker participation at Lordstown are as telling as its successes. GM revealed its lack of commitment to democracy and true worker participation by outsourcing jobs and increasing the use and abuse of contingent labor during the 1990s. Temporary "summer help" became a year-round practice. Under the guise of cost cutting, GM sent cushion production to an outside supplier situated close to the factory site. Although the union negotiated a temporary compromise to allow offsite production with union labor, workers fought back with direct action. GM tried to fire Alli in 1996 but succeeded only in provoking a wildcat strike reminiscent of the 1970s.

These events illustrate broader patterns in the rocky relationship between adversarial politics and worker participation. The success of worker-participation programs seems to depend upon a rough equality of power that only class struggle can create. Outrage over corporate profiteering and arrogance, an improving economy, growing calls for reform within the labor movement, and the rise of the antiglobalization movement provoked a tougher stance toward corporations. Workers at Lordstown and elsewhere began, once again, to adopt more adversarial politics in the 1990s.

The period of worker participation in the 1980s nonetheless augmented the adversarial politics of the labor/capital accord, because a more democratic vision of enterprise emerged. It is no coincidence that a new vision for industry was most clearly articulated by Irving Bluestone, labor's foremost advocate of worker participation.[71] This consumer- and worker-centered view seeks to promote consumer demand, full employment, and job security by winning market share through plentiful high-quality, low-priced products. As a leader at Lordstown observed: "The most important thing that effects our job security is the quality of the product."[72]

The working-class perspective on industry claims that economic democracy is consistent with efficiency, technological innovation, quality, and even profit making. Only the single-minded pursuit of the maximum possible profit remains inimical to a more democratic economy.

Labor's view of enterprise is vitally important, because it poses a practical alternative that allows us to imagine the transition from existing reality to conditions of economic and political justice. Without an alternative plan or vision, social movements may continue to be critics of the world but will never become its authors.

At Lordstown and across the country, the vision of a more democratic economy began to take tangible shape in the late 1980s and 1990s. The desire to bring corporations into a new contract with the communities that made them wealthy was one of the prime motivations for the environmental, antiglobalization, community, and living-wage movements of the 1990s. A small but growing number of Americans agreed with Lordstown activist Joe Santiago's call for public control over corporate behavior: "We need a commitment from corporate America, that if they get tax breaks . . . tax abatements . . . , there's a commitment to take care of the community, not just pick up and leave anytime they feel like it. . . . They take my youth, they take the environment, they destroy the community . . . and there's no complication? Why not? . . . There's nothing until we have some commitment—some laws."[73]

Tested by decades of labor war and labor peace, Lordstown's workers asserted that control by sharing responsibility for management and production and by claiming their jobs as their property. Articulating a theme the union would make its standard for more than twenty years, shop leader Alli held: "These are jobs that should be passed on to our children and grandchildren." The failure to do so would be like "squandering the family fortune."[74]

The pursuit of economic democracy at Lordstown evolved from a sharp struggle to limit management's power to a more positive assertion of rights—including the right to control jobs as if they were the property of the workers.[75]

JOB PROPERTY RIGHTS

What are the broad historical implications of Lordstown's experiment in workplace democracy? How are we to interpret three decades of class conflict and negotiations centered on everyday working-class jobs? Lordstown offers us an opportunity to think about the relationship between jobs, property, and democracy.

Our concepts of property are historical.[76] Property rights evolved incrementally, rarely giving way to revolutionary changes such as when the Civil War ended slavery and millions of former slaves became citizens. If we consider the economic reorganization of the last half of the twentieth century, it could well be argued that the conditions for a practical, if gradual, redefinition of property rights and citizenship once again exists.

The legal requirements for job property rights were set out by two 1972 Supreme Court rulings, *Perry v. Sinderman* and *Board of Regents v. Roth.* Both cases considered disputes over academic tenure, one of the only forms of job property rights upheld by U.S. courts. In both cases, the justices wrote: "Property interests . . . are created . . . by existing rules or understandings . . . that secure certain benefits and that support claims of entitlement to those benefits."[77] Philosophically, the high court made way for us to reconsider jobs as property by asserting: "'Liberty' and 'property' are broad and majestic terms. They are among the great constitutional concepts . . . purposely left to gather meaning from experience. . . . They relate to the whole domain of social and economic fact."[78]

Job property rights emerged in practice from many decades of both adversarial and cooperative union/management relations. U.S. unions have conventionally placed jobs at the center of their concerns.[79] In his pioneering study of the International Typographical Union, Arthur R. Porter Jr. argued that "property rights have evolved in the composing rooms of the printing industry."[80] For Porter, these new rights grew out of routine union principles and procedures.

Job-centered unionism favored the creation of elaborate rules governing work that were enforced by contract. Seniority can be seen as a way to establish the connection between length of relationship and degree of equity accumulated in a job. Grievance procedures and job security clauses insisted that formal proceedings should make "just cause" the standard of judgment to fire someone in the same way the Fifth or Fourteenth Amendment demands due process of law before property or liberty is taken by the government. Severance pay, cash settlements, retraining grants, and relocation costs may all be interpreted as compensation for lost property.[81]

For more than a century, law, labor contracts, and precedent have laid one foundation for the emergence of property concepts in the job.[82] The practice, if not the theory, of U.S. unionism has always treated the job as a type of social property owned jointly by worker, union, capitalist, and community. While U.S. courts have rarely decided in favor of job property rights, a new economic context may, as Staughton Lynd has suggested, transform the meaning of the common working-class value placed on a job.[83]

When the members of Local 1112 ran the jobs bank, controlled manpower transfers, negotiated the job buyouts, limited management's right to demand layoffs, changed the workweek, and led the fight for product quality, they acted as owners of property have traditionally acted. When the UAW gave wage and benefit concessions to achieve job security, they paid for their jobs; GM recognized that workers owned their jobs by buying them back with cash settlements. By establishing long-standing and open control over jobs, and by creating reasonable expectations about such control or access in the future, the union asserted property rights.[84]

If jobs were treated as property, then workers could bring citizenship rights into the workplace. Just as important, labor history could then be more easily considered a chapter in the larger, and unfinished, history of American democracy.

CITIZENSHIP AND THE CITIZEN-WORKER

The citizen-soldier, yeoman farmer, and small proprietor of the eighteenth and nineteenth centuries served as powerful models of U.S. citizenship. These citizen figures were the "free and independent men" essential to the political traditions that evolved from the revolutionary era.[85] As Richard Hofstadter observed in his classic *Age of Reform*, the yeoman ideal was based on a series of interlocking concepts: "Land is the common stock of society to which every man has a right—what Jefferson called 'the fundamental right to labor the earth,' that since the occupancy and use of land are the true criteria of valid ownership, labor expended in cultivating the earth confers title to it; that since government was created to protect property, the property of working landholders has a special claim to be fostered and protected by the state."[86]

Labor, property ownership, and rights were bundled together as the indivisible foundation to revolutionary conceptions of citizenship. The Fifth Amendment expresses this view by twinning personal liberty and property and shielding them both with due-process protections.[87] The Bill of Rights did not, however, apply to conditions at the workplace but focused solely on the abuse of governmental power. Private property was conceived of only in positive terms, as a realm of rights and freedoms that good government dared not violate.[88] While we know that these freedoms did not apply to slaves, women, or the poor, the U.S. political tradition assumed that economic democracy, in the form of widespread property ownership, was absolutely necessary to the political freedom of its citizens, because it permitted economic security and independence of mind. The yeoman ideal became national ideology and functioned "as a depiction of reality as well as an assertion of an ideal."[89]

At the end of the nineteenth century, however, the rise of corporate capitalism reorganized property under the control of large bureaucracies and radically severed economic from political democracy. Most individuals no longer owned or controlled productive property and only could acquire consumer goods. These developments were often seen as a threat to democracy and a root cause for the decline of civic engagement. People without property were thought to have no stake in society and could be easily misled by bosses and tyrants. Given U.S. political values since the time of Thomas Jefferson, persons without property could not be model citizens.[90] By centralizing productive property, the modern corporation overthrew the original yeoman and proprietor figure and left the American political tradition in disarray.[91]

Although the corporations undercut the democratic aspect of the economy, they could not help but make their own private property and economic activities increasingly political and public.[92] The very existence of corporations as legal persons took its modern form in the judicial revolution of the 1890s, when U.S. courts redefined certain types of vital public activity as a private matter. For example, railroad companies began as special associations granted political privileges and charged with the public interest. Yet they were made financially feasible only by the free transfer of millions of acres of public lands to private hands.[93]

This confusion and fusion of the public and private accelerated as the twentieth century progressed. In response to the Great Depression and World War II, the welfare/warfare state was built to promote industry for war and to protect citizens against economic failure. Many forms of welfare followed; some, like veteran's benefits and Social Security, were for the benefit of common people. Yet it has been the military-industrial complex above all that has made public policy decisions and public expenditures essential to economic activity. The military-industrial complex is a socialized economy that protects industrial giants from market forces and transfers billions of public dollars to private coffers. In general, the public/private mix encouraged private access to national wealth.[94]

During the last half of the twentieth century, corporations and government merged many of their activities, as government promoted profits and corporations exercised sovereignty. The association between the two became systemic and routine through the corporate finance of

campaigns and political parties, by the exchange of high-level executives and managers, and through lobbying efforts. A half century of
vast public subsidies, government bailouts, immense military budgets,
low-interest loan guarantees, price supports, political favors, so-called
free-trade agreements, and billions of dollars in tax abatements helped
to cover costs for almost every major industry.[95] In the words of Daniel
Bell, private forms of corporate ownership are "simply a legal fiction."[96]
The economic requirements of the modern corporation no longer justify
its completely private control, for "when we see property as the creature
of the state, the private sphere no longer looks so private."[97] By the late
twentieth century, economic activity and work were thoroughly politicized. In this regard, property reassumed the form it took at the dawn of
the capitalist era when "the concept of property apart from government
was meaningless."[98]

By merging private enterprise and public government, current economic realities have ironically created the conditions under which
democracy at work, that is, economic democracy, and political democracy are also practically indistinguishable. That is, citizens must have
power in both realms or they will not have power at all. Job property
rights offer the possibility of exerting civic control over corporations
and government by repopulating the politicized workplace with citizen-workers. Once in possession of their jobs and protected by due process, citizen-workers could exercise their right to free speech, association, and participation in the governance of their enterprises.

The history of worker participation at Lordstown hints at the possible reinvention of classical citizen ideals through the traditional prerogatives of property ownership. For the citizen of old, widely distributed small property holdings safeguarded democracy. In our time, job
property rights could play the same symbolic and political role as productive property once did by protecting the citizen-worker's freedom to
participate in corporate and civil governance. Viewed from this perspective, struggles for workplace democracy, and other campaigns for
corporate responsibility and living wages, may best be understood as
part of the larger project of U.S. democracy.[99]

The idea of the citizen-worker will make sense, however, only if we
appreciate the interplay between novelty and tradition that animates
history. Our society will not realize its democratic promise unless it taps
the latent power of ancient and inherited belief and proposes a future
that is a coherent extension of the grand narratives of U.S. history. The
new citizen-worker I have discussed is a descendant of the American

Revolution, the Bill of Rights, the Civil War, and the 1960s, and the political traditions they represent. This is a revolutionary figure with a past, a present, and a project.

As we continue to reinterpret late-twentieth-century America and the social movements that made it distinctive, we might choose to understand this history as growing out of a tradition of citizenship that thrived whenever people struggled "to be a participator in government." Three decades of experimentation with workplace democracy at Lordstown point toward the possibility that a democratic practice and vision comparable to the traditions that moved America in its most liberating moments may once again be established.

NOTES

Acknowledgments: I would like to thank Martin Sklar, Stuart Eimer, and Hugh Hindman for commenting on early versions of this essay. Van Gosse and Eliza Reilly made many helpful suggestions, and Eliot Katz's editorial expertise was absolutely indispensable. I am very grateful to the American Council of Learned Societies for the generous fellowship that made this project possible. UAW documents reprinted from the Walter Reuther Library by permission of the library. Material from *See Here* courtesy of UAW Local 1112, Lordstown, Ohio.

1. Hannah Arendt, *On Revolution* (New York: Viking Press, 1963), 221–22, 123–29.

2. Arendt suggested that the local committees of the revolution were a model for a township system of "elementary republics" that would complement the national government (see ibid., chap. 6).

3. See David Brody, *Workers in Industrial America: Essays on the Twentieth Century* (New York: Oxford University Press, 1980), chaps. 5, 6; Barry Bluestone and Irving Bluestone, *Negotiating the Future: A Labor Perspective on American Business* (New York: Basic Books, 1992), chap. 2; Nelson Lichtenstein and Stephen Meyer, *On the Line: Essays in the History of Auto Work* (Urbana: University of Illinois Press, 1989), 1–16; Thomas A. Kochan, Harry Katz, and Robert B. McKersie, *The Transformation of American Industrial Relations* (New York: Basic Books, 1986), chap. 2; Kevin Boyle, *The UAW and the Heyday of American Liberalism, 1945–1968* (Ithaca: Cornell University Press, 1995); Kevin Phillips, *The Politics of Rich and Poor: Wealth and the American Electorate in the Reagan Aftermath* (New York: HarperPerennial, 1990); Jeffrey Madrick, *The End of Affluence: The Causes and Consequences of America's Economic Dilemma* (New York: Random House, 1995); Barry Bluestone and Bennett Harrison, *The Deindustrialization of America* (New York: Basic Books, 1982). Members of Local 1112 read about the redistribution of wealth thanks to John Russo, "Labor's Alternative to Reaganomics," *See Here*, May 1982, 8.

4. Harry Chester, "The Effect of the Vietnam War on Economic Growth and Inflation," UAW Inter-office Memo, July 14, 1970, UAW Research Collection,

box 76, folder 10, Archives of Labor and Urban Affairs, Wayne State University (hereafter, WSU-ALUA).

5. Robert M. Collins, "The Economic Crisis of 1968 and the Waning of the 'American Century,'" *American Historical Review* 101, 2 (April 1996): 396–422.

6. David Montgomery, *Worker's Control in America: Studies in the History of Work, Technology, and Labor Struggles* (Cambridge: Cambridge University Press, 1979), 162.

7. While precise figures vary according to different methodologies and ideological biases, the concentration of wealth and income in the 1990s was the most extreme in the industrialized world and the greatest in twentieth-century U.S. history since the eve of the Great Depression. On this wealth gap, see Edward N. Wolf, *Top Heavy: The Increasing Inequity of Wealth in America and What Can Be Done about It* (New York: New Press, 1996); Denny Braun, *The Rich Get Richer: The Rise of Income Inequality in the United States and the World* (Chicago: Nelson-Hall, 1991); James D. Smith, "Recent Trends in the Distribution of Wealth in the U.S.: Data, Research Problems, and Prospects," in Edward N. Wolff, ed., *International Comparisons of the Distribution of Household Wealth* (New York: Oxford University Press, 1987), 72–89; Richard B. Du Boff, *Accumulation and Power: An Economic History of the United States* (London: M. E. Sharpe, 1989); Keith Bradsher, "Gap in Wealth in U.S. Called Widest in West," *New York Times,* April, 17, 1995; Jason DeParle, "Census Report Sees Incomes in Decline and More Poverty," *New York Times,* October 6, 1995.

8. Bluestone and Bluestone, *Negotiating the Future,* 36–41. According to the authors, as few as four large producers in seventeen key industries had nearly 70 percent of all sales.

9. Ibid., 26–27, chap. 4; Madrick, *The End of Affluence,* 72.

10. Steve Jefferys, *Management and Managed: Fifty Years of Crisis at Chrysler* (Cambridge: Cambridge University Press, 1986), 34; Montgomery, *Worker's Control in America,* 6; Robert H. Zieger, *American Workers, American Unions: 1920–1985* (Baltimore: Johns Hopkins University Press, 1994), 169–70.

11. Dan Georgakas and Marvin Surkin, *Detroit: I Do Mind Dying* (New York: St. Martin's Press, 1975); James A. Geschwender, *Class, Race, and Worker Insurgency: The League of Revolutionary Black Workers* (New York: Cambridge Press, 1977); Heather Ann Thompson, "Auto Workers, Dissent, and the UAW: Detroit and Lordstown," in Robert Asher and Ronald Edsforth, eds., *Autowork* (Albany: SUNY Press, 1995), 181–208.

12. Annelise Orleck, *Common Sense and a Little Fire: Women and Working-Class Politics in the U.S., 1900–1965* (Chapel Hill: University of North Carolina Press, 1995), 303.

13. Kim Moody, *Workers in a Lean World: Unions in the International Economy* (New York: Verso, 1997), 4–5, 275–79; Brody, *Workers in Industrial America,* 209–10; Jefferys, *Management and Managed,* 33–46. See also the symposia "Sociology and the New Labor Movement," *Contemporary Sociology* 27, 2 (March 1998): 123–39; and Linda Chavez-Thompson, "Communities at Work: How New Alliances Are Restoring Our Right to Organize," *New Labor Forum,* fall/winter 1998: 110–17.

14. My account of Lordstown during the 1960s and early 1970s is deeply indebted to David Moberg's "Rattling the Golden Chains: Conflict and Consciousness of Auto Workers" (Ph.D. diss., University of Chicago, 1978). For other key works on Lordstown see Emma Rothschild, *Paradise Lost: The Decline of the Auto-Industrial Age* (New York: Vintage Books, 1973); Stanley Aronowitz, *False Promises* (New York: McGraw-Hill, 1973); Peter Herman, "In the Heart of the Heart of the Country: The Strike at Lordstown," in Root and Branch, ed., *Root and Branch: The Rise of Worker's Movements* (Greenwich, Conn.: Fawcett, 1975); Thompson, "Auto Workers, Dissent, and the UAW."

15. Wildcats that involved significant numbers of workers occurred at Lordstown some ten times from 1966 to 1970 (Paul Cubellis, interview by the author, Lordstown, Ohio, July 10, 1996).

16. Agis Salpukas, "G.M.'s Toughest Division," *New York Times*, April 16, 1972.

17. While the discussions of worker alienation were common among unionists, Lordstown drew the attention of government and media (see Department of Health, Education, and Welfare, *Work in America* [Washington, D.C.: U.S. Government Printing Office, 1972]; Philip Shabecoff, "H.E.W. Study Finds Job Discontent Is Hurting Nation" *New York Times*, December 22, 1972).

18. Minutes of Regular Membership Meeting, March 12, 1972, UAW 1112 Collection, box 3, folder 8, Archives of Labor and Urban Affairs, Wayne State University; Moberg, *Rattling the Golden Chains*, 43; Salpukas, "G.M.'s Toughest Division."

19. "The GM Efficiency Move That Backfired," *Business Week*, March 25, 1972, 47.

20. See petition from members of Local 719, UAW, to Local 1112, February 13, 1972, UAW 1112 Collection, box 8, folder 1, Archives of Labor and Urban Affairs, Wayne State University; Agis Salpukas, "Young Workers Disrupt Key G.M. Plant" *New York Times*, January 23, 1972.

21. Moberg, *Rattling the Golden Chains*, 432.

22. Ibid., 185.

23. Dan Clark, "Guilty until Proven Innocent: Discipline," *See Here*, November 1973, 6, Local 1112 Archive, Reuther/Scandy/Alli Hall, Lordstown, Ohio (hereafter, L1112 Archive).

24. Moberg, *Rattling the Golden Chains*, 188, 371.

25. Mike Aurilio, interview by the author, Lordstown, Ohio, June 20, 1997.

26. Moberg, *Rattling the Golden Chains*, 173.

27. "Sabotage Claim Halts GM Plants," *Dayton Daily News*, December 24, 1971; Ralph Orr, "War Brews at GM Vega Plant," *Detroit Free Press*, January 23, 1972.

28. Robert Daniels, "Mahoning UAW Gets Infusion of Youthful Leadership, Energy," *Cleveland Plain Dealer*, October 4, 1971. See also editorial, "A New-Breed Leader in UAW," *Cleveland Plain Dealer*, October 6, 1971.

29. Thompson, "Auto Workers, Dissent, and the UAW," 204; Russel W. Gibbons, "Showdown at Lordstown, *Commonweal*, March 3, 1972, 523.

30. Moberg, *Rattling the Golden Chains*, 291. See also letter to Mr. Robert A. Smith from Gary B. Bryner, President Local 1112, UAW Local 1112 Collection, box 6, folder 13, Archives of Labor and Urban Affairs, Wayne State University; Thompson, "Auto Workers, Dissent, and the UAW," 205.

31. Local Union Report and Request to Regional Director for Strike Authorization, UAW Local 1112 Collection, box 4, folder 18, Archives of Labor and Urban Affairs, Wayne State University.

32. Andrei Cvercko, "The Cover Up," *See Here*, October 1974, L1112 Archive. See also John Spain, "Quality 1 Issue at Lordstown," *See Here*, May 1973, L1112 Archive.

33. Raymond Hartley, Committeeman-at-Large, *See Here*, 5, 13 (February 1974).

34. "Press Release by Paul Cubellis—Shop Chairman of Bargaining Committee," UAW 1112 Collection, box 76, folder 10, Archives of Labor and Urban Affairs, Wayne State University.

35. Moberg, *Rattling the Golden Chains*, 372–73. In a survey, "job protection" was the highest-ranked response (89.3 percent) to those asked "What do you think you should get from being in the union?"

36. Gibbons, "Showdown at Lordstown," 523.

37. In addition to Montgomery, *Workers Control in America*, see Michael Merrill, "Labor Shall Not Be Property: The Horizon of Workers' Control in the United States," *Labor Studies Journal* 21, 2 (May 31, 1996): 27–50.

38. Nelson Lichtenstein, *The Most Dangerous Man in Detroit: Walter Reuther and the Fate of American Labor* (New York: Basic Books, 1995), 279–81; Zieger, *American Workers, American Unions*, chap. 4.

39. For discussion of workers' control between World War II and the late 1960s see Brody, *Workers in Industrial America;* and Rosemary Feurer,"William Senter, the UE, and Civic Unionism in St. Louis," in Steve Rosswurm, ed., *The CIO's Left-Led Unions* (New Brunswick N.J.: Rutgers University Press, 1992), 95–118.

40. On limitations of the UAW in relation to black nationalism see Thompson, "Auto Workers, Dissent, and the UAW," 181–208.

41. Richard Moser, *The New Winter Soldiers: GI and Veteran Dissent during the Vietnam Era* (New Brunswick, N.J: Rutgers University Press, 1996).

42. Orr, "War Brews at GM Vega Plant."

43. "Vietnam Veteran Kerry Blasts War," *UAW Solidarity*, May 1972, Solidarity Collection, Archives of Labor and Urban Affairs, Wayne State University.

44. Moberg, *Rattling the Golden Chains*, 350–51.

45. While the New Left may have had a general effect on Lordstown's workers, Moberg claims that, besides the UAW itself, there was no organized left-wing presence at the plant before the strike (*Rattling the Golden Chains*, 599).

46. Ibid., 139.

47. Ibid., 151–52.

48. Minutes of General Membership Meeting, April 9, 1972, UAW 1112 Collection, box 3, folder 8, Archives of Labor and Urban Affairs, Wayne State University.

49. Tape-recording no. 616A, Staughton Lynd, April 21, 1972, recorded by Francis Feely, State Historical Society of Wisconsin, Madison. Courtesy of State Historical Society of Wisconsin, Madison, Wisconsin.

50. Moberg, *Rattling the Golden Chains*, 196–98.

51. Harry Boyte, "On Silences and Civic Muscle," *Campus Compact Reader*, winter 2002, 21; Robert Pollin and Stephanie Luce, *The Living Wage: Building a Fair Economy* (New York: New Press, 1998), chap. 6.

52. Richard B. Freeman and James L. Medoff, *What Do Unions Do?* (New York: Basic Books, 1984), 202–5; Jefferys, *Management and Managed*, 39; Kochan, Katz, and McKersie, *Transformation of American Industrial Relations*, 67.

53. Thomas Ferguson and Joel Rogers, *Right Turn: The Decline of the Democrats and the Future of American Politics* (New York: Hill & Wang, 1986), 83–86, 130–39; Boyle, *Heyday of American Liberalism*, 1.

54. Phillips, *Politics of Rich and Poor*, chap. 4; Ferguson and Rogers, *Right Turn*, 138–39.

55. David M. Gordon, *Fat and Mean: The Corporate Squeeze of Working Americans and the Myth of Managerial "Downsizing"* (New York: Martin-Kessler Books, 1996). An American Management Association survey reported that 35 percent of companies surveyed admitted using electronic surveillance on workers (see Anne R. Carey and Jerry Mosemak, "Big Brother at Work," *USA Today*, July 20, 1998, B1).

56. See Joshua Freeman, ed., "Organizing Is a Civil Right," *New Labor Forum*, fall/winter 1998, 95–150, esp. David Brody, "A Question of Rights," 129–37.

57. Kathryn Marie Dudley, *The End of the Line: Lost Jobs, New Lives in Postindustrial America* (Chicago: University of Chicago Press, 1994); Kochan, Katz, and McKersie, *Transformation of American Industrial Relations*, chap. 3.

58. John Russo, "All Bets Are Off," *See Here*, August 1981, 3, L1112 Archive.

59. Joseph William Singer, "The Reliance Interest in Property," *Stanford Law Review* 40, 611 (1988): 614–749; Staughton Lynd, "The Genesis of the Idea of a Community Right to Industrial Property in Youngstown and Pittsburgh, 1977–1987," *Journal of American History* 74, 3 (1987): 926–58; Jeffrey R. Lustig, "The Politics of Shutdown: Community, Property, Corporatism," *Journal of Economic Issues* 19, 1 (1985): 123–52; Seymour Melman, *After Capitalism: From Managerialism to Workplace Democracy* (New York: Alfred A. Knopf, 2001), 382–84.

60. John Logue, "Rustbelt Buyouts: Why Ohio Leads in Worker Ownership," *Dollars and Sense*, September–October 1998, 34–37.

61. Ruth Milkman, *Farewell to the Factory*, 81.

62. For Local 1112's view of concessions see Al Alli, "Chairman's Report," *See Here*, April 1982, 3, L1112 Archive; Paul S. Terlesky, "GM Tells the Whole Truth Once Each Year" *See Here*, April 1982, 4; John Russo, "Actions to Influence the Outcome of Bargaining" *See Here*, May 1984, 12.

63. Jefferys, *Management and Managed*, 42.

64. QWL programs were also influenced by the Swedish and Japanese practices. These ideas were not entirely foreign and resonated well with management's paternalistic attempts at worker/management cooperation during the

1920s (Irving Bluestone, interview by the author, July 8, 1996); Bluestone and Bluestone, *Negotiating the Future*, 17; Katz, *Shifting Gears*, 74–76; Kochan, Katz, and McKersie, *Transformation of American Industrial Relations*, 42.

65. Katz, *Shifting Gears*, 74; Kochan, Katz, and McKersie, *Transformation of American Industrial Relations*, 44; Rosabeth Moss Kantor, "Work in a New America," *Daedalus* 1, 107 (winter 1978): 61.

66. Al Alli, "Shop Chairman's Report," *See Here*, October 1986, 5, L1112 Archive.

67. Paul Cubellis, interview by the author, Lordstown, Ohio, July 10, 1996.

68. Al Alli, "Shop Chairman's Report," *See Here*, 1987, 5 and *See Here*, November 1987, 4, L1112 Archive. For an account of the buyout program at GM's Linden, New Jersey, plant see Milkman, *Farewell to the Factory*.

69. Bob Price, interview by the author, July 11, 1996.

70. "Saving Jobs for the Valley Workers," *See Here*, June 1986, 1, L1112 Archive.

71. See Bluestone and Bluestone, *Negotiating the Future*. This strategy has antecedents from the 1940s before policy making was surrendered to management. In 1949, the UAW proposed a small, fuel-efficient, low-cost car ("Small Car Named Desire," *Ammunition* 7, 1 [January 1949]: 24–30, UAW Education Department Collection, Archives of Labor and Urban Affiars, Wayne State University).

72. Jim Tripp, interview by the author, July 10, 1996. See also Catherine L. Kissling, "Growing Up: Maturing Managers, Line Workers Forge Detente at GM Lordstown," reprinted with permission of *Crain's Cleveland Business* in *See Here*, December 1984, 16, L1112 Archive.

73. Joe Santiago, interview by the author, Lordstown Ohio, June 17, 1997.

74. Al Alli, "Shop Chairman's Report," *See Here*, April 1985, 5, and "Shop Chairman's Report," *See Here*, April 1996, 3, L1112 Archive.

75. I would like to thank Michael Merrill for introducing me to the concept of job property rights in the work of Arthur J. Porter; see *Job Property Rights*, (New York: King's Crown Press, Columbia University, 1954).

76. Singer, "Reliance Interest in Property," 621; Jennifer Nedelsky, *Private Property and the Limits of American Constitutionalism: The Madisonian Framework and Its Legacy* (Chicago: University of Chicago Press, 1990), 269.

77. *Roth*, 408 U.S. 577; *Perry*, 408 U.S. 601.

78. *National Ins. Co. v. Tidewater Co.*, 337 U.S. 582, 646 (Frankfurter, J. dissenting), cited in *Roth*, 571.

79. Selig Perlman, *A Theory of the Labor Movement* (New York: Macmillian, 1928).

80. Porter, *Job Property Rights*, 8.

81. Singer, "Reliance Interest in Property," 688; Moberg, *Rattling the Golden Chains*, 389.

82. Porter, *Job Property Rights*, 67.

83. Staughton Lynd, "Ideology and Labor Law," *Stanford Law Review* 36 (May 1984): 1287, 1293, and Lynd, "Genesis of the Idea." See also Donald H. J.

Herman and Yvonne S. Sor, "Property Rights in One's Job: The Case for Limiting Employment-at-Will," *Arizona Law Review* 24 (1982): 763–816; Phillip J. Levin, "Towards a Property Right in Employment," *Buffalo Law Review* 22 (1973): 1081–1110.

84. Singer, "Reliance Interest in Property," 665, 673.

85. Joyce Appleby, *Capitalism and a New Social Order: The Republican Vision of the 1790s* (New York: New York University Press, 1984), 78, 82, 86, 105, chap. 2.

86. Richard Hofstadter, *The Age of Reform* (New York: Vintage, 1955), 27.

87. James W. Ely, *The Guardian of Every Other Right: A Constitutional History of Property Rights* (New York: Oxford University Press, 1992), 9, 54.

88. Nedelsky, *Private Property,* 264.

89. Hofstadter, *The Age of Reform,* 30.

90. The most important exception is the citizen-solider, who can achieve citizenship without property but only at the price of heroic action in service to the republic (see Moser, *New Winter Soldiers,* chap. 2; J.G.A. Pocock, *The Machiavellian Moment: Florentine Political Thought and the Atlantic Republican Tradition* [Princeton: Princeton University Press, 1975]; Appleby, *Capitalism;* Montgomery, *Citizen Worker,* introduction, chap. 1; Livingston, *Pragmatism,* 275–79).

91. Nedelsky, *Private Property,* chap. 6.

92. This interpretation of corporate capitalism is derived from the work of Adolf A. Berle and Gardiner C. Means, *The Modern Corporation and Private Property* (New York: Harcourt, Brace & World, 1932); William A. Williams, *Contours of American History* (New York: World Publishing, 1961); Porter, *Job Property Rights;* Daniel Bell, *The Coming of Post-Industrial Society: A Venture in Social Forecasting* (New York: Basic Books, 1973); Martin Sklar, *The Corporate Reconstruction of American Capitalism, 1890–1916: The Market, the Law, and Politics* (New York: Cambridge University Press, 1988), and *The United States as a Developing Country: Studies in U.S. History in the Progressive Era and the 1920's* (New York: Cambridge University Press, 1992); and Livingston, *Pragmatism.*

93. Lustig, "The Politics of Shutdown,"139–44; William A. Williams, *The Contours of American History,* 289, 304.

94. I borrow the term "public/private mix" from Sklar, *United States as a Developing Country.* See also Daniel Bell, *The Cultural Contradictions of Capitalism* (New York: Basic Books, 1976), 224–27.

95. This relationship between government and business is often referred to by critics as "corporate welfare." That designation implies, however, that public support of private wealth is an aberrant aspect of our economy rather than its true basis. For studies on corporate welfare see Cato Institute, *Ending Corporate Welfare as We Know It* (Washington, D.C.: Cato Institute, 1996); Robert Sherill, "The Looting Decade, S&Ls, Big Banks, and Other Triumphs of Capitalism," *Nation,* November 19, 1990, 592–93; Stephen Pizzo, Mark Fricker, and Paul Mulo, *Inside Job: The Looting of America's Savings and Loans* (New York: Harper-Perennial, 1991); Mark Zepezauer and Arthur Naiman, *Take the Rich off Welfare* (Tucson, Ariz.: Odonian Press, 1996); David Bollier, *Silent Theft: The Private Plunder of Our Common Wealth* (New York: Routledge, 2002). The issue of corporate

welfare reached even the corporate media when *Time* magazine ran a three-article series in 1998.

96. Bell, *The Coming of Post-Industrial Society*, 294.

97. Nedelsky, *Private Property*, 263.

98. Porter, *Job Property Rights*, 1.

99. For a study of worker as citizen in the nineteenth century see David Montgomery, *Citizen Worker: The Experience of Workers in the United States with Democracy and the Free Market during the Nineteenth Century* (New York: Cambridge University Press, 1993). The more than sixty successful living-wage campaigns between 1994 and 2002 have won a measure of legal control over corporate property (David Reynolds and Jen Kern, "Labor and the Living Wage Movement," *Working USA*, winter 2001/2002, 19). For other strategies to modify corporate behavior see Steven Hill, "Stakeholders vs. Stockholders: An Antidote to NAFTA/GATT," *Blueprint for Social Justice* 47, 9 (May 1995): 1–7.

James Livingston

12   Cartoon Politics
The Case of the Purloined Parents

THE 1990s WERE an astonishing moment of innovation in animated film—indeed, the increasing use of special effects in every genre threatened, or promised, to make all movies an adjunct of animation. These innovations were not the results of an anticapitalist art-house sensibility, or of small, "independent" studios, because animated films are still labor-intensive, very expensive productions. They are still mass-market movies or television series that must appeal to many overlapping constituencies. So they typically register and rework most of the social conflicts and moral dilemmas specific to what we used to call "mass society." But because they are not realistic renditions of contemporary life, and because they often valorize the fears and fantasies of childhood, they are especially good at inhabiting and imagining changes in the "family romance" of our time.

And since the typical U.S. family changed so drastically in the aftermath of the sexual revolution and women's movements of the 1960s and 1970s—for example, females were finally freed from an exclusive preoccupation with domestic roles (as wives and mothers) and thus were able to ask new questions about the functions of families—animated filmmakers have had a lot to ponder. From *The Little Mermaid* and *Toy Story* to *The Princess Monanoke*, from *The Simpsons* to *South Park*, the question at issue is, What can we do with a past we've outgrown? or What are parents good for anyway? In animated film, however, these parents are never given by the past—they are not *just there* because they happened in the past, because they somehow precede us. Instead they get *created* by a narrative that can leave them out, or reconstitute them in weird disguises, or insert, even invent, them at inappropriate times, according to the bizarre but rule-bound logic of contradiction that regulates cartoons. They are always there, in other words, only not so that you would notice. They are mostly missing, like absent causes, or like

316

real parents who can't seem to show up when it counts but who shape our lives anyway. In the letter and postscript that follow, I look at the breakthrough Disney movies of the 1990s—*The Little Mermaid* and *Toy Story*—as brilliant exemplars of the animated films that feature these purloined parents. They are addressed to my daughter, but they were written with her brother and their friends in mind. Mine, too.

July 4, 1990
Dear Julia,

Last Sunday Mommy and I took you to see your first real movie in a real theater. The movie was *The Little Mermaid*, made by Walt Disney Studios. You liked the theater because it was old and dark and smelled good. And you got to eat lots of popcorn. But you were not impressed with the movie. It was too big and complicated for you—you don't yet have the skills to watch a movie without thinking about it, so that you can concentrate on the story.

But I've been going to movies for a long time now, and this one impressed me. I watched it for you and hope you'll read these notes on it someday, before you decide you're too grown up for cartoons.

The story of Ariel, the little mermaid, is pretty simple (it's a retelling of a fairy tale that was first written down and published about two hundred years ago). She lives in the ocean, so she has a big fish tail instead of legs, and she can breathe underwater. She's almost but not quite human—the people who made the movie try to tell us that by covering her breasts and making her look exactly like the big girls you see every day, except of course for her fish tail. The differences between her and the other mermaids (her sisters) are that she believes life is better among the human beings who walk around on the ground, on legs, and that she has a beautiful singing voice. She believes life is better above the water because she collects things from shipwrecks—things like forks, corkscrews, pipes—all kinds of stuff she can't use and doesn't understand, but stuff that seems wonderful to her, anyway.

Now, Ariel's father is Triton, the king of the ocean, who would like her to be the same as her sisters—they seem uninterested in other worlds and are eager to sing songs for him while they stand on big oyster shells. But she keeps on collecting human stuff and ignores his stern warnings about going to the surface. In fact, Ariel falls in love with a prince she sees on a ship and saves him from drowning in a storm. The prince never sees her clearly when she rescues him, but he remembers and falls in love with her voice.

When Ariel's father finds out about her rescue, and her love for the prince, he destroys her collection of human stuff and forbids her to go back to the surface. Ariel then goes to Ursula, the wicked sea witch—she's a big ugly octopus—and makes a bargain. The bargain is this: The witch gets Ariel's voice, but in return Ursula casts a spell giving Ariel legs to walk on and three days with the prince. If at the end of three days, the prince has not kissed Ariel, her soul becomes Ursula's property.

You can imagine how hard it is for Ariel in the next few days. She doesn't have the voice the prince remembers, so she can't tell him it was she that rescued him. And he keeps thinking about that voice. Even so, he does try to kiss her while they're rowing a boat through an ocean inlet. The kiss never happens because Ursula's helpers—two nasty eels named Flotsam and Jetsam—turn the boat over at the last second. Then Ursula, knowing she's about to lose her bet, casts another spell, turning herself into a dark-haired twin sister of Ariel who can sing with the voice the prince remembers. He is enchanted by the voice, of course, and decides to marry this twin right away.

Ariel and her friends prevent the marriage, but the sun sets on the third day before the prince can kiss her—and so Ursula takes her back down to the ocean floor, where Triton challenges the witch's claim to Ariel's soul. But he agrees the claim is valid (his daughter signed a contract, after all) and trades his soul for his daughter's. Ursula then inherits the king's magical powers and turns on the prince, who has dived down to free Ariel. Once more the prince is saved by Ariel, who now becomes the object of Ursula's anger. The witch turns herself into a giant octopus and stirs up a huge whirlpool that traps Ariel but also brings a wrecked ship to the surface. The prince steers the bowsprit (the mast at the front) of this wreck into Ursula's gigantic belly, killing her and restoring the king's powers.

Triton then finds Ariel gazing at the unconscious prince, who was washed up on shore after his battle with Ursula. The king finally understands how much his daughter wants to join the prince's earthly world and uses his magical powers to make her fully human, with legs and all. Ariel and the prince get married, and I suppose they live happily ever after.

These are the bare outlines—the plot—of a pretty simple story. Told like this, its meaning is equally simple: Girl wants boy, girls loses boy to wicked witch, girl gets boy. The prince is passive—he doesn't do much—until he knows that the voice he loves belongs in Ariel's body. At that point, he gets the point in every way. But it's Ariel's love story until the prince becomes the pilot of the wrecked ship (and remember that it's got to be the same wreck Ariel explores at the beginning of the movie).

The meaning of the movie isn't as simple as this, though, because there are all sorts of funny and interesting moments that aren't real events in the story the movie tells. To begin with, there are lots of songs and speeches that show us how the people and the fish might think and act later on—lots of words and music that show us where they stand between Ariel, who longs for the world above the surface, and Triton, who can't imagine a better world than his undersea kingdom. Even the ways the words are spoken and the songs are sung tell us something more than we get from the simple events that make the plot.

One of Ariel's friends, for example, is Sebastian the crab, who also serves as Triton's trusted advisor. He's torn between loyalty to the king's commands and sympathy for Ariel, just as a human being in his position would be. So he helps us see a difficult situation from both sides and makes the story more complicated by being caught in the middle of it. But he adds even more to the meaning of the story, because he speaks with a West Indian accent, and because, in his one big song, he tries to persuade Ariel to stay in the water by pointing out that "up dere" they work all the time.

All these little things like accents amount to what grown-ups call the discourse—the parts of the story that aren't exactly events in the story, yet somehow add meaning to the story anyway. Let's see how they do so by looking at the discourse of this movie.

Let's start with the songs. There are four big numbers, one by Ariel at the beginning of the story, two by Sebastian, and another by Ursula in the middle. Ariel starts by singing about all the things she's found in the wrecks she explores. She calls this stuff treasures, wonders, gadgets, gizmos, whose-its, what's-its, thingamabobs. She doesn't understand what any of it is for—how or why it gets used by people "up there"—but she's sure that all of it somehow fits together in a way of life that's very different from hers. When Ariel calls herself "the girl who has everything" (she's using a phrase common in the 1980s), she's really complaining that by themselves, as simple objects, her things don't have any meaning. She knows they would take on meaning—and proper names—only in the world "up there," where they are taken for granted but get used with specific purposes in mind. So when she goes on to sing "I want more," she doesn't mean more stuff. Instead she wants the way of life in which the stuff makes sense.

That's why she doesn't sing about her stuff in the rest of the song. Ariel sings instead about seeing, dancing, running, jumping, strolling—about walking upright on two feet, "wandering free." What would I give, she asks herself, "if I could live out of these waters?" But it's obvious that she can already wander more freely in the water than anybody her age can on the land. So she must have some ideas about freedom that involve more than moving about in space. She makes those ideas clear in the next part of the song. "Betcha on land," she sings, "they understand—bet they don't reprimand their daughters." She's thinking about how her father has scolded her and tried to keep her in her place, underwater. Then she switches from "they" to "we"—she identifies herself with other ambitious girls who don't want to stay in the same old place: "Bright young women, sick of swimmin', ready to stand." I think she means that girls everywhere are ready to stand up to their fathers, to face them as equals on their own two feet. I think that because she goes on to sing about the question she wants to ask the people up there: "What's a fire, and why does it—what's the word—burn?"

Fire, you may know, has been the symbol of human civilization for thousands of years. We have long believed that we became something more than animals when we were able to change the natural world by using tools, planting crops, building houses, and making fires. Without fire, we wouldn't have been able to make the tools, cook the food, or warm the houses, so it usually comes first in the stories we tell about how we became human beings. There is a wonderful story, for example, about how, once upon a time, a god named Prometheus brought the gift of fire to people on earth, and so let them copy the ways of the gods. When they did, they began to understand that the world up there in the heavens, among the gods, was different, and better, and they also began to want more of the gods' way of living. For it was a way of living in which the natural world presented no obstacle to freedom—no obstacle to becoming what you wanted to be when you grew up.

But there is another, more recent, set of stories that completes the myth of Prometheus. These stories are also part of the movie's discourse. They tell us that long ago, we evolved from—we grew out of—animals that swam in the sea, like whales and dolphins do now. Once upon a time, these stories go, we were similar to hairy apes and lived in trees. Then bad weather came and killed off the trees. There we were on the plains with no place to hide from the animals that would eat us. So the females among us—the mothers—led us into the water, where they could escape the flesh-eating creatures on the land and protect their babies. Because we stayed in the water for thousands of years, as swimming mammals, we lost our body hair except in the places where the water could not go as we swam.

But at some point, when the weather changed again, we came out of the water and took over the world. For the males among us—the fathers—had meanwhile learned how to use weapons to kill animals for food. They had spent a lot of time out of the water hunting animals. And so they were more hairy, and better at walking and running, than the females, who had stayed out of danger by staying in the water with their babies. Notice that it was the males who led us back to the footing of civilization on land, where fires could be started.

The many stories about mermaids we have heard and told over the years are a way of recalling this watery "past," this strange "moment" that remains in our memories because we keep telling the stories—this decisive "moment" at which we could choose to stay in the ocean or fight it out on the land. They are also a way of reminding us that these stories have always been told as if the choice that made fire (civilization) possible was between the fluid, formless, watery habitat of the females and the harder, rougher, grounded habitat of the males.

When Ariel sings she "wants more" and asks herself what she would give up to "live out of these waters," she is recalling that "moment," that choice. Only this time, she is doing the choosing—she is not being led out of the water by a man used to killing animals (the prince doesn't want to be a fop, a mere gentleman like his uncle, but it's clear that until he meets Ariel he has no purpose in life except riding around on boats). She wants to know what fire is, what it means, what it does. She wants to be ready to stand up to her father, but she can't unless she gets legs and leaves the fluid, formless, watery habitat where things don't have names. So her story is not just about growing up and getting married. The discourse of the movie tells us it's also about the weird relation between males, females, and what we think we mean when we talk about civilization. It's about how that relation has changed and is still changing.

Before I try to tell you how it has changed recently, and why the changes confuse us, let's listen to Sebastian's first song and think about how it, too, adds to the story's meaning. His accent, remember, is West Indian, and his big number has a tropical sound and rhythm that place it closer to calypso and reggae than to the African American music we call the blues. So the song makes a new connection between males, females, and civilization. For Sebastian is a male, but his accent tells us that if he were a human being, he would be a brown man from a part of the world that is much poorer than our country. Now, many people in our day think that if a country is poor, it can't be fully civilized. These people often say that poor countries stay poor and uncivilized because the brown men and women who live in them don't want to work hard or don't know how to. These same people also use a term that is nicer than "poor" or "uncivilized," but it means both. That term is "less-developed countries." And everyone who uses it agrees that the poorest of the "less-developed countries" are in Africa and, in our part of the world, in the West Indian islands of the Caribbean Sea.

So Sebastian's accent places him in historical time as well as space —he stands between Ariel and Triton, to be sure, but also between Africa, the ancient cradle of civilization, and our own most-developed country, the United States. And in his big song, he tries to convince Ariel to stay in that "less-developed" time and space—to stay in the water because it's a place where no work needs to be done. "Out in de sun," he sings, "dey slave away," and yet it's somehow "hotter down under de water." Nature is bountiful in the warmth of the ocean, he says—you don't have to work down here to be comfortable, to get food and shelter. So there's more energy available for playing music, for doing things without a purpose, for having fun with your body. In fact, Sebastian is telling Ariel to stay in her body by staying in the ocean. He can't see why she'd want to rise above her body or above the water. He can't see why anybody would want to go beyond what is naturally given by working harder, by changing the world. He can't (yet) understand the idea of development.

Sebastian is of course a stereotype. I mean that he speaks in a way that is familiar to people who know almost nothing about poor countries and their real problems. He is afraid of the world "up there" because even before his escape from the crazed French chef—"Zut alors! What eez zees?"—he knows that civilized people have terrific power; after all, they catch and cook and eat little fish. He also claims "we got no troubles" down under the water and so confirms the silly notion of "happy darkies" whose desires are simple, natural, and easily met. But his song is important because it lets us see that Ariel won't stand for the related stereotype that connects females and dark continents like "less-developed" Africa. It also lets us understand why you and your friends identify so strongly with the little mermaid even though you love Sebastian and his songs. For Ariel likes the idea of development, of rising above her body and the water. She rejects the idea that females are somehow trapped in their natural bodies—that their desires are simple, natural, and easily met, perhaps by piling up more stuff in their pantries. She wants to get beyond the fluid, formless, watery habitat that is her "less-developed" country, the place where no work is necessary and knowledge of other worlds is impossible.

And so she disappears before Sebastian is done singing. She's already on her way to make her bargain with the witch. Here the discourse of the movie again adds meaning to Ariel's simple story. For the bargain she strikes is the kind of pact with the devil that usually symbolizes the moment when plain old civilization becomes modern society through the mechanical use of natural science. The best-known example of this pact is in a book called *Doctor Faustus* from almost 250 years ago (although its author was borrowing from earlier legends and plays). The date is important, since it was about then that the differences between countries became obvious to educated people. They became obvious because in some countries, new inventions based on science were applied to the way people worked and produced goods. The result in those countries was the industrial revolution. In other countries, this application of science to goods production never happened—and they are the countries now called "less-developed." So Ariel's pact with the devil enlarges the meaning of her determination to escape the "less-developed" world that holds her sisters as well as Sebastian. It suggests that she wants the modern version of civilization, where progress is scary, and costly, and normal.

But until very recently, most people have believed that what Ariel wants is not something that females should want—because females are not supposed to rise above their bodies, like men seem to do, and to think abstractly or scientifically, without emotions or feelings. You may find this belief amazing, but it is still common sense among many grown-ups, including some of the most ardent champions of women's rights. And you should try to treat it as a belief that contains a certain kind of truth. For until very recently, females did not get much of a chance to think in these ways and weren't sure they wanted to. Males kept females out of places and jobs where they'd learn to think abstractly or scientifically—so most females had no motive and no way to use their reason exactly as males did. Besides, most women have long been suspicious of thinking that didn't take real bodies and real desires into account. As it turns out, they were right to be suspicious. We've finally realized that we think with our bodies. Our minds and thoughts are never far removed from emotions and feelings.

Ariel's choice is almost unsettling, then. She rejects the old view of females, the one that would keep them out of the world of work, scientific knowledge, and development. She also rejects the new view, the one that would suggest that work, scientific knowledge, and development are mental illnesses to which females have been somehow immune. She's not "the girl who has everything." She is the girl who wants it all. She is modern.

But she learns something important on the land. Or at least she teaches us something important. Back when our ancestors were learning how to walk and run on the land, they found that their abilty to see made a difference. They couln't smell their prey unless they were very close to it, and they couldn't hear as well as most flesh-eating creatures on the land. But their upright posture let them see farther than most four-legged animals and gave new meaning to the horizon. So vision was essential to the quick-footed hunters—the males—who led us out of the water, once upon a time, to build fires and civilization.

It became even more essential in the great leap from civilization to modern society. For modern society is built around stories, messages, and promises that are written or typed. Before ideas and possibilities could be stored in this way, on paper, the past was preserved in memory and the future was imagined in stories by talking and singing. So hearing was more essential than seeing, if you were doing something other than hunting animals to kill for food. And most people, especially females, spent most of their time doing something other than hunting. But about 250 years ago, when printed stories, messages, and promises finally replaced talking or singing as the way most people preserved their memories and imagined their futures, seeing became more essential than hearing. New vistas of silence opened up, and the menfolk started to the see the horizon as a frontier—a place where boyish beginnings could be endlessly repeated.

Now, hearing is complicated, because you have to listen to sounds made by someone or something else, and you usually have to respond somehow to those sounds, to let the other know you're paying attention. The logic of the gaze is simpler. You can stare at people or things as if they were mute objects. And since you can't see people or things up close or around corners, it's better to look at them from a distance or from above. Sooner or later, you begin to try to see things as if you were far away from them, and out of your own body as well. So vision is the forerunner and becomes the model of abstract reasoning or scientific thinking. And once this kind of reasoning becomes normal— again, about 250 years ago—it tends to make people believe that vision is more important than any of the other four senses, maybe even the only important one.

But vision can tell us only about surfaces. It can't get us inside people, where songs start out as sounds. It can't let us respond to someone unless we use the rest of our senses and other parts of our bodies, especially our voices—which of course come from within us. So we lose our ability to know each other well if we let vision stand in for all the ways we think with our bodies.

That is what Ariel learns and teaches us when she leaves the water for the first time. Her body has changed in two ways. She has legs— she walks upright—but she can't speak or sing. She can be an object in the prince's field of vision, but she can't turn herself inside out, so to speak, through her voice. For all practical purposes, she doesn't have an inside—she's all surfaces. So the prince, who remembers the sounds and song that once came from within her, is mostly puzzled by Ariel's appearance on the shore. He keeps looking at her and wondering why she stares at him.

You'll remember that he does try to kiss her. But he tries after Sebastian has put together a chorus of little animals to sing about how we think with our bodies when we fall in love—after music reminds the prince of the interiors that we can discover, express, and share only by talking to one another.

By this time, you're probably thinking, Jeez, Dad, it's only a cartoon. Why should we take a movie made for children so seriously? I'd say we have to just because it's made for children. It tells us something about what grown-ups believe—they made the movie, after all—and something about what children might grow up to believe. It does both because the people who made it wanted children to like it. So they had to make sure it wouldn't offend or trouble children. But they also used grown-up ideas in making the movie. They had to try to see the world the way children would, but they couldn't become children—like all parents in modern society, they had to see the world *as if* they were children.

They didn't make a simple movie. Its discourse is quite complicated. But the movie works because the stories and meanings embedded in it are familiar—they are part of the common sense grown-ups have to teach children, by example and with stories. You already know there's nothing natural about common sense, for you already know that it *tells* us what is natural and normal. Once upon a time, the common sense of Christians let them believe it was natural or normal to hurt and kill Jews. The common sense of the Europeans who invaded North America after 1500 let them believe it was natural or normal to kill Indians and make slaves out of Africans. And then there is the common sense that still tells us how natural or normal it is to believe that females cannot, do not, and should not want what males want—that it's pointless to think of women as the equals of men because the differences between them are so great.

Now, I happen to think that we won't know what females really want or need until women and men are equal—not the same, but equal (think about it: If we were all the same, if we had no differences, we wouldn't want or need to fuss about equality). But what I think about this matter is less important than what the makers of *The Little Mermaid* think, because their audience is so much bigger than mine. And they seem to think that it's both unnatural *and* good for Ariel to stand up to her father, get out of the water, and enter the habitat of males on her own two feet. If you don't like her and don't agree with her, the movie fails. But she does have to go beyond her natural body and her "less-developed" undersea world to get what she wants. Is there a new common sense in the making here?

To answer the question, we have to go back to what Ariel wants. She starts out wanting the way of life that would make sense of her stuff. But then she rescues the prince and falls in love with him. She sings a slower yet more confident version of her opening song: "Just you and me, someday I'll be . . . part of your world." This song announces that three changes are underway. First, the world up there becomes *his* world, a man's world. Second, what drives Ariel into that world is still her curiosity, her desire for knowledge, but she is now thinking with her body. Third, all the dangers of her departure from the "less-developed" undersea world—all the tensions and fears this departure might create—are tamed by the idea of marriage. Ariel is paired off with the prince, so the possible meanings of her ascent get contained by the familiar. Her goal becomes the start of a new family that marriage symbolizes.

This use of the familiar lets the moviemakers take chances with their mermaid story without offending or troubling their audience. They do question the common sense of our time. But they end up suggesting that marriage is the way to answer all the questions raised by the "bright young women" who are "sick of swimmin'" and ready to stand up to their fathers. And that is a way of suggesting that the important questions of our time can be addressed from *within* the family.

You may have noticed that Ariel seems to have no mother—no one to help her father decide what's best for her. But look closer. The only character in the movie who is Triton's equal is Ursula the sea witch. She competes directly with the king for control of Ariel's future, as if she were, in fact, the mermaid's mother. And she shows the daughter how to get the man she wants. She's the closest thing to a mother Ariel has. Now Ursula seems simply evil because what she's really after is the power of the king—*she used to live in Triton's castle,* she tells us, and wants to move back in. So it's clear that, once upon a time, just like the devil himself, she challenged the king's powers from within his home, his castle, and got kicked out for that reason.

No matter where we look in the movie, then, it seems that females, both mothers and daughters, have to leave the castle if they are going to stand up to the king as his equal. This departure is either the cause or effect of conflict with the father who rules the castle, but it happens to both Ariel and Ursula. Yet we're supposed to be able to tell the difference between them, apart from obvious differences of age, size, and shape. We're supposed to know that Ariel is good and Ursula is evil.

So we have to ask, What does Ursula want that makes her evil? What makes her rebellion so awful? And why is Ariel's rebellion acceptable in the end? Both stand up to the father, remember. But one is killed by Ariel's husband-to-be; the other is rewarded with entry into the enlightened world of men of earth. One is driven out of the king's castle; the other chooses to leave. One tries to change the inherited ("normal") relation between father and mother—and she's the one who sings about sex rather than marriage—the other wants to re-create this relation in a new family. One breaks the law of the father; the other upholds it. But how?

There is an ancient story about his law. Once upon a time, a king was told by a prophet that his queen would have a son, and that this son would grow up to murder him. So as soon as the son was born, the king told a servant to take him away and let him die in the open. But instead the servant gave the baby to a poor shepherd's family. When he had grown up, this son set out for the great city of his province. On his way, he came to a crossroads, where he met an older man who challenged him. They fought, and the younger man won—he killed the older man.

When the son arrived in the city, he met and married the queen, whose husband had recently died. Soon after, the city suffered a terrible plague that no one could explain except by saying that the gods were angry. The son—he was now the king of his adopted city—decided to find out why the gods were so angry. He found that the man he had killed at the crossroads was his father, the king, and that the woman he had married was his mother, the queen. He had broken the law of the father by taking his father's place within the original family. That is why the gods were angry.

This is the story of Oedipus the King. It is retold with a new twist in *The Little Mermaid*. For in the movie, the law of the father still works only if Ursula's rebellion gets punished by death. Only if the witch is removed can Ariel pair off with the prince in the enlightened world of men by calling on her father's great powers. But remember that Ursula is in effect the mermaid's mother. And remember that she is killed by the prince—the future son-in-law of the father, the king—with the bowsprit of the wreck Ariel found at the beginning of the movie. Everyone is cooperating, it seems, to aim this shaft at the belly of the beast—to kill the mother, to remove her from the scene she has tried to steal. By doing so, they preserve the law of the father and let Ariel ascend to earth.

I think that's what must happen if we believe that the important questions of our time can be answered from within the family. Something's got to give if we're confined to this small social space. *The Little Mermaid* suggests that either the law of the father or the mother herself will give way. The "bright young women" who are "sick of swimmin'" need new ground to stand on. But if that ground can be found only within the family, father or mother must be removed from the scene. And so the choice the movie lets us make is reduced to the kind we faced when, once upon a time, we hesitated at the water's edge— the choice between the fluid, formless, watery world of the mothers, and the harder, rougher, grounded world of the fathers.

But I have to think that the people who made this movie were troubled by the choosing they did for us. Otherwise they wouldn't have given such important choices to a girl who, like you and your friends, might grow up to be a mother.

Love,
Daddy

P.S. July 5, 2000. Well, Julia, here I am at the end of the 1990s, still astonished by the ambitions of mainstream animation since *The Little Mermaid*. Look at *The Simpsons*, one of the longest-running televison series ever. It's a loving parody—both imitation and criticism—of *Ozzie and Harriet*, the family sitcom of the 1950s, and a serious yet hilarious commentary on parental absences, mental and physical. Or look at *South Park*, the most idiotic, and thus the most appealing, animated series since MTV's *Beavis and Butthead*. Heh-heh. Notice the excremental vision of the world that guides the creators of both: Everything is shit, they seem to believe, and, to judge from their popularity, lots of kids your age and older agree. Do you? I hope not. But then I have to hope because I'm a parent—it's in the job description.

It seems that I'm not the only one on the job. As it turns out, there's a parental principle of hope at work in the mainstream animation of the Nineties. For example, look at the left-wing politics of *The Simpsons*, the series in which the only real villains are the characters who promote "family values" and free markets: Republicans all! Or look at Disney's *Beauty and the Beast* (the follow-up to *The Little Mermaid*), in which the female lead rejects the dumb jock and chooses the hairy intellectual with the big library—all in the name of redeeming her hapless father, the absent-minded professorial type who invents useless gadgets. A similar principle of hope is at work, I think, in the best Disney movie of the Nineties, *Toy Story*. At least that's what I argued in a letter to Frank Rich, a *New York Times* columnist, back in 1995. Let me share that letter with you, and then ponder the sequel.

Dear Mr. Rich,

In your recent column, you suggest that because fathers are absent from *Toy Story*, the moral of the story must be "more work for mother." I want to suggest that you're wrong about this absence—that the movie is about how fathers can and should reinsert themselves in the "family romance" that is modern U.S. culture. I mean that you're right to say that father's absence is the premise of the movie, but wrong to say that the writers leave it at that.

How so? Let's suppose that we treat Woody and Buzz, the toy cowboy and the toy astronaut who compete for the son's undivided attention, as the two sides of the U.S. male who emerged and evolved in the twentieth century—in movies and TV, as well as in the larger culture. Woody (voice by Tom Hanks, the Jimmy Stewart of our time) is the distant echo of the western hero who resists progress because he knows it means the eclipse of his independence, his unique and self-evident position in a fixed moral universe (think of John Wayne in *Red River*, but more poignantly in *The Man Who Shot Liberty Valence;* or try *Butch Cassidy and the Sundance Kid*). But Woody also stands at the end of a long line of suburban middle managers who crowded TV screens in the 1950s and 1960s, pretending that "father knows best" (think of the staff meeting Woody holds before the son's birthday party). So he represents a hybrid of male images drawn from film and TV, the most characteristic cultural media of the twentieth century.

Buzz (voice by Tim Allen, a stand-up comic who became the star of a hit TV series in the mid-Nineties) is Thorstein Veblen's engineer, Vince Lombardi's shoulder-padded poet, and Tom Wolfe's astronaut rolled into one—the ex-jock with the right stuff who hates the past and believes almost religiously in progress and its technological armature. He wants to go to the moon and thinks he already has the equipment he needs—like Tim Allen's other alter ego, in his sitcom role, his credo is "More power!" He represents "the machine," the favorite metaphor of U.S. writers, but he reminds us of cheesy Saturday-morning cartoons, too, and not just because he recognizes himself in a TV commercial.

Together, and only together, Woody and Buzz are the missing father the son needs. At the outset, Woody is simply afraid of the future—he might be displaced by a new toy—and Buzz is just contemptuous of the past, when space travel was science fiction. By itself, neither side of the modern U.S. male can make the family whole again, by restoring the father to his proper place at its head. And each is vulnerable to Sid, the nasty boy next door. This boy is the mad scientist from the past—you know, the young Frankenstein, except he's not funny—and he's perverted modern technology. Like the folks who are exploring the human genome, he takes things apart and reassembles them as if he's trying to invent brand-new species (think of the disfigured baby doll's head on Erector Set spider legs). In doing so, he scares everybody, but especially parents, who like to think that they are the origin of the next generation.

For this kid's goal is to downsize Dad (Woody and Buzz) by dividing him up and dispersing his parts. Sid represents the hard side of Microsoft, I'd say—he's bound for glory in Silicon Valley, or wherever computer scientists congregate these days, by depriving dads of the good jobs they had when baby boomers (like me) were dutiful sons and daughters (when Disneyland got its start as a destination). Like the audience—like dads everywhere—Woody and Buzz experience this threat of a jobless future as dismemberment, perhaps even as impending castration. Only by joining forces, only by coming together and trading on each other's strengths, can these two sides of U.S. manhood (thus fatherhood) defeat the perversions of technology and familial relations that Sid represents. Only then can they resurrect the mangled toy soldiers, the heroic fathers from World War II, who were buried by Sid in the sandbox—buried, that is, in the Vietnam memories of their postwar children. Only then can they reappear, courtesy of old-fashioned rocket science, at the son's side, just as his family reaches the horizon of no return.

THAT WAS the end of my letter to Frank Rich. In writing it, I was trying to say that *Toy Story* was a great deal more complex, and frightening, than another parable of "more work for mother," or another evasion of the question, "Where's Dad?" I was trying to say that this movie spoke directly and productively to the sense of loss—the loss of jobs, the decline of "typical" families, the fear of the future—that permeated our culture back then. But you will rightly say, Dad, what about now? I'll answer by looking at *Toy Story 2*, a movie released early on in the new millennium, when you were getting to be a teenager.

The delightful cast of toy characters came back, to be sure, and its mission was accomplished by the reunion of Woody and Buzz (played again by Tom Hanks and Tim Allen). In fact, the reconciliation of their different personalities *just is* this movie's mission. Woody still fears the future in which Andy (the same but older son) will outgrow his favorite fatherly toy. He fears it so much that he has decided to retire to a museum of TV memorabilia, the cartoon equivalent of a nursing home, where he won't have to beg for attention. Buzz understands Woody's fear, but he's willing to let go, even to be put on the shelf where childish things languish and get forgotten until the garage sale—he's willing to let this son grow up and decide for himself what's worth keeping and caring for.

Before Woody can leave for the museum, he's kidnapped by the cartoon version of Jerry Seinfeld's postal nemesis. Buzz then leads the other toys on a rescue mission. When the leading men are finally reunited, Buzz convinces Woody that it's too early for retirement from fatherly duties, and they return to their proper place just in time to welcome Andy home from camp. So the movie's mission is accomplished by the mere juxtaposition of the main characters, not by any change in their attitudes toward history.

Bear with me now, Julia. The original *Toy Story* taught us that a usable model of fatherhood and family can't be imagined by committing ourselves to the past *or* the future, as if these are the terms of an either/or choice. It taught us that we exile ourselves from the present, and from our families, whether we try to stay in the past along with Woody or try to flee the past along with Buzz. In the end, they understood that each had to adopt an attitude toward history that allows for both previous truth and novel fact—an attitude that lets each of them *change* the other, and so makes their cooperative effort, their unison, greater than the sum of its parts. They taught us that the point is to keep the conversation going between the past and the future, not to choose between them. The point is to live forward but understand backward.

So the sequel is less hopeful, more elegiac (more funereal, more nostalgic), than the original. It speaks directly, but not very productively, to the sense of an ending that our strange millenial moment afforded us. For it suggests that you can't teach an old toy new attitudes. All you can do is get older and watch as your kids grow up, move out, move on. And pretty soon you'll be on the shelf like your own father, diminished ("downsized") not by technology but by time—by the growing gaps of memory you share with people who believe that history is bunk. Such weary resignation probably seems realistic as the baby boomers (your parents) start thinking about how to finance their retirement. Even so, *Toy Story 2* inadvertently advertises another and more useful truth, which I'd put this way: It is only when our attitudes toward history become fixed that both the past and the future look the same—that is, impervious to change.

The moral of the story? I don't know. Isn't it still in the making, as we keep retelling and reinterpreting? Good night, Julia. Tomorrow is a Sunday. Let's go see another matinee.

ELIOT KATZ

13   At the End of the Century

Written for Allen Ginsberg at his 70th birthday

Ah century that has embraced me these past 39 years, that has set
before my eyes so much tumult and catastrophe, that has taken too
many of my friends and ravaged the calendar with my mother's
mother's blood, that has wormed a hole

from earth's core through ozone layer to the sun, I have but one
wish for you: Die my century! why wait? early to bed with you!
Take early retirement, take your granite eyes, your fully paid
tombstone, your electrified casket, your four billion odes to death,

burn your damn books those dastardly lies, lay your plutonium
shroud over leftover legacy, let's be done with you. Artists around
here in all watercolors have prefigured many paths to follow—
choose one: no-warning aneurism during peaceful sleep, drunken

liver rot, kidney explosion at top of donor wait list, youthful breast
cancer, no-holds-barred immune system surrender, sudden leap off
college dormitory roof—if you don't like local Jersey methods, why
not blow your brains out

like Russia's Mayakovsky, you betrayed his dreams as much as
anyone's, over & over & over, so go ahead, straight to your grave,
die my century! It's your time, the signs all there, all 500 TV
channels are screaming bloody random murder,

—"Lester Leaps In" now
playing on my CD, these the jazz rhythms A.G. had in mind while

writing angelic "Howl," while swinging for the century's fences, ah
Allen's 70th birthday last week, maybe the books are worth

saving from the bonfire, maybe some twentieth-century visions to carry,
some ways to connect—maybe, my century, you never intended to
fuck us up? maybe never intended to walk into the bar wearing the
death mask? Whatever your intentions, you're through!

Die my century, we're growing impatient, no need to prolong this
multiperspectival agony, leave now so rebirth may arrive soon, too
many cannot afford to wait—Goldie's kidneys can't take it much
longer, you've already killed her, what more do you want?

For her, there was too much apartheid far & near, too many youth
shot, too many communities allowed to go broke, too many
pharmaceutical giants allowed to roughshod concrete boots through
city's historic gardens—for Mark, too many fathers

dying ridiculous wars, too many mothers scrambling for shelter, too
many hungry children deserving songs of their own—audrey's
landlord never let her pick up her clothes, robbery by the propertied
class plain and simple, an old-fashioned crime

your courts never learned to solve—what good were you? Your
patriarchal capitalisms grew immeasurable tumors, you threw out
socialized medicine before inventing an alternate cure, Ethan leapt
off the balcony & nobody knows why, too many too manys,

cover that body, cover that experimental beard, hide that loud
music, cover cover cover blood blood blood cover—now I've got
this throbbing headache, like a hammer at the back of the head
banging from the inside, could be sinus

infection, how am i supposed to be sure when no doctor will see
anyone for days—southern black churches are burning,
Woodbridge's fiery oil storage tanks at this very moment spewing
huge toxic clouds, hawks drop Mid-East bombs on infant ribs,

FBI looks up the wrong files, Vietnam's lessons & veterans remain
locked outside our nation's checkbook memory, celebrities endorse

sexy underwear sewn by starved Guatamala teens, Nigeria is
hanging its writers, Philadelphia prefers to lethally inject—

how beautiful Lester's rhythms of earthly engagement, dead friends'
divine energies digging those sounds, they lived spread out &
diverse, they lived this century as well as died it, they rode the
universe's internationalist intergenerational bus along

your potholed highways & loved out loud many of your bumpy
struggles, —My beloved pillowcase century! After yr breathing has
slowed, we who endure will send our compassionate imaginations
ahead, will keep our coalitions together with tough new thread,

our desire for change will survive the most callous assassins, so
send yr SS back to their self-made hells, toss torturers East & West
back into their flesh-eating ditches—let go yr thousand demons & yr
one gods, merciful death & even more merciful rebirth,

we will encounter a future, the fourway mirror will forgive,
emancipatory eyedrops will relieve the ache, after the sliding back
& the spiraling forth, the planet & the plan, after the redwood
keyboard & the meditative sprint, the bacbacbac back back

bacbacbac—sometime next century our sketches will come to life . . .

June 1996

About the Contributors

CHRISTOPHER CAPOZZOLA is an assistant professor of history at the Massachusetts Institute of Technology. He completed a Ph.D. at Columbia University in 2002 with a specialty in U.S. twentieth-century political and cultural history and has published widely in journals and periodicals.

ANNE ENKE is assistant professor of history and women's studies at University of Wisconsin–Madison. She helped design the university's new LGBT Studies Certificate Program and is building an interdisciplinary graduate curriculum in sexualities/bodies/health. Her book in progress is "Locating Feminist Activism: Sexuality, Race, and Contested Space in the Upper Midwest, 1960–1980."

JEFFREY ESCOFFIER is editing an anthology of writings from the 1960s and 1970s on the sexual revolution. He is the author of *American Homo: Community and Perversity* and a biography of John Maynard Keynes, and he recently published a book on the choreographer Mark Morris. He develops mass media and public health education campaigns in New York City.

SARA EVANS is Distinguished McKnight University Professor of History at the University of Minnesota. Among her books are *Tidal Wave: How Women Changed America at Century's End* (2003) and *Born for Liberty: A History of Women in America* (2d ed., 1997). She has served as the director of the Center for Advanced Feminist Studies and on the Board of Editors of *Feminist Studies*.

ANDREW FEFFER is associate professor of history and director of American studies at Union College. He is the author of *The Chicago Pragmatists and American Progressivism* (1993) and is writing a book on the political culture of Philadelphia in the 1970s.

VAN GOSSE has written widely on post-1945 politics, including *Where the Boys Are: Cuba, Cold War America and the Making of a New Left* (1993). His current research concerns twentieth-century black politics. He has taught at Wellesley, Trinity, and Franklin and Marshall Colleges and is a member of the *Radical History Review* Editorial Collective.

ELIOT KATZ is the author of three books of poetry, including *Unlocking the Exits* (1999). He is a coeditor of *Poems for the Nation* (2000), a collection of contemporary political poems compiled by the late poet Allen Ginsberg, and he is currently serving as poetry editor of the online politics journal *Logos* (http://www.logosjournal.com/).

KITTY KRUPAT is associate director of the Queens College–CUNY Labor Resource Center and a doctoral candidate in American Studies at New York University, where she was a founding member of the Graduate Student Organizing Committee–UAW. She is co-editor of *Out at Work: Building a Gay-Labor Alliance* (2001). Her essays have appeared in a number of publications.

JAMES LIVINGSTON teaches American history at Rutgers, the State University of New Jersey. His most recent book is *Pragmatism, Feminism, and Democracy: Rethinking the Politics of American History* (2001). His book in progress is "The Origins of Our Time: Sources of the American Centuries, 1896–1946, or The Political Economy of Cultural Hegemony."

TINA LOO teaches at Simon Fraser University and is currently writing a monograph on nature conservancy in Canada. She and Carolyn Strange work on a project on historic sites of punishment now reinvented as tourist sites (prisontourism.net).

RICHARD MOSER is a national field representative of the American Association of University Professors. He taught American history at Middle Tennessee State University and is the author of *The New Winter Soldiers: GI and Veteran Dissent during the Vietnam Era.*

ANDREW SCHROEDER is an assistant professor of communications at the University of Wisconsin–Oshkosh. He received his Ph.D. in the American Studies program at New York University and is the author of a forthcoming book, "Technologies of Transnationalism: Tsui Hark and the Legends of *Zu*."

CAROLYN STRANGE specializes in the history of punishment and its representations and teaches at the University of Toronto. She and Tina Loo work on a project on historic sites of punishment now reinvented as tourist sites (prisontourism.net).

NATASHA ZARETSKY is an assistant professor of American history and women's history at Southern Illinois University at Carbondale. Her essay is drawn from a larger project on the relationship between narratives of national decline and family decline in the United States during the 1970s.